# Outlooks

## Readings

## for

## Environmental Literacy

*Edited by*

**Michael L. McKinney and Parri Shariff**
*University of Tennessee, Knoxville*

**Jones and Bartlett Publishers**
*Sudbury, Massachusetts*
Boston   London   Singapore

*Editorial, Sales, and Customer Service Offices*

Jones and Bartlett Publishers
40 Tall Pine Drive
Sudbury, MA  01776
508-443-5000
info@jbpub.com
http://www.jbpub.com

Jones and Bartlett Publishers International
Barb House, Barb Mews
London W6 7PA
UK

ISBN 0-7637-0658-2

**Acknowledgment**

The editors and Jones and Bartlett Publishers wish to express their sincere thanks to the many freelance authors, magazines, and journals for allowing us to reprint their articles.

Production services: Dean W. DeChambeau
Cover Image: Redwood State Park, California. © 1996 Dean W. DeChambeau

Printed in the United States of America
01 00 99 98 97   10 9 8 7 6 5 4 3 2 1

# Contents

# SECTION FOUR: SOCIAL SOLUTIONS

# Section One

# Overview

**1**

*The average citizen is increasingly informed about environmental problems, but more education is needed. Environmental education is especially urgent for young people, who will be the decision makers of the future. More classes on environmental sustainability must be implemented in primary and secondary school education. Liberal arts educators in colleges and universities must work harder to integrate environmental literacy courses into their curricula. Ideally, these courses should cover the impacts that the environment and society have on one another. They must also describe environmental issues and their affects on both the local and the global level. Cooperation will be needed from administrators and faculty members to implement this curricula.*

# Turning Curricula Green
## Jonathan Collett and Stephen Karakashian

**The Chronicle of Higher Education, February 23, 1996**

*Raising the environmental consciousness of the liberal arts.*

As some Republican lawmakers have discovered, many ordinary citizens care a good deal about the environment and oppose proposals to roll back federal laws protecting it. The environment is indeed in great danger, with pollution increasing, species becoming extinct, and overpopulation leading to growing demands for more food and fuel. Human behavior is responsible for our planet's current predicament, and only a change in the ways we think and act can begin to repair the damage and avoid future depredations.

These sobering realities are gaining increased attention among academics, despite some conservatives' sniping that "ecocentrism" now has joined race, gender, and class as touchstones among the politically correct. But higher education has lagged behind primary and secondary schools in some states, particularly those that have mandated study of environmental concerns in public-school curricula.

"We cannot ignore the urgent call for environmental literacy," says David Ehrenfeld, professor of biology at Rutgers University, in his foreword to a book we have edited, *Greening the College Curriculum: A Guide to Environmental Teaching in the Liberal Arts* (Island Press, 1996). "This is not merely a clash of rival cultures that we are about to witness, important as that may be; no 'Western Civilization 101' versus 'Native American Cultures 111.' This time, survival is the issue."

Many students need no convincing. In the 1995 annual survey of college freshmen conducted by the Higher Education Research Institute at the University of California at Los Angeles, 83.5 percent of the respondents agreed that "the federal government is not doing enough to control environmental pollution." Raised with a stronger environmental consciousness than their teachers, students are eager to study one of their main concerns. And the number of environmental-studies programs at colleges and universities is rising rapidly. The 1996 edition of *Peterson's Guide to Four-Year Colleges* lists more than 750 programs in institutions across the country offering majors in environmental studies, environmental sciences, or related subjects.

Yet all those programs still will reach only a minority of undergraduates. Students who choose such popular majors as sociology, communications, or literature, for example, are not likely to confront issues of the biosphere and sustainable development and may never enroll in an environmental-studies course, either because the classes are too full or students' schedules are too tight.

•••

Faculty members must change this situation by integrating the study of the environment and pressures for development into the liberal-arts disciplines. A good example of how to do this is the general-education requirement in environmental literacy recently adopted by the University of Wisconsin at Stevens Point. The faculty and chancellor have approved objectives that any course accepted for the requirement must achieve. For example, each course must describe the impact that human society and the ecosystem have on each other and also must demonstrate the local and global importance of a variety of environmental issues. This approach is a demanding one, since it requires many faculty members in various disciplines to become environmentally literate themselves, but it is the best way to make sure that all students become educated about the biosphere.

In the 1970s and '80s, during the development of academic programs and courses about gender, race, and class, we learned that active opposition from faculty members opposed to changing the curriculum was not the only obstacle to adding new perspectives and subject matter. It also was hard to get sympathetic faculty members to take the time to restructure their own thinking, learn the basic facts about new topics, find appropriate texts, and make room in their syllabi for new material.

•••

With this in mind, about five years ago we began asking eminent professors who see the need to integrate environmental teaching into the liberal arts to write a guide for faculty members in their particular disciplines. First, they presented a rationale for how basic concepts in their discipline could be illustrated through the use of material on ecology. (For example, in economics, students can learn to add a new dimension, ecological costs and assets, when considering the economic factors used to construct supply-and-demand curves.) Then we asked the scholars to prepare sample syllabi introducing environmental material into full courses or parts of courses at both the introductory and upper-division levels.

They concluded with an annotated list of print and non-print resources. The results appear in *Greening the College Curriculum.*

The interdependent character of the earth and its living systems leads quite naturally to a healthy reexamination of the basic assumptions and definitions of several disciplines. In some cases quite a radical rethinking may result. Two examples, whose implications for teaching are explored in depth in our book, are instructive.

In the humanities, notes one of the our contributors, Steven C. Rockefeller, professor of religion at Middlebury College, ecological thinking has led to a resurgence of interest in religions—especially Eastern traditions such as Hinduism and Buddhism, but also Native American spirituality—that stress the interdependence of all things. This interest cannot be dismissed, as it sometimes is, as simply a New Age fad; it builds on religious traditions that predate the Christian era.

In anthropology, says William Balée, associate professor of anthropology at Tulane University, an ecological approach quickly leads one into an examination of the interaction between human culture and the environment. Which one has more influence on the other? Are humans inherently destructive of their environment, or do some societies truly live in balance with their immediate surroundings? Pursuing those questions in depth soon involves students in the study of human nature, which an astute professor can combine with an examination of the philosophical underpinnings of the social sciences.

Instructors may be surprised to discover that fresh teaching methods also emerge naturally from the interdisciplinary nature of environmental issues. John Opie, professor of environmental-policy studies at the New Jersey Institute of Technology, and the environmental historian Michael Black have taken students into Newark to analyze an intersection or a commercial block, after they have read about the history of the area and looked at old maps. The students are asked to untangle the web of political and economic decisions and technological actions over time that account for present conditions. Then they are directed to construct their own cities from the ground up, using the popular computer simulation game "SimCity 2000," in which they must make decisions about zoning, traffic, and taxes, as well as cope with an occasional natural disaster.

Students themselves are leading the way at some institutions. Students from all 50 states and 22 other countries organized the "Campus Earth Summit" at Yale University in 1994. The participants drew up 10 recommendations, beginning with a call to "integrate environmental knowledge into all relevant disciplines." A follow-up conference in February 1995 drew more than 1,000 students to the University of Pennsylvania.

•••

Several national organizations, including the Campus Ecology Program, Campus Green Vote, and the Student Environmental Action Coalition, help coordinate hundreds of student environmental groups. Their activities range from urging implementation of the Yale conference's recommendations, to supporting local and national "green" candidates and legislation. And students can find plentiful information about the environment on EcoNet, Envirolink (started by a student at Carnegie Mellon University), and other on-line sites.

A sign that the growing concern about the environment cuts across racial boundaries can be found in an EcoNet listing of the "People of Color Environmental Groups Directory," which includes more than 200 groups, organized by geographic area. These groups could provide material for an academic unit on "environmental racism," the bias in environmental policy making that has led to less enforcement of pollution laws in communities with large numbers of low-income people and members of minority groups, and the deliberate placement of toxic-waste dumps in such communities.

•••

The environmental crisis challenges college and university faculty members and administrators to re-educate themselves, and then to devise ways to teach students new patterns of thinking and acting. These changes should invigorate the classroom by showing students the connections between what they are studying and their lives as local and world citizens. Colleges and universities either should require students to take specific courses on the environment or should make environmental perspectives so integral a part of the whole curriculum that students inevitably are exposed to them. No one pretends that either approach will make all students into environmental experts, but we should be sure our graduates are at least equipped to assess the arguments of the specialists. Such environmental literacy will benefit us all. ❏

---

**Questions**

1. What is responsible for the planet's current predicament?

2. To repair the damage done to the environment and to avoid future devastation, what must be done?

3. How are students leading the way to environmental literacy?

*Answers are at the back of the book.*

**2** *Since the invention of television, people have been influenced by media coverage. Today, it is the single largest factor influencing the political debate on the future of the Earth and its environment. However, media coverage of environmental issues has declined by 60 percent since 1989 on the three major networks. Two factors shape environmental coverage. The first is the attitudes of the cable or broadcast television owners toward environmental concerns. The second is the fact that opponents of the environmental movement substantially fund media sources, whereas the foundations that support the environmental causes do not contribute at all to the media. The environmental movement must make stronger appeals to the media about the future of the environment and what the cost of complacency will be for the next generation.*

# Television Misses the Picture
## Carl Pope

*Sierra*, March/April 1996

Since Sam Donaldson of ABC News owns a ranch in New Mexico, it's not surprising that the conversation turned to the environment when he appeared recently as a guest on the David Letterman show. Donaldson took the opportunity to rail against plans for the reintroduction of the Mexican wolf: "Now the people who live in New York City, God love you all, think it would be fun to have wolves in New Mexico. You'll never see a Mexican wolf on my land," he promised. "You may see newly spaded ground."

It's hard to imagine a print journalist so candidly advertising his or her biases. Even former *New York Times* environmental reporter Keith Schneider, who lionized the anti-environmentalist Wise Use movement and claimed that exposure to dioxin was no worse than sunbathing, still zealously presented himself as an objective journalist. But Donaldson doesn't have to worry because Donaldson is a celebrity, and in television celebrity is more important than objectivity.

Therein lies a dilemma for the environmental movement. Media coverage is the single biggest factor shaping the political debate on the future of the planet. In the print world, with the Republican leadership of the 104th Congress in deep trouble over its attempt to dismantle the country's major environmental laws, the environmental beat is suddenly hot again. Reporters who cover it can get their stories on page one, and editorials and editorial cartoons have been flaying the wreckers and polluters as they haven't since the heyday of James Watt.

But aside from a few shining exceptions like Ted Turner's outlets, television still finds the environment a big yawn. Environmental coverage on the three networks has declined 60 percent since 1989, and in fact TV's hardest-hitting environmental reporter is found in newspapers: the cartoon character Roland Hedley in *Doonesbury*. The decline certainly isn't due to a dearth of visual material or a lack of conflict. Is it then, as viewers might reasonably conclude, something about the cowboy-chic opinions of Eastern celebrity newspeople with weekend ranches in the West?

It's not that simple. Ted Turner has a large ranch in Montana, and so does Tom Brokaw, who recently spoke on the *Tonight* show about his strong environmental feelings and his love of the land. And, surprisingly, the environmental reporting on Donaldson's ABC has been marginally better than that on CBS or NBC, which devoted nearly 40 percent of last year's evening news to the O. J.

Simpson trial. Television's obsession with celebrity has grown at the same time that the resources it devotes to news and current-affairs programming has declined; tabloid TV and "infotainment," once embarrassing anomalies in the broadcast world, are now becoming the norm. Why bore people with corporate America's assault on environmental protection when they can be entertained instead?

What we see—or don't see—on television is governed by a complex chemical reaction of influences. Yes, the personal attitudes of reporters and editors matter; Brokaw and Donaldson, even while striving for objectivity, will flavor the debate differently. But even more important are the attitudes of the owners. Ted Turner's cable outlets cover the environment and population issues in much more depth than the competition because Turner has made it clear that he cares and is interested in these subjects.

But there is little room for independent voices in an industry increasingly dominated by impersonal forces, as media operations and entire networks are swallowed into larger and larger corporate empires. Recently, House Speaker Newt Gingrich advised these media conglomerates to make sure that their news coverage reflected their business and economic interests. It is easy to see evidence that his advice is being followed. At the same time that CBS was merging with Westinghouse, for example, it spiked a *60 Minutes* segment on the health effects of tobacco, citing fear of lawsuits from the tobacco industry. A short while later, CBS's parent Loews Corporation purchased six cigarette companies.

Corporate radio fares no better; ABC canceled former Texas Agricultural Commissioner Jim Hightower's weekend radio talk show, one of the few progressive efforts to challenge the monopoly of Rush Limbaugh and his clones. (Before he was canned, Hightower had criticized the takeover of ABC by the Disney Corporation, demonstrating that it is unwise to bite the mouse that feeds you.) Hightower's departure leaves the commercial radio world as a self-reinforcing market for right-wing talk: hosts tell anti- environmental listeners and corporate advertisers what they want to hear, and they in turn support the programs with their wallets.

Another factor shaping environmental coverage on TV and radio is that our opponents take these media seriously. Right-wing funders pour money into media operations (the Reverend Sun Myung Moon alone subsidizes an entire newspaper, *The Washington Times*), while most foundations that give to environmental causes fund no media at all. The other side also puts great energy into influencing reporters and editors, down to critiquing their choice of words. In the Medicare debate, for instance, when news anchors or correspondents used what Newt Gingrich and Company considered the "wrong" word, they received chiding calls from Republican PR flacks. "White House aides express admiration for Gingrich's communications monolith," the *Washington Post* reported, "marveling especially at the way the Republicans pressured the news media."

What the White House marvels at we can learn from. Media people are subject to persuasion, as the Sierra Club has demonstrated over the last year in its letters-to-the-editor campaign. Generating thousands of letters from Club members all over the country has gotten hundreds of them published. More importantly, it convinces assignment editors and editorial boards that their readers care about the environment and want to read about it. So do visits to the editorial board, and calls suggesting local environmental angles. It is partly due to such pressure that the print media have covered the environment as well as they have.

Our next challenge is to confront the electronic media and find their pressure points. We need to speak out to the managers, editors, and, yes, anchors and reporters of radio and television news shows, and let them know that we are more concerned about our children's future than about the latest celebrity scandal. If we don't make our voices heard, the critical environmental issues of the day will remain buried as deep as a wolf who makes the mistake of trespassing on Sam Donaldson's ranch. ❑

## Questions

1. What is the dilemma for the environmental movement?

2. Why is there little room in television for independent voices?

3. What are some forms of persuasion that have been used on the media to encourage the coverage of environmental issues?

*Answers are at the back of the book.*

**3** *Technology has accelerated the flow of information in a way that is often referred to as* fast knowledge. *Knowledge that has accumulated slowly over time is often called* wisdom *or* slow knowledge. *Fast knowledge, which is defended on the altruistic belief that we must meet the needs of an increasing population, has reshaped most of our social institutions. However, fast knowledge can create problems faster than we can solve them. Although fast knowledge is important for solving immediate technological and other problems, slow knowledge is essential for truly sustainable long-term solutions.*

# Slow Knowledge
## David W. Orr

*Conservation Biology*, **June 1996**

Between 1978 and 1984 the Asian Development Bank spent $24 million to improve agriculture on the island of Bali. The target for improvement was an ancient agricultural system organized around 173 village cooperatives linked by a network of temples operated by "water priests" working in service to the water goddess, Dewi Danu, a diety seldom included in the pantheon of development economists. Not surprisingly, the new plan called for large capital investment to build dams and canals and to purchase pesticides and fertilizers. The plan also included efforts to make idle resources, both the Balinese and their land, productive year-round. Old practices of fallowing were ended, along with community celebrations and rituals. The results were remarkable but inconvenient: yields declined, pests proliferated, and the village society began to unravel. On later examination (Lansing 1991), it turns out that the priests' role in the religion of Agama Tirtha was that of ecological master planners whose task it was to keep a finely tuned system operating productively. Western development experts dismantled a system that had worked well for more than a millennium and replaced it with something that did not work at all. The priests have reportedly resumed control.

The story is a parable for much of the history of the twentieth century, in which increasing homogenized knowledge is acquired and used more rapidly and on a larger scale than ever before and often with disastrous and unforeseeable consequences. The twentieth century is the age of fast knowledge driven by rapid technological change and the rise of the global economy. This has undermined communities, cultures, and religions that once slowed the rate of change and filtered appropriate knowledge from the cacophony of new information.

The culture of fast knowledge rests on many assumptions:

- only that which can be measured is true knowledge;
- the more of it we have the better;
- knowledge that lends itself to use is superior to that which is merely contemplative;
- the scale of effects of applied knowledge is unimportant;
- there are no significant distinctions between information and knowledge;
- wisdom is an indefinable, hence unimportant, category;
- there are no limits to our ability to assimilate growing mountains of information, and none to our ability to separate essential knowledge from that which is trivial or even dangerous;
- we will be able to retrieve the right bit of knowledge at the right time and fit it into its proper social, ecological, ethical, and economic context;

- we will not forget old knowledge, but if we do, the new will be better than the old;
- whatever mistakes and blunders occur along the way can be rectified by yet more knowledge;
- the level of human ingenuity will remain high;
- the acquisition of knowledge carries with it no obligation to see that it is used responsibly;
- the generation of knowledge can be separated from its application;
- all knowledge is general in nature, not specific to or limited by particular places, times, and circumstances.

Fast knowledge is now widely believed to represent the very essence of human progress. While many acknowledge the problems caused by the accumulation of knowledge, most believe that we have little choice but to keep on. After all it's just human nature to be inquisitive. Moreover, research on new weapons and corporate products is justified on the grounds that if we don't do it, someone else will and so we must. Others, of course, operate on identical assumptions. And, increasingly, fast knowledge is justified on purportedly humanitarian grounds that we must hurry the pace of research in order to meet the needs of a growing population.

Fast knowledge has a lot going for it. Because it is effective and powerful it is reshaping education, communities, cultures, lifestyles, transportation, economies, weapons development, and politics. For those at the top of the information society it is also exhilarating, perhaps intoxicating, and, for the few at the very top, it is highly profitable.

The increasing velocity of knowledge is widely accepted as sure evidence of human mastery and progress. But many if not most of the ecological, economic, social, and psychological ailments that beset contemporary society can be attributed directly or indirectly to knowledge acquired and applied before we had time to think it through carefully. We rushed into the fossil-fuel age only to discover problems of acid precipitation and climate change. We rushed to develop nuclear energy without the faintest idea of what to do with the radioactive wastes. Nuclear weapons were created before we had time to ponder their full implications. Knowl-

edge of how to kill more efficiently is rushed from research to application without much question about its effects on the perceptions and behavior of others, on our own behavior, or about better and cheaper ways to achieve real security. CFCs, a host of carcinogenic, mutagenic and hormone-disrupting chemicals, too, are products of fast knowledge. High-input, energy-sensitive agriculture is also a product of knowledge applied before much consideration of its full ecological and social costs. Economic growth is driven in large measure by fast knowledge, with results everywhere evident in environmental problems, social disintegration, unnecessary costs, and injustice.

Fast knowledge undermines long-term sustainability for two fundamental reasons. First, for all of the hype about the information age and the speed at which humans are purported to learn, the facts say that our *collective* learning rate is about what it has always been: rather slow. A half-century after their deaths, for example, we have scarcely begun to fathom the full meaning of Gandhi's ideas about nonviolence or that of Aldo Leopold's land ethic. Nearly a century and a half after *The Origin of Species* we are still struggling to comprehend the full implications of evolution. And several millennia after Moses, Jesus, and Buddha we are about as spiritually inept as ever. The problem is that the rate at which we collectively learn and assimilate new ideas has little to do with the speed of our communications technology or with the volume of information available to us, but it has everything to do with human limitations and those of our social, economic, and political institutions. Indeed, the slowness of our learning—or at least of our willingness to change—may itself be an evolved adaptation; shortcircuiting this limitation reduces our fitness.

Even if humans were able to learn more rapidly, the application of fast knowledge generates complicated problems much faster than we can identify them and respond. We simply cannot foresee all of the ways complex natural systems will react to human-initiated changes at their present scale and velocity. The organization of knowledge by a minute division of labor further limits our capacity to comprehend whole-systems effects, especially when the creation of fast knowledge in one area creates problems elsewhere at a later time. Consequently, we are playing catch-up, but falling farther and farther behind. Finally, for reasons once described by Thomas Kuhn, fast knowledge creates power structures whose function it is to hold at bay alternative paradigms and world views that might slow the speed of change to manageable rates. The result is that the system of fast knowledge creates social traps in which the benefits occur in the near term while the costs are deferred to others at a later time.

The fact is that the only knowledge we've ever been able to count on for consistently good effect over the long run is knowledge that has been acquired slowly through cultural maturation. Slow knowledge is knowledge shaped and calibrated to fit a particular ecological and cultural context. It does not imply lethargy but rather thoroughness and patience. The aim of slow knowledge is resilience, harmony, and the preservation of "patterns that connect." Evolution is the archetypal example of slow knowledge. Except for rare episodes of punctuated equilibrium, evolution seems to work by the slow trial-and-error testing of small changes. Nature seldom, if ever, bets it all on a single throw of the dice. Similarly, every human culture that has artfully adapted itself to the challenges and opportunities of a particular landscape has done so by the patient and painstaking accumulation of knowledge over many generations; an "age-long effort to fit close and ever closer" into a particular place.* Unlike fast knowledge generated in universities, think-tanks, and corporations, slow knowledge occurs incrementally through the process of community learning motivated more by affection than by idle curiosity, greed, or ambition.

The worldview inherent in slow knowledge rests on beliefs that

- wisdom, not cleverness, is the proper aim of all true learning;

---

*The words are those of George Sturt, one of the last English wheelwrights, quoted from his *The Wheelwright's Shop* (p. 66, 1923/1984) Cambridge University Press, Cambridge, United Kingdom.

- the velocity of knowledge is inversely related to the acquisition of wisdom;
- the careless application of knowledge can destroy the conditions that permit knowledge of any kind to flourish (a nuclear war, for example, made possible by the study of physics, would be detrimental to the further study of physics);
- what ails us has less to do with lack of knowledge but with too much irrelevant knowledge and the difficulty of assimilation, retrieval, and application, as well as lack of compassion and good judgment;
- the rising volume of knowledge cannot compensate for a rising volume of errors caused by malfeasance and stupidity generated in large part by inappropriate knowledge;
- the good character of knowledge creators is not irrelevant to the truth they intend to advance and its wider effects;
- human ignorance is not an entirely solvable problem; it is, rather, an inescapable part of the human condition.

The differences between fast knowledge and slow knowledge could not be more striking. Fast knowledge is focused on solving problems, usually by one technological fix or another; slow knowledge has to do with avoiding problems in the first place. Fast knowledge deals with discrete things; slow knowledge deals with context, patterns, and connections. Fast knowledge arises from hierarchy and competition; slow knowledge is freely shared within a community. Fast knowledge is about know-how; slow knowledge is about know-how *and* know-why. Fast knowledge is about "competitive edges" and individual and organizational profit; slow knowledge is about community prosperity. Fast knowledge is mostly linear; slow knowledge is complex and ecological. Fast knowledge is characterized by power and instability; slow knowledge is known by its elegance, complexity, and resilience. Fast knowledge is often regarded as private property; slow knowledge is owned by no one. In the culture of fast knowledge "man is the measure of all things." Slow knowledge, in contrast, occurs as a co-evolutionary process among humans, other species, and a shared habitat. Fast knowledge is often abstract and theoretical, engaging only a portion of the mind. Slow knowledge engages all of the senses and the full range of our mental powers. Fast knowledge is always new; slow knowledge often is very old. The besetting sin inherent in fast knowledge is hubris, the belief in human omnipotence now evident on a global scale. That of slow knowledge can be parochialism and resistance to needed change.

Are there occasions when we need fast knowledge? Yes, but with the caveat that many of the problems we now attempt to solve quickly through complex and increasingly expensive means have their origins in the prior applications of fast knowledge. The point, as every accountant knows, is the difference between gross and net. After all of the costs of fast knowledge are subtracted, the net gains in many fields have been considerably less than we have been led to believe.

What can be done? Until the sources of power that fuel fast knowledge run dry, perhaps not a thing. Then again, maybe we are not quite so powerless as that. The problem is clear: we need no more fast knowledge cut off from its ecological and social context—no more ignorant knowledge. In principle, the solution is equally clear: We need to discover and sometimes rediscover the knowledge of things like how the Earth works, how to build sustainable and sustaining communities that fit their regions, how to raise and educate children to be decent people, and how to provision ourselves justly and within ecological limits. We need to remember all of those things as means by which to repair a world fractured by competition, fear, greed, and shortsightedness. If there is no quick cure, neither are we without the wherewithal to create a better balance between the real needs of society and the pace and kind of knowledge generated. For colleges and universities, in particular, I propose the following steps aimed at improving the quality of knowledge by slowing its acquisition to a manageable rate.

First, scholars ought to be encouraged to include practitioners and those affected in setting priorities and standards for the acquisition of knowledge. Professionalized knowledge is increasingly isolated from the needs of real people and, to that extent, it is dangerous to our larger prospects. It makes no sense to rail about participation in the political and social affairs of the community and nation while allowing the purveyors of fast knowledge to determine the actual conditions in which we live without so much as a whimper. Knowledge has social, economic, political, and ecological consequences as surely as any act of Congress, and we ought to demand representation in the setting of research agendas for the same reason that we demand it in matters of taxation. Inclusiveness would slow research to more manageable rates while improving its quality. And there are good examples of participatory research involving practitioners in agriculture (Hassanein & Kloppenburg 1995), forestry (Banuri & Marglin 1993), land use (Appalachian Land Ownership Task Force 1983), and urban policy (Bryant 1995). There should be many more.

Second, faculty ought to be encouraged in every way possible to take the time necessary to broaden their research and scholarship to include its ecological, ethical, and social context. They ought to be encouraged to rediscover old and true knowledge and to respect prior wisdom. And colleges and universities could do much more to encourage and reward efforts by their faculty to teach well and apply existing knowledge to solve real problems in their communities.

Third, colleges and universities ought to foster a genuine and ongoing debate about the velocity of knowledge and its effects on our larger prospects. We bought in to the idea that faster is better without taking the time to think it through. Increasingly, we communicate electronically by quick-mail and Internet. As a consequence, I believe that one can detect a decline in the salience of our communication and perhaps in its civility in direct proportion to its velocity and volume. It is certainly possible to detect a growing frustration among faculty with the time it takes to service the rising deluge of electronic messages, pronouncements, and directives, and to separate chaff from grain. For comparison, consider the collected correspondence of, say, Thomas Jefferson and James Madison, letters written slowly by quill pen, perhaps by candlelight, delivered by horse, and still full of magic and power nearly 200 years later. Would that magic and power be present still had Tom and James corresponded by e-mail? Somehow, I doubt it.

## Conclusion

Fast knowledge has played havoc in the world because *Homo Sapiens* is not smart enough to manage everything that it is possible for the human mind to discover and create. In Wendell Berry's words, there is a kind of idiocy inherent in the belief "that we can first set demons at large, and then, somehow, become smart enough to control them" (Berry 1983:65).

Slow knowledge really isn't slow at all. It is knowledge acquired and applied as rapidly as humans can comprehend it and put it to consistently good use. Given the complexity of the world and the depth of our human frailties, true knowledge takes time, and it always will. "There is no hurry, there is no hurry whatever."

## Literature Cited

The Appalachian Land Ownership Task Force. 1983. *Who owns Appalachia?* University of Kentucky Press, Lexington.

Banuri, T., and A. Margin. 1993. *Who will save the forests?* ZED, London.

Berry, W. 1983. *Standing by words*. North Point Press, San Francisco.

Bryant, B. 1995. *Pollution prevention and participatory research as a methodology for environmental justice*. Virginia Environmental Law Journal.

Hassanein, N., and J. Kloppenburg. 1995. *Where the grass grows again*. Unpublished.

Lansing, S. 1991. *Priests and programmers*. Princeton University Press, Princeton, New Jersey. ❑

---

## Questions

1. What two factors drive the twentieth century?

2. What does fast knowledge represent?

3. What kind of knowledge have we been able to count on consistently?

*Answers are at the back of the book.*

---

**4**

*Overpopulation seems so overwhelming because it has so many complex causes and consequences. Population problems are entangled with economics, the environment, and culture. The population's increasing natural resource consumption affects the Earth's ecology and the environment. The marine environment is in trouble because of factory fishing and the disposal of pollutants in water. Wetland destruction and deforestation are causing a decrease in biodiversity and the release of carbon into the atmosphere. These factors and many more are the results of increasing population. However, the information, technology, and knowledge are available to stabilize the population enough to establish an environmentally sustainable economy.*

# We *Can* Build a Sustainable Economy
## Lester R. Brown

*The Futurist,* July/August 1996

---

***The keys to securing the planet's future lie in stabilizing both human population and climate. The challenges are great, but several trends look promising.***

The world economy is growing faster than ever, but the benefits of this rapid growth have not been evenly distributed. As population has doubled since midcentury and the global economy has nearly quintupled, the demand for natural resources has grown at a phenomenal rate.

Since 1950, the need for grain has nearly tripled. Consumption of seafood has increased more than four times. Water use has tripled. Demand for beef and mutton has tripled. Firewood demand has tripled, lumber demand has more than doubled, and paper demand has gone up sixfold. The burning of fossil fuels has increased nearly fourfold, and carbon emissions have risen accordingly.

These spiraling human demands for resources are beginning to outgrow the earth's natural systems. As this happens, the global economy is damaging the foundation on which it rests.

To build an environmentally sustainable global economy, there are many obstacles, but there are also several promising trends and factors in our favor. One is that we know now what an environmentally sustainable economy would look like. In a sustainable economy:

- Human births and deaths are in balance.
- Soil erosion does not exceed the natural rate of new soil formation.
- Tree cutting does not exceed tree planting.
- The fish catch does not exceed the sustainable yield of fisheries.
- The number of cattle on a range does not exceed the range's carrying capacity.
- Water pumping does not exceed aquifer recharge.
- Carbon emissions and carbon fixation are in balance.
- The number of plant and animal species lost does not exceed the rate at which new species evolve.

We know how to build an economic system that will meet our needs without jeopardizing prospects for future generations. And with some trends already headed in the right direction, we have the cornerstones on which to build such an economy.

## Stabilizing Population

With population, the challenge is to complete the demographic transition, to reestablish the balance between births and deaths that characterizes a sustainable society. Since populations are rarely ever precisely stable, a stable population is defined here as one with a growth rate below 0.3%. Populations are effectively stable if they fluctuate narrowly around zero.

Thirty countries now have stable populations, including most of those in Europe plus Japan. They provide the solid base for building a world population stabilization effort. Included in the 30 are all the larger industrialized countries of Europe—France, Germany, Italy, Russia, and the United Kingdom. Collectively, these 30 countries contain 819 million people or 14% of humanity. For this goal, one-seventh of humanity is already there.

The challenge is for the countries with the remaining 86% of the world's people to reach stability. The two large nations that could make the biggest difference in this effort are China and the United States. In both, population growth is now roughly 1% per year. If the global food situation becomes desperate, both could reach stability in a decade or two if they decided it were important to do so.

The world rate of population growth, which peaked around 2% in 1970, dropped below 1.6% in 1995. Although the rate is declining, the annual addition is still close to 90 million people per year. Unless populations can be stabilized with demand below the sustainable yield of local ecosystems, these systems will be destroyed. Slowing growth may delay the eventual collapse of ecosystems, but it will not save them.

The European Union, consisting of some 15 countries and containing 360 million people, provides a model for the rest of the world of an environmentally sustainable food/population balance. At the same time that the region has reached zero population growth, movement up the food chain has come to a halt as diets have become saturated with livestock products. The result is that Europe's grain consumption has been stable for close to two decades at under 160 million tons—a level that is within the region's carrying capacity. Indeed, there is a potential for a small but sustainable export surplus of grain that can help countries where the demand for food has surpassed the carrying capacity of their croplands.

As other countries realize that continuing on their current population trajectory will prevent them from achieving a similar food/population balance, more and more may decide to do what China has done—launch an all-out campaign to stabilize population. Like China, other governments will have to carefully balance the reproductive rights of the current generation with the survival rights of the next generation.

Very few of the group of 30 countries with stable populations had stability as an explicit policy goal. In those that reached population stability first, such as Belgium, Germany, Sweden, and the United Kingdom, it came with rising living standards and expanding employment opportunities for women. In some of the countries where population has stabilized more recently, such as Russia and other former Soviet republics, the deep economic depression accompanying economic reform has substantially lowered birth rates, much as the Great Depression did in the United States. In addition, with the rising number of infants born with birth defects and deformities since Chernobyl, many women are simply afraid to bear children. The natural decrease of population (excluding migration) in Russia of 0.6% a year—leading an annual population loss of 890,000—is the most rapid on record.

Not all countries are achieving population stability for the right reasons. This is true today and it may well be true in the future. As food deficits in densely populated countries expand, governments may find that there is not enough food available to import. Between fiscal year 1993 and 1996, food aid dropped from an all-time high of 15.2 million tons of grain to 7.6 million tons. This cut of exactly half in three years reflects primarily fiscal stringencies in donor countries, but also, to a lesser degree, higher grain prices in fiscal 1996. If governments fail to establish a humane balance between their people and food supplies, hunger and malnutrition may raise death rates, eventually slowing population growth.

Some developing countries are beginning to adopt social policies that will encourage smaller families. Iran, facing both land hunger and water scarcity, now limits public subsidies for housing, health care, and insurance to three children per family. In Peru, President Alberto Fujimori, who was elected overwhelmingly to his second five-year term in a predominantly Catholic country, said in his inaugural address in August 1995 that he wanted to provide better access to family-planning services for poor women. "It is only fair," he said, "to disseminate thoroughly the methods of family planning to everyone."

### Stabilizing Climate

With climate, as with population, there is a disagreement on the need to stabilize. Evidence that atmospheric carbon-dioxide levels are rising is clear-cut. So, too, is the greenhouse effect that these gases produce in the atmosphere. That is a matter of basic physics. What is debatable is the rate at which global temperatures will rise and what the precise local effects will be. Nonetheless, the consensus of the mainstream scientific community is that there is no alternative to reducing carbon emissions.

How would we phase out fossil fuels? There is now a highly successful "phase out" model in the case of chlorofluorocarbons (CFCs). After two British scientist discovered the "hole" in the ozone layer over Antarctica and published their findings in *Nature* in May 1985, the international community convened a conference in Montreal to draft an agreement designed to reduce CFC production sharply. Subsequent meetings in London in 1990 and Copenhagen in 1992 further advanced the goals set in Montreal. After peaking in 1988 at 1.26 million tons, the manufacturer of CFCs dropped to an estimated 295,000 tons in 1994—a decline of 77% in just six years.

As public understanding of the costs associated with global warming increases, and as evidence of the effects of higher temperatures accumulates, support for reducing dependence on fossil fuels is building. As the March 1995 U.N. Climate Convention in Berlin, environmental groups were joined in lobbying for a reduction in carbon emissions by a group of 36 island communities and insurance industry representatives.

The island nations are beginning to realize that rising sea levels would, at a minimum, reduce their land area and displace people. For some low-lying island countries, it could actually threaten their survival. And the insurance industry is beginning to realize that increasing storm intensity can threaten the survival of insurance companies as well. When Hurricane Andrew tore through Florida in 1992, it took down not only thousands of buildings, but also eight insurance firms.

In September 1995, the U.S. Department of Agriculture reported a sharp drop in the estimated world grain harvest because of crop-withering heat waves in the northern tier of industrial countries. Intense late-summer heat had damaged harvests in Canada and the United States, across Europe, and in Russia. If farmers begin to see that the productivity of their land threatened by global warning, they too, may begin to press for a shift to renewable sources of energy.

As with CFCs, there are alternatives to fossil fuels that do not alter climate. Several solar-based energy sources, including wind power, solar cells, and solar thermal power plants, are advancing rapidly in technological sophistication, resulting in steadily falling costs. The cost of photovoltaic cells has fallen precipitously over the last few decades. In some villages in developing countries where a central grid does not yet exist, it is now cheaper to install an array of photovoltaic cells than to build a centralized power plant plus the grid needed to deliver the power.

Wind power, using the new, highly efficient wind turbines to convert wind into electricity, is poised for explosive growth in the years ahead. In California, wind farms already supply enough electricity to meet the equivalent of San Francisco's residential needs.

The potential for wind energy is enormous, dwarfing that of hydropower, which provides a fifth of the world's electricity. In the United States, the harnessable wind potential in North Dakota, South Dakota, and Texas could easily meet national electricity needs. In Europe, wind power could theoretically satisfy all the continent's electricity needs. With scores of national governments planning to tap this vast resource, rapid growth in the years ahead appears inevitable.

## A Bicycle Economy

Another trend to build on is the growing production of bicycles. Human mobility can be increased by investing in public transportation, bicycles, and automobiles. Of these, the first two are by far the most promising environmentally. Although China has announced plans to move toward an automobile-centered transportation system, and car production in India is expected to double by the end of the decade, there simply may not be enough land in these countries to support such a system and to meet the food needs of their expanding populations.

Against this backdrop, the creation of bicycle-friendly transportation systems, particularly in cities, shows great promise. Market forces alone have pushed bicycle production to an estimated 111 million in 1994, three times the level of automobile production. It is in the interest of societies everywhere to foster the use of bicycles and public transportation—to accelerate the growth in bicycle manufacturing while restricting that of automobiles. Not only will this help save cropland, but this technology can greatly increase human mobility without destabilizing climate. If food becomes increasingly scarce in the years ahead, as now seems likely, the land-saving, climate-stabilizing nature of bicycles will further tip the scales in their favor and away from automobiles.

The stabilization of population in some 30 countries, the stabilization of food/people balance in Europe, the reduction in CFC production, the dramatic growth in the world's wind power generation capacity, and the extraordinary growth in bicycle use are all trends for the world to build on. These cornerstones of an environmentally sustainable global economy provide glimpses of sustainable future.

## Regaining Control of Our Destiny

Avoiding catastrophe is going to take a greater effort than is now being contemplated by the world's political leaders. We know what needs to be done, but politically we are unable to do it because of inertia and the investment of powerful interests in the status quo. Securing food supplies for the next generation depends on an all-out effort to stabilize population and climate, but we resist changing our reproductive behavior, and we refrain form converting our climate-destabilizing, fossil-fuel based economy to a solar/hydrogen-based one.

As we move to the end of the century and beyond, food security may well come to dominate international affairs, national economic policy making, and—for much of humanity—personal concerns about survival. There is now evidence from enough countries that the old formula of substituting fertilizer for land is no longer working, so we need to search urgently for alternative formulas for humanely balancing our numbers with available food supplies.

Unfortunately, most national political leaders do not even seem to be aware of the fundamental shifts occurring in the world food economy, largely because the official projections by the World Bank and the U.N Food and Agriculture Organization are essentially extrapolations of past trends.

If we are to understand the challenges facing us, the teams of economists responsible for world food supply-and-demand projections at these two organizations need to be replaced with an interdisciplinary team of analysts, including, for example, an agronomist, hydrologist, biologist, and meteorologist, along with an economist. Such a team could assess and incorporate into projections such things as the effect of soil erosion on land productivity, the effects of aquifer depletion on future irrigation water supplies and the effect of increasingly intense heat waves on future harvests.

The World Bank team of economists argues that, because the past is the only guide we have to the future, simple extrapolations of past trends are the only reasonable way to make projections. But the past is also filled with a body of scientific literature on growth in finite environments, and it shows that biological growth trends typically conform to an S-shaped curve over time.

The risk of relying on these extrapolative projections is that they are essentially "no problem" projections. For example, the most recent World Bank projections, which use 1990 as a base and which were published in late 1993, are departing further from reality with each passing year. They show the world grain harvest climbing from 1.78 billion tons in 1990 to 1.97 billion tons in the year 2000. But instead of the projected gain of nearly 100 million tons since 1990, world grain production has not grown at all. Indeed, the 1995 harvest, at 1.69 billion tons, is 90 million tons below the 1990 harvest.

One of the most obvious needs today is for a set of country-by-country carrying-capacity assessments. Assessments using an interdisciplinary team can help provide information needed to face the new realities and formulate policies to respond to them.

## Setting Priorities

The world today is faced with an enormous need for change in a period of time that is all too short. Human behavior and values, and the national priorities that reflect them, change in response to either new information or new experiences. The effort now needed to reverse the environmental degradation of the planet and ensure a sustainable future for the next generation will require mobilization on a scale comparable to World War II.

Regaining control of our destiny depends on stabilizing population as well as climate. These are both key to the achievement of a wide array of social goals ranging from the restoration of a rise in food consumption per person to protection of the diversity of plant and animal species. And neither will be easy. The first depends on a revolution in human reproductive behavior; the second, on a restructuring of the global energy system.

Serving as a catalyst for these gargantuan efforts is the knowledge that if we fail our future will spiral out of control as the acceleration of history overwhelms political institutions. It will almost guarantee a future of starvation, economic insecurity, and political instability. It will bring political conflict between societies and among ethnic and religious groups within societies. As these forces are unleashed, they will leave social disintegration in their wake.

Offsetting the dimensions of this challenge, including the opposition to change that is coming from vested interests and the momentum of trends now headed in the wrong direction, are some valuable assets. These include a well-developed global communications network, a growing body of scientific knowledge, and the possibility of using fiscal policy—a potentially powerful instrument for change—to build an environmentally sustainable economy.

## Policies for Progress

Satisfying the condition of sustainability—whether it be reversing the deforestation of the planet, converting a throwaway economy into a reuse-recycle one, or stabilizing climate—will require new investment. Probably the single most useful instrument for converting an unsustainable world economy into one that is sustainable is fiscal policy. Here are a few proposals:

• **Eliminate subsidies for unsustainable activities.** At present, governments subsidize many of the very activities that threaten the sustainability of the economy. They support fishing fleets to the extent of some $54 billion a year, for example, even though existing fishing capacity already greatly exceeds the sustainable yield of oceanic fisheries. In Germany, coal production is subsidized even though the country's scientific community has been outspoken in its calls for reducing carbon emissions.

• **Institute a carbon tax.** With alternative sources of energy such as a wind power, photovoltaics, and solar thermal power plants becoming competitive or nearly so, a carbon tax that would reflect the cost to society of burning fossil fuels—the costs, that is, of air pollution, acid rain, and global warming—could quickly tip the scales away from further investment in fossil fuel production to investment in wind and solar energy. Today's fossil-fuel-based energy economy can be replaced with a solar/hydrogen economy that can meet all the energy needs of modern industrial society without causing disruptive temperature rises.

• **Replace income taxes with environmental taxes.** Income taxes discourage work and savings, which are both positive activities that should be encouraged. Taxing environmentally destructive activities instead would help steer the global economy in the environmentally sustainable direction. Among the activities to be taxed are the use of pesticides, the generation of toxic wastes, the use of virgin raw materials, the conversion of cropland to nonfarm uses, and carbon emissions.

The time may have come also to limit tax deductions for children to two per couple: It may not make sense to subsidize childbearing beyond replacement level when the most pressing need facing humanity is to stabilize population.

The challenge for humanity is a profound one. We have the information, the technology, and the knowledge of what needs to be done. The question is, Can we do it? Can a species that is capable of formulating a theory that explains the birth of the universe now implement a strategy to build an environmentally sustainable economic system?

*This article is based on* State of the World 1996, *by Lester R. Brown (W.W. Norton, 1996).* ❏

## Questions

1. At what point are populations effectively stable?

2. What entity provides a model for the rest of the world of an environmentally sustainable food/population balance?

3. What type of energy could replace the use of fossil fuels in the future?.

*Answers are at the back of the book.*

**5** *The world's supply of national resources is diminishing. Now we must conserve what we have and find other ways of meeting our needs with a minimum of materials and energy usage. During the last 50 years, the production of raw materials has brought extreme ecological destruction. Industrial logging has more than doubled since 1950 and is responsible for the destruction of primary rain forests in Central Africa and Southeast Asia. Overall, nearly one fifth of the Earth's forested area has been cleared. The United States, in particular, has an unquenchable thirst for energy that greatly attributes to global warming, acid rain, the flooding of valleys, and the destruction of rivers for hydroelectric dams. Collection systems must be developed to collect waste and transform it into new products. Such systems can work if public policies encourages sharing, maintains the value of materials, and promotes the design of efficient goods and services. If 60 percent of all materials were recycled, it would be the equivalent of 315,000,000 barrels of oil a year.*

# Mankind Must Conserve Sustainable Materials

## John E. Young and Aaron Sachs

*USA Today Magazine*, July 1995

*As the supply of natural resources dwindles, the world must focus on meeting human needs with a minimum of materials and energy usage.*

The culture of consumption that has spread from North America to Western Europe, Japan, and a wealthy few in developing countries has brought with it an unprecedented appetite for physical goods and the materials from which they are made. People in industrial countries account for 20% of global population, yet consume 86% of the world's aluminum, 81% of its paper, 80% of its iron and steel, and 76% of its timber.

Sophisticated technologies have let extractive industries produce these vast quantities of raw materials and have helped to keep most materials prices in decline. However, the growing scale of those industries also has exacted an ever-increasing cost. Raw materials production has brought about unparalleled ecological destruction during the last half-century.

The environmental costs of waste disposal, ranging from toxic incinerator emissions to the poisoning of groundwater by landfills, have been docu- mented with increasing frequency. Even greater damage is caused by the initial extraction and processing of raw materials by an immense complex of mines, smelters, petroleum refineries, chemical plants, logging operations, and pulp mills. Just four primary production industries—paper, plastics, chemicals, and metals—account for 71% of the toxic emissions from all U.S. manufacturing. The search for virgin resources increasingly has collided with the few indigenous peoples who had remained relatively undisturbed by the outside world.

Though not many of the world's mostly city-dwelling consumer class comprehend the impacts and scale of the extractive economy that supports their lifestyles, the production of virgin materials alters the global landscape at rates that rival the forces of nature. Mining moves more soil and rock—an estimated 28,000,000,000 tons per year—than is carried to the seas by the world's rivers. Mining operations often result in increased erosion and siltation of nearby lakes and streams, as well as acid drainage and metal contamination by ores containing sulfur compounds. Entire mountains, valleys, and rivers have been ruined by mining. In the U.S.,

59 former mineral operations are slated for remediation under the Federal Superfund hazardous-waste cleanup program, at a cost of billions of dollars.

Cutting wood for materials plays a major role in global deforestation, which has accelerated dramatically in recent decades. Since 1950, nearly one-fifth of the Earth's forested area has been cleared. Industrial logging has more than doubled since 1950, and is particularly culpable in the destruction of primary rain forests in Central Africa and Southeast Asia. Production of agricultural materials has dramatic environmental impacts as well. In the former Soviet republics of Kazakhstan and Uzbekistan, for instance, decades of irrigated cotton production have contaminated large areas of farmland with toxic chemicals and salt.

The chemical industry has become a major source of materials, including plastics, which increasingly have been substituted for heavier materials, and synthetic fibers, which have become crucial to the textile industry. The impacts of chemical production— from hazardous-waste dump sites such as Love Canal to industrial accidents like the release of dioxin from a Seveso, Italy, plant in 1977—generally are more familiar than those from mining, logging, and agriculture, since chemical facilities usually are located closer to urban areas.

Raw materials industries are among the planet's biggest consumers of energy. Mining and smelting alone take an estimated five to 10% of global energy use each year. Five primary materials industries— paper, steel, aluminum, plastic and container glass— account for 31% of U.S. manufacturing energy use. This thirst for energy contributes significantly to such problems as global warming, acid rain, and the flooding of valleys and destruction of rivers for hydroelectric dams.

Despite the environmental impacts of the materials economy, the principal subject of debate over materials policy in the last several decades has been how soon Earth is likely to run out of nonrenewable resources. Yet, the ecosystems that provide renewable resources could collapse long before that point is reached.

Since the 1970s, growth in industrial nations' raw materials consumption has slowed. Some observers believe that these countries have reached a consumption plateau, for much of their materials-intensive infrastructure—roads and buildings—already is in place, and markets for cars, appliances, and other bulky goods largely are saturated. The plateau they sit on is a lofty one, though, and the consumer culture still is going strong.

Materials use has reached extraordinary levels in industrial countries because of an outdated global economic framework that depresses virgin materials' prices and, most important, fails to account for the environmental costs of their extraction and processing. Prices have continued to fall even as ecological expenses of the global materials economy have risen sharply. During the past decade, almost every major commodity has gotten significantly cheaper throughout the world—a trend that, in turn, allowed consumption rates to continue their steady growth.

International trade rules and the policies of industrial nations tend to reinforce materials consumption patterns that date back to the colonial era, when empires were assembled to secure access to raw materials for manufacturing industries in home countries. The development assistance policies of former colonial powers tend to favor the production and export of primary commodities, which they often still receive in large quantities from the countries they once ruled. World Bank and International Monetary Fund planners generally advise commodity-exporting developing nations—many of which are deeply in debt—to invest in those sectors to gain foreign exchange. Such policies, combined with tariffs that are lower for primary commodities than for processed intermediates or manufactured goods, have tended to depress prices of primary material commodities as compared with recovered materials.

At the other end of the cycle, industrial countries commonly subsidize waste disposal as well. In the U.S., where national policy officially favors waste reduction, reuse, and recycling over landfilling and incineration, actual practice has been the reverse. Local communities have spent billions of dollars to finance construction of disposal facilities, while cheaper, more environmentally sound waste management options have received little funding. A large share of these waste disposal costs are hidden in property taxes or utility assessments, rather than being paid for directly per unit of waste. Thus, there is little incentive not to throw things away.

Favoring disposal over waste reduction, re-use, and recycling squanders not only materials, but the large amounts of energy embodied in products that are buried or burned. A 1992 study of recycling and incineration found that, while significant amounts of energy can be recovered through burning, three to five times more can be saved by recycling municipal solid waste. Increasing the recovery of materials in U.S. solid waste so that at least 60% of all materials are recycled could save the equivalent of 315,000,000 barrels of oil a year.

Preserving the natural resource base will require the creation of an economy that produces much less waste and can function with relatively small inputs of virgin materials. Sooner or later, of course, the over-all efficiency of the system will have to improve on a massive scale; all the goods and services the economy produces will have to be designed to need far fewer materials. On a more immediate level, though, it is necessary to look at "wastes" and secondary materials in an entirely different light. The throwaway culture of "convenience" and planned obsolescence must be discarded in favor of an approach that seeks value in products even after people think they have finished using them.

The practical consequences of this attitude will be complex and varied. Perhaps most important, entrepreneurial and employment opportunities would grow rapidly in the recovery and reprocessing of used materials. A wide variety of items—from bottles to shipping containers—could be reused dozens of times, then collected for remanufacturing. Car owners might bring their tires to a local auto parts dealer to get retreaded and, later perhaps, melted down into completely different products. Composted kitchen, yard and, sewage wastes would be plowed back into gardens and farms. Recycled-paper mills would outnumber those equipped only for virgin fiber, and smelters fed by recycled metals would replace a major share of mining operation. In general, cities—where used resources, factories, and labor are concentrated—would become a more important source of materials than rural mines or forests.

Bringing about change on this scale is going to require more than today's incremental increases in governments' environmental budgets, curbside pickup of newspapers and the occasional trip to the community bottle bank. The job demands an infusion of capital, design skill, imagination, and public commitment comparable to America's economic mobilization during World War II. Like that process, this one will have to proceed from public policies, but its principal players will be industrialists, financiers, engineers, designers, and thousands of small businesses. In the long run, efficient use of materials should mean not only less environmental damage, but also a more stable economy, better long-term investment opportunities, and more skilled jobs, especially in design industries.

The most obvious place to start is with the current subsidization of virgin materials extraction. Raw material production should be taxed, not subsidized. A reformed tax system could force industries to cover the full environmental costs of their activities, instead of leaving the bill for the public to pay. By raising prices to more realistic levels, such a system would provide strong incentives not to degrade the natural resource base in the first place. Market forces need to be aligned for, rather than against, materials efficiency.

A related policy could force households and businesses to pay the full cost of disposing of their waste—with the clear understanding that a more efficient economy would make it well worth their while.

Truly taking responsibility for garbage will involve far more than just paying a little extra for its disposal. The ultimate goal is to develop comprehensive systems for collecting waste and transforming it into new products, which will be possible only if many consumer goods are redesigned to be reused and recycled easily.

Recovering secondary materials and re-integrating them into the economy will be crucial in the struggle to reduce the need for virgin resources. Over the long term, though, it will be necessary to make basic design changes in the materials economy to eliminate materials needs and wastes at the source.

Two decades ago, when the world faced an energy crisis, skeptics scoffed at the idea that efficiency was the key to a sustainable energy policy. Since then, new lighting, heating, cooling, insulation, and manufacturing technologies have made it possible to cut energy use by three-fourths or more in many applications. The improved technologies often are cheap enough to make energy efficiency a better investment than energy production.

Houses can be designed to save materials without sacrificing comfort. Even the boards they are made of could be produced more efficiently. In recent years, managers of industrial sawmills, frustrated at how much wood was being lost as sawdust, determined that they could realize considerable savings simply by using thinner blades to saw logs; the thinner blades cut just as well as the originals but left more of the wood intact. By combining similar technologies already available—ranging from two-sided copying in offices to the adoption of efficient architectural techniques—the U.S. could cut its wood consumption in half.

Efficiency policies will have to cover a wide range of issues, but on the most basic level they all need to spark smarter design. Three principles may help designers, architects, engineers, planners, and builders work together to make that happen.

The first is to promote sharing. For years, consumers have obtained reading materials from free public libraries instead of buying increasingly expensive books that they probably would read only once. Many people likely would welcome the opportunity to apply the same concept of sharing and re-use to thousands of other everyday items—power tools, bottles and jars, cars, or computer data, for example.

A second principle is to maintain the value added to materials. Extraction, processing, refining, and manufacturing all add value to a raw material. These processes also have major environmental costs. If a computer becomes worthless a few months after its purchase because a much better, cheaper model has hit the market, the economy has wasted all the effort and environmental damage that went into the device's manufacture. The item would lose value much more slowly if it were designed specifically to be repaired or upgraded easily. The more durable a product is, the less frequently the cycle of processing or reprocessing has to start over again.

The third is to design goods and services in context. A product design is most likely to be mate-rials- and-energy efficient if it is considered as part of the entire system in which it functions. It often is more efficient to substitute a broad systemic change for an individual product.

Synergistic gains between components of design are not realized simply by plugging in energy-efficient technologies or materials. They emerge only when design professionals work together from beginning to end—as they did, for example, when the National Audubon Society built its new headquarters in New York City. Audubon achieved massive improvements in lighting, heating, cooling, ventilation, and over-all indoor air quality. The architects drew up floor plans to take full advantage of natural light; the contractor installed windows that let just the right amount of light and heat pass through them, the lighting technician knew, accordingly, that the building would need fewer lamp fixtures; and the interior designer arranged surfaces and finishes to get the most out of the lamps.

Such integrated design costs perhaps three times as much as conventional design. Nevertheless, according to Amory Lovins, whose Rocky Mountain Institute has done pioneering studies on the subject, the resulting efficiency improvements can yield as much as 25% more floor space in a building of the same size. The extra expense may be recovered immediately in materials savings—fewer ducts will be necessary, for instance, if climate-control systems are smaller—and a good design would yield substantial energy-saving dividends over the life of the structure.

This truly thoughtful design no doubt would be more common if society rewarded it more directly. An engineer's commission usually is based on a percentage of the overall project budget—a practice that in many cases rewards oversizing. Taking the opposite approach, the Canadian utility Ontario Hydro recently announced that it would reward design that met certain energy-efficiency standards with a rebate equivalent to three years' energy savings, to be shared by the developer, architect, and consulting engineers. By basing the rebate on the finished product—the building's actual energy performance—the utility was adding an incentive for the design professionals to stay involved and ensure that their ideas were executed properly during the structure's construction, operation and maintenance. Although materials efficiency is harder to measure than energy efficiency, similar methods of compensating designers for work that reduces materials intensiveness could be just as effective.

Even with such incentives, smarter design will remain difficult until information systems are in place that give fuller descriptions of products and materials. The "green labels" now seen in several countries are intended to encourage purchases of environmentally preferable products, but they provide little detailed data and are directed primarily at consumers. More promising would be in-depth green labeling for designers and builders. Information on a material's origin, its capacity for re-use and recycling, the environmental costs of its production, etc., will have to become an essential part of its design specifications.

Systematically reworking materials specifications to include environmental information would be a step in the right direction. Accomplishing this reform on a broad scale, though, will require a much clearer understanding of how materials production and use actually affect the environment. Currently, detailed information on that topic is just as scarce as information about waste. Yet, materials-efficient design ultimately will be impossible without it. Data must be developed at every level of society, from corporate materials audits—which should help firms identify opportunities for efficiency improvements—up to national and international accounting of materials flows. These statistics also need to be linked with data on the amount of energy, pollution, and economic activity associated with materials production and use.

There have been at least a few promising initiative in this area. In the U.S., the Bureau of Mines has started compiling limited, but extremely useful, information on materials production, consumption, and recycling. The eventual goal is to track comprehensively the quantities of materials flowing into and out of the American economy, allowing progress in materials efficiency to be measured. Similarly, the Department of Energy has begun to collect more detailed energy-use statistics. Combining the two data sets undoubtedly will uncover valuable opportunities for saving energy through more efficient materials use.

Data on pollution and hazardous waste generation from production processes, exemplified by the information collected annually in the U.S. Toxics Release Inventory (TRI), also has been useful. Unique in the world, the Environmental Protection Agency's TRI lists the reported output of several hundred toxic substances by American manufacturers. Data are available by the specific facility or company, by geographical area or industrial sector, or by chemical. The TRI has its flaws—including limited coverage of industries and chemicals, and poor quality control on its data—but it is a good starting point for the sort of comprehensive system that is needed. It would be very useful if such a system included data on raw materials that flow into industrial facilities—a reform Massachusetts has implemented on a limited basis through its toxics use reduction law.

In the long run, materials-data collection efforts—like energy-use tracking—make sound economic sense, since they could inspire efficiency improvements that would far outweigh the cost of amassing the information. They could also help in making materials choices by facilitating quick assessments of the energy use, pollution, jobs, and waste associated with production of a given material or product—a virtually impossible task today. ❑

## Questions

1. Name five primary materials industries and the problems they contribute to.

2. Explain what would need to be done in order to take responsibility for garbage.

3. Why has materials use in industrial countries reached extraordinary levels?

*Answers are at the back of the book.*

**6** *With the advent of technological innovations, the world's death rate has decreased and life expectancy increased. These factors, combined with the third world countries' steadily increasing birth rate, are placing maximum demand on the world's resources. The world needs more energy, materials, land, water, labor, and capital. This article addresses the question, Can technology help us expand the productivity of these resources and help create a sustainable economy in the long run? We would need a smoke-free system of generating hydrogen and electricity that is highly proficient, higher yielding crops, a reduction in materials intensity which would preserve natural resources and decrease human exposures to hazardous materials, and a more efficient water system.*

# Can Technology Spare the Earth?
## Jesse H. Ausubel

*American Scientist*, March/April 1996

*Evolving efficiencies in our use of resources suggest that technology can restore the environment even as population grows.*

Technologies have enabled us to expand our range and transform the earth. In 1909 Peary sledded to the North Pole and in 1911 Amundsen reached the South. Improved navigational aids and ships that could withstand the pack ice made the poles accessible to men and dogs. Less than a century later we worry about the environmental purity of the polar regions and the ozone that shields them. My fundamental question is whether the technology that has conquered the earth can also spare it.

To answer this question, I shall examine secular trends in what technology does with four paramount resources: energy, materials, land and water. I focus on the evolving efficiency of use of these resources. Economists call such resources "factors of production," along with labor and capital.

Customarily, technology's relation to environment is considered by evaluating lists of devices and machines: cars, oil tankers, nuclear power stations, windmills, wastewater-treatment plants, spray cans and chain saws. My approach is more basic. I ask whether technology enables us to obtain services more efficiently and, if so, at what rates. The answers indicate the feasibility of greatly diminishing our environmental burdens by increasing the productivity of our resources.

Analysts, eager to assimilate the latest information, live life on the tangent, extrapolating brief fluctuations to eternity. To counter this tendency, I search for stable signals amid the noise of the daily news. The historical analyses shared here, many contributed to an ongoing project at The Rockefeller University on technological trajectories and the human environment, seek the inherent lifetimes of processes of technological development, which can extend generations and centuries. Recognizing and formally analyzing incomplete developmental processes and the rhythmic patterns of processes permits confident prediction.

Identifying secular trends also enables me to frame answers to a second question: what distinguishes the last half-century or so with regard to environment and technology? The years around 1970 marked the maximum rate of growth of human population in modern times. Have we more generally passed a point of inflection in the curve of human development? Finally, what present actions will wave us toward sweet, greener days?

Two basic arguments weigh against technology. One is that technology's success is self-defeating. Technology makes the human niche elastic. If we solve problems, our population grows and creates further, eventually insurmountable problems. The cardinal case is the conquest of death in the developing countries. Public-health measures and modern medicine defeat mortality, while fertility declines at a much slower pace, and so population explodes. Before closing, I shall consider technology's relation to population. Population is always the catch.

The second argument contra-technology is the paucity of human wisdom. Technology creates handguns and hydrogen bombs, and these kill. We can use science and technology to provide goods and services for human sustenance and comfort and other purposes worth for the planet. But technology powers good and evil. Some would feel more comfort with less power. I leave it to others to discuss the cultural controls to assure constructive use of science and technology.

A subordinate, manageable argument is that unanticipated consequences of the introduction of technologies diminish their value. Chlorinated fluorocarbons solved the problem of explosive and inefficient ammonia-based refrigerators, but turned out 40 years after their introduction to threaten life's stratospheric filter. The appropriate response is a feedback system: Assess technologies early in their prospective social penetration, watch them thereafter for surprises and tailor designs to fit changing needs and tastes.

I outline a global picture, with most detail from the United States. For more than a century the United States has on average adopted technologies earliest, diffused them fullest and documented the outcomes. The symptoms and cures show.

## Energy

Energy systems extend from the mining of coal through the generation and transmission of electricity to the artificial light that enables the reader to see this page. For environmental technologists, two central questions define the energy system. First, is the efficiency increasing? Second, is the carbon used to deliver energy to the final user declining?

Energy efficiency has been gaining in many segments, probably for thousands of years. Think of all the designs and devices to improve fireplaces and chimneys. Or consider the improvement in motors and lamps. About 1700 the quest began to build efficient engines, at first with steam. Three hundred years have increased the efficiency of generators from 1 to about 50 percent of the apparent limit, the latter achieved by today's best gas turbines. Fuel cells can advance efficiency to 70 percent. They will require about 50 years to do so, if the socio-technical clock continues to tick at its established rate. In 300 years, physical laws many finally arrest our engine progress.

Whereas centuries measure the struggle to improve generators, lamps brighten with each decade. A new design proposes to bombard sulfur with microwaves. One such bulb the size of a golf ball could purportedly produce the same amount of light as hundreds of high-intensity mercury-vapor lamps, with a quality of light comparable to sunlight. The current 100 year pulse of improvement will surely not extinguish ideas for illumination. The next century may reveal quite new ways to see in the dark. For example, nightglasses, the mirror image of sunglasses, could make the objects of night visible with a few milliwatts.

*Segments* of the energy economy have advanced impressively toward local ceilings of 100 percent efficiency. However, modern economies still work far from the limit of *system* efficiency because the system efficiency is multiplicative, not additive. In fact, if we define efficiency as the ratio of the theoretical minimum to the actual energy consumption for the same goods and services, modern economies probably run at less than 5 percent efficiency for the full chain from extracting primary energy to delivery of the service to the final user. So, far from a ceiling, the United States has averaged about 1 percent less energy to produce a good or service each year since about 1800. At that pace of advance, total efficiency will still approach only 15 percent by 2100. Because of some losses difficult to avoid in each link of the chain, the thermodynamic efficiency of the total system in practice could probably never exceed 50 percent. Still, in 1995 we are early in the game.

What about the decarbonization of the energy system? Carbon matters because it blackens lungs, causes air pollution and oil spills and regulates climate. Carbon is also a surrogate for sulfur, heavy metals and other environmental bads that attach to it in the dirty fossil fuels. Carbon enters the energy economy bonded with hydrogen as wood (and other biomass), coal, oil, and natural gas. Per unit of energy, wood weighs most heavily in carbon followed by coal, and then oil, with natural gas following as much the lightest.

One can measure decarbonization in several different ways. Plentiful natural gas, efficient turbines and thrifty end-use devices promise more energy delivered with less carbon during the next decades.

Uranium also decarbonizes. At the end of 1993 432 operating nuclear reactors provided almost 20 percent of the world's electricity. Even if a fraction of the 48 listed in the 1994 as under construction never operate, the remainder assure a continuing nuclear contribution to decarbonization. The radioactive reactor products, which are toxic and also hard and slow to degrade, and potentially powerful explosives, must of course be safely isolated. Solar sources also decarbonize but continue to stumble over obstacles in energy storage and transport.

Consider decarbonization also as the diminishing carbon intensity of the economics of a range of countries. Measured as the ratio of kilograms of carbon to gross domestic product and taking into account fuelwood and other renewable sources of energy, the decarbonization of dozens of nations studied, including Turkey, Thailand and China as well as the United Kingdom, Germany and Japan, has advanced almost in parallel. Countries begin at different times from different situations, but once they begin to decarbonize, they advance at about the same rates, and irreversibly, so far. Between 1970 and 1993, even the gas-guzzling United States more than doubled the ratio of its income to carbon use, decarbonizing about 3 percent per year. The spectrum of achievement, from about 3 kilograms of carbon per dollar of output in China to less than 0.2 in Japan and France, shows the distance most of the world economy stands from leading practice. The carbon intensity of the Chinese and Indian economies resembles the Japanese, American and European at the onset of industrialization in the 19th century.

Fundamentally, decarbonization tracks a technological competition between combustible elements.

In the hydrocarbons, the truly desirable element for energy generation is not the carbon but the hydrogen. The evolution of the atomic ratio of hydrogen to carbon in the world fuel mix displays the gradual and unrelenting penetration of the energy market by the number one element of the periodic table.

All these analyses imply that during the next 100 years the human economy will clear most of the carbon from its system and move, via natural gas, to hydrogen metabolism. Hydrogen, fortunately, is the immaterial material. It can be manufactured from something abundant, namely water, it can substitute for most solid, liquid and gaseous fuels in use, and the product of its combustion, water vapor, does not pollute. The next decades will see a vigorous growth in the hydrogen industry. Nightly nuclear heat seeking a market outlet can efficiently steam-reform natural gas into hydrogen and carbon dioxide, the latter permanently reinjected into the gas fields from whence it came. Later, hear, nuclear or solar, can neatly decompose water.

Hydrogen, of course, requires a partner, electricity, to provide action at a distance in a clean energy system. Since Edison began the commercial industry in the 1880s, the electrical system has grown in two neat pulses each lasting about 50 years, synchronized with long cycles of economic growth. A new pulse of growth should soon begin, in which electricity powers not only more information products but also more of the transport system, using linear motors. The magnetically levitated train soon to operate between Hamburg-Berlin inaugurates the way.

Combining analyses of efficiency and decarbonization startles many with the fact that national energy systems with the fact that national energy systems ranging from India to South Korea to France are heading in the right direction, toward micro-emissions. The way is long, but we are on the right path.

### Land

Of all human activities, agriculture transforms the environment most widely. Crops and pasture occupy at least one-fifth the land surface, at least ten times as much as cities, towns and roads. Agriculture has consumed forests, drained wetlands, erased habitats and favored some plants over others in fierce green warfare. Farms, or course, also feed us.

Yields per hectare measure the productivity of land and the efficiency of land use. To 1940, yields per hectare of most crops advanced little, and more mouths required more land to feed them. During the past half century, ratios of crop to land for the world's major grains—maize, rice, soybean and wheat—have climbed, fast and globally. The rise in wheat in India, Egypt, Ireland and the U.S. shows the inception and the spread of the trend.

A cluster of innovations including tractors, seeds, chemicals and irrigation, joined through timely information flows and better organized markets, raised yields to feed billions more without clearing new fields. In fact, since mid-century global, cropland has remained stable. Expansion in developing countries has offset contraction in Europe and North America.

As the century draws to a close, the earth is at a historic turning point in land use. The continuing diffusion high yields and efficient land use permits the absolute reversal of the destruction of nature that has occurred for many centuries.

Societies chronically fear exhaustion of the potential to increase food supply. In reality, the agricultural production frontier is still spacious, even without invoking the engineering of plants with new molecular techniques. For many decades in Iowa, while yields have risen steadily, the average corn grower has managed only half the yield of the Iowa master grower, and the work grows only about 20 percent of the top Iowa farmer. The production ratio of the performers has not changed much since 1960. In Iowa the average performer lags more than 30 years behind the state of the art.

Even where diffusion proceeds at a moderate pace, the effects accumulate dramatically. In India, for example, by raising wheat yields farmers spared 42 million hectares, about the size of Sweden or California, if we compare the land actually harvested in 1991 with the land the farmers would have harvested at 1961-66 yield for the actual production. Globally, the land spared since 1960 by raising yields of grain, which make up more than half of all calories, equals the Amazon basin.

A single-minded concentration on land raises concern that side effects will harm the nature we seek to preserve. In fact, land requires little more clearing, tilling and cultivating for high yields than for low ones. Protecting lush foliage needs little more pesticide and usually less herbicide than sparse foliage. Luxuriant foliage also protects soil better from erosion. The law of diminishing returns applies to fertilizers, which farmers tend to use abundantly. In many area yield gains now come by optimizing inputs such as nitrogen and phosphorus in step and lowering total application. In sum, careful management of the land we do use is likely to diminish the total fallout from food production. Most fallout is coextensive with land use.

What is a reasonable outlook for the land cropped for future population? Future calories per capita will likely lie between the 3,000 per day of vegetarian diet and the 6,000 that include meat (counting dietary calories plus the calories fed to food and draft animals and not recovered in milk, meat and so on). Let us consider, as Paul Waggoner has done (Waggoner 1994), how much cropland a population of 10 billion, almost twice the present, could spare for wilderness or other purposes with that range of calories per capita. If farmers fail to raise global average yields form the present 2 tons grain equivalent per hectare, people will have to lower their daily portions to 3,000 calories to avoid further land clearing. But Irish wheat and American corn now average 8 tons per hectare. If farmers can lift the global average to 5, 10 billion people on average can enjoy the diet 6,000 calories bring, and spare a quarter of the *present* 1.4 billion hectares of cropland. The quarter spared is about twice the size of Alaska. If future farmland on average yielded today's U.S. corn, 10 billion eating an American diet could allow cropland the area of Australia to revert to wilderness.

Per hectare, annual world grain yields in fact rose 2.15 percent 1960-1994. If dynamics continue as usual, farmers will grow 8 tons per hectare around 2060, at the end of the decade in which the United Nations projects population to reach 10 billion. From the Great Plains of America to the Great Plains of China, reversion of farms and ranches to woods and grasses will be spreading, major environmental feature of the next decades, and beyond. And governments will avidly seek rationales to subsidize agriculture to keep it from contracting more rapidly than culture will allow.

## Materials

We can reliably project more efficient energy, decarbonization and effectively landless agriculture. What about a companion dematerialization? I will define dematerialization primarily as the decline over time in weight of materials used to perform a given economic function.

Dematerialization would matter enormously for the environment. Excluding water and oxygen, in 1990 each American mobilized on average about 50 kilograms per day. Reducing the materials intensity of the economy could preserve landscapes and natural resources, lessen garbage and reduce human exposures to hazardous material.

Over time new material substitute for old. Successful new materials usually show improved properties per ton, thus leading to a lower intensity of use for a given task. The idea is as old as the epochal succession from stone to bronze to iron. Our century has witnessed the relative decline of wood and the traditional metals and the rise of aluminum and especially plastics.

Modern examples of dematerialization abound. Since the early 19th century, the ratio of weight to power in industrial boilers has decreased almost 100 times. Within the steel industry, powder metallurgy, thin casting, ion beam implantation and directional solidification as well as drop and cold forging have allowed savings up to 50 percent of material inputs in a few decades. In the 1970s a mundane invention, the radial tire, directly lowered weight and material by one-quarter below the bias-ply tire it replaced. An unexpected and bigger gain in efficiency came form the doubling of tire life by radials, so halving the use of material (and the piles of tire carcasses blighting landscapes and breeding mosquitoes). Lightweight optical fibers with 30 to 40 times the carrying capacity of conventional wiring and invulnerability to electromagnetic interference are ousting copper in many segments of the telecommunications infrastructure. The development of high-fructose corn syrup (HFCS) in the 1960s eliminated sugar from industrial uses in the United States. HFCS has five times sugar's sweetening power on a unit-weight basis, with a proportional impact on agricultural land use.

Certainly many products—for example, cars, computers and containers—have become lighter and often smaller. Compact discs selling for less than $100 now contain 90 million home phone numbers of Americans, equivalent to the content of telephone books once costing $60,000 and weighing 5 tons. At midcentury, glass bottles dominated. In 1953 the first steel soft-drink can was marketed. Cans of aluminum, one-third the density of steel, entered the scene a decade later and by 1986 garnered more than 90 percent of the beer and soft-drink market. Between 1973 and 1992 the aluminum can itself lightened 25 percent. In 1976 polyethylene terephthalate resins began to win a large share of the market, especially for large containers previously made of glass.

Recycling, of course, diminishes the demand for primary materials and may thus be considered a form of dematerialization. No longer limited to resource-poor individuals and regions during the past couple of decades recycling has regained standing as a generalized social practice in the U.S. and other societies with huge material appetites.

Difficulties arise in the more complex "new material society" in which the premium lies on sophisticated materials and their applications. Alloys and composites with attractive structural properties can be hard to separate and recycle. Popular materials can be lighter but bulkier or more toxic. Reuse of plastics may be less economical than burning them (cleanly) for fuel or otherwise extracting their chemical energy. Most important, economic and population growth has multiplied the volume of products and objects. Thus, total wastes have tended to increase while declining per unit of economic activity.

By weight, construction materials makeup about 40 percent of the materials Americans consume and thus form a significant metric. Although absolute use of physical-structure materials by weight has fluctuated, consumption per unit of economic activity has trended downward since 1970. Because energy materials such as petroleum constitute another 40 percent of our materials diet, increased in energy efficiency could also markedly dematerialize economies.

As yet, trends with respect to dematerialization are equivocal. Better and more complete data on materialization and dematerialization over long periods for the United States and the rest of the world need to be assembled and analyzed. Moreover, the heterogeneity of purpose of material will never permit the performance of the materials sector to be summarized as simply as kilowatts and carbon can summarize energy, or tons per hectare summarize land. A kilogram of iron does not compare with one or arsenic. But the promise clearly exists for what Robert Frosch, I and our colleagues call a superior "industrial ecology," in which the materials intensity of economy declines, wastes lessen and the wastes that are created become nutritious in new industrial food webs.

## Water

We can get more value from each unit of energy, land and material. Can we squeeze more from a drop of water?

Total per capita water withdrawals quadrupled in the United States between 1900 and 1970, and overall personal consumption increased by one-third between just 1960 and the early 1970s. However, since 1975, per capita water use has fallen appreciably, at an annual rate of 1.3 percent. Absolute water withdrawals peaked about 1980.

Industry, alert to technology as well as costs, exemplifies the progress, although it consumes a small fraction of total water. Total industrial water withdrawals plateaued a decade earlier than total U.S. withdrawals and have dropped by one-third, more steeply than the total. More interesting, industrial withdrawals per unit of GNP (in 1982 dollars) have dropped steadily since 1940, when 14 gallons of water flowed into each dollar of output. Now the flow is less than 3 gallons per dollar. The steep decline taps many sectors, including chemicals, paper, petroleum refining, steel and food processing. After adjusting for production levels, not only intake but discharges per unit of production are perhaps one-fifth of what they were 50 years ago.

In manufacturing, technology as well as law and economics have favored frugal water use. More efficient use of heat and water usually go together, through better heat exchangers and the recirculation of cooling water. Legislation, such as the U.S. Clean Water Act of 1972, encouraged reduction of discharges and recycling and conservation as well as shifts in relative price. Although water treatment may cost only about 5 percent of production, wastewater-treatment systems are expensive capital investments.

Despite the gains, the United States is far from most efficient practice. Water withdrawals for all users in the countries making up the Organization for Economic Cooperation and Development range tenfold, with the U.S. and Canada the highest. Allowing for differences in major uses (irrigation, electrical cooling, industry, public water supply), large opportunities for deductions remain. In the late 1980s over 90 percent of measured U.S. hazardous wastes were still wastewaters.

In the long run, with much higher thermodynamic efficiency for all processes, removing impurities to recycle water will require small amounts of energy. Dialytic membranes open the way to such efficient purification systems. Because hydrogen will be, with electricity, the main energy carrier, its combustion (if from seawater) may eventually provide another important source of fresh water, perhaps 200 liters per person per day at the level of final consumers, about one-forth the current withdrawal in water-prudent societies such as Denmark. Importantly, as agriculture contracts spatially and irrigates more frugally, its water demand will shrink.

## Population

I have demonstrated a revolution in factor productivity, whether energy, land, materials or water. The game to get more from less is old. In energy, global progress is documented for centuries. With land, the Chinese started long ago, but most of the world began only about 1940. 1940 also appears to have marked a crossing point for new material. In water, U.S. industry joined the search about 1940, and the population more generally about 1970.

The catch for *homo faber* is that our technology not only spares resources but also expands our niche. Technology further adds to population by increasing longevity and decreasing mortality. Although fertility has also declined greatly, the role of new birth-control technologies in the decline has been small. Feedbacks may well also occur between population growth and density on the one hand and invention and innovation on the other.

Population provides a multiplier that determines total consumption. So far I have stressed ratios, not absolutes.

To see graphically how technology can change carrying capacity, consider the population history of Japan. From the establishment of the Tokugawa Shogunate about 1600 Japan insulated itself from outside technology until 1854 when American Commodore Matthew Perry reopened trade. In 1868 the Meiji restoration lessened the isolationist policy of the former imperial party, and Japan entered a period of great borrowing from the Occident. Japanese population growth since 1100 sorts perfectly into two pulses of growth. Tokugawa technology (and culture) and its medieval predecessors accommodated a gradual addition of 28 million over about five centuries to Japan's earlier population of about 5 million. Meiji and Western technology keyed the opening of the niche to another 100 million or so in one century.

Reasoning about the link between technology and carrying capacity from the Japanese case, my colleague Perrin Meyer and I have speculated about the growth of the population of the U.S. We hypothesize a sequence of overlapping pulses of population growth centered on times of rapid economic expansion, the midpoints of tentatively identified 50-year-long waves of economic growth. Technological innovations affecting resources, processes and products cluster in each economic wave and expand carrying capacity. The first pulse of population growth associates with wood, iron, steam, canals, and wool and cotton textiles; the second with coal, steel, railways, telegraphy and early electrification; and the third with oil, plastics, autos, widespread electrification, telephony, computers and pharmaceuticals. The fourth emerging pulse revolves around natural gas, aviation and a host of information and molecular technologies. Daring to extrapolate our reasoning with a "superlogistic" curve using the center points of the growth pulses as the base points, we find the U.S. population saturating around 400 million in 2100, a total consistent with projections made by conventional demographic methods.

Clearly the limits to human numbers keep shifting. In any case, analysis of historic population data shows that the global rate of growth peeked at about 2.1 percent per year around 1970, as noted near the outset of the article. Fertility rates, the key factor, have been falling in most nations and are below the levels needed to replace current population in Europe and Japan. The difficulty is that we have no logic to predict future fertility, and simply fitting an equation, as we did for the U.S., is chancy. Globally, the pervasive economic and social effects of the information revolution could allow the increase in human numbers to 15 or 50 or 100 billion, or influence the fertile to choose not to reproduce. The question of future population appears quite open, as reflected in the spray of projections.

## Conclusion

Population frames the challenge for green technologists. To maintain current levels of cleanliness with the 50 percent increase in population I think likely for the United States and the current level and kind of economic activity, emissions per unit of activity would need to drop by one-third. That is an easy target. An improvement of 1.5 percent per year reaches the target by 2020, 80 years early.

The challenge is much harder taking into account growing consumption. If economic activity doubles per capita roughly every 30 years, as it has since about 1800 in the industrialized countries, the result is an eightfold increase by 2100. Multiplied by population, the United States would have 12 times today's emissions and demands on resources, other things being equal. This scenario of the "dirty dozen" requires micro- or zero emissions per unit of economic activity to maintain or enhance environmental quality. In other words, Americans need to clean processes by more than one order of magnitude. More reassuringly, the annual cleaning need be about 2.5 percent.

In Europe and Japan population is stable or even shrinking, easing the magnitude of their environmental challenges. The rest of the world, where most people live, faces the twin pressures of enlarging economies and populations. So in absolute terms the technical gains must be enormous.

But we have seen the outlines of how the gains can be made. In the long run, we need a smoke-free system of generating hydrogen and electricity that is highly efficient from generator to consumer, food decoupled from acreage, materials smartly designed and selected for their uses and recycled, and carefully channeled water. In short, we need a lean, dry, light economy.

In truth, I exaggerate the challenge. With respect to consumption, multiplying income will not cause an American to eat twice as much as today in 2020 or eight time more in 2100, and even a mouth moving today from Lima to Los Angeles only triples its original caloric intake. With respect to production, history shows that the economy can grow from epoch to epoch only according to a new industrial paradigm, not by inflating the old. High environmental performance forms an integral part of the modern paradigm of total quality. The past half-century signals the preferred directions: the changeover from oil to gas, the contraction of crops in favor of land for nature, the development of a new ecology of materials use in industry, and diffusion of more efficient water use to farmers and residents as well as industries.

Economists always worry about trading off benefits in one area for costs in another. Hearteningly, we have seen that, in general, efficiency in energy favors efficiency in material; efficiency in materials favors efficiency in land; efficiency in land favors efficiency in water; and efficiency in water favors efficiency in energy. The technologies that will thrive, such as electricity, will concert higher resource productivity. Prone to fail is a technology, such as biomass farming for energy, which brings into conflict the goal to spare land with the goal to spare carbon.

Some worry that the supply of a fifth major resource, ingenuity, will run short. But nowhere do averages appear near the frontier of current best practice. Simply diffusing what we know can bring gains for several decades. Moreover, science and technology are young. Aggressively organized research and development (R&D) is another innovation of the past 50 years. Many industries have systematized their search for better practice ("endogenized R&D" in the economics jargon) and have the productivity gains to show for it. Other industries, including much of the service sector which now forms the bulk of modern economies, and the enlarging public and non-profit sectors have improved slowly. Overall, society hardly glimpses the theoretical limits of performance.

Inevitably, sectors and societies will advance at unequal pace. We will continue to have laggards as well as pioneers. Problems will arise from the distribution of goods, the actions and interactions of bads, shocking and poorly tailored innovations and social traps such as the well-known "tragedy of the commons," which today sadly entangles the wild stocks of fish. Yet the long history of technical progress and its reach into more sectors during recent decades encourage. Perhaps the first Earth Day in 1970 was an inflection point.

Policy can interfere wastefully with dynamics-as-usual, where they are benign. For example, decarbonization mandates the phasing out of the coal industry worldwide over the next decades; the political system might prudently assist those who lose their livelihoods, but not with dollars for actual coal. Wise policy favors science, experimentation and fluidity, while addressing inequity and security and insuring against catastrophe.

Families named Smith, Cooper, and Miller people our nation because until not long ago most of us beat metal, bent casks, and ground grain. Now few workers hold such jobs. So far, except in video, we are not named Programmer, Sub-Micron, and Genesplicer. We easily forget how much the modern world has changed and yet how early our day is. We forget the power of compounding our technical progress, even at one or two percent per year. Knowledge can grow faster than population and provide abundant green goods and services. The message from history is that technology, wisely used, can spare the earth. You can click on it. ❑

**Questions**

1. What are two basic arguments against technology?

2. List the factors of production.

3. Approximately what year marked the maximum rate of growth of human population in modern times?

*Answers are at the back of the book.*

*Deforestation, soil erosion, desertification, wetland degradation, and insect infestation are some of the major indicators of how severe environmental degradation is in sub-Saharan Africa. As poverty runs rampant throughout the area, the inhabitants of Africa have to overexploit natural resources, thereby causing environmental degradation simply to survive. Three elements that increase degradation in this area are demographics, foreign debt, and the absence of democracy. Population has been a source of contention as well. During the last 25 years, social services, especially in education and health care, have led to a decrease in infant mortality and an increase in population. The developmental strategies attempted in these countries not only caused destruction to the environment at large, but did not improve the average standard of living. Furthermore, even though sub-Saharan Africa has a large natural resource base, degradation is still prevalent. But perhaps the most significant element is that the information on the environment and its degradation remains insufficient. Hope for sub-Saharan Africa lies with institutional development, which can reduce poverty and conserve the environment by encouraging democracy, fostering human rights, and enlarging the information base so that environmental concerns can be decided upon. If these institutional developments can be implemented, the people of sub-Saharan Africa can turn the economic hardships of their countries around and improve the attributes of their environment.*

# The Environmental Challenges of Sub-Saharan Africa

## Akin L. Mabogunje

*Environment,* May 1995

Sub-Saharan Africa suffers from some serious environmental problems, including deforestation, soil erosion, desertification, wetland degradation, and insect infestation. Efforts to deal with these problems, however, have been handicapped by a real failure to understand their nature and possible remedies. Conventional wisdom views the people of this region as highly irresponsible toward the environment and looks to the international community to save them from themselves. It tends to blame all of the region's environmental problems on rapid population growth and poverty. Yet, there is no conclusive evidence that Africans have been particularly oblivious to the quality of the environment, nor has the international community shown any genuine concern for it until recently. Clearly, protecting the environment of sub-Saharan Africa is an issue that needs to be examined more carefully and incorporated into an overall strategy of sustainable economic development.

Formulating such a strategy will not be easy: In the closing years of the 20th century, virtually every country in this region is slipping on almost every index of development. The heady post-independence period of the 1960s and early 1970s, when development was considered simply a matter of following a plan formulated by Western experts, has now been succeeded by a time of fiscal crises and international marginalization. The region now finds itself afflicted by the consequences of inappropriate policies, as well as by almost endemic political instability, an inability to manage its economies effectively, and an increasingly hostile external economic milieu. As simple survival has become more problematical, it has become increasingly difficult to avoid overexploiting natural resources and degrading the envi-

*Environment,* Vol. 37, No. 4, pp. 4–35, May 1995. Reprinted with permission of the Helen Dwight Reid Educational Foundation. Published by Heldref Publications, 1319 Eighteenth St., NW, Washington, DC 20036-1802. Copyright © 1995.

ronment. Analysts are now concerned that this will compromise the prospects for sustainable development in the near future.[1]

To understand the full dimensions of the problem, it will first be necessary to examine the factors that predispose sub-Saharan Africa to serious environmental degradation. This will permit a detailed investigation of the environmental problems caused by humans in both rural and urban areas, along with a suggestive comparison between those problems and ones caused solely by nature. It will then be possible to look at the question of environmental protection in terms of sustainable development in the region and to suggest the roles that the state and international assistance ought to play. The present situation offers an important opportunity to redirect development strategy in ways that will not only improve the social and economic well-being of people in this region but also enhance the quality of the environment in which they live.

### Factors Predisposing to Environmental Degradation

There are three factors that strongly increase the threat of environmental degradation in sub-Saharan Africa: its demographics, its heavy burden of foreign debt, and the absence of democracy. Throughout the region, the end of the colonial period saw a tremendous expansion of social services, especially in the areas of education and healthcare. This led to a sharp decline in infant mortality and to a rapid increase in population. During the last 25 years, annual growth rates of 2.5 to 3.5 percent have caused the population of sub-Saharan Africa to double (to 570 million); at the current rate of increase, it should double again in the next 25 years.[2]

An increase of this magnitude within a relatively short time span implies a rising proportion of children in the population and thus a heavier burden on those who must care for them. This has led to mass migration to the cities (particularly by adult males) and other efforts to supplement family income through nonfarm employment. As a result, there has been less time for farm work, and more labor-saving but environmentally harmful shortcuts are being taken. In forested areas, for instance, cleared land is used continuously, even though allowing it to lie fallow from time to time would result in greater productivity and less degradation. In dryland regions, cultivation has been extended into marginal lands that are more easily cleared and cultivated.

Turning to the second factor, countries in sub-Saharan Africa incurred large foreign debts in their efforts to industrialize and to provide their rapidly growing populations with modern social services. Most of these loans have been long-term ones from official sources and on concessional terms; as the need for borrowing has become more urgent, however, countries have turned increasingly to private, short-term loans at market rates. Thus, while in 1970 the region's total official debt (excluding that of South Africa and Namibia) was slightly more than $5 billion (U.S. dollars), by 1990 it had risen to nearly $140 billion. Total private debt, which was zero in 1970, was more than $20 billion in 1990. (With other external loans, the total indebtedness of the region was more than $171 billion by 1990.[3])

The problem, however, lies not so much in the rising level of debt as in the region's dwindling ability to service it. High dependence on the export of primary products left sub-Saharan African countries vulnerable to the long decline of commodity prices that began in the late 1970s. The total value of the region's agricultural exports has fallen dramatically, with the decline averaging 0.8 percent a year from 1975 to 1980, 2.9 percent a year from 1980 to 1985, and 2.5 percent a year from 1986 to 1988. (For some countries the decline has been even more pronounced.[4]) As a result, the burden of debt has risen markedly for most countries in the region. Between 1980 and 1989, the total external debt rose from 27 percent to 97 percent of gross national product and from 97 percent to 362 percent of exports.[5]

Not unexpectedly, most countries in sub-Saharan Africa have had to undergo major structural adjustments. This has entailed not only a drastic compression of imports and a sharp devaluation of national currencies but also the retrenchment of a sizable portion of the wage- and salary-earning population. As living conditions deteriorated, more people turned to survival agriculture, both in urban and rural areas. At the same time, sharply rising prices for imported energy products forced many families to fall back on wood and charcoal for their domestic energy needs. Clearly, these developments put acute strain on the environment everywhere in the region.

The performance of most African governments in implementing the reforms necessary to turn their economies around has also been a source of serious concern. The international community spent the years immediately following independence rationalizing (and sometimes applauding) the necessity for authoritarian one-party or military rule. Over time, these regimes have become inordinately corrupt and have managed the countries' economies without due concern for transparency and accountability. In most countries, this has led to a high level of political instability and social alienation that has impaired both development efforts and environmental protection. There is a growing realization that economic reforms cannot be achieved without a much greater degree of decentralization and democratization in the political process.

Much of the debate about sustainable development in sub-Saharan Africa has focused on the region's severe poverty. There is no question that poverty has become widespread. The World Bank estimates that between 1985 and 2000, the number of persons living below the poverty line will rise from 180 million to 265 million.[6] By 1990, the combination of rapid population growth and an economy in crisis had lowered per capita gross national product to $340, making this region one of the least developed in the world.

For neo-Malthusians, this poverty stems directly from overpopulation; in their view, the two will inevitably lead to an increase in land fragmentation, overutilization of agricultural and grazing land, more frequent famines, lower life expectancy, and considerable environmental degradation.[7] By contrast, the renowned agricultural economist, Ester Boserup, and others argue that population growth need not result in such dire consequences. In their view, population growth can promote more intensive agricultural practices and induce more favorable attitudes toward technological and organizational innovation that will not only increase productivity but improve environmental quality as well.[8]

Two considerations suggest that the second view is more applicable to the situation prevailing in sub-Saharan Africa. First, over the period 1600 to 1900, this region lost a large part of its population to internecine warfare and the slave trade. As a result, by 1900 the region was more sparsely populated than it had been earlier. Second, at 23 persons per square kilometer, the region's current population density is still low compared to that of Asia or Europe.

This is not to imply that there is no cause for concern about the environment in sub-Saharan Africa. One needs to keep a sense of perspective in addressing the question, however. The proper focus is on the region's poverty per se (as opposed to its population growth) and on the impact this has on the environment in both rural and urban areas.

**Poverty and the Rural Environment**

Despite its pervasive poverty, sub-Saharan Africa has substantial natural recourses in its rural areas, including forests and grasslands, wetlands, cultivable soils, and other biological resources.[9] Although only 40 percent of the total land area is under cultivation or used for pasture, much of it is threatened by one form of damage or another.

Three types of environmental damage are occurring in sub-Saharan Africa: deforestation, degradation, and fragmentation. Deforestation is defined as "the temporary or permanent clearance of forest for agriculture or other uses, resulting in the permanent depletion of the crown cover of trees to less than 10 percent."[10] Degradation, on the other hand, refers to the temporary or permanent deterioration in the density or structure of vegetation cover or species composition.[11] It results from the removal of plants and trees important in the life cycle of other species, from erosion, and from other adverse changes in the local environment. Fragmentation arises from road construction and similar human intrusions in forest areas; it leaves forest edges vulnerable to increased degradation through changes in microclimates, loss of native species and the invasion of alien species, and further disturbances by human beings.

While there is no doubt that all three processes are taking an increasingly heavy toll on the forest and woodland areas of sub-Saharan Africa, there is considerable controversy over the exact rate at which this is occurring. Estimates based on the subjective judgment of experts or on data from low-resolution sensors on weather satellites are generally higher than those based on the more accurate data from high-resolution sensors on the Landsat and Spot satellites.[12] Until more of the latter data are available, the actual extent of deforestation will remain uncertain.

The United Nations Food and Agriculture Organization (FAO) estimates that forested land was converted to agricultural uses at increasing rates over the period 1981 to 1990 and that such changes accounted for 25 percent of the changes in forest cover during the period.[13] These changes were concentrated in the moist and dry forest lowland areas, where the average annual conversion rate was higher than in tropical rain forest areas. Except for the dry forest areas, however, conversion rates in sub-Saharan Africa are lower than those in Latin America and the Asia-Pacific region.

Degradation and fragmentation involve a much larger area than deforestation and pose a greater threat to the diversity of plant and animal life. Selective logging and the failure to pursue a systematic program for forest regeneration (either natural or artificial) are the two major factors promoting rapid degradation of the forest and woodland environment. Owing to the desperate need for foreign exchange, the rate of logging in sub-Saharan Africa rose more than 34 percent between 1979 and 1991, compared with a global average of only 19 percent. Similarly, the lack of foreign exchange to purchase petroleum has led to a rapid rise in the production of fuelwood and charcoal.[14]

There are no firm estimates of the harm resulting from degradation and fragmentation in the region. Two factors suggest that it is considerable, however: First, the ratio of forest regeneration to deforestation is as low as 1:32 in sub-Saharan Africa, compared with ratios of 1:2 in Asia and 1:6 in Latin America.[15] Second, one out of every six species in the tropical moist forests has some economically valuable, nontimber use.[16]

Nowhere is this loss of biological resources more marked than in the region's wetlands. These wetlands include river floodplains, freshwater swamps and lakes, and coastal and estuarine environments. They provide a number of valuable resources, including wood; foraging, hunting, and fishing opportunities; and land for crops and pasture. They also contribute significantly to aquifer recharge and flood control, as well as providing habitat for migratory birds and other organisms.

Degradation of these wetlands is due not to population growth or poverty but to modern development, principally the construction of major dams on important rivers. These dams control water flow over much of the rivers' length and impair the agricultural value of wetlands both by lowering water quality and by altering the extent and timing of floods.[17] In Nigeria's Benue floodplain, for instance, the reduction in flooding caused by the Lagdo Dam led to a 50 percent reduction in the area used for environmentally friendly flood-recession sorghum farming in the dry years of the mid-1980s.[18] Similarly, the Diama Barrage on the Senegal River, built to prevent incursion of salt water during periods of low river flow, is expected to cause the loss of some 7,000 tons of shrimp and fish, while Manantali Dam is expected to greatly reduce the fish catch in that river.

If wetlands are being degraded by inappropriate development, grasslands and other relatively dry areas are being degraded by both rapid population growth and inappropriate technology and land-use practices. Recent studies, however, highlight the resilience of dryland ecosystems and caution against confusing natural changes due to recurring droughts with the long-term degradation caused by human activities.[19] They also argue against the simplistic application of the general concepts of overgrazing and carrying capacity in dryland environments.

This is not to say that such factors as overgrazing, overcultivation, and excessive use of wood for fuel have not contributed to the degradation of drylands. Rather, it is to stress that degradation occurs only where these activities lead to detrimental changes to the soil system itself as well as to plant cover. Damage to the soil system results either from erosion or from physical and chemical changes in the soil itself. Erosion by wind or water is a serious problem in dryland areas because the naturally thin soil and its slow rate of formation make recovery difficult. Such erosion accounts for nearly 86 percent of the total degradation of dryland areas in sub-Saharan Africa.[20] The remainder is primarily due to the loss of nutrients from excessive cultivation and lack of fertilization.

Estimates based on the GLASOD (Global Assessment of Soil Degradation) approach indicate that by 1992 nearly 320 million hectares of drylands in sub-Saharan Africa had degraded soils, ranging from light and moderate (77 percent) to strong and extreme (23 percent).[21] These estimates, however, represent a considerable (almost two-thirds) reduction in the area previously thought to be suffering desertification as a result of human activities. Improved monitoring capabilities are making it increasingly clear that climatic variations are responsible for much of the degradation of soils in the region.

Even so, the loss of biological diversity—due to habitat destruction, the introduction of exotic species, overharvesting, pollution, and other activities that affect natural ecosystems—is a growing problem in sub-Saharan Africa. This is especially significant because biodiversity is greatest in the tropics. According to one estimate, between 40 and 90 percent of all plant and animal species are found in tropical forests.[22] Based on current trends in habitat destruction, as many as 11 percent of total species may become extinct during every 10-year period from 1975 to 2015.[23]

Despite international agreements such as the Convention on International Trade in Endangered Species of Flora and Fauna (CITES), hunting of elephants, rhinoceroses, and alligators is still a major problem in some African countries. The situation is even more serious in the case of birds, because widespread pollution is destroying their habitats, often in imperceptible ways. Tragically, although most endangered species are technically under government protection, as a practical matter they are resources free for the taking.

## Poverty and Urban Environments

Although sub-Saharan Africa is the least urbanized region in the world, its urban population is growing quite rapidly. In 1965, urban areas accounted for only 14 percent of the total population of the region; by 1990, however, such areas accounted for 29 percent, and by 2020, the figure should be more than 50 percent. Already, there are 27 metropolitan areas with populations greater than 1 million and 1 (Lagos) with a population of at least 10 million.[24]

Consequently, even in urban areas, the widespread poverty exerts a strong negative impact on air, water, and land resources. The ongoing economic crisis has intensified the level of air pollution in most countries. Most households can no longer afford to use petroleum or gas products for fuel and are relying increasingly on charcoal or wood. This has greatly increased the amount of carbon dioxide generated by cities in the region. While in 1991 the region accounted for just 2 percent of global carbon dioxide emissions from industrial processes, its total contribution to global carbon dioxide emissions (from both urban and rural areas) was 19 percent.[25] Also contributing to the problem is the increased use of substandard industrial equipment and motor vehicles, made necessary because the region lacks the funds to invest in more environmentally responsible devices. Thus, three countries in the region—South Africa, Zaire, and Nigeria—are now ranked among the top 50 countries in terms of their 1991 contributions to global greenhouse emissions.[26]

Air pollution, both indoor and outdoor, exposes the population to serious health hazards, especially from suspended particulate matter and lead. Most sub-Saharan African cities do not yet suffer from serious outdoor pollution. Nonetheless, the increased use of wood and charcoal in household kitchens is exacerbating indoor air pollution and heightening the risk of acute respiratory infections, particularly among infants and children. In some areas, lead pollution from substandard vehicles is also starting to increase the risks of hypertension, heart attacks, and strokes.

Access to clean water is also a major problem throughout sub-Saharan Africa. Although the region as a whole has large water resources, a number of countries in the drier areas have experienced serious shortages. Within these countries, some 35 percent of the urban population has no source of drinking water within 200 meters of their homes. For 13 of the 18 countries for which data are available, the proportion of the population with ready access to water has declined since the 1970s;[27] in countries without data, the situation is probably worse.

Safe water, however, is a premium everywhere

in the region. Water pollution, largely from human waste, has become a serious health hazard because the economic crisis is preventing most countries from providing adequate water treatment. Diseases such as typhoid, cholera, and diarrhea are spread by drinking contaminated water, while bilharzia, guinea worm, roundworm, and schistosomiasis are spread by bathing in it. Water pollution thus exacts a tremendous toll on the population of sub-Saharan Africa, raising infant mortality rates and impairing the health of all age groups.[28]

Degradation of land resources, mainly from improper disposal of solid and toxic wastes, is another problem. Although the volume of such wastes is much lower than in industrial countries, most of the region lacks even rudimentary collection and disposal facilities. Refuse is simply dumped along roads and other public places or into waterways, contributing to the spread of disease. Although toxic wastes are not yet widespread and exposure is fairly localized, there is fear of surreptitious trade in and dumping of such wastes in some countries.

## Natural Disasters

In addition to human-induced degradation, geophysical events (such as droughts, floods, tornadoes, windstorms, and landslides) and biological events (such as locust and pest invasions) greatly affect the environment and the well-being of people in sub-Saharan Africa. The two most important geophysical events are probably drought and floods. Drought is defined as a period of two or more years during which rainfall is well below average.[29] In ecological terms, it is simply a dry period to which an ecosystem may be adapted and from which it often recovers quickly. Drought should be distinguished from dryland degradation, which, as pointed out earlier, is brought about by inappropriate land-use practices under delicate environmental conditions.

Unlike dryland degradation, however, drought inflects acute distress on human beings and animals, forcing mass migrations from the affected areas. Given the region's poverty and its inability to invest in new techniques, plant strains, storage facilities, and so on, the capacity to deal with drought is severely limited. As a result, many countries have become dependent on international assistance; this is especially true for small countries, but even large ones like Ethiopia (where a drought occurred in the midst of a prolonged civil war) have needed significant help. However, once normal rainfall resumes, recovery takes place quickly and people tend to return to their native areas.

Floods, on the other hand, stem from periods of heavy rainfall, either in the immediate locality or upstream of it. They are most common in river valleys and floodplains. In rural areas, their effects can be beneficial as well as harmful. Although flash floods destroy crops, livestock, and settlements, they provide ideal conditions for certain fish and for cultivating crops such as paddy rice, millet, sorghum, and vegetables. In urban areas, however, especially where there has been indiscriminate building on floodplains or where channels are blocked, floods pose a real danger to life and property. In Ibadan, Nigeria, for instance, the flood of 31 August 1980 claimed about 200 lives, displaced about 5,000 persons, and damaged property worth millions of dollars.[30]

Insects are the most important biological hazard in sub-Saharan Africa. According to Thomas Odhiambo, the leading African entomologist, "The insect world in tropical Africa is a rich and diverse one."[31] Although some species confer benefits such as pollinating trees and other plants, many others are pests to plants or serve as vectors in the transmission of disease. Serious study of insects began only recently. The initial emphasis has been on combating plant pests through heavy pesticide use—with all the deleterious environmental consequences this implies. Fortunately, most farmers in the region cannot afford to use pesticides to any great degree.

As the entomology of the region becomes better understood, there is growing appreciation of the potential for biological control of pests. The best example so far is the cassava mealybug program. Mealybugs were inadvertently introduced into sub-Saharan Africa from South America in the early 1970s. Within less than a decade, they had cut cassava yields by two-thirds in most parts of the region. However, biologists eventually found a natural enemy of the mealybug; specially bred in laboratories and distributed throughout the cassava-growing areas, it has brought losses substantially under control. Thus, this program not only saved a staple on which so many people depend but also prevented major harm to the environment.

## The Potential for Sustainable Development

Three points stand out clearly from this review of environmental challenges in the rapidly growing but poor countries of sub-Saharan Africa. First, the development strategy pursued in most of these countries has wrought serious havoc on the environment without necessarily improving the average person's standard of living. Second, this has taken place despite the region's relatively ample natural resources. Third, and perhaps most important, knowledge about the region's environment and its degradation remains inadequate.

Nowhere is this last point more true than in the attempt to explain environmental degradation in terms of population growth. This Malthusian argument depends on there being a "carrying capacity" beyond which the environment will inevitably suffer. But as already pointed out, in most of sub-Saharan Africa the population density is relatively low. Furthermore, some prime agricultural lands are clearly "undersettled," while areas less suited to agriculture are densely populated.[32]

A recent study of the relationships among population growth and density, the intensification of agriculture, and the implications for sustainability offers some useful insights on this issue.[33] The study focused on 10 areas with relatively dense populations (ranging from 150 to more than 1,000 persons per square kilometer). Five of these were in East Africa (in Kenya, Rwanda, Uganda, and Tanzania), while the remaining five were in West Africa, mainly Nigeria. In all of these areas, the study found that "contrary to much conventional wisdom that portrays the African smallholders as wrecking their physical resources, particularly in the face of land-intensive conditions…farmers…made considerable investments in resource-based capital, thereby protecting their farms from major environmental deterioration and the negative impacts of intensification and production that usually follow."[34]

Similar conclusions have been reached regarding other aspects of the population-environment equation in sub-Saharan Africa. Contrary to conventional wisdom, detailed field investigations in Nigeria have found that the rising demand for fuelwood has not led to greater deforestation or desertification. Far from "overcutting their trees," farmers have been maintaining their tree stocks by planting and by protecting spontaneous seedlings. The area studied showed "a 2.3 percent per annum increase in tree density between 1972 and 1981, in the wake of the disastrous drought of the late 1960s and early 1970s when pressure on woody vegetation from human and natural sources must have been very intense."[35] Field investigations in Uganda and Mali drew similar conclusions.[36]

This is not to imply that there have been no instances of severe environmental degradation. These have only occurred under three special circumstances, however: where the population density was greater than 500 per square kilometer; where the area itself was physically or biologically vulnerable; and where socioeconomic conditions impeded the implementation of conservation measures. Indeed, decreases in well-being (indicated by reduced food availability) are attributable not to rapid population growth but to the persistence of customary land tenure arrangements, misguided macroeconomic policies, and inadequate infrastructure. According to the World Commission on Environment and Development, chaired by Gro Harlem Brundtland in 1987, sustainable development is "a process of change in which the exploitation of resources, the direction of investments, the orientation of technological development, and institutional change are *in harmony* [emphasis added] and enhance both current and future potential to meet human needs and aspirations."[37] Included in the concept of harmony, of course, is the access of producers to the various factors of production, especially land.

The problem of land tenure, like many of the other problems besetting the development process in sub-Saharan Africa, probably stems from the region's incomplete transition from one mode of production to another. Colonialism attempted to shift the economies of these countries from a precapitalist mode of production (based largely on kinship relations) into a global capitalist mode (based on "commoditized" factors of production whose prices were subject to the forces of supply and demand in a self-regulating market). Though praiseworthy in many ways, these efforts failed signally in the one major area where they could have made a real difference: the patterns of land ownership in rural areas. By and large, colonial administrators left the traditional patterns intact, thus introducing a major contradiction into the development process.

While capitalism requires well-established individual property rights, most smallholders in sub-Saharan Africa have no such rights, even though they have longstanding rights to the use of communal land. Smallholders thus have no "economic assets" in the conventional sense of the term.[38] Second, they have no real collateral against which to borrow and thus no access to the credit they need to invest in improved farm infrastructure, new cultigens, and modern technologies generally. When one considers the heavy investment that went into producing the polders of the Netherlands or the wheat-lands of North America, the disability under which African farmers labor becomes readily apparent.

Consequently, much as colonial and post-colonial governments tried to make farmers more market oriented, the fact that one of their major inputs lies outside the market system has always limited the success of this effort. In many cases, farmers have chosen simply to "opt out" of the system, especially now that governments make little attempt to ensure that they receive fair prices for their output.[39] The unnecessary liabilities under which farmers labor probably account for a large part of the poverty in sub-Saharan Africa.

Other aspects of the macroeconomic policies pursued by most African governments simply served to deepen the poverty under which the majority of their rural populations labored and exacerbated the negative impact of their activities on the environment. Widening budget deficits eroded the value of national currencies, fueled inflation, undermined peoples' real income, and encouraged excessive exploitation of natural resources to maintain even a subsistence level of existence.

### The Roles of the State and International Assistance

It is clear that the environmental challenges in sub-Saharan Africa are more complex than the simple model linking environmental degradation to population growth and inappropriate macroeconomic policies indicates. Because of this complexity, no easy solutions are available. But whatever policies are adopted, to succeed they must increase peoples' interest in protecting the environment by involving them directly in the process; reduce the incidence of poverty to reduce the pressure on natural resources; and show people how a high level of resource use can go hand-in-hand with the maintenance of environmental quality.

The state can play an important role in promoting sustainable development and improvement of the environment. By setting the correct investment priorities, it can provide needed infrastructure, services, and education. In urban areas, it should focus on providing safe water, collecting and disposing of solid wastes, and improving the physical layout of congested places; in the rural areas, it should focus on health education and basic sanitation.

Regulatory measures, however, may be more important than public investment. In this regard, the state should set environmental standards that are realistic in terms of the country's particular socio-economic circumstances. For example, setting strict standards for indoor air pollution when most people cannot afford less-polluting energy sources simply makes enforcement impossible. Regulatory measures should also aim to remove those distortions in the economy that tend to penalize producers and/or promote overconsumption. Important examples include underpricing agricultural commodities and subsidizing public goods and services, both of which favor the urban population at the expense of the rural population. Such distortions, of course, are partly responsible for the economic collapse of many countries in sub-Saharan Africa. Although structural adjustments now taking place may improve matters, the governments' lack of commitment has left the situation far from satisfactory.

Conservation measures have been important in protecting most natural resources from excessive use or degradation. Through its power of eminent domain, the state has been able to set aside sizable tracts of land to protect watersheds, prevent soil erosion, allow natural regeneration to take place,

41

and preserve habitats, species, and biodiversity. As of 1993, there were 663 public reserves or parks in sub-Saharan Africa, totally 125.2 million hectares.[40] This, however, is no more than 4.6 percent of the total land area of the region, much less than the 6 percent for the world as a whole. Moreover, the 1992 Caracas Action Plan of the World Parks Congress set a goal of protecting at least 10 percent of each of the world's major biomes; sub-Saharan Africa currently falls far short of this standard.

Simply setting land aside, however, does not mean being able to manage it properly. Many governments in the region lack the staff or financial resources to administer their protected areas, much less invest in new ones. Innovative strategies, such as involving private groups and nongovernmental organizations, are being considered and may provide another option for conservation management. Such groups are believed to be better able to raise funds to purchase land, to support conservation activities in existing parks and reserves, to incorporate the local population in management decisions, and to negotiate land-use disputes within and between communities.

Important as public investment, regulation, and conservation are, however, it is institutional development that offers the most hope for alleviating poverty and protecting the environment. Three aspects of institutional development are paramount: promoting democracy, expanding individual property rights, and increasing the knowledge base.

Decentralization and democratization must go down to the community level and must entail not only giving people a voice in decisions but also ensuring that they can raise the revenues necessary to translate their desires into reality. It is this that will promote transparency and accountability in government and foster a proprietary interest in the quality of the environment.[41]

The importance of expanding property rights was made clear earlier. Although it is often claimed that land tenure in sub-Saharan Africa is so complex that nothing can be done about it, it is difficult to believe that meaningful reforms cannot be introduced. The most serious mistake that many governments have made, however, was to resort to nationalization.[42] From a conservation standpoint, nationalization often fails to distinguish between traditional communal property systems (which promote sound management of natural resources) and open-access systems (which result in excessive exploitation). When land and water have been nationalized and sound management practices disturbed, the environmental consequences have often been very severe.[43]

Nationalism has also led governments to give short shrift to titling and registration. Yet, until such procedures clearly define rights to land (on either a freehold or a leasehold basis), much of the region's natural resources are bound to be treated as common property and therefore suffer degradation and "the tragedy of the commons."

The third aspect of institutional development relates to the knowledge available for making decisions on environmental matters. People in sub-Saharan Africa have been adapting to the region's various environments for thousands of years. In the process, they have accumulated valuable information that should be incorporated into more formal analyses of sustainable development.[44] Along with such knowledge, of course, must go the collection and analysis of field data by modern techniques. This is necessary to correct the "hallowed but mistaken" notions of conventional wisdom and to give governments in the region better appreciation of the causes and effects of environmental damage as well as the costs and benefits of different policy options. In this regard, independent commissions provide a useful way for governments to draw on technical expertise both within and outside of their countries; they can also be instrumental in bringing the results of advanced research to bear on local problems.

As mentioned earlier, current knowledge of the ecology of tropical forests and grasslands is still rudimentary. The rich biological resources of these areas—and the ways in which humans relate to them—have yet to receive as much study as they deserve. Given the shortage of funds and trained personnel in most sub-Saharan African countries, this is an area where bilateral and multilateral assistance could make a real difference. The Convention on Biological Diversity, signed by 153 countries at the 1992 United Nations Conference on Environment and Development (UNCED) in Rio de Janeiro, is correct in insisting that tropical countries be compensated for protecting biological diversity from which others benefit.[45] If such compensation became the order of the day, some of it should be used to finance further study of tropical ecosystems.

Poor countries in sub-Saharan Africa could also use international assistance in reforming their environmental laws and in selecting optimal strategies for environmental management. Not enough emphasis has been given to the role of law in alleviating poverty and protecting the environment. Particularly in the area of pollution charges, the experience of developed countries could be invaluable. But countries in the tropics that are being asked to protect biodiversity and genetic resources partly for the benefit of others also need technical assistance in legally defining and protecting their rights regarding these resources.

Consequently, management strategies must go beyond assessing the impact of individual projects, as this tends to address the symptoms rather than the root causes of environmental problems. Such strategies must pay greater attention to broader issues and recognize intersectoral links and intergenerational concerns. This would entail integrating natural resource management with national economic planning as well as tailoring international assistance to specific aspects of resource conservation. To implement such strategies, African countries must strive to secure broad consensus and support, both nationally and internationally.

## Conclusion

In the closing years of the 20th century, most countries in sub-Saharan Africa find themselves almost returning to the drawing board. Three decades of trying to drive their economies according to Western models have left them prostrate, their people wallowing in poverty, and their environment exposed to many hazards. More importantly, the international indebtedness of these countries and their present unattractiveness to foreign investors are forcing them to rethink the whole question of development.

The next 25 years thus offer real opportunities for improvement, beginning with population control. At the household level, the economic crisis is inducing a reassessment of the viability of large families; at the governmental level, political inertia and indifference to family planning programs are being replace by more effort and initiative. Already, fertility has begun to decline in some countries, such as Zimbabwe, Kenya, and Cameroon.[46] Although the future remains uncertain, there is every likelihood that this trend will spread across the region.

A decline in fertility, however, will not completely eliminate the momentum that has built up in the years of rapid population growth. The number of people will continue to increase, raising the population density all over the region. But as already emphasized, there is growing evidence that the African environment is more resilient than conventionally thought and can probably support a higher level of population and more intensive agriculture. Technological innovations and institutional developments are thus more important to maintaining a sound environment in sub-Saharan Africa than are efforts to reduce population pressure. If the focus of development shifts from mere economic growth to eradicating the widespread poverty, the people as a whole can play a more decisive role, not only in turning the economic fortunes of their countries around but also in enhancing the quality of the environment.

## Notes

1. World Bank, *Sub-Saharan Africa: From Crisis to Sustainable Development: A Long Term Perspective Study* (Washington, D.C., 1989), 22.
2. United Nations Centre for Human Settlements, *Global Report on Human Settlements 1986* (New York: Oxford University Press, 1987), table 1.
3. World Bank, *World Development Report 1992* (New York: Oxford University Press, 1992), 258–59.
4. W.B. Morgan and J.A. Solarz, "Agricultural Crisis in Sub-Saharan Africa: Development Constraints and Policy Problems," *Geographical Journal* 160, no. 1 (1994); 57–73.
5. World Bank, note 3 above, pages 250–51.
6. World Bank, *World Development Report 1990* (New York: Oxford University Press, 1990), 139.
7. A.S. MacDonald, *Nowhere to Go But Down? Peasant Farming and the International Development Game* (London: Unwin Hyman, 1989).

8. E. Boserup, *The Conditions of Agricultural Growth* (Chicago: Aldine, 1965); and E. Boserup, *Population and Technological Change: A Study of Long-Term Trends* (Chicago: University of Chicago Press, 1981). See also R.W. Kates and V. Haarmann, "Where the Poor Live: Are the Assumptions Correct?" *Environment*, May 1992, 4.

9. World Bank, note 3 above, page 201.

10. A. Grainger, "Quantifying Changes in Forest Cover in the Humid Tropics: Overcoming Current Limitations," *Journal of World Forest Resource Management* 1 (1984): 3–63.

11. World Resources Institute, *World Resources 1994–95* (New York: Oxford University Press, 1994), 133. See also A. Grainger, *Controlling Tropical Deforestation* (London: Earthscan Publications, 1993).

12. A. Grainger, "Rates of Deforestation in the Humid Tropics: Estimates and Measurements," *Geographical Journal* 159, no. 1 (1993): 33–44.

13. Food and Agriculture Organization, *Forest Resources Assessment 1990: Tropical Countries,* FAO Forestry Paper 112 (Rome, 1993), 38.

14. World Resources Institute, note 11 above, page 310.

15. A.D. Jones, "Species Conservation in Managed Tropical Forests," in T.C. Whitmore and J.A. Sayers, eds., *Tropical Deforestation and Species Extinction* (London: Chapman and Hall, 1992), 3.

16. J. Davidson, *Economic Use of Tropical Moist Forests*, Commission on Ecology Paper No. 9 (Gland, Switzerland: International Union for Conservation of Nature and Natural Resources, 1985), 9.

17. B.R. Davies, "Stream Regulation in Africa," in J.V. Ward and J.A. Stanford, eds., *The Ecology of Regulated Streams* (New York: Plenum Press, 1979). For more information on one such project in Botswana, see the review by C.W. Howe of *The IUCN Review of the Southern Okavango Integrated Water Development Project, Environment*, January/February 1994, 25.

18. C.A. Drijver and M. Marchand, *Taming the Floods: Environmental Aspects of Floodplain Development in Africa* (Leiden, the Netherlands: University of Leiden, 1985).

19. A. Warren and M. Khogali, *Assessment of Desertification and Drought in the Sudano-Sahelian Region 1985–1991* (New York: United Nations Sudano-Sahelian Office and United Nations Development Programme, 1993).

20. D.S.G. Thomas, "Sandstorm in a Teacup? Understanding Desertification," *Geographical Journal* 159, no. 3 (1993): 318–31. See also United National Environment Programme, *World Atlas of Desertification* (London: Edward Arnold, 1992).

21. D.S.G. Thomas, note 20 above, page 328.

22. P.H. Raven, "Biological Resources and Global Stability," in S. Kawano, J.H. Connell, and T. Hidaka, eds., *Evolution and Coadaptation in Biotic Communities* (Tokyo: University of Tokyo, 1988), 16–23.

23. W.V. Reid, "How Many Species Will There Be?" in T.C. Whitmore and J.A. Sayers, note 15 above, table 3.2.

24. United Nations Centre for Human Settlements, note 2 above, table 6. See also G. McGranahan and J. Songsore, "Wealth, Health, and the Urban Household: Weighing Environmental Burdens in Accra, Jakarta, and Sao Paulo," *Environment*, July/August 1994, 4.

25. World Resources Institute, note 11 above, pages 362–65. See also K.R. Smith, "Air Pollution: Assessing Total Exposure in Developing Countries," *Environment*, December 1988, 16.

26. World Resources Institute, note 11 above, p. 201.

27. United Nations Development Programme, Environment & Natural Resources Group, *The Urban Environment in Developing Countries* (New York: United Nations, 1992), 29.

28. D. Satterthwaite, "The Impact on Health of Urban Environments," *Environment and Urbanization* 5, no. 2 (1993): 87–111. For another side of this, see J. Briscoe, "When the Cup Is Half Full: Improving Water and Sanitation Services in the Developing World," *Environment*, May 1993, 6.

29. D. Wilhite and M. Glantz, "Understanding the Drought Phenomenon: The Role of Definitions," in D. Wilhite and W. Easterling, eds., *Planning for Drought* (London: Westview Press, 1987), 1130.

30. A.B. Oguntola and J.S. Oguntoyinbo, "Urban Flooding in Ibadan: A Diagnosis of the Problem" *Urban Ecology* 7 (1982): 39–46.

31. T.R. Odhiambo, "Insect Pests," in E.S. Ayensu and J. Marton-Lefevre, eds., *Proceedings of the Symposium on the State of Biology in Africa* (Washington, D.C.: International Biosciences Network, ICSU [International Council of Scientific Unions]), 115.

32. A.J. Dommen, *Innovation in African Agriculture* (Boulder, Colo.: Westview Press, 1988), 115–17.

33. B.L. Turner II, G. Hyden, and R. Kates, eds., *Population Growth and Agricultural Change in Africa* (Gainesville, Fla.: University Press of Florida, 1993).

34. Ibid., page 422. See also M. Mortimore and M. Tiffen, "Population Growth and a Sustainable Environment: The Machakos Story," *Environment*, October 1994, 10.

35. R.A. Cline-Cole, H.A.C. Main, and J.E. Nichol, "On Fuelwood Consumption, Population Dynamics and Deforestation in Africa," *World Development* 18 (1990): 522–23. The conventional view is presented in E. Eckholm, G. Foley G. Barnard, and L. Timberlake, *Firewood: The Energy Crisis that Won't Go Away* (London: Earthscan, 1994); and E. Eckholm and L. Brown, *Spreading Deserts: The Hand of Man*, Worldwatch Paper 13 (Washington, D.C.: Worldwatch Institute, 1977).

36. H.P. Andersen, "Land Use Intensification and Landscape Ecological Changes in Budondo Sub-County, Uganda," (Master's thesis, University of Oslo, 1993); and T.A. Benjaminsen, "Fuelwood and Desertification: Sahel Orthodoxies Discussed on the Basis of Field Data from the Gourma Region of Mali," *Geoforum* 24, no. 4 (1993): 397–409.

37. World Commission on Environment and Development, *Our Common Future* (New York: Oxford University Press, 1987), 46.

38. World Bank, note 6 above, pages 31–32.

39. A.O. Hirschman, *Exit, Voice and Loyalty* (Cambridge, Mass.: Harvard University Press, 1990); see also G. Hyden, *No Shortcuts in Progress: African Development Management in Perspective* (London: Heineman, 1983).

40. World Resources Institute, note 11 above, page 316.

41. See R.L. Paarlberg, "The Politics of Agricultural Resource Abuse," *Environment*, October 1994, 6.

42. A.L. Mabogunje, *Perspective on Urban Land and Urban Management Policies in Sub-Saharan Africa*, Technical Paper No. 196 (Washington, D.C.: World Bank, 1992), 15–22.

43. World Bank, note 3 above, page 12.

44. P. Richards, *Indigenous Agricultural Revolution: Ecology and Food Production in West Africa* (London: Hutchinson, 1985).

45. J.A. Tobey, "Toward a Global Effort to Protect the Earth's Biological Diversity," *World Development* 12, no. 12 (1993): 1931–45.

46. World Resources Institute, note 11 above, page 30. See also the articles in the January/February 1995 issue of *Environment*. ❏

## Questions

1. Name three types of environmental damage in sub-Saharan Africa.

2. Based on current statistics, what percentage of species in sub-Saharan Africa may become extinct from 1975 to 2015?

3. What three countries are ranked in the top 50 in terms of global greenhouse emissions?

*Answers are at the back of the book.*

**8**

*In September 1994, the third United Nations population conference was held in Cairo, Egypt. It was called the International Conference on Population and Development (ICPD). Its approach was gender-sensitive and covered such areas as sustainable human development, family planning in regard to population control, socioeconomic development, education, the environment, and migration. The conference attracted participants from over 150 countries, including governmental delegatates, representatives from international agencies, academics, feminists, environmentalists, and members of the press. During the conference, the official delegations negotiated a 16-chapter, 113-page World Programme of Action (WPOA) that set guidelines for attaining population stabilization, educating girls, and setting up a universal high-quality health care system that would improve child survival and instigate reproductive health care services. The final agreements focused on sustainable development and gave priority to reproductive health, women's empowerment, and reproductive rights. Of the $17 billion allotted for population endeavors, $10 billion is designated for family planning. Overall, the Cairo conference provided a model for the management of global issues.*

# Women, Politics, and Global Management
## Lincoln C. Chen, Winifred M. Fitzgerald, and Lisa Bates

*Environment,* January/February 1995

The third United Nations population conference, held in Cairo last September, was a watershed global event. The International Conference on Population and Development (ICPD) succeeded in both shifting concern about world demographics into a gender-sensitive, peoples-centered approach of sustainable human development and propelling sensitive and ideologically charged population issues into the public domain.[1] Even more important, ICPD was a landmark in the management of complex global problems, such as population, through an imperfect international institutional machinery. The international consensus in Cairo, summarized in a World Programme of Action, was, despite fierce opposition to abortion and other sensitive subjects, a monumental achievement.

ICPD was the third decennial UN-sponsored world population conference. The first, held in Bucharest in 1974, saw the North and the South become polarized over the importance of demographics relative to other development concerns.[2] Led by the United States, Northern countries proposed vigorous family planning (contraception) programs to control rapid population growth, while many Southern governments, led by China and India, argued that, to attain global equity, higher priority should be given to socioeconomic development. Southern countries rejected the Northern assertions and insisted that the key to slowing population growth was through a more equitable distribution of resources between North and South. The South's assertions were captured in the phrase "development is the best contraceptive."

By the second conference, held in 1984 in Mexico City, the North-South dynamics had changed dramatically. After a decade of the fastest population growth in their histories, most Southern countries had adopted antinatalist policies, usually in the con-

*Environment,* Vol. 37, No. 1, pp. 5–33, January/February 1995. Reprinted with permission of the
Helen Dwight Reid Educational Foundation. Published by Heldref Publications,
1319 Eighteenth St., NW, Washington, DC 20036-1802. Copyright © 1995.

text of health and social development objectives. The United States had also switched its position. Under domestic political pressure from conservative and religious groups, the U.S. delegation opposed abortion and stated that demographic factors were "neutral," arguing that private markets would solve many population problems. In support of its position, the United States government withdrew financial support to several international organizations, such as the International Planned Parenthood Federation (IPPF) and the United Nations Population Fund.[3]

Given this history, few could have predicted the outcome at Cairo. Ten years after Mexico City, a broad and inclusive women-centered approach to population policies as part of sustainable human development was able to attract remarkable consensus in Cairo. Southern countries, after a "lost decade" of development associated with indebtedness and structural adjustment programs, were concerned over the dwindling concessional resource transfers from the North. They continued to view population both as an independent problem and as an important component of socio-economic development.[4] As for the United States, the Clinton administration was more supportive of environmental and women's issues than the previous administration and had reversed the Mexico City Policy after coming to office.[5] For Cairo, the United States supported a global consensus through active engagement with nongovernmental organizations (NGOs) and women's health groups.[6]

ICPD was structured along two parallel processes: official negotiations over the World Programme of Action and the NGO Forum for non-official participants. More than 1,500 organizations were represented by the estimated 10,000 participants who flocked to Cairo for the nine-day meetings.[7] The simultaneous processes drew participants from more than 150 countries who were part of the governmental delegations, international agencies, NGOs, academia, and the press. Although the battle over abortion received significant attention from the media, many other population-related issues were addressed, such as development, education, health, family planning, the environment, and migration.

At Cairo, certain North-South tensions evident at the Bucharest and Mexico City conferences appeared in the context of only a few issues, such as international migration and volume of foreign aid commitments. Furthermore, the vigorous dissent of the Holy See and extremist Islamic groups galvanized participants to leap across traditional divisions and to nurture common ground among most official and NGO groups.

During ICPD, official delegations negotiated the 16-chapter, 113-page World Programme of Action (WPOA)[8] that sets out recommendations for achieving population stabilization, educating girls and women, improving child survival and health, and providing universal access to high-quality reproductive health care services. As a UN statement about population problems and approaches, WPOA is not a treaty or a convention and thus has no legal force. However, it can become a powerful instrument for promoting national compliance through actions by citizenry and NGOs to hold governments accountable for pledges made and for attaining international standards.[9]

Before the negotiations at Cairo, the participating governments had agreed on about 92 percent of the WPOA text during three UN preparatory committee (PrepCom) meetings.[10] Left for finalization at Cairo were the more contentious issues, such as reproductive rights, sexuality and family structures, and abortion. Negotiations over these were not easy; indeed, there were times when consensus appeared beyond reach. Among the difficulties hampering the negotiations was the simultaneous use of the five official UN languages. Translating ambiguities and subtle nuances was a tedious and sometimes troublesome chore that occasionally proved helpful in reaching compromises on acceptable language.

## A Leap to Women's Priorities

The final World Programme of Action that was agreed on at Cairo is a major departure from previous mainstream discourse on population and development issues; it shifted the focus from population control and demographic targets to sustainable development that gives priority to reproductive health, women's empowerment, and reproductive rights.[11] "Reproductive health" is a term that encompasses health issues associated with human sexuality and reproduction: safe and effective contraception, maternal and child health and nutrition, safe obstetrical practices (safe motherhood), and control of reproductive tract infections, including sexually transmitted diseases and HIV/AIDS.[12] "Women's empowerment" refers to improving the status of women and achieving gender equity through education and economic opportunities, thereby allowing women to exercise greater control over their reproductive and productive lives. "Reproductive rights" can be viewed in terms of the power and resources that enable individuals and couples to make informed and safe decisions about their reproductive health.[13]

Moving beyond the customary emphasis on family planning, the Cairo agenda focused on an expanded range of high-quality reproductive health services responsive to the needs of clients, male participation in family planning, and male responsibility in sexual health and childrearing. Other social concerns were adolescent sexuality and violence against women.

The consensus achieved on advancing the health and safety of human reproduction and on promoting gender equity and empowerment was remarkable in light of the controversy over abortion, adolescent sexuality, and the definition of "family." In some instances, fierce resistance to the concept of women's rights was met with an equally defiant resolve to defend those rights.[14] Some religious groups voiced concern that "reproductive health" could become an umbrella term encompassing and condoning abortion or the promotion of unsupervised sex education for adolescents. They also argued that certain terminology could legitimize family structures beyond legal heterosexual unions. Reproductive rights were considered threatening in terms of empowering individuals to make their reproductive decisions without respecting the obligations and responsibilities of married couples and the community, including the laws and cultures of diverse nation states.[15]

Many terminology problems that persisted during the negotiations were resolved through adroit rewording. Often, successful negotiations on thorny issues were achieved by inserting qualifying language that respected the laws, religions, and cultural values of diverse countries; for example, by highlighting the statement "in no case should abortion be promoted as a method of family planning"; by changing "fertility regulation"—which could be interpreted to include abortion—to "regulation of fertility"; and by more carefully defining "adolescent sexuality" and "household structure."[16]

The Holy See's controversial role at Cairo was widely reported in the media. There were, however, several aspects of WPOA the Holy See did support, such as the broader population and development approach, the emphasis on the role of the family, and language against coercive practices. After tough negotiations and the fine-tuned editing of certain passages, the Holy See joined the consensus on several chapters of the document. Women's health activists were satisfied that sexual and reproductive health had been brought into the public domain and were addressed in the final document. ICPD also succeeded in highlighting long-neglected issues of adolescent needs and the roles and responsibilities of men.

Achieving global population stabilization was a broadly endorsed goal, but the paucity of debate at Cairo over its importance was markedly unlike the attention during the 1980s that focused on the causative role of population growth in economic development.[17] During the three PrepCom meetings leading up to ICPD, disagreements were largely settled between so-called population alarmists who advocated vigorous targeted action to slow population growth and those who argued that human welfare, not demographic targets, should be the focus of population programs. The two sides of this debate found common ground in the emphasis at Cairo on high-quality reproductive health services. For the "alarmists," the emphasis on a broader reproductive health approach supported the importance of birth control. These advocates, while concerned that resources not be diverted from family planning, could hardly object to high-quality, broadly inclusive services. For the human welfare advocates, the emphasis on health, individual welfare, and individual rights to be stressed in population programs satisfied their concerns to avoid an excessive focus on demographics that might result in coercive or abusive practices or that might deemphasize critical social development issues. Furthermore, the late intervention by conservative Christian and extremist Islamic forces accelerated the "patching up" of unresolved differences in the interest of meeting greater threats.[18]

Several other population-related issues also received comparatively less attention. Environmental quality and resource conservation, the potential role of demographics on political stability and ethnic strife, and urbanization were hardly discussed. Although structural global economy issues linking population to North-South disparities in economic development—especially mass poverty and the consequences of structural adjustment policies—were raised by some Third World women's groups, they were omitted from the official exchange. It is unclear why these issues received so little attention; it might have been because more than 92 percent of the document had been agreed on prior to the conference, time was insufficient due to the abortion controversy, or delegates had decided to abandon disagreements to represent a unified opposition to religious attacks.

One contentious issue requiring lengthy negotiations to resolve was the reunification of families separated as a result of international migration, a matter covered in other international conventions such as the Convention on Child Rights. Some Southern countries advocated that such reunification should be recognized as a "right." Industrialized countries—notably "receiving countries," such as the United States, Canada, and many European countries—resisted the inclusion of language that implied such obligations in their domestic efforts to control immigration. Delegations from the receiving countries succeeded in changing the text of WPOA on this topic such that it urges countries "to promote" family reunification, without making it an absolute right.[19]

### Women's NGOs: Influential and Vital

The most striking aspect of ICPD was the high level of participation by the nongovernmental community, building upon a process that characterized the Rio Earth Summit in 1992 and the Vienna Human Rights Conference in 1993.[20] ICPD attracted a diverse group of participants: population control advocates, feminist and health activists, academics and researchers, environmentalists, and religious groups. Some NGO participants were invited as members of their countries' official delegations. But unlike the official and NGO processes at the Rio conference, which were constrained by logistical barriers caused by the physical distance between the official conference site and the NGO Forum, these processes in Cairo were within walking distance of each other. This proximity allowed participants to move freely back and forth, promoting tremendous interconnectedness between the two processes.

The most visible and best organized in the NGO community were the women's health groups, which conducted a well-planned and well-coordinated advocacy effort.[21] A Women's Caucus coordinated women's NGO interactions, monitored the positions and negotiations of all delegations, advocated gender-sensitive positions, and proposed alternative language to bridge negotiation gaps.

Many women's groups worldwide had begun two years earlier to lay the groundwork for Cairo. In 1992, for example, women activists from the North and South developed and distributed the "Women's Declaration on Population Policies," which was reviewed, modified, and finalized by more than 100 women's organizations. It was additionally signed and endorsed by more than 2,500 individuals and organizations from over 110 countries.[22] In addition, networks of women from North and South as well as the Women's Caucus were widely acknowledged by the media, delegates, academics, and NGOs to have had a significant influence at PrepCom II in May 1993 by persuading government delegations to address reproductive health and rights, access to safe abortion, sexuality and gender equity, and broader socioeconomic development. In January 1994, about 200 women activists gathered in Rio de Janeiro to create a 21-point statement and to develop strategies for ensuring that women's perspectives and experiences were included at ICPD.[23] These strategies to influence and inform the public, official delegations, and the media were fine-tuned and applied throughout the process leading up to and at the Cairo conference itself. These efforts to harmonize diverse women's positions were vital for fostering North-South solidarity among women's NGOs during the Cairo deliberations.[24]

Conspicuously muted at the Cairo conference were tensions separating women's health groups from environmental scientists and activists—tensions that had been so prevalent at Rio. This relative quiescence can be partially attributed to concerted efforts by women's groups to seek common ground rather than to focus on their differences.[25]

Rather than targeting economic or political issues, the women's groups at Cairo focused on population issues. Until then, population had not been the highest priority issue of the global feminist movement, except perhaps in the United States, where the abortion debate is intense.[26] But over the past two decades, the international women's movement has increasingly recognized that sexuality and reproduction are critical issues in the struggle for gender equity. Without having control of their sexuality and reproduction, women argue, they will never achieve economic, social, and political equality.

Women have also felt compelled to become engaged in the population debate to redress the egregious abuses and failings they see in population policies and programs; among these are overemphasis on demographic goals at the expense of individual welfare, bureaucratic approaches to family planning that fail to address women's broader health needs, coercive practices, and no choice of contraceptive methods or an over-reliance on nonreversible methods.[27] Thus, even though the Social Summit in Copenhagen and the Women's Conference in Beijing are less than one year away, women's groups invested much time and effort to influence the Cairo proceedings and were tremendously successful.

Despite these successes, however, some NGOs, especially those from developing countries, claimed their views were overshadowed by those of well-organized lobbyists from the North.[28] Some groups argued that the burdens of limiting population growth still fall on the poor and that WPOA will result in conditions being attached to foreign aid for developing countries.

### The "Unholy Alliance"

Even before the Cairo conference, the Holy See and some Islamic countries had criticized the draft WPOA—especially the sections dealing with abortion, and reproductive and sexual health and rights—in what the media coined as an "unholy alliance." That criticism escalated with conservative Islamic groups calling for a boycott of the conference and

even threatening the safety of ICPD participants.

The Holy See's 15-member delegation fiercely attacked the draft document's recommendations on abortion, enlisting the support of several national delegations, including those from Argentina, Benin, Ecuador, the Philippines, Malta, Mauritius, Poland, and Slovakia. Nongovernmental "pro-life" activists and scientists, who advocated natural methods of birth control, also supported the Holy See's stance. Islamic criticism was articulated by Muslim scholars at Al-Ahzar University, the world's oldest Islamic university. In addition to abortion, their critique focused on the lack of attention given to poverty, the definition of family, and the treatment of extramarital sexuality, especially among adolescents.

To understand these religious concerns, it is necessary to understand how patriarchy and politics play into the issues involved. Some argue that the Holy See and fundamentalist Islam are basically patriarchal in their power structures and the norms they espouse. At Cairo, these religious groups resisted the strong women's agenda, underlined by feminist language, and succeeded in polarizing various participants over different social values and ethical norms. The divisions at Cairo were therefore more ideological and gender-based than religious or geographical.

The politics of the debate differed for the Holy See and Islamic groups. ICPD was held in Cairo, where longstanding anti-UN and anti-Western feelings in the Arab world had been exacerbated by the Gulf War and the incomplete peace accord between the Israelis and the Palestinians. Severe poverty and deeply entrenched social alienation characterize the development situation of the vast majority of the people living in countries governed by secular, Western-oriented elites. The Islamic arguments, therefore, could be interpreted as being about population issues more than as being a criticism of the Western modernization strategy of the secular governments in power in the region, such as that of Egypt. Recognizing the domestic implication of this threat, the Egyptian government went to great lengths to host a successful conference by ensuring the security of participants and enlisting the support of the Chief Cleric in Egypt (the Grand Mufti), who delivered a message of tolerance to Forum participants. Some argue that without the Egyptian government's strong political commitment, the conference could have been easily derailed.[29]

The Holy See's delegation at Cairo, after staking its position with moral absolutism and being overwhelmingly rejected by both official delegations and NGO groups, left the conference with its principles intact but its image seriously tarnished. By taking its dogmatic and unyielding stance, the Holy See has prompted queries about its status as a UN nonmember state and a permanent observer. For example, questions have been raised about why the Holy See has the privileged status that other religions do not.

Unlike after the Rio conference, the United States emerged from Cairo as a strong leader. Led by Undersecretary of State Timothy Wirth, the U.S. delegation played a constructive, consensus-building role during ICPD. Despite some criticism that the United States was leading "imperialist" attempts to impose homosexual and abortion rights on demand and to promote sexual promiscuity among teenagers, anti-U.S. rhetoric was generally absent. The U.S. delegation gained credibility with and the trust of both the NGO community and Southern delegates for several reasons. First, throughout the Cairo process, the U.S. delegation—more than half of which consisted of representatives from NGOs and the private sector, most of whom were women—sought the input and involvement of NGOs, especially women's health groups. Second, by bridging the North-South divide, the women's alliance, as described earlier, had created an environment that made it easier for delegates to encourage an exchange of ideas and to seek compromises among many Northern and Southern delegates. Third, the United States acknowledged politically sensitive issues, such as the "right to development" and the problem of overconsumption in industrialized countries. Finally, the U.S. government agreed to increases of financial commitments, albeit modest, for population programs overseas.

## WPOA: An Unfinished Agenda
As a political statement and the product of global negotiations, WPOA is a lengthy and sometimes redundant document. Nonetheless, what emerges from its pages is a refreshingly new direction for population policies emphasizing reproductive health, the empowerment of women, and an endorsement of reproduction as part of universal human rights. As such, WPOA is a seminal document in dramatically shifting the central focus of population studies.

The challenge now is for governments, international organizations, and NGOs to translate WPOA's rhetoric into action. Implementation at the local and national levels will be difficult and cumbersome because it will require the support of the UN system, extensive bilateral and multilateral funding, committed follow-up by NGOs, and the engagement of academia, business, and the media. Many women's NGOs left Cairo with strategic plans to monitor the performance of donors and governments in implementing the WPOA—demanding transparency in donor and governmental activities—and to hold these accountable for the pledges they have made. How these follow-up activities will be executed is unclear. What seems likely, however, is that the next decade will witness considerable public evaluation and debate over the direction of all implementation efforts.

WPOA estimates that resource requirements to implement population activities will increase to $17 billion by the year 2000. Of this total, $10 billion is slated for family planning and $7 billion for reproductive health, sexually transmitted diseases and HIV/AIDS, and social investments such as the education of girls and women. WPOA proposes that developing countries meet about two-thirds of these required resources. Foreign aid, currently 25 percent of the total population expenditures, is suggested to increase to 33 percent of the total. This will require an increase of nearly six-fold in population aid by the year 2000: from about $1 billion to nearly $6 billion.[30]

In a larger context, the Cairo conference can be seen to have provided a model for the planetary management of complex global problems. Increasingly, the scale of some of these problems overwhelms the global community's institutional capacity to address them. Transnational problems are beyond the capacity of individual states to resolve. Thus, as demonstrated by Cairo, we are likely to witness a steady stream of piecemeal negotiations on certain global problems pressingly important at specific times, with the involvement of governments and concerned NGOs, presented to the public through the media. While these processes will be fluid and dynamic, with unpredictable outcomes, they can be viewed as part of a process of global democratization with the increasing participation of concerned global citizens through their governments and private associations. Cairo made a major contribution toward advancing international understanding and global problem solving.

### Acknowledgments

We gratefully acknowledge the support of the John D. and Catherine T. MacArthur Foundation, the Global Stewardship Initiative of the Pew Charitable Trusts, and the Swedish International Development Authority. The views in this article are the authors' and not necessarily the views of their affiliated organizations.

### Notes

1. The media coverage of ICPD was extensive. The Communications Consortium Media Center in Washington, D.C., has collected press clips on the coverage of ICPD and is preparing a videotape of network news coverage.

2. J.L. Finkle and B. B. Crane, "The Politics of Bucharest: Population, Development, and the New International Economic Order," *Population and Development Review* 1 (1975): 87–114.

3. Sharon L. Camp, "The Politics of U.S. Population Assistance," in Laurie Mazur, ed., *Beyond the Numbers* (Washington, D.C.: Island Press, 1994), 122–34.

4. G. Sen, "Development, Population, and the Environment: A Search for Balance," in G. Sen, A. Germain, and L.C. Chen, *Population Policies Reconsidered: Health, Empowerment, and Rights* (Cambridge, Mass.: Harvard University Press, 1994), 68.

5. See Camp, note 3 above.

6. "Cairo Conference Showcases Work of NGOs," *Christian Science Monitor*, September 8 1994.

7. *POPULI* 21, no. 9 (October 1994): 4.

8. United Nations, *World Programme of Action: International Conference on Population and Development* (New York: United Nations Population Fund, September 1994).

9. R. Boland, S. Rao, and G. Zeidenstein, "Honoring Human Rights in Population Policies: From Declaration to Action," in Sen, Germain, and Chen, note 4 above, pages 89–105.

10. The first PrepCom meeting, held in March 1991, defined the objectives and themes of ICPD; the second meeting in May 1993 was to agree on the form and substance of the final document to be adopted at Cairo; at the third meeting in April 1994, delegates attempted to agree on as much of the draft WPOA as possible.

11. R. Cassen, *Population and Development: Old Debates, New Conclusions,* Policy Perspectives no. 19 (Washington, D.C.: Overseas Development Council, 1994).

12. A. Germain, S. Nowrojee, and H.H. Pyne, "Setting a New Agenda: Sexual and Reproductive Health and Rights," in Sen, Germain, and Chen, note 4 above.

13. S. Corrêa and R. Petchesky, "Reproductive and Sexual Rights: A Feminist Perspective," in Sen, Germain, and Chen, note 4 above, page 107. See also S. Corrêa, *Population and Reproductive Rights, Feminist Perspectives from the South* (London: Zed Press, 1994).

14. Carmen Barroso, the John D. and Catherine T. MacArthur Foundation, personal communication with the authors, September 1994.

15. P. Chasek, *Earth Negotiations Bulletin* 6, no. 39 (Washington, D.C.: International Institute for Sustainable Development, September 14 1994).

16. Ibid.

17. National Academy of Sciences, *Population Growth and Economic Development: Policy Questions* (Washington, D.C.: National Academy Press, 1986).

18. Susan Sechler, the Pew Global Stewardship Initiative, personal communication with the authors, September 1994.

19. The final text in Chapter X, "International

Migration," states that "all Governments, particularly those of receiving countries, must recognize the vital importance of family reunification and promote its integration into their national legislation in order to ensure the protection of the unity of the families of documented migrants." *World Programme of Action,* note 8 above.

20. Y. Kakabadse and S. Burns, "Movers and Shapers: NGOs in International Affairs," *International Perspectives on Sustainability* (Washington, D.C.: World Resources Institute, May 1994). See also *Environment,* October 1992, pages 6, 12 for further discussions of UNCED.

21. Many issues related to women's health— population policy, family planning, sexual and reproductive health, violence against women, and others—are part of the women's health movement, involving organizations ranging from national feminist NGOs to grassroots groups of varying sizes. Like all social movements, the women's health movement is shaped by many political, cultural, and socioeconomic factors. As such, the movement is by no means homogeneous, and there were indeed many debates at Cairo. For the purposes of this article, discussion of the role of the international women's movement at ICPD refers to the groups that did reach agreement. For further information on the women's health movement, see C. Garcia-Moreno and A. Claro, "Challenges from the Women's Health Movement: Women's Rights Versus Population Control," in Sen, Germain, Chen, note 4 above, pages 46–61. See also "Women's Groups Coalesce in Cairo," *Christian Science Monitor,* September 8 1994.

22. In September 1992, women's health advocates representing women's networks in Asia, Africa, Latin America, the Caribbean, the United States, and Western Europe met to discuss how women's perspectives might best be included during the preparations for the 1994 ICPD and during the conference itself. The group suggested that a strong positive statement from women worldwide would make a unique contribution to reshaping the population agenda to better ensure reproductive health and rights. The declaration outlines fundamental ethical principles, minimum program requirements in the design and implementation of policies and programs, and the requisite conditions for women to control their own sexuality and reproductive health. See A. Germain, S. Nowrojee, and H.H. Pyne, "Setting a New Agenda: Sexual and Reproductive Health and Rights," in Sen, Germain, and Chen, note 4 above, pages 31–34.

23. International Women's Health Coalition and Citizenship, Studies, Information, Action, *Reproductive Health and Justice* report of the International Women's Health Conference (Rio de Janeiro, Brazil, January 24–28, 1994).

24. Garcia-Moreno and Claro, note 21 above.

25. Many environmentalists argue that population growth is a major cause of environmental degradation, while many women's health advocates argue that population growth, by itself, is not a major contributor to global environmental problems. In the past, some women's health groups feared that sounding a population "alarm" could legitimize a range of family planning abuses against women. See Sen, note 4 above, pages 63–73. See also S. A. Cohen, "The Road from Rio to Cairo: Toward a Common Agenda," *International Family Planning Perspectives* 19, no. 2 (Washington, D.C.: Alan Guttmacher Institute, June 1993).

26. Carmen Barroso, personal communication with the authors, November 1994.

27. Sen, note 4 above, pages 63–73. See also R. Dixon-Mueller, *Population Policy and Women's Rights: Transforming Reproductive Choice* (Westport, Conn.: Praeger Publishers, 1993), and B. Hartmann, *Reproductive Rights and Wrongs: The Global Politics of Population Control and Contraceptive Choice* (New York: Harper & Row, 1987).

28. See, for example, three articles from India: "Third World Feels Betrayed," *Telegraph,* September 29 1994; "Foetal Distractions: Reductionisms by the West Are Threatening the Rights of Third World Women," *Tele-*

*graph*, October 7 1994; "What Cairo Did Not Discuss," *Down to Earth*, October 15 1994.

29. Barbara Ibrahim, Population Council, Cairo, Egypt, personal communication with the authors, September 1994.

30. *World Programme of Action*, note 8 above. ❑

## Questions

1. What does the term *reproductive rights* refer to?

2. What common ground did the "population alarmists" and the "human welfare advocates" find?

3. What two issues in the women's movement for gender equity are critical, and without which women will never achieve economic, social, and political equality?

*Answers are at the back of the book.*

**9**

*Overpopulation is often identified as the single greatest cause of environmental destruction. Overpopulation has been a latent fear over the centuries. In 1798, Thomas Malthus was very concerned with the theory of a doubling of population within a specific unit of time. However, population statistics show a recent decline in population trends, due in part to better education. Worldwide poverty and overpopulation are interrelated. By effectively dealing with one of these issues, we can alleviate the other. For instance, reducing population growth will help diminish poverty worldwide. Conversely, diminishing poverty will diminish population growth. The consequences of not addressing these problems could be grave. They could eventually lead to a society that must enforce a reduction in fertility or one where death rates will increase.*

# Ten Myths of Population
## Joel E. Cohen

*Discover*, April 1996

*How do we save the world from the burden of too many people? We can start by clearing up a few misconceptions.*

Fears about Earth's burgeoning human population have long been at the back of many people's minds. Now, it seems, as the threat of nuclear annihilation recedes from the headlines, those fears can move up to claim center stage. Moving along with the anxiety, of course, is a great deal of confusion, not the least of which is about how to recognize a population problem when you see one. Population problems are entangled with economics, the environment, and culture in such complex ways that few people can resist the temptations of unwarranted simplification. The result is a loose and widely accepted collection of myths, all of which wrap a heavy coating of fiction around a nugget of truth. During the 30 years I have spent studying population dynamic, I have become quite familiar with these myths, in all their guises. Here, in their essential form, are ten of the ones that I have encountered most often.

### 1. The human population grows exponentially.
In 1978 the Reverend Thomas Robert Malthus wrote that any human population, "when unchecked," doubles in a certain unit of time, and then keeps on doubling in the same unit of time. For example, according to his statistics, in "the English North American colonies, now the powerful People of the United States of America,... the population was found to double itself in 25 years."

The fact is that hardly any human populations keep doubling in the same unit of time for very long. Two thousand years ago, there were about 250 million people on this planet. It took about 1,650 year for the population to double to 500 million. But the next doubling took less than 200 years—by 1830 Earth's human population had passed 1 billion. After that the doubling time continued to shrink: just another 100 years to reach 2 billion, then only 45 more to get to 4 billion. Never before the twentieth century had any human being lived through a doubling of Earth's population.

But things have begun to change. In 1965 the global population growth rate peaked at around 2 percent per year (a rate sufficient to double the global population in 35 years, if it were sustained) and then began to fall. It has now dropped to 1.5 percent per year, which yields a doubling time of 46 years. For the first time in human history, the population growth slowed, despite a continuing drop in death rates, because people were having fewer children. The myth of exponential growth misses this human triumph.

## 2. Scientists know how many people there will be 25, 50, and 100 years from now.

Most demographers no longer believe they can accurately predict the future growth rate, size, composition, or distribution of populations. It's not that demographers are a particularly humble bunch, it's simply that so many of their past predictions have failed. Researchers could not and cannot predict changes in birthrates or the changes wrought by large migrations of peoples, nor did any of them anticipate that the death rates in poor countries would fall as rapidly as they did after World War II.

Yet demographers can safely predict some things. They know, for example, that everyone who will be at least 18 years old 18 years from now is already born, and that everyone who will be 65 years old or older 20 years from now is at least 45 today. This means that if death rates do not change abruptly, demographers can predict with some confidence how many people of working age there will be at 18 years from now, and how many potentially retired people 20 years hence.

## 3. There is a single factor that limits how many people Earth can support.

This myth has a long, distinguished history. In 1679, Antoni van Leeuwenhoek, the inventor of the microscope, estimated how many people the planet could support. He assumed that what limited Earth's population was population density alone—that is, the number of people per unit of land area. He further assumed that Earth could not be more densely inhabited than the Holland of his day, which had an estimated 1 million people at the density of around 300 per square mile. He calculated that Holland then occupied one part in 13,400 of Earth's habitable land. Therefore, he concluded, the planet could support at most 13.4 billion people.

Things turned out to be more complex than Leeuwenhoek imagined. In 1989 a third of the world population lived at densities greater than 300 people per square mile. People, it turns out, can and will live at higher population densities when technologies and environments make it possible, economic incentives and trade make it affordable, and cultural values make it acceptable or even desirable.

Just behind the "standing room" hypotheses in popularity—at least, among those who have not thought much about the problem or the facts—is the belief what limits global population is the availability of food. In fact, except for people who are actually starving, humans today do not have more or fewer children according to whether they have more or less food. On the contrary, the average number of children per woman is lowest in the rich countries where food is most abundant (such as in Japan and in Europe and North America) and is highest where food availability per person is lowest (as in Africa south of the Sahara).

Since Leeuwenhoek, some 65 estimates of how many people Earth can support have been published, using a wide range of limiting factors—everything form food to land to freshwater, phosphorus, photosynthesis, fuel, nitrogen, waste removal, and human ingenuity. The estimates have ranged from fewer than 1 billion to more than 1 trillion, and in the past few decades they have grown increasingly divergent. But there are a number of problems with all these studies. The advocates of a single limiting factor can rarely determine whether some other factors might intervene before the assumed constraint comes into play. Moreover, even if these determinations were scientifically possible, many of the isolated factors are not independent of one another. True, the amount of available water determines how productive the land will be, but it itself is partially determined by how much energy is available for pumping the water or desalinating it. And that energy capacity depends in part on the amount of water available to flow through hydroelectric dams and to cool nuclear reactors. Everything affects everything else.

Most important, many limiting factors are subject to changing cultural values. If a peasant farmer in Kenya believes that educating her children matters greatly, and if school fees begin to rise, then she may choose to have fewer children not because land is scarce but because she values her children's future more than their labor as farmhands.

### 4. Earth's population problems can be solved by colonizing outer space.

Let's review the numbers: the world's population of 5.7 billion people is currently growing by roughly 1.5 percent per year. Now, let's say you wanted to use space travel to bring the growth rate down a tiny notch to 1.4 percent. That would require .001 x 5.7 billion = 5.7 million astronauts to blast off in the first year—and increasing numbers in years that followed. Space shuttle launches cost $450 million apiece, so if you ferried ten people to space in each shuttle, the cost per person would be $45 million. Exporting 5.7 million people would cost $257 trillion, roughly ten times the world's annual economic product. Your mass migration would bankrupt the remaining Earthlings, who would still be saddled with a population that doubles every 50 years.

Demographically speaking, space is not the place.

### 5. Technology can solve any population problem.

People once feared that shipbuilding would be hampered by the scarcity of tall trees for sailing masts, that railroads would be crippled by a shortage of timber for railroad ties, and that the U.S. economy would grind to a halt with the exhaustion of coal. Yet people figured out how to switch to metal masts (and then steam power); they invented concrete railroad ties and built super highways; and they found better ways to extract coal, as well as oil, gas, and other fuels. But these solutions brought new problems, such as acid rain, dramatically rising atmospheric carbon dioxide, stripped lands, and oil spills. Still, technological optimists argue that industrial societies will go on solving problems as they arise.

In technology, as in comedy, timing is everything. For every timely success of technology, doubters can point to problems where solutions did not come in time to avert great human suffering and waste. For example, medical technology's solution for tuberculosis so far is partial at best. One in three humans are infected with tuberculosis (including half the population of Africa), and 3 million of them are dying of it every year. Yet despite decades of medical research, drug-resistant forms of the disease are spreading. Technology will take time to solve such problems—which are ultimately related to population through culture, the environment, and the economy—if it can solve them at all.

### 6. The United States has no population problem.

When people are born whose parents don't want them, there is definitely a population problem, and the United States suffers this problem in a big way: in 1987, of the 5.4 million pregnancies among American women about 3.1 million (57 percent) were unintended at the time of conception. Of these, about 1.6 million were aborted; 1.5 million resulted in live birth. Young and poor women were more likely than average to have unintended pregnancies. In 1987, 82 percent of pregnancies among American teenagers 15 to 19 years old were unintended, as were 61 percent of pregnancies among women 20 to 24 years old. Women with family incomes below poverty level in 1987 reported that 75 percent of their pregnancies were unintended. The trend is not good: among all U.S. women 15 to 44 years old, the fraction of all births that resulted from intended pregnancies shrank from 64 percent in 1982 to 61 percent in 1988 to 55 percent in 1990.

The inability of the United States to assure that every conception is an intended one is entwined with other social problems. The United States ranks first or second (always behind Australia) among industrial countries in rates of intentional homicides by males, reported rapes of women aged 15 to 59, drug crimes, injuries from road accidents, income disparity between the richest 20 percent of households and the poorest 20 percent, prisoners, and divorces. Unintended births are partly a cause and partly an effect of all these other troubles.

### 7. Population problems of developing countries are not a problem for the United States.

The myth that the United States is immune to the population problems of the rest of the world ignores migration, infectious diseases, international labor markets, and the shared global commons of crust, oceans, atmosphere, and wildlife. Refugees and immigrants are driven from home by political upheavals, ethnic conflict, poverty, and environmental degradation—all problems that may be exacerbated by rapid population growth—and already play visible roles in the domestic politics of Florida, Texas, and

California, as well as in American foreign policy. The health of Americans depends on the health of people outside our borders—infectious diseases do not carry a passport. The rapid population growth of developing countries, leading to fierce wage competition, may even play some role in the movement of jobs out of the United States, although the extent of this role is still controversial because it has not been accurately measured. American workers may do well to recognize their self-interested stake in lowering population growth rates of developing countries.

## 8. The Roman Catholic Church is responsible for the population explosion.

In some countries church policies have certainly hindered access to contraception and have posed serious obstacles to family planning programs. In practice, however, religion isn't the critical factor for fertility levels among Catholics, not to mention Muslims, Jews, or members of most other religions. Last year Spain and Italy—two Catholic countries—tied with Hong Kong for the lowest levels of fertility in the world, with an average of 1.2 children per woman. In largely Catholic Latin America, fertility has fallen rapidly to the world average of 3.1 children per woman, thanks mainly to modern contraceptive methods. The fertility of American Catholics had gradually converged over the years with that of Protestants. Polls show that nearly four-fifths of them think that couples should make up their own minds about family planning and abortion.

Within the church hierarchy, Catholicism shelters a diversity of views. In 1994, for example, the Italian bishops' conference issued a report stating that falling mortality and improved medical care "have made it unthinkable to sustain indefinitely a birthrate that notably exceeds the level of two children per couple." By promoting literacy for adults, education for children, and the survival of infants in developing countries, the church has helped bring about social conditions that favor a decline in fertility.

## 9. Plagues, famines, and wars are nature's (or God's) way of solving population problems.

This venerable myth traces back at least to 1600 B.C. According to an ancient Babylonian history, when human commotion disturbed the gods' peace and quiet, the gods inflicted plagues to rid the Earth of humans.

Plagues, of course, are directly cause by viruses, bacteria, and other microorganisms that take advantage of human behavior in a favorable environment. After the last ice age, when sedentary agriculture greatly increased the population density in permanent human settlements, the inhabitants became surrounded by their own wastes and those of their domestic animals and hangers-on like rats and fleas. By the time the Babylonians recorded their creation myths a few thousand years later, people could well have observed that denser settlements were subject to strange new infectious diseases and could have interpreted these diseases as divine interventions. Now we know that humble humans can at least partially control disease. Inexpensive public health measures controlled lethal infectious diseases of childhood in developing countries after World War II, and population growth then accelerated in an unprecedented way.

Modern epidemics, while causing great suffering, have yet to show any probability of putting a brake on population growth. The highly reported Ebola outbreak last year killed 244 people—fewer than are born every minute. As for AIDS, a 1994 United Nations report on the 15 countries in central Africa where it is most prevalent estimated that by 2005 their population growth rate would be 2.88 percent per year in the presence of AIDS. If AIDS were not present, it would be 3.13 percent. These rates correspond to doubling times of 24 years and 22 years, respectively.

Famines today are only partly a result of natural events. Many readers may remember a Pulitzer Prize-winning photograph from 1993, showing a starving Sudanese girl collapsed on a trail, with a vulture looming behind her. At the time, the Sudanese government was just opening parts of its famine-stricken country-side—the scene of a long-running civil war—to relief operations. If aid workers had gotten in sooner, they could have prevented a crop failure from leading to a famine, but the Sudanese government stopped relief from reaching its own people. This is not divine intervention or an act of nature.

Finally, war has not been a major obstacle to human population growth. It's a safe estimate that fewer than 200 million people have been killed in the wars of this century (combined, World Wars I and II may have killed 90 million people, including civilians; since World War II, perhaps 50 million people have lost their lives on conventional battlefields). Yet the population increased from fewer than 1.7 billion in 1900 to 5.7 billion today. This 4-billion-person increase is more than 20 times greater than the number killed by wars.

## 10. Population is a women's issue, and women are the key to solving it.

If we don't improve the education, welfare, and legal status of women, there is little hope of solving many population problems. Women bear babies, and they are obviously key players in improving the survival of children and lowering fertility. But they are not the only key players. In most of the world, men too need similar help. As demographer Uche Isiugo-Abanihe of the University of Ibadan in Nigeria has pointed out, it is as important to educate African men about the consequences of high fertility as it is African women. In the United States, a 1995 report on unintended pregnancy by the Institute of Medicine concluded that "the prevailing policy and program emphasis on women as the key figures in contraceptive decision-making unjustly and unwisely excludes boys and men." Scientists have discovered it take two to tango.

Last October a neurophysiologist I was chatting with claimed that the people of India are poorer, more miserable, and more fecund than ever. I quoted him statistics showing that India's average gross national product per person rose 3 percent per year from 1980 to 1993 and that its life expectancy rose from 39 years during the period of 1950 to 1955 to 58 years during the period of 1985-1990. I added that in that same period of time the average number of children per woman fell from 6 to 4.1. "Oh, that doesn't matter!" he said. Population myths have a life of their own.

Yet behind the neurophysiologist's exaggerations are valid, urgent concerns. Too many people in India and around the world are far poorer than the means available require them to be. Too many children are born without the prospect of sufficient love, food, health, education, or dignity in living and dying. But only by clearing the myths from our vision of population can we focus on the real problems and find hope without complacency. One way or another, human population growth on Earth must ultimately end. Ending it through voluntary reduction in fertility will make it easier to reduce the poverty of the 4.5 billion people who live on an average of $1,000 a year. At the same time, reducing poverty will make it easier to end population growth through voluntary reductions in fertility. The alternatives are coerced reduction of fertility or the misery of rising death rates. The choice is ours, for now. ❏

---

## Questions

1. What factor was responsible for the decrease in population growth around 1965?

2. Why can most demographers not accurately predict future population growth rates?

3. What are limiting factors subject to?

*Answers are at the back of the book.*

---

**10** *The degradation of the environment, the depletion of natural resources, and the slow-down of yield-raising technologies have contributed to the reduction of food production in recent decades. With seafood, we are approaching natural limits as fishing exceeds capacity. Rangelands are being overgrazed at or beyond capacity worldwide, and water is being depleted at an alarming rate. In the United States alone, more than one-fourth of cropland is irrigated, but aquifer depletion will eventually put an end to irrigation. In 1992, the U.S. National Academy of Sciences and the Royal Society of London issued a report that expressed concern over continued population growth. The Earth can only support a limited number of people, and the food supply will be the dominant factor in determining the number. Recognizing food scarcity as the primary threat to the future is an important step in working toward a solution. Governments can introduce family planning programs, which would decrease fertility rates, reduce illiteracy, and diminish poverty. This would also help conserve the environment and the natural resources by protecting the soil and water, which in turn would help stabilize agriculture and help protect and sustain the food supply.*

# Earth Is Running Out of Room
## Lester R. Brown

*USA Today Magazine*, **January 1995**

**Food scarcity, not military aggression, is the principal threat to the planet's future.**

The world is entering a new era, one in which it is far more difficult to expand food output. Many knew that this time would come eventually; that, at some point, the limits of the Earth's natural systems, cumulative effects of environmental degradation on cropland productivity, and shrinking backlog of yield-raising technologies would slow the record increase in food production of recent decades. Because no one knew exactly when or how this would happen, food prospects were debated widely. Now, several constraints are emerging simultaneously to slow that growth.

After nearly four decades of unprecedented expansion in both land-based and oceanic food supplies, the world is experiencing a massive loss of momentum. Between 1950 and 1984, grain production expanded 2.6-fold, outstripping population growth by a wide margin and raising the grain harvested per person by 40%. Growth in the fish catch was even more spectacular—a 4.6-fold increase between 1950 and 1989, thereby doubling seafood consumption per person. Together, these develop-

ments reduced hunger and malnutrition throughout the world, offering hope that these biblical scourges would be eliminated one day.

In recent years, these trends suddenly have been reversed. After expanding at three percent a year form 1950 to 1984, the growth in grain production has slowed abruptly, rising at scarcely one percent annually from 1984 until 1993. As a result, grain production per person fell 12% during this time.

With fish catch, it is not merely a slowing of growth, but a limit imposed by nature. From a high of 100,000,000 tons, believed to be close to the maximum oceanic fisheries can sustain, the catch has fluctuated between 96,000,000 and 98,000,000 tons. As a result, the 1993 per capita seafood catch was nine percent below that of 1988. Marine biologists at the United Nations Food and Agriculture Organization report that the 17 major oceanic fisheries are being fished at or beyond capacity and that nine are in a state of decline.

Rangelands, a major source of animal protein, also are under excessive pressure, being grazed at or beyond capacity on every continent. This means that rangeland production of beef and mutton may not increase much, if at all, in the future. Here, too, availability per person will decline indefinitely as population expands.

With both fisheries and rangelands being pressed to the limits of their carrying capacity, future growth in food demand can be satisfied only by expanding output from croplands. The increase in demand for food that was satisfied by three food systems must now be satisfied by one.

Until recently, grain output projections for the most part were simple extrapolations of trends. The past was a reliable guide to the future. However, in a world of limits, this is changing. In projecting food supply trends now, at least six new constraints must be taken into account:

- The backlog of unused agricultural technology is shrinking, leaving the more progressive farmers fewer agronomic options for expanding food output.
- Growing human demands are pressing against the limits of fisheries to supply seafood and rangelands to supply beef, mutton, and milk.
- Demands for water are nearing limits of the hydrological cycle to supply irrigation water in key food-growing regions.
- In many countries, the use of additional fertilizer on currently available crop varieties has little or no effect on yields.
- Nations that already are densely populated risk losing cropland when they begin to industrialize at a rate that exceeds the rise in land productivity, initiating a long-term decline in food production.
- Social disintegration by rapid population growth and environmental degradation often is undermining many national governments and their efforts to expand food production.

## New Technologies Are Not Enough

In terms of agricultural technology, the contrast between the middle of the 20th Century and today could not be more striking. When the 1950s began, a great deal of technology was waiting to be used. Except for irrigations, which goes back several thousand years, all the basic advances were made between 1840 and 1940. Chemist Justus von Liebig discovered in 1847 that all nutrients taken from the soil by crops could be replaced in mineral form. Biologist Gregor Mendel's work establishing the basic principles of heredity, which laid the groundwork for future crop breeding advances, was done in the 1860s. Hybrid corn varieties were commercialized in the U.S. during the 1920s, and dwarfing of wheat and rice plants in Japan to boost fertilizer responsiveness dates back a century.

These long-standing technologies have been enhanced and modified for wide use through agricultural research and exploited by farmers during the last four decades. Although new developments continue to appear, none promise to lead to quantum leaps in world food output. The relatively easy gains have been made. Moreover, public funding for international agricultural research has begun to decline. As a result, the more progressive farmers are looking over the shoulders of agricultural scientists seeking new yield-raising technologies, but discovering that they have less and less to offer. The pipeline has not run dry, but the flow has slowed to a trickle.

In Asia, rice crops on maximum-yield experimental plots have not increased for more than two decades. Some countries appear to be "hitting the wall" as their yields approach those on the research plots. Japan reached this point with a rice yield in 1984 at 4.7 tons per hectare (2.47 acres), a level it has been unable to top in nine harvests since then. South Korea, with similar growing conditions, may have run into the same barrier in 1988, when its rice yield stopped rising. Indonesia, with a crop that has increased little since 1988, may be the first tropical rice-growing nation to see its yield rise lose momentum. Other countries could hit the wall before the end of the century.

Farmers and policymakers search in vain for new advances, perhaps from biotechnology, that will lift food output quickly to a new level. However, biotechnology has not produced any yield-raising technologies that will lead to quantum jumps in output, nor do many researchers expect it to. Donald Duvick, for many years the director of research at Iowa-based Pioneer Hi-Bred International, one of the world's largest seed suppliers, makes this point all too clearly: "No breakthroughs are in sight. Biotechnology, while essential to progress, will not produce any sharp upward swings in yield potential except for isolated crops in certain situations."

The productivity of oceanic fisheries and range-lands, both natural systems, is determined by nature. It can be reduced by overfishing and overgrazing or other forms of mismanagement, but once sustainable yield limits are reached, the contribution of these systems to world food supply can not be expanded. The decline in fisheries is not limited to developing countries. By early 1994, the U.S. was experiencing precipitous drops in fishery stocks off the coast of New England, off the West Coast, and in the Gulf of Mexico.

With water—the third constraint—the overpumping that is so widespread eventually will be curbed to bring it into balance with aquifer recharge. This reduction, combined with growing diversion of irrigation water to residential and industrial uses, limits the amount of water available to produce food. Where farmers depend on fossil aquifers for their irrigation water—in the southern U.S. Great Plains, for instance, or the wheat fields of Saudi Arabia—aquifer depletion means an end to irrigated agriculture. In the U.S., where more than one-fourth of irrigated cropland is watered by drawing down underground water tables, the downward adjustment in irrigation pumping would be substantial. Major food-producing regions where overpumping is commonplace include the southern Great Plains, India's Punjab, and the North China Plain. For many farmers, the best hope for more water is from gains in efficiency.

Perhaps the most worrisome emerging constraint on food production is the limited capacity of grain varieties to respond to the use of additional fertilizer. In the U.S., Western Europe, and Japan, usage has increased little if at all during the last decade. Utilizing additional amounts on existing crop varieties has little or no effect on yield in these nations. After a tenfold increase in world fertilizer use from 1950 to 1989—from 14,000,000 to 146,000,000 tons—use declined to the following four years.

A little-recognized threat to the future world food balance is the heavy loss of cropland that occurs when countries that already are densely populated begin to industrialize. The experience in Japan, South Korea, and Taiwan gives a sense of what to expect. The conversion of grainland to nonfarm uses and to high-value specialty crops has cost Japan 52% of its grainland; South Korea, 42%; and Taiwan, 35%.

As the loss of land proceeded, it began to override the rise in land productivity, leading to declines in production. From its peak, Japan's grain output has dropped 33%; South Korea's, 31%; and Taiwan's, 74%.

Asia's densely populated giants, China and India, are going through the same stages that led to the extraordinarily heavy dependence on imported grain in the three smaller countries that industrialized earlier. In both, the shrinkage in grainland has begun. It is one thing for Japan, a country of 120,000,000 people, to import 77% of its grain, but quite another if China, with 1,200,000,000, moves in this direction.

Further complicating efforts to achieve an acceptable balance between food and people is social disintegration. In an article in the February 1994 Atlantic entitled, "The Coming Anarchy," writer and political analyst Robert Kaplan observed that unprecedented population growth and environmental degradation were driving people from the countryside into cities and across national borders at a record rate. This, in turn, was leading to social disintegration and political fragmentation. In parts of Africa, he argues, nation-states no longer exist in any meaningful sense. In their place are fragmented tribal and ethnic groups.

The sequence of events that leads to environmental degradation is all to familiar to environmentalists. It begins when the firewood demands of a growing population exceed the sustainable yield of local forests, leading to deforestation. As firewood become scarce, cow dung and crop residues are burned for fuel, depriving the land of nutrients and organic matter. Livestock numbers expand more or less apace with the human population, eventually exceeding grazing capacity. The combination of deforestation and overgrazing increases rainfall runoff and soil erosion, simultaneously reducing aquifer recharge and soil fertility. No longer able to feed themselves, people become refugees, heading for the nearest city of food relief center.

Crop reports for Africa now regularly cite weather and civil disorder as the key variables affecting harvest prospects. Not only is agricultural progress difficult, even providing food aid can be a challenge under these circumstances. In Somalia, getting food to the starving in late 1992 required a UN peacekeeping force and military expenditures that probably cost 10 times as much as what was distributed.

As political fragmentation and instability spread, national governments no longer can provide the physical and economic infrastructure for development. Countries in this category include Afghanistan, Haiti, Liberia, Sierra Leone, and Somalia. To the extent that nation-states become dysfunctional, the prospects for humanely slowing population growth, reversing environmental degradation, and systematically expanding food production are diminished.

Other negative influences exist, but they have emerged more gradually. Among those that affect food production more directly are soil erosion, the waterlogging and salting of irrigated land, and air pollution. For example, a substantial share of the world's cropland is losing topsoil at a rate that exceeds natural soil formation. On newly cleared land that is sloping steeply, soil losses can lead to cropland abandonment in a matter of years. In other situations, the loss is slow and has a measurable effect on land productivity only over many decades.

## Growing Pessimism

Until recently, concerns about the Earth's capacity to feed ever-growing numbers of people adequately was confined largely to the environmental and population communities and a few scientists. During the 1990s, however, these issues are arousing the concerns of the mainstream scientific community. In early 1992, the U.S. National Academy of Sciences and the Royal Society of London issued a report that began: "If current predictions of population growth prove accurate and patterns of human activity on the planet remain unchanged, science and technology may not be able to prevent either irreversible degradation of the environment or continued poverty for much of the world."

It was a remarkable statement, an admission that science and technology no longer can ensure a better future unless population growth slows quickly and

the economy is restructured. This abandonment of the technological optimism that has permeated so much of the 20th century by two of the world's leading scientific bodies represents a major shift, though perhaps not a surprising one, given the deteriorating state of the planet. That they chose to issue a joint statement, their first ever, reflects the deepening concern about the future within the scientific establishment.

Later in 1992, the Union of Concerned Scientists issued a "World Scientists' Warning to Humanity," signed by some 1,600 of the planet's leading scientists, including 102 Nobel Prize winners. It observes that the continuation of destructive human activities "may so alter the living world that it will be unable to sustain life in the manner that we know." The scientists indicated that "A great change in our stewardship of the earth and the life on it is required, if vast human misery is to be avoided and our global home on this planet is not to be irretrievably mutilated."

In November, 1993, representatives of 56 national science academies convened in New Delhi, India, to discuss population. At the end of their conference, they issued a statement in which they urged zero population growth during the lifetimes of their children.

Between 1950 and 1990, the world added 2,800,000,000 people, and an average of 70,000,000 a year. Between 1990 and 2030, it is projected to add 3,600,000,000 or 90,000,000 a year. Even more troubling, nearly all this increase is projected for the developing countries, where life-support systems already are deteriorating. Such population growth in a finite ecosystem raises questions about the Earth's carrying capacity. Will the planet's natural support systems sustain such growth indefinitely? How many people can the Earth support at a given level of consumption?

Underlying this assessment of population carrying capacity is the assumption that the food supply will be the most immediate constraint on population growth. Water scarcity could limit population growth in some locations, but it is unlikely to do so for the world as a whole in the foreseeable future. A buildup of environmental pollutants could interfere with human reproduction, much at DDT reduced the reproductive capacity of bald eagles, peregrine falcons, and other birds at the top of the food chain. In the extreme, accumulating pollutants in the environment could boost death rates to the point where they would exceed birth rates, leading to a gradual decline in human numbers, but this does not seem likely. For now, it appears that the food supply will be the most immediate, and therefore the controlling, determinant of how many people the Earth can support.

Grain supply and demand projections for the 13 most populous countries—accounting for two-thirds of world population and food production—show much slower growth in output than the official projections by the Food and Agriculture Organization and the World Bank. If those projections of relative abundance and an continuing decline of food prices materialize, governments can get by with business as usual. If, on the other hand, the constraints discussed above continue, the world needs to reorder priorities.

The population-driven environmental deterioration/political disintegration scenario described by Robert Kaplan not only is possible, it is likely in a business-as-usual world. However, it is not inevitable. This future can be averted if security is redefined, recognizing that food scarcity, not military aggression, is the principle threat to the future. Government must give immediate attention to filling the family planning gap; attacking the underlying causes of high fertility, such as illiteracy and poverty; protecting soil and water resources; and raising investment in agriculture. ❑

## Questions

1. During what time frame were most of the basic technological advances made?

2. What two food systems are determined by nature?

3. What do crop reports for Africa cite as determining factors affecting harvest possibilities?

*Answers are at the back of the book.*

**11** *Approximately 1,600 years ago, the Polynesians stepped ashore on Easter Island and found a paradise. The famous gigantic stone statues they left behind indicate a complex, social society made possible by abundant natural resources. Archaeologists estimate that the 64-square mile island had a population of 7,000 and may have supported up to 20,000. This would not have been unreasonable considering the fertility of the island. But records show that the Polynesians were destroying their forests by the year 800. Preserved statuettes with sunken cheeks and visible ribs show that the people were starving. Within a few short centuries, the forests were gone, the animals had disappeared, and so had the people. All that remains today is an impoverished and barren grassland. Could similar events occur on a global or regional scale? Some people think so.*

# Easter's End
## Jared Diamond

*Discover*, August 1995

*In just a few centuries, the people of Easter Island wiped out their forest, drove their plants and animals to extinction, and saw their complex society spiral into chaos and cannibalism. Are we about to follow their lead?*

Among the most riveting mysteries of human history are those posed by vanished civilizations. Everyone who has seen the abandoned buildings of the Khmer, the Maya, or the Anasazi is immediately moved to ask the same questions: Why did the societies that erected those structures disappear?

Their vanishing touches us as the disappearance of other animals, even the dinosaurs, never can. No matter how exotic those lost civilizations seem, their framers were humans like us. Who is to say we won't succumb to the same fate? Perhaps someday New York's skyscrapers will stand derelict and overgrown with vegetation, like the temples at Angkor Wat and Tikal.

Among all such vanished civilizations, that of the former Polynesian society on Easter Island remains unsurpassed in mystery and isolation. The mystery stems especially from the island's gigantic stone statues and its impoverished landscape, but it is enhanced by our associations with the specific people involved: Polynesians represent for us the ultimate in exotic romance, the background for many a child's, and an adult's, vision of paradise. My own interest in Easter was kindled over 30 years ago when I read Thor Heyerdahl's fabulous accounts of his *Kon-Tiki* voyage.

But my interest has been revived recently by a much more exciting account, one not of heroic voyages but of painstaking research and analysis. My friend David Steadman, a paleontologist, has been working with a number of other researchers who are carrying out the first systematic excavations on Easter intended to identify the animals and plants that once lived there. Their work is contributing to a new interpretation of the island's history that makes it a tale not only of wonder but of warning as well.

Easter Island, with an area of only 64 square miles, is the worlds most isolated scrap of habitable land. It lies in the Pacific Ocean more than 2,000 miles west of the nearest continent (South America), 1,400 miles from even the nearest habitable island (Pitcairn). Its subtropical location and latitude—at 27 degrees south, it is approximately as far below the equator as Houston is north of it—help give it a rather mild climate, while its volcanic origins make its soil fertile. In theory, this combination of blessings should have made Easter a miniature paradise, remote from problems that beset the rest of the world.

The island derives its name from its "discovery" by the Dutch explorer Jacob Roggeveen, on Easter (April 5) in 1722. Roggeveen's first impression was not of a paradise but of a wasteland: "We originally, from a further distance, have considered the said Easter Island as sandy; the reason for that is this, that we counted as sand the withered grass, hay, or other scorched and burnt vegetation, because its wasted appearance could give no other impression than of a singular poverty and barrenness."

The island Roggeveen saw was a grassland without a single tree or bush over ten feet high. Modern botanists have identified only 47 species of higher plants native to Easter, most of them grasses, sedges, and ferns. The list includes just two species of small trees and two of woody shrubs. With such flora, the islanders Roggeveen encountered had no source of real firewood to warm themselves during Easter's cool, wet, windy winters. Their native animals included nothing larger than insects, not even a single species of native bat, land bird, land snail, or lizard. For domestic animals, they had only chickens.

European visitors throughout the eighteenth and early nineteenth centuries estimated Easter's human population at about 2,000, a modest number considering the island's fertility. As Captain James Cook recognized during his brief visit in 1774, the islanders were Polynesians (a Tahitian man accompanying Cook was able to converse with them). Yet despite the Polynesians' well-deserved fame as a great seafaring people, the Easter Islanders who came out to Roggeveen's and Cook's ships did so by swimming or paddling canoes that Roggeveen described as "bad and frail." Their craft, he wrote, were "put together with manifold small planks and light inner timbers, which they cleverly stitched together with very fine twisted threads…. But as they lack the knowledge and particularly the materials for caulking and making tight the great number of seams of the canoes, these are accordingly very leaky, for which reason they are compelled to spend half the time in bailing." The canoes, only ten feet long, held at most two people, and only three or four canoes were observed on the entire island.

With such flimsy craft, Polynesians could never have colonized Easter from even the nearest island, nor could they have traveled far offshore to fish. The islanders Roggeveen met were totally isolated, unaware that other people existed. Investigators in all the years since his visit have discovered no trace of the islanders' having any outside contacts: not a single Easter Island rock or product has turned up elsewhere, nor has anything been found on the island that could have been brought by anyone other than the original settlers or the Europeans. Yet the people living on Easter claimed memories of visiting the uninhabited Sala y Gomez reef 260 miles away, far beyond the range of the leaky canoes seen by Roggeveen. How did the islanders' ancestors reach that reef from Easter, or reach Easter from anywhere else?

Easter Island's most famous feature is its huge stone statues, more than 200 of which once stood on massive stone platforms lining the coast. At least 700 more, in all stages of completion, were abandoned in quarries or on ancient roads between the quarries and the coast, as if the carvers and moving crews had thrown down their tools and walked off the job. Most of the erected statues were carved in a single quarry and then somehow transported as far as six miles—despite heights as great as 33 feet and weights up to 82 tons. The abandoned statues, meanwhile, were as much as 65 feet tall and weighed up to 270 tons. The stone platforms were equally gigantic: up to 500 feet long and 10 feet high, with facing slabs weighing up to 10 tons.

Roggeveen himself quickly recognized the problem the statues posed: "The stone images at first caused us to be struck with astonishment," he wrote, "because we could not comprehend how it was possible that these people, who are devoid of heavy thick timber for making any machines, as well as strong ropes, nevertheless had been able to erect such images." Roggeveen might have added that the islanders had no wheels, no draft animals, and no source of power except their own muscles. How did they transport the giant statues for miles, even before erecting them? To deepen the mystery, the statues were still standing in 1770, but by 1864 all of them had been pulled down, by the islanders themselves. Why then did they carve them in the first place? And why did they stop?

The statues imply a society very different from the one Roggeveen saw in 1722. Their sheer number and size suggest a population much larger than 2,000 people. What became of everyone? Furthermore, that society must have been highly organized. Easter's resources were scattered across the island: the best stone for the statues was quarried at Rano Raraku near Easter's northeast end; red stone, used for large crowns adorning some of the statues, was quarried at Puna Pau, inland in the southwest; stone carving tools came mostly from Aroi in the northwest. Meanwhile, the best farmland lay in the south and east, and the best fishing grounds on the north and west coasts. Extracting and redistributing all those goods required complex political organization. What happened to that organization, and how could it ever have arisen in such a barren landscape?

Easter Island's mysteries have spawned volumes of speculation for more than two and a half centuries. Many Europeans were incredulous that Polynesians—commonly characterized as "mere savages"—could have created the statues or the beautifully constructed stone platforms. In the 1950s, Heyerdahl argued that Polynesia must have been settled by advanced societies of American Indians, who in turn must have received civilization across the Atlantic from more advanced societies of the Old World. Heyerdahl's raft voyages aimed to prove the feasibility of such prehistoric transoceanic contacts. In the 1960s the Swiss writer Erich von Däniken, an ardent believer in Earth visits by extraterrestrial astronauts, went further, claiming that Easter's statues were the work of intelligent beings who owned ultramodern tools, became stranded on Easter, and were finally rescued.

Heyerdahl and Von Däniken both brushed aside overwhelming evidence that the Easter Islanders were typical Polynesians derived from Asia rather than from the Americas and that their culture (including their statues) grew out of Polynesian culture. Their language was Polynesian, as Cook had already concluded. Specifically, they spoke an eastern Polynesian dialect related to Hawaiian and

Marquesan, a dialect isolated since about A.D. 400, as estimated from slight differences in vocabulary. Their fishhooks and stone adzes resembled early Marquesan models. Last year DNA extracted from 12 Easter Island skeletons was also shown to be Polynesian. The islanders grew bananas, taro, sweet potatoes, sugarcane, and paper mulberry—typical Polynesian crops, mostly of Southeast Asian origin. Their sole domestic animal, the chicken, was also typically Polynesian and ultimately Asian, as were the rats that arrived as stowaways in the canoes of the first settlers.

What happened to those settlers? The fanciful theories of the past must give way to evidence gathered by hardworking practitioners in three fields: archeology, pollen analysis, and paleontology.

Modern archeological excavations on Easter have continued since Heyerdahl's 1955 expedition. The earliest radiocarbon dates associated with human activities are around A.D. 400 to 700, in reasonable agreement with the approximate settlement date of 400 estimated by linguists. The period of statue construction peaked around 1200 to 1500, with few if any statues erected thereafter. Densities of archeological sites suggest a large population; an estimate of 7,000 people is widely quoted by archeologists, but other estimates range up to 20,000, which does not seem implausible for an island of Easter's area and fertility.

Archeologists have also enlisted surviving islanders in experiments aimed at figuring out how the statues might have been carved and erected. Twenty people, using only stone chisels, could have carved even the largest completed statue within a year. Given enough timber and fiber for making ropes, teams of at most a few hundred people could have loaded the statues onto wooden sleds, dragged them over lubricated wooden tracks or rollers, and used logs as levers to maneuver them into a standing position. Rope could have been made from the fiber of a small native tree, related to the linden, called the hauhau. However, that tree is now extremely scarce on Easter, and hauling one statue would have required hundreds of yards of rope. Did Easter's now barren landscape once support the necessary trees?

That question can be answered by the technique

of pollen analysis, which involves boring out a column of sediment from a swamp or pond, with the most recent deposits at the top and relatively more ancient deposits at the bottom. The absolute age of each layer can be dated by radiocarbon methods. Then begins the hard work: examining tens of thousands of pollen grains under a microscope counting them, and identifying the plant species that produced each one by comparing the grains with modern pollen from known plant species. For Easter Island, the bleary-eyed scientists who performed that task were John Flenley, now at Massey University in New Zealand, and Sarah King of the University of Hull in England.

Flenley and King's heroic efforts were rewarded by the striking new picture that emerged of Easter's prehistoric landscape. For at least 30,000 years before human arrival and during the early years of Polynesian settlement, Easter was not a wasteland at all. Instead, a subtropical forest of trees and woody bushes towered over a ground layer of shrubs, herbs, ferns, and grasses. In the forest grew tree daisies, the rope-yielding hauhau tree, and the toromiro tree, which furnishes a dense, mesquite-like firewood. The most common tree in the forest was a species of palm now absent on Easter but formerly so abundant that the bottom strata of the sediment column were packed with its pollen. The Easter Island palm was closely related to the still-surviving Chilean wine palm, which grows up to 82 feet tall and 6 feet in diameter. The tall, unbranched trunks of the Easter Island palm would have been ideal for transporting and erecting statues and constructing large canoes. The palm would also have been a valuable food source, since its Chilean relative yields edible nuts as well as sap from which Chileans make sugar, syrup, honey, and wine.

What did the first settlers of Easter Island eat when they were not glutting themselves on the local equivalent of maple syrup? Recent excavations by David Steadman, of the New York State Museum at Albany, have yielded a picture of Easter's original animal world as surprising as Flenley and King's picture of its plant world. Steadman's expectations for Easter were conditioned by his experiences elsewhere in Polynesia, where fish are overwhelmingly the main food at archeological sites, typically accounting for more than 90 percent of the bones in ancient Polynesian garbage heaps. Easter, though, is too cool for the coral reefs beloved by fish, and its cliff-girded coastline permits shallow-water fishing in only a few places. Less than a quarter of the bones in its early garbage heaps (from the period 900 to 1300) belonged to fish; instead, nearly one-third of all bones came from porpoises.

Nowhere else in Polynesia do porpoises account for even 1 percent of discarded food bones. But most other Polynesian islands offered animal food in the form of birds and mammals, such as New Zealand's now extinct giant moas and Hawaii's now extinct flightless geese. Most other islanders also had domestic pigs and dogs. On Easter, porpoises would have been the largest animal available—other than humans. The porpoise species identified at Easter, the common dolphin, weighs up to 165 pounds. It generally lives out at sea, so it could not have been hunted by line fishing or spearfishing from shore. Instead, it must have been harpooned far offshore, in big seaworthy canoes built from the extinct palm tree.

In addition to porpoise meat, Steadman found, the early Polynesian settlers were feasting on seabirds. For those birds, Easter's remoteness and lack of predators made it an ideal haven as a breeding site, at least until humans arrived. Among the prodigious numbers of seabirds that bred on Easter were albatross, boobies, frigate birds, fulmars, petrels, prions, shearwaters, storm petrels, terns, and tropic birds. With at least 25 nesting species, Easter was the richest seabird breeding site in Polynesia and probably in the whole Pacific.

Land birds as well went into early Easter Island cooking pots. Steadman identified bones of at least six species, including barn owls, herons, parrots, and rail. Bird stew would have been seasoned with meat from large numbers of rats, which the Polynesian colonists inadvertently brought with them; Easter Island is the sole known Polynesian island where rat bones outnumber fish bones at archeological sites. (In case you're squeamish and consider rats inedible, I still recall recipes for creamed laboratory rat that my British biologist friends used to supplement their diet during their years of wartime food rationing.)

Porpoises, seabirds, land birds, and rats did not complete the list of meat sources formerly available on Easter. A few bones hint at the possibility of breeding seal colonies as well. All these delicacies were cooked in ovens fired by wood from the island's forests.

Such evidence lets us imagine the island onto which Easter's first Polynesian colonists stepped ashore some 1,600 years ago, after a long canoe voyage from eastern Polynesia. They found themselves in a pristine paradise. What then happened to it? The pollen grains and the bones yield a grim answer.

Pollen records show that destruction of Easter's forests was well under way by the year 800, just a few centuries after the start of human settlement. Then charcoal from wood fires came to fill the sediment cores, while pollen of palms and other trees and woody shrubs decreased or disappeared, and pollen of the grasses that replaced the forest became more abundant. Not long after 1400 the palm finally became extinct, not only as a result of being chopped down but also because the now ubiquitous rats prevented its regeneration: of the dozens of preserved palm nuts discovered in caves on Easter, all had been chewed by rats and could no longer germinate. While the hauhau tree did not become extinct in Polynesian times, its numbers declined drastically until there weren't enough left to make ropes from. By the time Heyerdahl visited Easter, only a single, nearly dead toromiro tree remained on the island, and even that lone survivor has now disappeared. (Fortunately, the toromiro still grows in botanical gardens elsewhere.)

The fifteenth century marked the end not only for Easter's palm but for the forest itself. Its doom had been approaching as people cleared land to plant gardens; as they felled trees to build canoes, to transport and erect statues, and to burn; as rats devoured seeds; and probably as the native birds died out that had pollinated the trees' flowers and dispersed their fruit. The overall picture is among the most extreme examples of forest destruction anywhere in the world: the whole forest gone, and most of its tree species extinct.

The destruction of the island's animals was as extreme as that of the forest: without exception, every species of native land bird became extinct. Even shellfish were overexploited, until people had to settle for small sea snails instead of larger cowries. Porpoise bones disappeared abruptly from garbage heaps around 1500; no one could harpoon porpoises anymore, since the trees used for constructing the big seagoing canoes no longer existed. The colonies of more than half of the seabird species breeding on Easter or on its offshore islets were wiped out.

In place of these meat supplies, the Easter Islanders intensified their production of chickens, which had been only an occasional food item. They also turned to the largest remaining meat source available: humans, whose bones became common in late Easter Island garbage heaps. Oral traditions of the islanders are rife with cannibalism; the most inflammatory taunt that could be snarled at an enemy was "The flesh of your mother sticks between my teeth." With no wood available to cook these new goodies, the islanders resorted to sugarcane scraps, grass, and sedges to fuel their fires.

All these strands of evidence can be wound into a coherent narrative of a society's decline and fall. The first Polynesian colonists found themselves on an island with fertile soil, abundant food, bountiful building materials, ample lebensraum, and all the prerequisites for comfortable living. They prospered and multiplied.

After a few centuries, they began erecting stone statues on platforms, like the ones their Polynesian forebears had carved. With passing years, the statues and platforms became larger and larger, and the statues began sporting ten-ton red crowns—probably in an escalating spiral of one-upmanship, as rival clans tried to surpass each other with shows of wealth and power. (In the same way, successive Egyptian pharaohs built ever-larger pyramids. Today Hollywood movie moguls near my home in Los Angeles are displaying their wealth and power by building ever more ostentatious mansions. Tycoon Marvin Davis topped previous moguls with plans for a 50,000-square-foot house, so now Aaron Spelling has topped Davis with a 56,000-square-foot house. All that those buildings lack to make the message explicit are ten-ton red crowns.) On Easter, as in modern America, society was held together by a complex political system to redistribute locally available resources and to integrate the economies of different areas.

Eventually Easter's growing population was cutting the forest more rapidly than the forest was regenerating. The people used the land for gardens and the wood for fuel, canoes, and houses—and, of course, for lugging statues. As forest disappeared, the islanders ran out of timber and rope to transport and erect their statues. Life became more uncomfortable—springs and streams dried up, and wood was no longer available for fires.

People also found it harder to fill their stomachs, as land birds, large sea snails, and many seabirds disappeared. Because timber for building seagoing canoes vanished, fish catches declined and porpoises disappeared from the table. Crop yields also declined, since deforestation allowed the soil to be eroded by rain and wind, dried by the sun, and its nutrients to be leeched from it. Intensified chicken production and cannibalism replaced only part of all those lost foods. Preserved statuettes with sunken cheeks and visible ribs suggest that people were starving.

With the disappearance of food surpluses, Easter Island could no longer feed the chiefs, bureaucrats, and priests who had kept a complex society running. Surviving islanders described to early European visitors how local chaos replaced centralized government and a warrior class took over from the hereditary chiefs. The stone points of spears and daggers, made by the warriors during their heyday in the 1600s and 1700s, still litter the ground of Easter today. By around 1700, the population began to crash toward between one-quarter and one-tenth of its former number. People took to living in caves for protection against their enemies. Around 1770 rival clans started to topple each other's statues, breaking the heads off. By 1864 the last statue had been thrown down and desecrated.

As we try to imagine the decline of Easter's civilization, we ask ourselves, "Why didn't they look around, realize what they were doing, and stop before it was too late? What were they thinking when they cut down the last palm tree?"

I suspect, though, that the disaster happened not with a bang but with a whimper. After all, there are those hundreds of abandoned statues to consider. The forest the islanders depended on for rollers and rope didn't simply disappear one day—it vanished slowly, over decades. Perhaps war interrupted the moving teams; perhaps by the time the carvers had finished their work, the last rope snapped. In the meantime, any islander who tried to warn about the dangers of progressive deforestation would have been overridden by vested interests of carvers, bureaucrats, and chiefs, whose jobs depended on continued deforestation. Our Pacific Northwest loggers are only the latest in a long line of loggers to cry, "Jobs over trees!" The changes in forest cover from year to year would have been hard to detect: yes, this year we cleared those woods over there, but trees are starting to grow back again on this abandoned garden site here. Only older people, recollecting their childhoods decades earlier, could have recognized a difference. Their children could no more have comprehended their parents' tales than my eight-year-old sons today can comprehend my wife's and my tales of what Los Angeles was like 30 years ago.

Gradually trees became fewer, smaller, and less important. By the time the last fruit-bearing adult palm tree was cut, palms had long since ceased to be of economic significance. That left only smaller and smaller palm saplings to clear each year, along with other bushes and treelets. No one would have noticed the felling of the last small palm.

By now the meaning of Easter Island for us should be chillingly obvious. Easter Island is Earth writ small. Today, again, a rising population confronts shrinking resources. We too have no emigration valve, because all human societies are linked by international transport, and we can no more escape into space than the Easter Islanders could flee into the ocean. If we continue to follow our present course, we shall have exhausted the world's major fisheries, tropical rain forests, fossil fuels, and much of our soil by the time my sons reach my current age.

Every day newspapers report details of famished countries—Afghanistan, Liberia, Rwanda, Sierra Leone, Somalia, the former Yugoslavia, Zaire—where soldiers have appropriated the wealth or where central government is yielding to local gangs of thugs. With the risk of nuclear war receding, the threat of our ending with a bang no longer has a chance of galvanizing us to halt our course. Our risk now is of winding down, slowly, in a whimper. Corrective action is blocked by vested interests, by well-intentioned political and business leaders, and by their electorates, all of whom are perfectly correct in not noticing big changes from year to year. Instead, each year there are just somewhat more people, and somewhat fewer resources, on Earth.

It would be easy to close our eyes or to give up in despair. If mere thousands of Easter Islanders with only stone tools and their own muscle power sufficed to destroy their society, how can billions of people with metal tools and machine power fail to do worse? But there is one crucial difference. The Easter Islanders had no books and no histories of other doomed societies. Unlike the Easter Islanders, we have histories of the past—information that can save us. My main hope for my sons' generation is that we may now choose to learn from the fates of societies like Easter's. ❏

---

**Questions**

1. What was the most common tree in the forest? What was it used for?

2. What were some of the meat sources during Easter Island's heyday?

3. What replaced those meat sources when they disappeared?

*Answers are at the back of the book.*

# Section Two

# Problems of Resource Scarcity

**12** *People generally like to support charismatic animals and majestic landscapes that are in need of environmental protection. Society generally appreciates aesthetically pleasing sights. However, we should pay equal attention to areas that do not necessarily excite us. For example, wetlands are largely unappreciated but very important ecologically. The general population is unaware of what thrives in a wetland—all they know is that it is an area they generally do not wish to visit. Wetlands provide a habitat for five thousand species of plants, 190 kinds of amphibians, and one-third of all bird species in the United States. Wetlands also purify groundwater, stabilize shorelines, improve water quality, and help control flooding. Different types of wetlands include swamps, bogs, and estuaries. Swamps contain some of the most diverse habitats. Their biological variety equals that of the rainforests. Bogs consume immense amounts of carbon dioxide. Estuaries are among the most naturally productive habitats in the world. The general public needs to understand what a wetland is and how it works. Once wetlands are destroyed, there is no way to know and replace what has been lost.*

# What Is a Wetland?
## Bruce Selcraig

*Sierra*, May/June 1996

---

***The best way to find out is to wade right in.***

One person's pristine prairie pothole worthy of eternal protection is another's mosquito-choked mudflat fit only for a shopping mall. The dreams of wheat farmers and golf course tycoons—not to mention ecologists—often ride on wildly different readings of the land.

To clear up the confusion caused by some 50 different wetland definitions in use, a National Research Council committee spent two years to produce this delicacy: "A wetland is an ecosystem that depends on constant or recurrent shallow inundation or saturation at or near the surface of the substrate." In other words, wetlands are usually wet.

There's more about "physiochemical, biotic, or anthropogenic factors," but for now let's say a wetland will probably have standing water on its surface or wet soil most of the year, or it will at least contain soils and plants typically found in aquatic environments. The ground may be dry at times, and saturated at others. Water levels may vary from zero to six feet.

If this majestic prose doesn't exactly inspire you to chain yourself to a lily pad, you understand the fundamental problem of wetland protection: marshes and bogs rarely excite the general public. To the hurried eye of the wilderness-calendar connoisseur, wetlands—at least those without a million flamingos rising out of them—are often unappealing and inaccessible ho-hum landscapes of gray and muddy brown, attracting neither poets nor company picnics. What fame wetlands do have is quietly whispered among duck hunters and birdwatchers.

Yet some of nature's most magnificent processes thrive among the reeds and rushes. Wetlands provide habitat for 5,000 species of plants, 190 kinds of amphibians, and one-third of all the bird species in the United States. The very elements that make some wetlands unpleasant for humans—mud, heat, humidity, bugs—create the perfect nursery for turtles, whooping cranes, and dragonflies.

But wetlands do good for humans too. They help purify groundwater and stabilize shorelines. Their dense vegetation and sediments improve water quality by filtering out pollutants. And wetlands do an enormous job helping control floods. By storing and gradually releasing floodwaters, wetlands have helped spare whole communities from devastation. Conversely, the mammoth flooding of the Mississippi in 1993 was made all the worse by the fact that farm-filled states like Iowa, Indiana, and Missouri have drained all but a small percentage of their wetlands. The United States has lost more than half of its wetlands (about 360,000 square miles) since the days of George Washington—who, in 1763, set up a company to drain the Great Dismal Swamp of Virginia and North Carolina.

## How Wetlands Work

Though the hydrology of any particular wetland can get somewhat complex, the most important factor for the health and function of wetlands is water movement. A coastal salt marsh typically floods twice a day with the tides; a major river delta may flood for days at a time, while the water level of a bog may stay just below the peat surface for the entire year, rising and falling only inches during dry periods. Whatever the amount of water, each wetland ecosystem must receive it in regular fashion or its fisheries, vegetation, and wildlife migrations will be impaired.

Water not only flushes nutrients into the wetland, but also provides the needed transportation for migratory fish species, which may depend upon flooding to reach otherwise dry spawning areas.

## Evolving Wetlands

Linked as they are to rivers and ocean coastlines, wetlands are constantly changing and are usually among the youngest of geologic features in any landscape. Change in a river's flow or direction, subsidence, or erosion can all cause the eventual demise of a wetland. But often wetlands simply evolve into drylands, a transformation brought about by plants. A freshwater lake's or pond's first plant community might be a floating species such as duckweed. In time, decaying plant material and sediments build up around the edges, and as the water becomes shallower, emergent species like reeds and rushes begin to take hold. These trap even more sediment and open the way for shrub-like growth. Slowly, often over decades or centuries, the pond is naturally changed into a dryland habitat. The process can be speeded up considerably, and unnaturally, by introducing a system of drains, river diversion, or, say, the pumping of a nearby aquifer.

## Swamps

Of all the wetlands varieties, swamps are probably most in need of a public-relations overhaul. Snakey, inhospitable, and associated in popular culture with dark, watery evil, swamps are among nature's most productive habitats. Acre for acre they often equal rainforests in biological variety. Swamps have standing or gently moving water either seasonally or for long periods, though the water table may at times drop below the rooting zone of vegetation. They are marked by flood-tolerant trees and shrubs, such as red maples in the northeast, and cypress and hardwoods like water gum in the south. Swamps are often transitional environments between large open water and higher, drier land, so it's not unusual to see species from both extremes in or near them.

## Bogs

In the cool, damp, once-glaciated regions of North America, vegetation doesn't decompose as quickly as it would in, say, a rainforest. Here the accumulation of dead plant material overwhelms the rate of decomposition, creating a stagnant, acidic, nutrient-poor ecosystem filled with peat and sphagnum moss—what we call a bog. These waterlogged wetlands are home to small shrubs and stunted spruce, but more commonly known for their wild cranberries. (Massachusetts' bogs produce about half the world's supply.) The abundance of decaying material makes bogs, which cover about one percent of the earth's surface, tremendous consumers of carbon dioxide. But they're also oxygen-starved, making them great for preserving dead bodies. Two thousand Iron Age corpses have been found in eastern Europe's bogs; one Florida bog yielded human brains, complete with DNA, dating back 7,000 years.

Peatlands can be found on all continents and at all latitudes. Canada holds about one-third of the world's peatlands; the best examples in the United States are in Alaska, the Great Lakes, and the Northeast, especially northern Maine's Great Heath.

## Prairie Potholes

Ten to fifteen thousand years ago, receding glaciers scraped out hundreds of thousands of shallow basins across the north-central United States and south-central Canada. More than half of North America's ducks know these prairie potholes as way stations for food, rest, and breeding. A summer trip to the Dakotas might find a pothole dotted with mallards and canvasbacks, northern shovelers and green-winged teals. These freshwater marshes are monuments to diversity, smorgasbords of invertebrates and aquatic life, and support elegant stands of sedges, cattails, and hardy grasses. Agriculture has devastated them, however. Usually surrounded by rich farmland, they have been drained by the thousands in the Dakotas and Minnesota, despite their important role in recharging aquifers and providing duck breeding grounds. Canada has lost over 70 percent of its prairie potholes.

## Estuaries

Estuaries are found all over the world. Whether salt marshes, mud flats, or mangrove forests, these inland marine waters are among the most naturally fertile habitats in the world.

Common along the sandy, sloping coasts of the Eastern Seaboard and Gulf of Mexico, estuarine salt marshes are dominated by grass or grass-like plants and usually lie behind barrier islands and beaches. Fed by nutrient-rich tides, coastal marshes provide a banquet for shellfish as well as spawning grounds for many fish species. Vegetation varies widely in marshes depending upon whether the marsh is flooded regularly or irregularly and the degree of salinity. In a coastal salt marsh flooded only in spring and during storm tides one might find spikegrass, black grass, salt hay cordgrass, black needlerush, sea ox-eye, and a host of reeds and bulrushes.

## Mitigation Banking

Over the past decade a policy called wetlands mitigation banking has taken root among government agencies responsible for overseeing wetlands. It allows property owners to restore or create a wetland in order to offset an action that will destroy one. An agency such as the U.S. Army Corps of Engineers assigns a certain number of "credits" to participating landholders, who can then withdraw them as "debits" when there will be an "unavoidable, necessary" loss of wetlands in the future. Utility companies, loggers, and land developers have taken a shine to the policy, often showcasing their "created" wetlands in corporate publications and on news media tours.

Many biologists and conservationists aren't so sure these complex economic and scientific experiments are working. In many cases bird habitat, once destroyed, can't be restored for years, and nutrient quality of the new site remains poor. Dr. Joy Zedler, professor of biology at San Diego State and a member of the National Research Council committee that worked two years to define wetlands, believes that biodiversity almost certainly suffers with the increase of "created" wetlands. There is no evidence that a created wetland can match the richness of one that is destroyed, because it's virtually impossible to inventory every living thing in order to know what you've lost. ❑

---

**Questions**

1. What is the fundamental problem of wetland protection?

2. How much of the wetlands has the United States lost since 1763?

3. What factors can contribute to the destruction of a wetland?

*Answers are at the back of the book.*

*Natural gas is on the rise and could shape the future of energy. It is a relatively clean and versatile hydrocarbon and has the potential to replace substantial amounts of coal and oil. Because of its lower carbon content, natural gas produces 30 percent less carbon dioxide per unit of energy than oil and 43 percent less than coal. It is easier to process and transport than coal. It is also more adaptable than coal or oil and can be utilized in more than 90 percent of energy applications. Natural gas is the most popular heating fuel in North America, and now natural gas is becoming common in other energy markets, including electricity generation. Low costs and low emissions permitted natural gas to dominate the market for new power plants in the United States and the United Kingdom in the early 1990s. Natural gas could become the primary fuel for new power plants in other countries, as well. Natural gas is a shift toward a more efficient and clean energy system.*

# The Unexpected Rise of Natural Gas
## Christopher Flavin and Nicholas Lenssen

*The Futurist*, May/June 1995

***With growing advantages to its use, natural gas may usurp oil as the world's energy resource of choice.***

When the U.S. Senate called a hearing in 1984 to assess the prospects for natural gas, almost everyone expected a gloomy session. At the time, gas production in the United States had been falling for 12 years and prices had tripled in a decade. It seemed a textbook example of a rapidly depleting resource.

Few were surprised when Charles B. Wheeler, senior vice president at Exxon—the world's largest oil company—told the Senate that natural gas was essentially finished as a major energy source. "We project a shortfall of economically available gas from any source," said Wheeler.

Only one voice interrupted the gloom that pervaded the hearing room—that of Robert Hefner, an iconoclastic geologist who headed a small Oklahoma gas-exploration company and grandson of one of the earliest oil wildcatters. Hefner told those in attendance, "My lifetime work requires that I respectfully have to disagree with everything Exxon says on the natural-gas resource base."

A decade later, legions of government and industry analysts have had to eat their words, while Hefner has turned his contrarian views on natural gas into a comfortable fortune. Natural-gas prices in the United States fell sharply after 1986, and production climbed. By 1993, the nation was producing 15% more gas. For the world as a whole, gas production has risen 30% since the mid-1980s, with increases recorded in nearly every major country.

The world now appears to be in the early stages of a natural gas boom that could profoundly shape our energy future. If natural-gas production can be doubled or tripled in the next few decades (as Hefner and a growing number of geologists believe), this relatively clean and versatile hydrocarbon could replace large amounts of coal and oil. Because it is easy to transport and use—even in small, decentralized technologies—natural gas could help accelerate the trend toward a more-efficient energy system and, over the long run, the transition to renewable sources of energy.

### Advantages of Natural-Gas Use
The environmental advantages of natural gas over other fossil fuels were a strong selling point from the start. Methane is the simplest of hydrocarbons—a carbon atom surrounded by four hydrogen atoms—

with a higher ratio of hydrogen to carbon than other fossil fuels. Natural gas helped reduce the dangerous levels of sulfur and particles in London's air during the 1950s. In fact, these two contaminants are largely absent from natural gas by the time it goes through a separation plant and reaches customers. Natural-gas combustion also produces no ash and smaller quantities of volatile hydrocarbons, carbon monoxide, and nitrogen oxides than oil or coal do. And, unlike coal, gas has no heavy metals.

As a gaseous fuel, methane tends to be combusted more thoroughly than solids or liquids are. Due to its lower carbon content, natural gas produces 30% less carbon dioxide per unit of energy than oil does and 43% less than coal, thus reducing its impact on the atmosphere. It is also relatively easy to process compared with oil and less expensive to transport (via pipeline) than coal, which generally moves by rail.

To be fair, methane gas is not entirely benign. When not properly handled, it can explode. And as a powerful greenhouse gas in its own right, it can contribute to the warming of the atmosphere. But with careful handling, both of these problems can be reduced dramatically.

### Gas as a Power Generator

Natural gas is far more versatile than either coal or oil, and with a little effort can be used in more than 90% of energy applications. Yet, until recently, its use has been largely restricted to household and industrial markets, in which it has thrived. In North America, for example, natural gas is far and away the most popular heating fuel. By the early 1990s, nearly two-thirds of the single-family homes and apartment buildings built in the United States has such heating systems.

In recent years, new technologies such as gas-powered cooling systems and heat pumps have even allowed this energy source to challenge electricity's dominance of additional residential and commercial applications. More significantly, natural gas has begun to find its way into energy markets from which it was excluded in the past, including electricity generation.

Gas has always been an attractive fuel for electric power generation, but high prices and legal strictures deterred its use by utilities during the 1970s and 1980s. Most of the plants built then were fueled by coal or nuclear power. By 1990, gas constituted only 8% of the fuel used in electricity generation in North America and only 7% in Europe.

Until recently, most power plants used a simple Rankine cycle steam turbine. The heat that was generated by burning a fuel produced steam, which spun a turbine connected to an electricity generator. Although this technology had progressed steadily for decades, by the 1960s its efficiency in turning the chemical energy of fossil fuels into electricity had leveled off at about 33%, meaning that nearly two-thirds of the energy was still dissipated as waste heat. The inefficiency of this process made it desirable to use as cheap a fuel as possible. Until recent years, natural gas did not fit the bill.

This situation changed, however, as natural-gas prices fell and turbine technologies improved during the 1980s. Much of the recent gas turbine renaissance is focused on the combined-cycle plant—an arrangement in which the excess heat from a gas turbine is used to power a steam turbine, thus boosting efficiency. Combined-cycle plants reached efficiencies of more than 40% during the late 1980s, with the figure climbing to 45% for a General Electric plant opened in South Korea in 1993. At about the same time, Asea Brown Boveri announced plans for a combined-cycle plant with an efficiency of 53%.

These generators are inexpensive to build (roughly $700 per kilowatt, or a little more than half as much as the average coal plant) and can be constructed rapidly. The huge 1,875 megawatt Teeside station completed in the United Kingdom in 1992 took only two and a half years to complete.

Natural gas powered turbines and engines are also helping to drive the growing use of combined heat and power systems, in which the waste heat from power generation is used in factories, district heating systems, or even individual buildings. Small-scale "cogeneration" has already become popular in Denmark and other parts of northern Europe.

Gas turbines plants also have major environmental advantages over conventional oil or coal plants, including no emissions of sulfur and negligible emissions of particulates. Nitrogen-oxide emissions can be cut by 90% and carbon dioxide by 60%. Indeed, the combination of low cost and low emissions has allowed natural gas to dominate the market for new power plants in the United States and the United Kingdom during the early 1990s. Even larger markets are unfolding in southern Asia, the Far East, and Latin America.

In the future, this technology could spur utilities to convert hundreds of aging coal plants into gas-burning combined-cycle plants—for as little as $300 per kilowatt. Worldwide, some 400,000 megawatts worth of gas turbine plants could be built by 2005, according to forecasts by General Electric. Units are already up and running in countries as diverse as Austria, Egypt, Japan, and Nigeria. A secondary result of this boom could be the emergence of natural gas as the dominant fuel for new power plants in many countries.

**On the Road to Natural Gas**
Interest in natural gas as a vehicle fuel blossomed in the early 1990s as cities such as São Paulo and Mexico City struggled to cope with intractable air pollution. In the United States, many state and local governments began to promote natural-gas vehicles in public and private fleets, while car manufacturers built gas-powered versions of some of their auto and light truck models, and gas-distribution companies converted gasoline-powered cars to the use of natural gas. In many regions, natural gas has eclipsed both ethanol and methanol, the two new automotive fuels that commanded most of the attention in the 1980s. An industry study estimates that as many as 4 million natural-gas vehicles could be on U.S. roads by 2005.

Natural gas is beginning to break oil's stranglehold on the transportation market. Compared with gasoline and diesel fuel, natural gas has both economic and environmental advantages. In the United States, for instance, its wholesale price was less than half that of gasoline in 1993, a disparity caused in part by the cost of refining gasoline. As in other applications, the chemical simplicity of methane is a major advantage, reducing emissions and allowing for less engine maintenance. Until recently, compress-gas vehicles were confined to just a few countries—nearly 300,000 on Italy's roads, and more than 100,000 on New Zealand's.

The main challenge in using natural gas in motor vehicles lies in storing the fuel in the car—usually in cylindrical, pressurized tanks. While early tanks were bulky and heavy, manufacturers are now producing lightweight cylinders made of composite materials that will make it possible to build virtually any kind of natural-gas vehicle with a range similar to a gasoline-powered one. Engineers believe they can design a tank into the smallest passenger car without even sacrificing trunk space.

Switching to natural gas will be even easier for buses, trucks, and locomotives, as their size means that finding room for the tanks is not an issue. Many local bus systems are already switching over, in order to avoid the cancer-causing particulates and other pollutants that flow from current diesel-powered engines. Operators of local delivery services are moving in the same direction. The United Parcel Service in the United States, for example, is testing natural gas in its vehicles. The idea of switching train locomotives from the currently dominant diesel-electric systems to gas-electric ones is just beginning to be studied. In the United States, Union Pacific and Burlington Northern are both testing the use of liquefied natural gas in their engines. Preliminary data indicates favorable economics and excellent environmental performance.

Converting service stations so that they can provide natural gas is also straightforward, and several oil companies have begun to do this. In Europe and North America, virtually all cities and many rural areas have gas pipes running under almost every street, and they simply need to provide service stations with compressors for putting the gas into pressurized tanks. And it may well be possible for residential buildings, millions of which are already hooked up to gas lines, to be fitted with compressors, meaning fewer trips to a service station. As of early 1994, about 900 U.S. service stations were selling natural gas, with four of five more joining their ranks each week.

**How Long Will It Last?**
Geologists disagree vehemently about how much natural gas remains to be found, but the trend is clear—as knowledge grows, the estimated size of the resource base expands with it. The U.S. experience provides insights, since it has the most-extensive gas industry and its resources are the most heavily ex-

ploited. The sharp increase in U.S. gas production since the mid-1980s has been accompanied by a reevaluation of the resource base. A 1991 National Research Council study of official estimates made by the U.S. Geological Survey (USGS) found that, "after a detailed examination of the [USGS's] databases, geological methods, and statistical methods, the committee judged that there may have been a systematic bias toward overly conservative estimates."

As with virtually all other energy technologies, the techniques for locating and developing new gas fields are advancing rapidly. Part of this is due to the advent of computer software that makes it possible to generate three-dimensional seismic images of the subsurface geology and to determine how much gas may be there. As a result, the real cost of finding and extracting gas has declined markedly.

U.S. gas resources are only a tiny fraction of the world total, and discoveries are now proceeding more rapidly in other regions. During the past two decades, enormous amounts of natural gas have been discovered in Argentina, Indonesia, Mexico, North Africa, and the North Sea, among other areas. Each either is or could become a major exporter of natural gas. In addition, some of the former Soviet republics in central Asia have extensive gas resources, which are relatively inaccessible but are being studied by major Western oil and gas companies.

Russia, the former seat of Soviet power, is one of the keys to the global gas outlook. It is the largest producer and has the most identified reserves. While oil production has declined catastrophically with the collapse of the communist economic system, the flow of gas has fallen only slightly. Western experts have reassessed the Russian data and decided that the gas fields are even richer than previously believed. According to estimates by USGS scientists, the total Russian resource is close to 5,000 exajoules—enough to meet current world demand for 60 years. Because it is located in Siberia and other remote areas, much of this gas must be moved long distances. But it is still within reach of more than half of the world's energy consumers, including the 1.8 billion who live in China, Japan, and Europe. And at least 50 additional countries have natural-gas reserves that are minor on a global scale but sufficient to fuel their economies for decades.

Even as reliance on natural gas grows during the next few decades, one of its most important features will become apparent: It is the logical bridge to what some scientists believe will become our ultimate energy carrier—gaseous hydrogen produced from solar energy and other renewable resources. Because these two fuels are so similar in their chemical composition—hydrogen can be thought of as methane without the carbon—and in the infrastructure they require, the transition could be a relatively smooth one. Just as the world shifted early in this century from solid fuels to liquid ones, so might a shift from liquids to gases be under way today—thereby increasing the efficiency and cleanliness of the overall energy system. ❑

---

**Questions**

1. What environmental advantages do gas turbine plants have over conventional oil and gas plants?

2. What is the main problem in using natural gas in motor vehicles?

3. What country could feasibly meet current world demands for natural gas for the next 60 years, and why?

*Answers are at the back of the book.*

**14**   *Wind power is an attractive alternative to other energy sources currently being used. It does not produce air pollution, acid rain, or carbon dioxide, which is the leading greenhouse gas destabilizing the world's atmosphere. For this reason, along with its decreasing cost, wind power may become a significant energy source for many nations within the next ten years. Currently, it supplies 1 percent of the world's energy and is the fastest growing energy source. In developing countries, wind power is governed by a growing need for electricity, which is in short supply. Although it cannot completely replace fossil fuels, it can surpass the 20 percent of world electricity produced by hydropower. Together with other renewable energy sources, wind power has the capability to transform the world's electricity system. This would allow the replacement of coal and nuclear power.*

# Windpower
## Small, but Growing Fast
## Christopher Flavin

*World Watch*, September/October 1996

Wind power is now the world's fastest growing energy source. Global wind power generating capacity rose to 4,900 megawatts at the end of 1995, up from 3,700 megawatts a year earlier. Since 1990, total installed wind power capacity has risen by 150 percent, representing an annual growth rate of 20 percent.

By contrast, nuclear power is growing at a rate of less than 1 percent per year, while world coal combustion has not grown at all in the 1990s.

If the world's roughly 25,000 wind turbines were spinning simultaneously, they could light 122 million 40-watt light bulbs or power over a million suburban homes. In the windy north German state of Schleswig-Holstein, wind power already provides 8 percent of the electricity.

Although it now generates less than 1 percent of the *world's* electricity, the rapid growth and steady technological advance of wind power suggest that it could become an important energy source for many nations within the next decade. The computer industry has demonstrated the potentially powerful impact of double digit growth rates. The fact that personal computers provided less than 1 percent of world computing power in 1980 did not prevent

them—a decade later—from dominating the industry, and changing the very nature of work.

Wind power is being propelled largely by its environmental advantages. Unlike coal-fired power plants, the leading source of electricity today, wind power produces no health-damaging air pollution or acid rain. Nor does it produce carbon dioxide—the leading greenhouse gas now destabilizing the world's atmosphere.

In many regions, wind power is now competitive with new fossil fuel-fired power plants. At an average wind speed of 6 meters per second (13 miles per hour) wind power now costs 5–7 cents per kilowatt-hour, similar or slightly lower than the range for new coal plants. As wind turbines are further improved, with lighter and more aerodynamic blades as well as better control systems, and as they are produced in greater quantity, costs could fall even further, making wind power one of the world's most economical electricity sources.

The modern wind power industry established its roots in Denmark and California in the early 1980s. Spurred by government research funds, generous tax incentives, and guaranteed access to the electricity grids, a sizable wind industry was created. However, development slowed dramatically at the end of the decade as government tax incentives were withdrawn and utilities became more resistant to higher-cost electricity.

Even as political support for wind power waned in the late 1980s, the technology continued to mature. Many of the small turbines installed in the early days were expensive and unreliable, but the lessons learned from those first generation turbines were soon translated into new and improved models. The turbines that entered the market in the early 1990s incorporated advanced synthetic materials, sophisticated electronic controls, and the latest in aerodynamic designs.

In an effort to make wind power more economical, most companies have built larger and larger turbines. In Germany, the average turbine installed in 1995 had a capacity of 480 kilowatts, up from 370 kilowatts in 1994 and 180 kilowatts in 1992. Several manufacturers will soon introduce machines that can generate between 1,000 and 1,500 kilowatts— with blade spans as great as 65 meters.

The 1,290 megawatts of wind generating capacity added in 1995 was almost double the capacity added a year earlier, and up sixfold from the 1990 figure. In 1995, the country with the most new capacity was again Germany, which added 505 megawatts, the most any country has ever installed in a single year. India added 375 megawatts, followed by Denmark with 98 new megawatts, Netherlands with 95, and Spain with 58.

The European wind industry is now growing at an explosive pace: altogether, Europe had 2,500 megawatts of wind power capacity at the end of 1995, up nearly threefold from 860 megawatts in 1992. The United States still led the world with 1,650 megawatts of wind power capacity at the end of 1995, but Germany was closing in fast with 1,130 megawatts. Denmark ranked third with 610 megawatts, and India fourth at 580 megawatts.

Europe is now home to most of the world's leading wind power companies, which are introducing larger and more cost-effective models. Unlike the United States, where most development has consisted of large groups of 20 to 100 turbines, called "wind farms," Denmark and Germany have pursued a decentralized approach to wind power development. Most of their machines are installed one or two at a time, across the rural landscape. This has made them popular with local communities, which benefit from the additional income, public revenues, and jobs that result.

Europe's leadership also stems from the financial incentives and high purchase prices established for renewable energy in response to concern about the atmospheric pollution caused by fossil fuel-fired power plants. In Germany, this approach has allowed determined investors and environmental advocates to beat back efforts by the electric utilities to reverse the 1991 "electricity in-feed law," which provides a generous price of about 11 cents per kilowatt-hour to electricity generators relying on solar, wind, and biomass energy. In a landmark vote in 1995, the Bundestag decided to uphold the law, though it remains under review by the courts.

Wind energy is also advancing rapidly in the Netherlands, Spain, and the United Kingdom. The U.K. has Europe's largest wind power potential, and hundreds of megawatts of projects are now being planned. European wind industry leaders are also hopeful that sizable wind power markets will soon emerge in Finland, Greece, Ireland, and Sweden, each of which has a large wind resource. Even France, the last bastion of the European nuclear industry, embarked on a sizable wind power development plan in 1995, aimed at adding 250 to 450 megawatts of wind power over the next decade.

Just as wind energy development is taking off in Europe, it has stalled in the United States, where the industry is buffeted by uncertainty about the future structure of the electricity industry. In fact, the country's total wind capacity has hardly increased since 1991. The country that led the world into wind power in the 1980s actually saw a net decline of 8 megawatts in its installed capacity in 1995. Some 50 megawatts were added—mainly in Texas—but 58 megawatts of old turbines were torn down in California. Kenetech, the leading U.S. wind power company, filed for bankruptcy in May 1996 after the combined effects of a slow market and mechanical problems with its new turbine led to large financial losses.

Prospects for developing nations are far brighter. Although most wind turbines are currently installed in industrial countries, much of the world's wind power potential is in the developing world. The leader so far is India, which is the first developing country with a real commercial market for wind power. India's roughly 3,000 wind turbines have virtually all been installed since the government opened the electricity grid to independent power producers and enacted tax incentives for renewable energy investments in the early 1990s. According to the government, 730 megawatts had been installed by April 1, 1996, which would make India the world's most active wind market in early 1996. However, uncertainty surrounding the Indian elections in May has slowed the pace of development since then.

Some of India's wind turbines are being imported, but others are manufactured in India, either by domestic companies or in joint ventures with foreign companies. Already, the Indian industry has more than 20 indigenous manufacturers and suppliers. In the windy southern state of Tamil Nadu, hundreds of jobs have been created as a result.

Many other developing countries, including Argentina, Brazil, China, Egypt, Mexico, and the Philippines are surveying their wind resources and installing small numbers of turbines on an experimental basis. Although none of these countries has yet encouraged or even permitted the development of a sustained, market-driven wind industry, some may be on the verge. China, for example, has just 36 megawatts installed but has plans to reach 1,000 megawatts by the year 2000.

In most developing countries, wind power development will be driven not by environmental concerns, as it is in industrial countries, but by a desperate need for electricity, which is in short supply throughout the Third World. In areas such as western China and northeast Brazil, wind power is the only indigenous source of electricity ready to be developed on a large scale.

The global wind energy potential is roughly five times current global electricity use—even excluding environmentally sensitive areas. In the United States, where detailed surveys have been conducted, it appears that wind turbines installed on 0.6 percent of the land area of the 48 contiguous states—mainly in the Great Plains—could meet one-fifth of current U.S. power needs—double the current contribution of hydropower. By comparison, the total cropland used to grow corn in the United States is nearly 3 percent of the country's land area. And unlike corn, wind power does not preclude the land from being used simultaneously for other purposes, including agriculture and grazing.

Other countries that have enough wind potential to supply most or all their electricity include Argentina, Canada, Chile, Russia, and the United Kingdom. China's wind energy potential is estimated by the government at 253,000 megawatts, which exceeds the country's current generating capacity from all sources by 40 percent. Much of that potential is located in Inner Mongolia, near some of the country's leading industrial centers.

India's potential is estimated at 80,000 megawatts, which equals the country's total current generating capacity. Europe could obtain between 7 and 26 percent of its power from the wind, depending on how much land is excluded for environmental reasons. Offshore potential in Europe's North and Baltic Seas is even greater.

Wind power cannot fully replace fossil fuels, but it has the potential to meet or exceed the 20 percent of world electricity provided by hydropower. Moreover, though wind power is more abundant in some areas than others, it is in fact one of the world's most widely distributed energy resources. More countries have wind power potential than have large resources of hydropower or coal.

Combined with other renewable energy sources such as solar and geothermal power, and by a new generation of gas-fired micro-power plants located in office and apartment buildings, wind power could help transform the world electricity systems. These technologies could quickly replace coal and nuclear power—which together now supply two-thirds of the world's electricity—and allow a sharp reduction in world carbon emissions. ❑

## Questions

1. What are the environmental advantages of wind power?

2. What developing nation is the leader in the use of wind power?

3. Why is wind power so important to most developing countries?

*Answers are at the back of the book.*

**15**

*Can sea power provide cheap energy? Sea power is expressed in waves, currents, and tides. A square mile of surface water contains more energy than 7,000 barrels of oil. Ocean thermal energy conversion (OTEC) theorists believe that the technology can extract stored heat energy from the sea directly. OTEC generates electricity by using the temperature difference between the surface of tropical waters and the frigid depths below. OTEC plants could supply enough power and water to tropical areas to make them independent of expensive fuel imports. An advantage of OTEC is that as long as the sun continues heating the ocean, the "fuel" is free. However, OTEC has a very low thermal efficiency rating. In order for OTEC to run efficiently, researchers must develop a system that produces more energy than is needed to run the plant. During the 1970s, the U.S. government allotted $260 million to OTEC research, but since 1980 federal support has foundered. OTEC has immense potential, but it also has enormous engineering and cost issues. Once these issues have been overcome, some futurists see OTEC as an essential part of a global change from petroleum to hydrogen fuels.*

# Sea Power
## Mariette DiChristina

*Popular Science*, May 1995

The world's largest solar collector absorbs an awesome amount of the sun's energy: equal to 37 trillion kilowatts annually—or 4,000 times the amount of electricity used by all humans on the planet. A typical square mile of that collector—otherwise known as the surface waters of Earth's vast oceans—contains more energy than 7,000 barrels of oil.

From the earliest water wheels, humans have sought to tap sea power, expressed in waves, currents, and tides. But a more promising idea extracts that stored heat energy directly: Ocean Thermal Energy Conversion, or OTEC, generates electricity by using the temperature differences between tropical waters drawn from the sun-warmed surface, and those from the chilly 2,500-foot depths below. Near lush Kailua-Kona, on an old black-lava bed on Hawaii's west coast, a test plant produces up to 100 kilowatts net. Rather than creating air pollutants or spent radioactive fuel, OTEC's by-product is not only harmless, it's downright useful: 7,000 gallons per day of desalinated ocean water with a crisp taste that rivals the best bottled offerings.

Using largely conventional components, OTEC plants built on costs or moored offshore could pro-

vide enough power and water to make tropical areas, including the Hawaiian islands, independent of costly fuel imports, say proponents. On drawing boards are plans by Sea Solar Power of York, Pa., for a 100-megawatt floating OTEC plant off the Indian state of Tamil Nadu. Other proposals include smaller plants in the Marshall and Virgin Islands. Some 98 tropical nations and territories could benefit from the technology, according to one study.

OTEC has advantages over other ocean-energy schemes. The largest wave-powered devices have produced only a few kilowatts, for example. Waves and currents have low energy potential—that is, they are not consistently vigorous enough to provide much power to run generators. Tides have greater power potential, but the technology to tap them is costly and limited to a few coastal spots where the tide regularly rises and falls at least 16 feet and can be harnessed. One, built across an estuary in Brittany, can generate 240 megawatts. The only North American demonstration project, on Nova Scotia's Annapolis River, can produce 50 megawatts.

OTEC isn't affected by capricious tides and waves, however. The solar energy stored in the seas is always available. Better yet, "that 'fuel' is free as long as the sun hits the ocean," adds Luis Vega, the shorts-clad director of the Kailua-Kona demonstration project.

That turns out to be a necessary bit of good fortune for OTEC. Tropical-ocean surface waters are typically some 80°F, while those far below hover several degrees above freezing. That temperature gradient gives OTEC a typical energy conversion of 3 or 4 percent. As any engineer knows, the greater the temperature difference between a heat source (in this case, the warm water), the greater the efficiency of an energy-conversion system. In comparison, conventional oil- or coal-fired steam plants, which may have temperature differentials of 500°F, have thermal efficiencies around 30 to 35 percent.

To compensate for its low thermal efficiency, OTEC has to move a lot of water. That means OTEC-generated electricity has a glut of work to do at the plant before any of it can be made available to the community power grid. Some 20 to 40 percent of the power, in fact, goes to pump the water through intake pipes in and around an OTEC system. While it takes roughly 150 kilowatts of juice to run the Kailua-Kona test plant, larger commercial plants would use a lower percentage of the total energy produced, says Vega.

That's why, a century after the idea was first conceived, OTEC researchers are still striving to develop plants that consistently produce more energy than is needed to run the pumps, and that operate well enough in the corrosive marine climate to justify the development and construction. "It's a beautiful process," says Vega. "But it needs large, costly components." During the 1970s the U.S. government invested $260 million in OTEC research. After the 1980 election, federal support fizzled.

One thing is not in doubt: The theory works. Georges Claude, a frenchman who also invented the neon sign, proved it. In 1930, Claude designed and tested an OTEC plant on Cuba's north coast. His patented invention, a version of OTEC called open cycle, generated 22 kilowatts of power—but consumed more than that in operating, partly because of the poor site choice. Claude's next attempt, a floating plant off Brazil, was thwarted by storm damage

to an intake pipe; the luckless inventor died virtually bankrupt from his OTEC efforts.

It's been smoother sailing for the Kailua-Kona plant, operated by the Pacific International Center for High Technology Research of Honolulu. Las September, the Kailua-Kona project took Claude's open-cycle concept to an OTEC world record, generating 255 kilowatts gross of electricity, and 104 net. Operated in a $12-million, five-year project, the plant's power is used by neighboring enterprises at the Natural Energy Laboratory, a Hawaiian facility devoted to developing solar and ocean resources.

Imagine a boiling hurricane. That's essentially what you see through the circular viewing portal when the Kailua-Kona OTEC plant is running. Inside a chamber, air froths from ocean water, forming whitecaps on the turbulent surface. More seawater—9,000 gallons a minute—pours in from 13 upright white plastic pipes. As the pressure inside drops to that of the atmosphere at 70,000 feet, the water abruptly goes ballistic, and 72°F steam shoots about. "That steam is cool enough to touch," a technician advises, "but in that vacuum your hand would blow apart."

After the resulting steam rushes through a turbine-generator, it's condensed back to liquid—desalinated water—by frigid deep-ocean water pulled from other pipes. Less than 0.5 percent of the incoming ocean water becomes steam. So large amounts of water must be pumped through the plant to create enough steam to run the large, low-pressure turbine. That limits an open-cycle system to no more than three megawatts of gross power; the bearing/support system needed for larger, heavier turbines may not be practical. Vega has a solution for this problem, however. "I was influenced by the movie *The Graduate*," he says, referring to the promising career path suggested to a young college graduate. "You know—plastics." Designed with new kinds of lighter-weight plastic or composite turbines, a series of open-cycle-system modules might together create ten-megawatt-size plants, he says. That's still not impressive as conventional power plants go. A large nuclear reactor, for example, can produce 1,000 megawatts.

Another type of OTEC system, called closed cycle, can more easily be scaled up to a larger industrial size; it can theoretically reach 100 megawatts. In 1881, French engineer Jacques Arsene d'Arsonval (who was later to become Claude's teacher and friend) originally conceived this version, although he never tested it.

In closed-cycle OTEC, warm surface water vaporizes pressurized ammonia via a heat exchanger. The ammonia vapor then drives a turbine-generator. The cold deep-ocean water condenses the ammonia back to liquid at another heat exchanger. Closed cycle's high-water mark to date was a floating test plant called Mini-OTEC that produced 18 kilowatts of net power in 1979.

Turbines are already commercially available for use with a pressurized-ammonia system, which gives closed cycle an advantage for installations that would require large amounts of electricity. The technology nonetheless requires large, expensive heat exchangers. New heat exchangers will begin testing next January at a 50-kilowatt (gross) closed-cycle experimental plant that is soon to be constructed at the Kailua-Kona site. The heat-exchanger will employ roll-bonded aluminum, which is less costly than the titanium previously used in OTEC experimental plants.

Researchers there will also monitor the aquaculture tanks located downstream. They want to determine the effects on marine life from any ammonia that might escape from the plant, as well as from the small amounts of chlorine added to the ocean water to prevent equipment fouling from algae and other varieties of marine creatures.

The Kailua-Kona test plants will also help reveal the answer to one of the biggest OTEC unknowns: the eventual life cycle of components, which are continuously besieged by the ocean's corrosive salt spray and biofouling. "We're discovering how to deal with rust," says Vega.

Because open cycle doesn't scale up easily, and closed cycle produces no drinking water, "the jury's out on which way to go—open or closed," says Vega.

Combining the two systems may yield the best of both: A hybrid OTEC could first produce electricity by closed cycle. Then, the hybrid system could desalinate the resulting warm and cold seawater effluents using the open-cycle process. Adding such a second stage to an open-cycle plant could also double water production.

Ultimately, OTEC has great potential—along with a generous share of remaining engineering and cost issues. Futurists see OTEC as an essential part of a worldwide switch from petroleum to hydrogen fuels; ocean-based OTEC plantships could electrolyze water for hydrogen. "OTEC is environmentally benign and could provide all of humanity's energy needs," declares Tom Daniel, scientific/technical program manager of the Natural Energy Laboratory.

Funding for the Kailua-Kona open-cycle plant runs out after 1995. The next step, as Vega sees it, must be to construct a scaled commercial plant of about five megawatts, and to operate it for one to two years. Such a plant could cost about $100 million over a five-year construction and development period—a stiff price, perhaps, for the tropical locales that would most benefit from OTEC's eventual use. "We need to go through a money-losing proposition to prove the money-making one," emphasizes Daniel. "That's where I believe the government should come in."

Like other forms of renewable energy, OTEC won't play well if that government considers only the immediate bottom line. Large OTEC plants could become cost-competitive if oil doubles from its current $18 or so a barrel, says Vega. Oil prices don't include what Vega and others call "externalities," such as money spent coping with the polluting effects of burning hydrocarbons or military defense of oil fields. Factoring in oil defense alone would make oil's "true" cost $100 a barrel, says energy guru Amory Lovins. (Among the closed-cycle test plant's funders is the Department of Defense Advanced Research Projects Agency, which consider the development of new fuel sources to be of importance to the nation's defense.)

Like every other method of generating power, OTEC is not entirely innocent of environmental consequences. The flow of water from a 100-megawatt OTEC plant would equal that of the Colorado River. And that water would also be some 6°F above or below the temperature it was when it was originally drawn into the plant. The resulting changes in salinity and temperature could have unforeseen consequences for the local ecology.

Can the tide turn for OTEC? A self-acknowledged dreamer, Vega professes to have no illusions. "Some people think I'm conservative, and some think I'm crazy," he sighs. "The truth is somewhere in between." ❏

---

## Questions

1. How must OTEC compensate for its low thermal efficiency?

2. Briefly explain OTEC's "open cycle."

3. Briefly explain OTEC's "closed cycle."

*Answers are at the back of the book.*

---

**16**  *The large expanse of land surrounding the Chernobyl nuclear power station, Reactor 4, which exploded nine years ago, is inhabited—not by people, but by genetically altered plants, insects, and field mice. Wild boar, roe deer, herons, and swans are in plentiful evidence. Ironically, the worst nuclear catastrophe in history is providing scientists with a rare opportunity to study how wildlife adapts to severe adversity. The multitude of evolutionary deviations some of the animal species have been going through since the accident is greater than would typically occur in 10 million years. The genetic impact of this disaster, for the animals and for the people who once lived close to Chernobyl, is far from clear.*

# The Truly Wild Life around Chernobyl
## Karen F. Schmidt

*U.S. News & World Report,* July 17, 1995

*Many animals are in evolutionary overdrive.*

At first glance, the glistening marshes of Glebokye Lake in Ukraine appear to be paradise. Wild boars stomp by, roe deer leap through the waist-high grass and myriad herons and swans feed in the shallows. Look on the horizon, though, and the skyline of Pripyat, a ghost city abandoned by 45,000 people, is visible. So is the red-and-white-striped tower of the Chernobyl nuclear power station's infamous Reactor 4, which exploded nine years ago. Paradise? Not even close. Glebokye is one of the most radioactive lakes in the world.

There is no disputing that the worst nuclear disaster in history was a human tragedy. But paradoxically, it is providing scientists with a unique opportunity to study how life adapts to extreme adversity. For more than two years, researchers affiliated with the University of Georgia's Savannah River Ecology Laboratory—armed with respirators, dosimeters and protective clothing—have gone to Ukraine to study Chernobyl's flourishing wildlife. On a recent trip, they allowed a *U.S. News* reporter unprecedented access to observe their work. "All your life you're told of the dangers of radiation, and here are all these organisms living with it," says team leader Ronald Chesser. "How are they managing to survive?"

One clue is being revealed this week at a meeting of the Society for the Study of Evolution in Montreal. Robert Baker of Texas Tech University in Lubbock, and a member of Chesser's group, is presenting startling evidence that Chernobyl field mice are undergoing an extremely rapid rate of evolution. Indeed, he says the amount of evolutionary change in some animal species since the accident is greater than would normally occur in 10 million years.

### Life Altering
Investigating how small creatures such as Chernobyl field mice are adapting and evolving is part of an emerging scientific discipline called evolutionary toxicology—the study of how radioactive and chemical pollutants alter the life course of species. "Man is deflecting the path of evolution; 200 years from now, we may be living with organisms that are genetically quite different from today's," says John Bickham of Texas A&M University at College Station.

Few predicted a swift comeback of wildlife around the Chernobyl plant. Flaws in the reactor's design combined with judgment errors by the operators caused an explosion on April 26, 1986, which belched into the atmosphere at least 10 times the amount of radiation released by the atomic bomb dropped on Hiroshima in 1945. More than 5 million acres of prime farmland were contaminated, and more than 160,000 people were forced to abandon their homes. The accident also caused nearly 1,500 acres of the surrounding forest to die almost immediately. (Pine trees have large chromosomes that are particularly sensitive to radiation.) Soviet researchers noted steep declines in wild animals and die-offs of small insects and worms living in the forest litter. Cattails with two and three "heads" became common.

Today, much of the original radioactivity has disappeared. Contaminants with short half-lives, such as radioiodine, have completely decayed and longer-lived ones, such as plutonium, radiocesium and radiostrontium, have settled deep into soils, says Richard Wilson, a physicist at Harvard University and a Chernobyl expert. However, high surface radioactivity remains in patches, and contaminants still circulate within the food chain. Mushrooms and berries set Geiger counters screaming. And boars, deer and mice captured in the zone have taken up radiocesium in their muscles and radiostrontium in their bones.

The abundance of wildlife is a puzzle, given what is known about the biological effects of radiation. Indeed, high-tech probing of the cells of animals from the region challenges the conventional wisdom that animals cannot tolerate a high rate of genetic change. Here's why: Extensive studies from Hiroshima and cold war laboratories have shown that radiation breaks chromosomes and the strands of the DNA double helix, which contain the blueprints for making the body's proteins. Most of the time, genetic damage signals a cell to die a programmed death, or else it enlists repair enzymes to restore the genetic code. Problems arise when genetic mistakes aren't fixed or are repaired incorrectly, and persist as mutations. In the body, such genetic errors can lead to birth defects in offspring and cancer. More subtly, mutations can cause cells to produce faulty proteins, such as those important for immunity.

While Chernobyl mice don't look like "mutants," on closer inspection, they have many breaks in their DNA strands and a phenomenally high mutation rate. Baker and Ron Van Den Bussche at Texas Tech analyzed DNA from five voles—a type of field mouse—captured within the contaminated zone and compared it with DNA from voles living outside the zone. To search for signs of genetic mutation, they read the code of a gene called cytochrome b that, because it is passed down directly from mother to offspring and changes slowly, is used by scientists as a sort of "genetic clock" for estimating genetic relatedness. As expected, the voles from the area outside the zone had essentially the same cytochrome b gene. But among the Chernobyl voles, the gene sequences as well as the proteins from all five animals were different. Indeed, the differences in the genes between two Chernobyl voles were greater than those normally found between mice and rats, two species that diverged about 15 million years ago.

### How Adaptable?

During mammalian evolution, the rate of spontaneous mutation of one letter in the genetic code has been estimated at 1 in a billion per generation, says David Hillis, who studies molecular evolution at the University of Texas at Austin. But at Chernobyl, the mutation rate in the cytochrome b gene is 1 in 10,000. The important question now is whether rapid mutation observed in the cytochrome b gene is also occurring in other genes. "If that kind of high mutation rate can be tolerated across the entire genome," says Hillis, "it would indicate that mammals in particular are a whole lot more resilient than anyone ever guessed."

Still, the full impact on the mice of this rapid rate of mutation is far from clear. While populations seem to thrive in the Chernobyl environment, individual mice may be living on the edge of their ability to adapt to stress or paying a price with shorter life spans, says Chesser. His lab is now investigating whether Chernobyl mice have had to maximize their resistance to cancer by keeping a well-known tumor suppressor gene called p53 turned on full throttle.

People from the region are clearly paying a heavy price for the accident as cancer and other disorders related to genetic mutations are rising in those who received the heaviest doses. Last month, scientists reported in the journal *Nature* that rates of thyroid cancer in Ukrainian children have climbed fivefold overall and 30-fold in those who lived nearest to Chernobyl. Higher rates of spontaneous abortion and birth defects have been documented in Belarus, but it's not clear that radiation exposure is the primary cause, says Martin Cherniack, an associate professor of medicine and international health at Yale University. Researchers also expect at least a small increase in leukemias and other cancers to show up over the years, but that, too, may be hard to trace to the Chernobyl accident.

The human toll triggers a conflict of emotions for Chesser. "The research potential is very exciting, but I also feel the sadness of all the people who were betrayed," he says. The picturesque landscape near Chernobyl will be repopulated in the coming years, but more by genetically adapted plants, insects and field mice than by people. ❑

## Questions

1. Define evolutionary toxicology.

2. If rapid mutation observed in the cytochrome b gene is occurring in other genes, what would this indicate?

3. What factors contributed to the Chernobyl explosion, and how much radiation was released compared to that of the atomic bomb dropped on Hiroshima?

*Answers are at the back of the book.*

**17** *The Florida Everglades, an area of incredible biological diversity, has become America's most endangered national park. To control flooding in the Kissimmee Valley, engineers reconstructed the 103-mile-long Kissimmee River, causing the destruction of 45,000 acres of swampland. Farms and suburban areas have replaced half of the marshes in the Everglades. This reduction in swampland caused a decline in evaporation, which accounts for 70 to 90 percent of South Florida's summer rainfall, and the intensity of its droughts. There are many plans for restoration, but due to diverse interests, restoration will take a long time. The conflict between wilderness preservation and development will determine the fate of the Florida Everglades.*

# Immersed in the Everglades
## Ted Levin

*Sierra*, May/June 1996

*Forget Miami Beach: If you want to see the real Florida, follow the Everglades' web of wetlands, rivers, and aquifers from its headwaters to the sea.*

On a jeweled January night, I stand in the spell of the Everglades, wet to my waist in sawgrass, listening to an owl's lusty pronouncements and the riotous jamming of frogs. My sandaled feet stuck in four-inch muck, I am part of the diversity of Everglades National Park, the first national park in the world established for its biological bounty rather than spectacular scenery. Yet that diversity now depends on an ugly reality—a wholly fabricated water-delivery system. Lacerated and balkanized by 1,400 miles of canals, dikes, and levees, the greater Everglades (of which the national park makes up only 20 percent) has become a computer-controlled watershed as artificial as Disney World, 200 miles to the north.

South Florida is a checkerboard-flat, two-dimensional landscape, but it is extremely complex. The Everglades seems more like a river than a marsh, one that in its heyday measured as much as 50 miles across, a sheet of water flowing lazily toward the sea. Imperceptibly tilted south at less than two inches per mile, the Everglades is so level that I could have stood in the sawgrass all night and all day and not noticed a current. At five-feet, ten-inches tall, I could walk most of the 300-mile-long watershed from the source of the Kissimmee River to Florida Bay without wetting my hair.

Wetlands here are measured in "hydroperiods," the length of time each year that a piece of land has standing water. Some areas are visibly soggy all or most of the year; others, like the pinelands, usually appear to be bone dry, but may be inundated for a month or more each year. Beneath the surface, water and aquatic animals move through a maze of tunnels and caverns in porous limestone. This is land on the verge of water, water on the verge of land.

Nothing in South Florida is more uncertain than its weather. Although the seasons are Caribbean—six months wet, six months dry—they are not reliable. On average, a quarter of the yearly rainfall occurs during the winter dry season, and the seam between the seasons is periodically obliterated by cycles of flood and brutal drought that sometimes last for years.

Many life-forms can tolerate these swings. Some even rely on them. The seeds of cypress and sawgrass, for example, germinate only on dry ground, even though their parent plants survive an inundation of nine or ten months. Six species of frogs spawn only during the first rains of the wet season, which, in some years, fails to appear. Drought favors the spread of wildfire, which rejuvenates marshes and pinelands, and annihilates hardwood trees. Hurricanes pitch trees and level jungles, all the while casting seed.

The whims of South Florida's weather place the snail kite, a red-legged, crow-sized hawk, and the wood stork at opposite ends of a meteorological seesaw. Wet years favor kites, which troll for snails above the deeper marshes. Dry years favor storks, which gorge on fish concentrated in vanishing pools. Who could imagine a more unusual natural system than one that supports two species of birds, each dependent on periodic and divergent meteorological swings? In fact, the breeding behavior of most species of wading birds—the spectacular wood storks, white ibis, and sundry species of herons and egrets— is cued as marshes on the higher, drier Atlantic Coastal Ridge (home to Miami and Ft. Lauderdale) begin to dry out in early winter. Only later in the season do the birds move inland to the deeper sloughs of the interior Everglades.

Humans have tried for most of the last century to make the Everglades more predictable. Ever since 1884, when William Harney described in *Harper's New Monthly Magazine* how to make the Everglades less sodden, the motto of most regional politicians and entrepreneurs has been: dam it, dike it, drain it, divert it. In 1905, Napoleon Bonaparte Broward was elected governor of Florida on his promise to wring the last drop of water out of that "pestilence-ridden swamp."

Half the original Everglades is gone, replaced by farms, suburban lots, and a dense tangle of alien trees. Water laden with agricultural runoff flowing through the remaining marshland must go through the underpasses of two east-west highways. In the interest of flood control and agricultural and urban expansion, water destined for the Everglades is locked in diked "water conservation areas" or sent directly to the sea. Within a morning's drive of a wilderness that stretches without a road 40 miles in any direction, four-and-a-half million people brush their teeth in water originally meant for spoonbills and crocodiles.

At the southern end of the watershed, 1.5-million-acre Everglades National Park has the dubious distinction of being "the park at the end of the pipe," America's most imperiled national park. Critical ecological relationships, like that of the seasonal wetlands on the eastern apron to the deeper marshes of the interior, are long gone. And with them went 90 percent of the Everglades' wading birds.

Monumental problems have begotten mammoth restoration proposals. In November 1994 the U.S. Army Corps of Engineers announced six possible plans for Everglades restoration. The cheapest, at a modest $6 million, would simply reroute some ocean-bound canal water back into the natural system. The most elaborate, costing $2 billion, would reconnect Lake Okeechobee to the Everglades by purchasing thousands of acres of abused marshland and farm-land, dismantling levees, filling canals, and building a 40,000-acre filtration pond and a three-mile-wide flow-way south from the lake. The effort, an attempt to coordinate the work of no fewer than three federal and four state agencies, is hampered by bickering, politicking, and turf-grabbing. According to Bob Johnson, the park's chief hydrologist, "Everglades restoration won't occur in my lifetime."

No matter. It took a century to disrupt the Everglades' flow; people here are ready to work that long to heal it.

• • •

Before rooting myself in that small remaining patch of wild South Florida, I traveled the vast watershed from its headwaters on Shingle Creek in suburban Orlando (within sight, appropriately, of a sewage treatment plant) down the Kissimmee River to Lake Okeechobee. There, the true Everglades begins, a 6,000-square-mile, island-studded marsh extending more than a hundred miles from the lake to Florida Bay.

My first stop is River Woods, a pink-carpeted, excessively mirrored ranch house built by a bass-fishing retiree from Ohio. I am the guest of the new owner, the South Florida Water Management District, overseer of the surface and underground water from Disney World to the Keys. Recently purchased by eminent domain, River Woods sits on the old floodplain of the Kissimmee, only a good cast away from a stagnant oxbow slated for resuscitation. In several years, when the river reconnects to its oxbow, the house will be torn down.

In 1947, after hurricanes flooded thousands of acres in the Kissimmee Valley and on the east coast near Ft. Lauderdale, Congress approved a huge public-works project to control the flow of the Everglades. (Ironically, Harry Truman dedicated Everglades National Park the same year.) The Army Corps of Engineers proceeded to beeline the 103-mile-long Kissimmee River, which had wandered a mile east or west for every mile it flowed south. Renamed C-38 (but nicknamed "The Ditch" by environmentalists) the 56-mile-long, 30-foot-deep canal proved to be an ecological lobotomy. Forty-five thousand acres of swamplands withered, causing a decline in evaporation, which accounts for 70 to 90 percent of South Florida's summer rainfall, and increasing the ferocity of droughts. Before the death of the swamps, more than a million ducks wintered here. One January day several years ago, a biologist surveying the river tallied just eight.

Now, after years of lobbying by the Sierra Club and other environmental organizations, the Corps and the water management district have begun to restore approximately 40 miles of the Kissimmee's original oxbows, including the one down the road from River Woods. Neighboring cattle ranchers, who stand to lose thousands of acres of pasture, oppose the plan.

The Kissimmee Valley drains about 3,000 square miles of wet prairie and pineland, the heart of central Florida's cattle industry. Between 1958 and 1972, over half of the unimproved pasture was drained and planted in Bahia grass, at the expense of native forage. After a series of big freezes in central Florida in the early 1980s, citrus plantations moved into the region from the north. Land that once spawned bobcats and sandhill cranes now grows cattle and oranges.

To see a vestige of the former valley I visit the National Audubon Society's Kissimmee Prairie Preserve, 8,000 acres of wire grass interspersed with oak and cabbage-palm hammocks, marshes, and ponds. An island in a sea of exotic grasses, the once extensive Kissimmee Prairie existed because of wildfire. The lightning that comes with the wet season would torch a knot of wire grass and fire would spread, consuming old, brittle growth, killing shrubs and small trees that would have otherwise choked the prairie. At the refuge, a biologist sets controlled burns and then monitors population trends of grasshopper sparrows and eastern meadowlarks, both species favored by periodic fire. After a burn, flowers bloom in profusion, as they must have in 1513 when Ponce de Leon named the region *La Florida,* Land of Flowers.

The soft mud in my path displays a montage of animal tracks: bobcat, spotted skunk, striped skunk, round-tailed muskrat, gray fox, and various species of frogs, beetles, and snails. A young water moccasin, its yellow-tipped tail twitching to lure a frog within striking distance, lies coiled along a lane of tracks. I find the spoor of wild hog, an exotic that has been rooting up Florida for more than four centuries. To control the beasts, the preserve contracts with students from the local high school, big boys from the cheerleading squad who throw pompom girls up in the air and provide food for the family's table by wrasslin' hogs.

I meet several locals who are harvesting and grinding sugarcane by hand. I pitch in and quickly tire. These lifelong residents hunt the Kissimmee Valley, fish Okeechobee, grow their own vegetables and fruit, make molasses, and are as much a manifestation of rural South Florida as the sandhill cranes that bugle in the distance. They wish the Corps would go home. "Them engineers shoulda left the Kissimmee alone in the first place and they sure as hell can't fix it now. The government don't live here," says one, and half a dozen heads nod. But what they have is a canal when what they need is a river, and unfortunately only the Corps of Engineers is capable of undoing a problem as grand as the one it created.

Next I visit Bill Berman, whose dairy was one of 40 to relocate in the Kissimmee Valley in the 1950s and 1960s after a growing Miami forced them off the coastal ridge. In the late 1980s Berman accepted a $400,000 grant from the water district to build a concrete feeding pad and a series of retention lagoons. The lagoons recycle manure flushed from the pad, keeping nutrients out of C-38 and Lake Okeechobee, where phosphorus from Kissimmee ranches has triggered massive algal blooms.

A single cow unloads a tenth of a pound of phosphorus into the watershed every day. "If you've got fifty dairies, each with over a thousand cows, you've got a problem," reasons Al Goldstein, head of the water district's Okeechobee office. Berman's pad makes it easier to feed cattle, while the lagoons recover nutrients. Berman's success has prompted others in the cattle-raising community to follow his lead.

I visit a Kissimmee River restoration site, where plugs and weirs along C-38 send water back into a series of oxbows. The estimated price for restoring less than half of the river is $500 million, 14 times what it cost to obliterate it.

We airboat north on C-38, a straight, wide, boring aquatic interstate, then enter a functioning oxbow. An alligator slides off a fallen cypress. Moss-covered oaks line the higher banks and verdant marsh plants spread from the shore. At the far end of the oxbow, after several serpentine miles of travel, I look back down C-38 to where we had entered and realize that our beautiful twisting, turning, curving course represents a net gain of about 300 yards.

• • •

If peninsular Florida were the outstretched neck of a turtle, Lake Okeechobee, the state's most recognizable natural feature, would be its troubled blue eye— 733 square miles of fresh water that ferments in a shallow, wedge-shaped depression inland from West Palm Beach. In the late 1920s, a pair of hurricanes whipped the lake up on its hind legs, overwhelming an earthen dam that protected towns along its southern margins. Two thousand people died and many more were left homeless. In response, the Corps cinched Okeechobee behind a lime-rock levee called Herbert Hoover Dike. Prior to that, the lake expanded during a wet year to perhaps 850 square miles, and shrank during a drought. A stand of cypress and red maple half a mile north of the lake marks the former shoreline. The old south shore, which once merged into the northern Everglades, is virtually gone, and the deep, rich muck is the heart of the 700,000-acre Everglades Agricultural Area. What was once a three-mile-wide swamp of pond apple—a shapely West Indian hardwood—is now under cultivation. I spot a pond-apple stump in the reeds too big to wrap my arms around, mute testimony to a rich ribbon of long-gone swamp.

Formerly, when water overflowed the lake's southern rim during flood years, the pulse of nutrients fed the swamp and the northern glades, growing sawgrass 10 feet tall and building a bed of peat 12 feet deep. Forty years ago the lake had such large hatches of mayflies, a species whose aquatic larvae require sandy bottoms and clean, oxygen-rich water, that snowplows were used to push the heaps of delicate cadavers off nearby roads. But Okeechobee was given a death sentence when the Kissimmee River became The Ditch and the agricultural area began to back-pump fertilized water into the lake. Today, mayflies have been replaced by pollution-tolerant segmented worms, which now account for 80 percent of the bottom fauna.

A line of glossy ibis labors in the wind, almost suspended in mid-flight above Indian Prairie Canal, a tributary on the northwest corner of the lake. Below them, gargantuan mats of torpedo grass, an import from Australia, clog the littoral zone. Torpedo grass is the lake's most recent crisis—it has replaced thousands of acres of water lilies, virtually eliminating dissolved oxygen and the aquatic insects that need it to survive.

Farther down the western shore, another Australian transforms the littoral zone. A jungle of melaleuca saplings, white, papery bark peeling and glinting in the morning light, thrives in altered wetlands. Well-mannered at home, fast-growing and water-hungry melaleuca was imported in 1906 as an ornamental and later planted to help drain the Everglades. Prospering in the absence of natural enemies, it now infests more than a half million acres, 47,000 of which support virtually no other plant life. It grows everywhere, is tolerant of flood, drought, and fire, flowers up to five times a year, casts millions of airborne seeds when disturbed, and sprouts when felled.

Chaperoned by representatives of four government agencies, our airboat roars up to three Guatemalan laborers standing in the cool, waist-deep water, wearing hip waders and baseball caps, their machetes hacking melaleucas. *Chop . . . chop . . . chop . . .* : the metronome of the morning. When a sufficient number of trees have been girdled, the men paint the exposed cambium blue with Arsenal, a biodegradable herbicide originally developed as an antihistamine. Behind the cutters looms a dark wall of melaleuca. Thus far, two crews of six to eight men have treated two-and-a-half million trees and pulled five-and-a-half million seedlings on Lake Okeechobee alone.

Nearby, the Army Corps coordinates a volunteer melaleuca-removal team on Hoover Dike. Unfortunately, the melaleuca removal effort often goes awry. If a fallen tree isn't treated with Arsenal in 48 hours, it releases seeds. A week later they sprout. If you cut down one tree, ten days later you may face thousands of seedlings. The good news is that melaleuca seeds are only viable for a year, and high water greatly reduces successful germination—further encouragement for those promoting the restoration of natural water-flows in the lake basin and across the remaining Everglades. Even so, Dan Thayer, the water district's director of vegetation management, hopes only for containment. Eradication is out of the question.

• • •

The Everglades Agricultural Area, the upper quarter of the original Everglades, is where every fourth teaspoon of sugar consumed in this country is grown, on land drained, sold, and subsidized by the federal government. It's a region and an industry known simply as Big Sugar.

The Fanjul brothers never intended to farm Florida. After four generations of cane-growing in Cuba, their operation was nationalized during the 1959 Cuban revolution. In 1960, together with several other families whose property was confiscated, the Fanjuls bought 4,000 acres south of Lake Okeechobee. U.S. federal and state governments sweetened their prospects of success by placing a tariff on foreign sugar imports, implementing price controls, and reducing land and water taxes—benefits that amounted to $64 million for the 1993–1994 growing season alone. By 1970, the Fanjuls owned 180,000 acres of the EAA, created Flo-Sun Incorporated, and have become America's sugar kings.

The hydrologic malady that began when the federal government encouraged construction of South Florida's first canal in 1881 has increased exponentially with the efforts to keep the agricultural area dry. Four canals that lowered Lake Okeechobee by five feet contribute mightily to the 3 to 4 million acre-feet of water pumped into the Atlantic every year without reaching the Everglades. Although Big Sugar uses only 200,000 acre-feet a year (about 70

billion gallons) for irrigation, without the lower level of the lake the EAA would grow sawgrass, not sugar and vegetables.

Big Sugar's big problem is water quality. Farming the Everglades' partially decomposed organic matter releases stored phosphorus and nitrogen, overloading Everglades waters with nutrients. Until 1979, water from the EAA was regularly back-pumped into Lake Okeechobee, exacerbating the lake's phosphorus troubles. To spare the lake, the water district began pumping untreated EAA runoff into the Everglades. Phosphorus-loving cattails, normally benign natives, have spread southeast from the EAA into the Loxahatchee National Wildlife Refuge, overwhelming the less-competitive sawgrass at a rate of 50 acres a day. When cattails replace sawgrass, dissolved oxygen decreases and the algal and microbial communities change, tearing apart a delicate food web.

If Big Sugar were a manufacturing company it would have been forced to clean up its act years ago. But no one, until very recently, wanted to move against agriculture. "It's like being against motherhood and apple pie," says Johnson. Sugar is grown more cheaply and cleanly in the Caribbean, and without jeopardizing a priceless wetland. In the Everglades sugar exists because of corporate welfare.

One of the most important elements of Everglades restoration is the construction of the 40,000-acre retention pond that will remove nutrients before polluted water reaches the sawgrass, much like Bill Berman's cattle lagoons. Flo-Sun is the only company in the EAA that agreed to pay up to $100 million over 20 years to help finance the pond, but many people still feel the sugar giant got off easy. Taxpayers sold public land cheaply, financed its drainage, and buy its price-controlled product. Now they're being asked to help clean EAA's wastewater. If the deluxe version of the Corps' Everglades restoration is implemented, a three-mile-wide flowway will be built from Lake Okeechobee across the canefields. Taxpayers will pay yet again, because the market value of the land it crosses will inevitably be inflated by all those federal subsidies.

Continuing south again, past the walled-off water conservation areas, past Dade County farms, in and out of hurricane-torn Homestead, I arrive at the

East Everglades. This is home to northeast Shark Slough and the Rocky Glades, the last undeveloped "short hydroperiod" wetlands in Dade County. In 1989, Congress authorized the purchase of 108,000 acres here that were critical to the recovery of the adjacent park. So far, though, only 40 percent of the lands designated for purchase have been acquired. There are thousands of landowners to deal with, victims of real-estate scams who bought parcels sight unseen from out of state. This ecologically vital transition zone between the urban and agricultural fringe to the east and the more persistent "long hydroperiod" marshes to the west is the last available land where wading birds once convened at the onset of the dry season. To the north, marshes are buried beneath tract housing, malls, and melaleuca woodlots, and are laced by highways whose names— Sawgrass Expressway, Palmetto Expressway—are the only hint of the past.

Much of the Rocky Glades is abused. Canals have shortened already brief hydroperiods, a levee cleaves the area from the rest of the national park, and thickets of non-native melaleuca, Brazilian pepper, and Australian pine crowd the marshes. But the Rocky Glades' most immediate problem is an 8.5-square-mile suburban tract that sits right in the middle of the marshland. Water levels can't be raised or surface flow increased until the land is protected.

"Protect home and business with Curtain Wall Technology," reads a full-page newspaper ad tacked up on Johnson's office bulletin board. The ad was paid for by the First National Bank of Homestead, which holds mortgages on many of the homes and farms that crowd the marshes. A vocal and influential minority—farmers, developers, bankers, local politicians—wants to wall off the Everglades from its suburban and agricultural neighbors by building an impermeable barrier, as though wrapping a leaky landfill in plastic.

Curtain-wall technology would protect Rocky Glades homeowners, but more significantly, it would allow development to push right to the edge of the Everglades. Its price tag is $3.6 million to $6.3 million per mile, at least two-and-a-half times what it would cost to buy all the undeveloped low-lying, flood-prone lands. Ecological costs would be far greater: the curtain would cut off groundwater flow east to Biscayne Bay, making the bay hyper-saline and prone to destructive algal blooms like those in nearby Florida Bay, stifle underground water flows to Dade County water wells, and cause the park to flood.

Only a few miles away, tentative efforts are being made to release the Everglades rather than restrict them. In February 1995, the water management district acquired the headwaters of Taylor Slough, the principal source of fresh water for Florida Bay. Euphemistically called the Frog Pond, this 5,200-acre parcel on the eastern frontier of the park currently benefits more tomatoes than amphibians.

I stand at the edge of the Frog Pond, unable to find my notion of Taylor Slough's headwaters—a gushing spring, a river issuing from a lake. What I see is a slight swale in the tomato fields, filled with willows and tall reeds, and a canal with a small pump-station that shoves water into Everglades National Park. The canal separates the park from the tomatoes, severing Taylor Slough, its water level kept low to drain the farmland. Inadvertently and unfortunately, the canal also drains the national park. The state planned to plug the canal, raise water levels across Taylor Slough, and send more fresh water into Florida Bay, where it belongs, rather than out the canal system to the east. But as soon as it took possession, the state leased the Frog Pond back to the very farmers it had planned to evict.

After two weeks of travel, I stand drenched in the Everglades, contemplating tomato vines running to the horizon and a mountain of sugar 600 yards long. How do you preserve and restore a functional remnant of these grassy miles? No matter how talented and committed the team of engineers, hydrologists, biologists; no matter how vocal and persistent the activists; no matter how eloquent the poets and helpful the politicians; the bulk of urban South Florida has no sense of what lies beyond its threshold. The salvation of the Everglades is and always has been determined by the conflict between wilderness and both urban and agricultural development. After all, this isn't Yosemite or Yellowstone tucked away at the sparkling sources of their respective watersheds, it's "the park at the end of the pipe."

The Everglades needs the sympathy of its human neighbors. Is that too much to ask? I watch a horned owl soar dark and silent beneath a sea of stars: it offers memory, a promise, and an invitation not to give up hope. ❑

---

**Questions**

1. How are wetlands measured?

2. Where does the true Everglades begin?

3. If curtain-wall technology is allowed, what will the ecological ramifications be?

*Answers are at the back of the book.*

---

**18** Biologists today face the challenge of educating the public to the immediate seriousness of biological diversity, climate change, and human population growth issues. By creating more effective means of interaction with social scientists, biologists can contribute significantly to sustainable development by integrating the biological processes model with the economics model. Population growth and economic degradation have continued unimpeded despite promising advances in ecosystem management and adaptive management. Limited human resources in the environmental sciences is the most difficult obstacle in managing global environmental problems. A basic knowledge of biology and its societal effects is necessary in order for the public to support policy initiatives. Unless biologists recognize that now is biology's moment in history and act to educate the public, the end result may be social chaos and conflicts over scarce resources.

# Will Expectedly the Top Blow Off?
## Environmental Trends and the Need for Critical Decision Making
### Thomas E. Lovejoy

*BioScience Supplement, 1995*

*The real challenge is how we as biologists can create a sense of urgency about biological diversity, climate change, and human population growth.*

Six years ago—when the population was 5.0 billion compared with today's 5.5 billion—I spoke at the AIBS annual meeting about environmental trends and the imperative to make critical decisions in the next decade (Lovejoy 1988). Today provides an opportunity to review how successful we have or have not been. On the face of the matter, it does not look very good. Trends in population growth, atmospheric levels of carbon dioxide, and deforestation continue largely unaltered. To these trends one can now add the lugubrious state of all major fisheries; as Hardy Eshbaugh of Miami University of Oxford, Ohio, expresses it, we have clear-cut the seas.

Let us begin, however, by looking at the population issue which can overwhelm all others. First, at the plus side of the ledger, in September 1994, sovereign states are to meet in Cairo for the International Conference on Population and Development.

The population policy of the United States has been revised into a humane, proactive effort to bring human numbers under control. The president of the United States—for what I believe to be the first time in history—has made a strong policy statement even though it has been ignored by the media. The role and empowerment of women are recognized as integral to any successful progress. We have learned that there are ways to make progress through education, particularly women's education, and through the availability of contraception. That is good news, because we cannot afford the increase in population that would follow were we to wait for the effects of increases in standards of living and declines in infant mortality. As with many aspects of the environmental challenge, to control the population we need to work on several fronts simultaneously. Arrayed against these encouraging steps are ideological forces that somehow manage to ignore the basic verity that abortion represents the failure of family planning.

In another positive step, the United States has reversed its awkward stance on the Biodiversity Convention. We have signed the convention despite its imperfections, and the ratification is now before the entire Senate due to the foreign affairs committee vote of 16–3 in its favor.[1]

In March 1994 the United States sent an entirely scientific delegation to the science meeting under the convention, signaling the constructive outlook of the new policy. The United States has not waited for ratification or formal international action before improving its national policy and actions with respect to biological diversity. In 1993 the Secretary of the Interior created the National Biological Survey[2] to consolidate into a single agency the field biology work of the US Department of the Interior. This agency has a large agenda and precious little new funding, and it has yet to receive appropriate statutory authority. Nonetheless, on Capitol Hill, its constructive scientific purpose is now better than it was initially understood. A first-class ecologist, Ron Pulliam, has been recruited as its first director. The new agency has indicated from the outset that it can only hope to succeed in its survey function through broad collaborative efforts within and without government.

If anything is now clear, it is that we in the United States—in fact, human society generally—can no longer approach environmental problems in unrelated increments and fragmented jurisdictions. Indeed, institutional fragmentation is as serious an environmental problem as habitat fragmentation. Nowhere is this situation clearer than in south Florida, where the accumulation of decades of decisions, each of which appeared reasonable in its own time and context but each made by institutions and interests largely in isolation from one another, has produced ecosystem degradation that is visible from space. Scarcely a drop of water of the Everglade's famous River of Grass flows naturally anymore, with ill consequences for south Florida, Florida Bay, and the reef system off the Keys.

The only possible way to address the problem is through collaborative planning and decision making, which is hardly easy once matters have gone so far. But there is no other solution to what we now call ecosystem management, which when successful maintains ecosystem function and characteristic biodiversity. The concept of ecosystem management, although grown from multiple roots, has as its essence just good common sense: If one approaches management of a large enough unit of landscape early, multiple options provide more flexibility for human aspirations to be met than if one considers small landscape fragments only after damage has been done. Ecosystem management recognizes that we must move from thinking of nature as something that can be set aside discretely and thus protected within a human-dominated landscape to thinking of human populations and activities as taking place within a natural landscape.

Equally profound, and perhaps of more interest to us as scientists, is the emergence of the concept of adaptive management, where management plans are designed as actual experiments. The results, both successes and failures, can thus be evaluated scientifically. In a way, this notion is inherent in the Biosphere Reserve concept of the Man and the Biosphere (MAB) program. The notion of a core area of undisturbed natural community against which one can compare the effects of manipulating a surrounding area makes good scientific sense. Indeed, an adequate network of biosphere reserves can become a national set of ecological standards. In this context, the importance of wilderness areas far transcends the recreational experience that a limited few enjoy within them, because these areas also provide the ultimate context for science and society to judge how the biology of the planet is being managed.

Biological survey, ecosystem management, and adaptive management all presuppose better, more effective, more coordinated, and more open science than US government programs have previously provided. That is not to say that there have not been some superb government science programs. But as the Committee for the National Institute for the Environment, in Washington, DC, has noted (CENR 1995), the programs have been far too fragmented, uneven in quality, and impervious to outside evaluation.

---

[1]The Senate failed to vote on ratification. It is clearly in the interest of US science and industry to do so, and we need to make this case to the new Congress.

[2]In January 1995, the name was formally changed to the National Biological Service.

These are problems that the Committee on Environment and Natural Resources (CENR), operating under the National Science and Technology Council chaired by President Clinton, is designed to address. A national forum was held at the National Academy of Sciences (NAS) in late March 1994 to assist in the development of a government-wide strategy in these areas of science, and most recently the CENR Subcommittee on Biodiversity and Ecosystem Dynamics shared working drafts of the implementation plan with the NAS Commission on Life Sciences. The CENR subcommittee has been particularly successful, no doubt due largely to the advances in thinking within the scientific community. Representative of these advances are the Sustainable Biosphere Initiative produced by the Ecological Society of America and the Systematics Agenda 2000, produced by a consortium of scientific societies. As someone who sometimes thinks of life and work in the nation's capital as a gigantic tableau of social primate behavior, I have in my participation in these developments never experienced less of a sense of territoriality between departments, agencies, and subcommittees. The ultimate test, of course, is the future meshing of the conceptual achievements of these documents with the reality of the budget process.

Promising as these advances may be, they nonetheless appear diminutive when compared to the unabated trends in population growth and environmental degradation and the glacially slow progress of the international multilateral environmental agenda. The North/South positions are too ritualized and the rhetoric too generalized and ideological to serve as meaningful solutions to the actual problems. Particularly disturbing is a trend, exemplified by the science meetings under the biodiversity convention, to subvert science with politics. It is essential for the scientific community to remain vigilant and vocal about the need for scientific assessment to proceed independently.

Too frequently opportunities to make progress on environmental problems run aground on the shoals of North/South posturing. Fingers are pointed at northern consumption patterns (of which those of the United States are amongst the highest), and sus-

picions are raised that the environmental concern emanating from industrialized nations is really a stalking horse to prevent the developing nations from attaining their God-given right to development and higher living standards. Why, it is asked, do you (the northern nations) point fingers at us (the southern nations) about population growth when you are the ones consuming so much of the world's resources? There is something to those accusations of course, but as clear as it is that 5.5 billion people cannot live US lifestyles, it is equally clear that 5.5 billion people cannot live as hunter-gatherers. Both population growth and consumption patterns are problems. We simply have to recognize that consumption does not equate one-on-one with quality of life and that the consumption patterns that might be labeled as *Yankee* occur in at least some segments of most countries in the world. The real point is that we urgently need to get on with solving these problems rather than engaging in deadlocking rhetoric. Because there is an ethical imperative for each individual to have some minimal level of quality of life, it is fundamentally easier to deal with the consumption issue than with the issue of additional population.

As biologists we have something to contribute to this discussion and this agenda. First, generally speaking, we are more aware of the state of the environment than anyone else. Biological diversity is, after all, the most sensitive indicator of environmental change. Furthermore, it is in our direct interest as scientists to be engaged in the discussion, because the biotic impoverishment of the planet automatically impoverishes the potential growth of the life sciences. Imagine the howls from astrophysicists if someone were to propose eliminating a number—a large number, somewhat at random but including some of the most interesting—of celestial bodies. Similarly, biologists need to stand up and be counted.

Biologists also have an extraordinary amount to contribute to the main solution to the environmental crisis, namely sustainable development. While some consider sustainable development an oxymoron, and while in fact no development will be sustainable if current patterns and bents continue, I believe it is abundantly clear that an important segment of sustainable development inevitably will be biologically based—in fact, derived from biological diversity.

I have made much in the last three years of the multibillions of dollars of economic activity that have derived from the enzyme from the Yellowstone hot spring bacterium *Thermus aquaticus,* which was described by Thomas Brock of the University of Wisconsin in Madison and which makes the polymerase chain reaction (PCR) possible. This reaction—so central to diagnostic medicine and forensic medicine (even making news in the murder trial of football star O. J. Simpson)—has already fed back into strengthened systematic science and population biology. The technique, and thus the enzyme, also is essential to the human genome project and all the incalculable potential that project holds for human society. Little wonder that Kary Mullis shared the 1993 Nobel Prize for chemistry for conceiving of this reaction.

Let us not forget that all this activity based on PCR is possible because of science concerned with biological diversity and because of biological collections (in this case the American Type Culture Collection). These scientific activities were coupled with the lucky accident that the scenic beauty captured in Thomas Moran's watercolors, rather than biological diversity, inspired the US Congress to set aside Yellowstone as the world's first national park in 1872. *Thermus aquaticus,* in fact, thus becomes an argument in itself for biological survey and ecosystem management.

Pursuing this chain of coincidence even further, it is important to bear in mind that the molecular scissors—the endonucleases—that the genetic engineers, biotechnologists, and molecular biologists employ for society's benefit also derive from a biological-diversity toolbox. In the end, molecular biology and the ability to generate wealth at the level of the molecule derive in significant degree from biological diversity.

Exciting new science and practical applications are resulting from the study of microorganisms with weird metabolisms and weird appetites. Bacteria that can break down aromatic compounds and chlorofluorocarbons (CFCs) have been discovered

in nature and—together with similar oddities—are part of bioremediation using biological processes for environmental clean-up. Some observers believe that bioremediation is likely to have a short flush of success and then become largely unnecessary when industries reduce pollution at the source. I believe that, to the contrary, bioremediation will be used to reduce pollution at the source. In addition, as industrial ecology grows in sophistication and in practice, bioremediation in the factory is likely to be used to make the waste stream of one industry acceptable feedstock for another.

Organisms and their enzymes are already being used in bioindustry to produce chemicals such as acrylamides. Biological processes for chemical manufacture eliminate the need for toxic catalysts and in some instances high-pressure processes. The biological processes are cheaper and cleaner, and when a more effective enzyme or organism is identified, there is no need to rebuild the factory to accommodate the substitute process.

As biologists, we have to find more effective ways to interact with social scientists. Biologists see the biosphere as ultimately run by biological processes largely driven by solar energy. Economists view the world as largely driven by economics, money, supply, and demand. I believe we should work together to integrate these two models.

There are interesting questions. How should the American oyster population of the Chesapeake Bay be valued? Is its value what it brings to market as seafood annually? Or is the value that the current population filters a volume of water equal to the entire bay once a year, and its value before degradation of the bay that it filtered that same enormous volume once a week? Our economies are riddled with such beneficial subsidies from nature, for which there is no current accounting. Similarly, our economies are riddled with subsidies and incentives that lead to environmental degradation. There is something akin to a Gordian knot here that can only be unraveled by biological and social scientists together.

In the midst of the environmental crisis, organismal biologists in particular are suddenly finding themselves moving from the shadow of the laboratory sciences to the spotlight of world issues. The

103

trick is to accept that responsibility and to be willing to bridge the gap (often a false one) between basic science and its application to societal problems. We particularly have to avoid what often seems like selfish yammering for money for research. While research is a true need, we are far more likely to attain a positive response from society if we are seen as wanting to develop the information necessary to produce good public policy rather than as wanting only to pursue our private, esoteric intellectual pleasures.

At the same time we are probably nanoseconds away—in terms of graduate training time—from recognizing that the toughest limiting factor in addressing global environmental problems is the limited human resources in the environmental sciences, particularly systematics and ecology. Now is the time to be bold and increase graduate training in these fields, even before the specific jobs are in sight.

We also need to seek ways to use experts' time more effectively. One way is to pursue the paramedic model, as Costa Rica's INBio has done with parataxonomists. Another way is to push the frontier of interactive electronic media, as has Australia's CSIRO. They have produced a CD-ROM, for example, that in essence permits anyone to determine the family or subfamily of any beetle larva. While creating these electronic products requires a large specialist contribution, as with the example of the expensive energy-efficient light bulb, the ultimate savings in specialists' time is staggering. These products are essentially redefining the boundary between the amateur and the specialist: empowering the amateur and parascientist while reserving the time of the specialist for those tasks for which that person is uniquely suited.

There also is a tremendous challenge before us with respect to education. Part of this challenge derives from the failure of our much-vaunted system of higher education to provide a minimal modicum of understanding about biology and how it relates to our existence. It is nothing short of scandalous that one can still graduate from most of our universities and colleges without that rudimentary knowledge. A basic knowledge of biology and its implications for society is requisite to responsible citizenship. Even if it were possible to quickly rectify this failing, it would not help the present citizenry make responsible decisions in the home or voting booth.

Every one of us has a particular responsibility to help with public education. There are some encouraging signs, such as the preliminary results of a study by the National Environment Education and Training Foundation showing that environment was a concern even for disadvantaged urban youth. But the discouraging reality is that probably 95% of US citizens do not understand even something as simple as exponential increase.

If that is the case, how can we expect the public to understand the threat of biotic impoverishment and global climate change and to support policy initiatives to address the threat? Those of us in the scientific community have a special responsibility to explain these issues to the public. These issues include explaining that:
- Biological diversity and ecosystems are important to science, to society, and to sustainable development;
- Artificially elevated levels of carbon dioxide are likely to cause ripples through the structure and function of biological communities, because there is no reason to expect every plant species to respond in the same way and degree; and
- Biological diversity, which is largely surviving in landscapes as isolated natural areas, is highly vulnerable to even natural climate change, because species will be unable to disperse and track their requisite climatic conditions.

Most important, we need to explain that even though uncertainty tends to be measured more effectively in science than in other forms of human endeavor, uncertainty is part of almost every kind of decision society makes. Rather than using uncertainty as an excuse for a blasé, lethargic approach to energy policy and greenhouse-gas emissions, we need to explain that the real policy issue is whether we oppose, or favor by default, total-planet experiments that bet the biosphere, if there is even a small chance we may regret the result. After all, there is not even an experimental control planet to colonize if we lose at biosphere roulette.

There is an important lesson to be learned from multilateral negotiations on the environment. One negotiation stands out as particularly successful in producing prompt action: the Montreal Protocol dealing with CFCs and the ozone layer. One can argue that the problem was relatively simple, and the solution was clear and inescapable. Those familiar with international obligations assert that a real sense of urgency was the more important factor in making the protocol work. I would assert that until there is such a sense of urgency about other environmental issues, international negotiation is likely to be dominated by short-sighted self service rather than long-term societal benefit.

The real challenge is how we as biologists can create that sense of urgency about biological diversity, climate change, and human population growth. These are problems that grow by increments and that may not seem of particularly great consequence, but which in aggregate are disastrous. No group is in a better position than are biologists to make this case and make it eloquently. It is likely to be hard, and maybe even impossible, to make significant progress unless we biologists enter the fray with greater energy and passion than we have so far. How can we possibly do otherwise with impending extinction rates projected at 10,000 times the past rates (May et al. in press)?

My speech six years ago was entitled "Will unexpectedly the top blow off?" borrowing from an Archibald MacLeish poem about a circus crowd so entranced by the show that nobody notices a problem until the entire big top of the circus tent blows off. My thesis in part was that environmental problems may grow so large, social chaos and quarreling over dwindling resources are likely to ensue, thwarting any possibility of remedial action—a notion that was given some flesh in R. D. Kaplan's *Atlantic Monthly* article (Kaplan 1994).

Today it is appropriate to pose the question differently: "Will expectedly the top blow off?" The answer, I believe, is yes, unless it is recognized that now is biology's moment in history. We biologists must recognize it first. We need to act now.

Now.

## References Cited

Committee on Environment and Natural Resources (CENR). 1995. CENR Integrated Strategy Document. The White House, Washington, DC.

Lovejoy, T.E. 1988. Will unexpectedly the top blow off? *BioScience* 38: 722–726.

Kaplan, R.D. 1994. The coming anarchy. *The Atlantic Monthly* 273(2): 44–63.

May, R.M., J.H. Lawton, and N.E. Stork. In press. Assessing extinction rates. In J.H. Lawton and R.M. Mays, ed. *Extinction Rates*. Oxford University Press, London, UK. ❏

---

## Questions

1. What is adaptive management?

2. What three programs provide more effective, more coordinated, and more open science than U.S. government programs?

3. What is the most sensitive indicator of environmental change?

*Answers are at the back of the book.*

**19** *Although forests once covered more than 40 percent of the land surface, they have since been decreased by one-third. Indeed, tropical forests have lost half of their initial area in the past 50 years. Forests shelter many different species, protect soils, affect hydrological cycles, and are crucial to the energy budget and reflectivity of Earth. Most species extinctions today result from deforestation. The causes of forest decline lie in the lack of understanding of forest values and lack of economic ability to measure their outputs. When we understand more about the intrinsic value of forests, then instituting policy measures will not be as inconvenient as living without the forests.*

# The World's Forests
## Need for a Policy Appraisal
## Norman Myers

*Science*, May 12, 1995

There is need for a fresh policy approach toward forests. An organization is soon to established for this purpose, the World Commission on Forests and Sustainable Development. It is hoped that the commission will move us beyond the negative clamor about forest destruction, and toward a constructive appraisal of how forests can best confer their manifold benefits on society, now and in the future.

Forests once covered more than 40% of Earth's land surface, but their expanse has been reduced by one-third. The most rapid decline has occurred since 1950—tropical forests have lost half their original expanse in the past 50 years, the fastest vegetation change of this magnitude in human history. Temperate forests are in steady state for the most part, but certain boreal forests have started to undergo extensive depletion. In the absence of greatly expanded policy responses, many of the world's forests appear set to decline at ever-more rapid rates, especially as global warming overtakes them.

Forests can supply such an exceptional array of goods and services that they should be reckoned among our most valuable natural resources. Only a few products are generally harvested, however, but with degradation of the forests' many other poten-tial outputs. Thus, forests are overexploited and underutilized.

The consequences of forest loss are far from being recognized in their full scope, especially by political leaders and policy-makers. Forests protect soils. They play a major role in hydrological cycles. They exert a gyroscopic effect in atmospheric processes and other factors of global climate, with an influence second only to that of the oceans. They are critical to the energy budget and the albedo (reflectivity) of Earth. And they harbor a majority of species on land.[1] Thus, there is a vital linkage between forests and the two recent conventions on climate and biodiversity, although the latter are of limited effectiveness without a parallel initiative for forests.[2]

A policy appraisal of forests should address both the scope of changes necessary for forests to undergo sustainable development, and the scope required for forests to contribute fully to sustainable development in the countries concerned and in the world at large. Both prospects can be facilitated by the new commission through an authoritative assertion of all forests' values to society. Forestry has so far been dominated by private interests, commercial for the most part. Certain of these interests could well have an expanded role in the future, but public interests deserve to be better represented in the policy arena, especially the fast-growing interests at a global level.[2]

In light of their exceptional potential to support humanity, why are forests allowed to decline? Well over half of all tropical deforestation is due to slash-and-burn agriculture by displaced landless peasants, sometimes known as "shifted cultivators" (by contrast with shifting cultivators of tradition, who cause no long-term injury to forest ecosystems).[3] Comprising several hundred million of the world's 1.3 billion people living in absolute poverty, these communities should have their plight relieved on humanitarian grounds, let alone to reduce deforestation. They are driven to migrate into the forests by poverty, population pressures, and land hunger, among other reasons.[4] Thus, the source of most tropical deforestation lies in an amalgam of factors that are usually far removed from the forests—and lie outside the purview of traditional forestry measures.

Boreal forests in Siberia are newly declining, primarily through clear-cut logging and fires.[5] The annual loss of these forests encompasses an area twice as large as deforestation in Brazilian Amazonia.[6] Boreal forests in northeastern North America and northern and central Europe are experiencing acid precipitation, with commercial losses of $30 billion a year in Europe alone.[7]

The ultimate source of forest decline lies both in our lack of scientific understanding of forests' overall values and our lack of economic capacity to evaluate many of their outputs. Instead of enjoying their proper place in the mainstream of development, forests tend to be relegated to the sidelines in the councils of power.[8] The Food and Agriculture Organization, the leading forestry agency in the United Nations, has reduced its budget allocation to forestry from a mere 5% in 1975 to 3% today. As a result of its "Cinderella status," forestry's case often falls through a plethora of institutional cracks.

The principal challenge for the commission will be to formulate a policy vision for forests, especially with regard to their role in the biosphere and the world. Here, I provide a selection of possible policy options.

First, the encouragement of sustainable development. Through the myriad goods and services they provide, forests should be enabled to support development sectors as diverse as energy, agriculture, fisheries, water, health, biodiversity, and climate. They can generally do this through their simple existence, and hence do it sustainably. In the spirit of this newly expansive approach with its emphasis on development both within and beyond forests, the maintenance of watershed functions should be seen as a form of "development" that ranks alongside timber harvesting. A national park is as legitimate a form of land use as a paper pulp plantation. Genetic reservoirs count together with agroforestry. Certain forest tracts can serve as extractive reserves. All forests constitute carbon sinks. In a few localities, development can even entail outright preservation of forest ecosystems, some of the most productive and diverse on Earth, for scientific research. Many of these functions can be served simultaneously as well as sustainably.

Second, enhancing forests' institutional status. When forests are treated as the poor relation by those in the corridors of power, forest policy is effectively set by departments of economic planning, agriculture, employment, human settlements, trade, and other entrenched bureaucracies. These agencies decide what forms of government investment, and hence of land use, will predominate, to the detriment of forests.[9] Although it is generally not recognized, basic forest policy is seldom formulated by foresters.

In order to dispel the Cinderella syndrome, policy planners need to appreciate forest outputs in their full scope, both actual and potential. A major reason why this is not done is that forest benefits often accrue to widely dispersed communities in the country concerned or to those in other countries, as in the case of watershed functions, biodiversity, and climate. Over half of the environmental and other eternality benefits of sustainable forest management in Costa Rica accrues to the global community.[10] A rational response would be for the global community to compensate forest countries that supply worldwide benefits, through a mechanism such as the Global Environment Facility. This organization already disburses $700 million per annum to make up the gap between what a country gains through environmental activities and what it loses in benefits to the global community.

Third, the removal of "perverse" subsidies. Much deforestation is fostered by government subsidies. In the United States, subsidies for below-cost timber sales alone amounted to $323 million in 1993, including $35 million for the Tongass National Forest,[11] a rainforest depleted through overlogging more rapidly than most rainforests in Amazonia or Borneo. Covert subsidies in the Philippines, in the form of the government's undervaluation of forest resources, led to revenue losses of $250 million in 1987. Much the same has applied in Indonesia, Malaysia, and the Ivory Coast, among other leading tropical timber countries. Subsidies for cattle ranching in Brazilian Amazonia caused commercial timber losses of $2.5 billion annually during the mid-1980s.[12] These perverse subsidies persist in part because certain governments remain unaware of the all-round and enduring value of their forests, and hence they view the forests as capital to be liquidated.

Fourth, calculating the costs of inaction. It is generally easy to calculate the costs of a specific action—for example, the budget for a fuelwood plantation—by using any of a number of marketplace indicators. It is less easy to calculate the concealed costs of inaction. Thus there is an asymmetry of evaluation. Nevertheless, it is possible to provide surrogate estimates of such costs. For instance, the opportunity costs of those who trek far afield to find fuelwood and thus utilize time that could otherwise have been spent on farm activities amounts to at least $50 billion per year.[13] This contrasts with the costs of tree planting to meet fuelwood needs—$12 billion per year— costs that, in the absence of a comparative evaluation, are viewed as "too high."

A similar reasoning applies to the costs of saving tropical forest biotas, in the absence of figures for the covert costs of losing them. Pharmaceuticals from tropical forest plants have a commercial value of $25 billion a year and an economic value at least twice as large,[14] but this reflects only a small part of the much greater biotic impoverishment that would ensue from grand-scale deforestation.[15] What price tag should we attach to the decline of watershed services in numerous deforested catchments? In India, annual flood damage attributable to deforested catchments amounted to $1 billion to $2 billion in the early 1980s.[16] What value will be lost if we reduce forests' stabilization of the global climate system? Tropical forests with the largest carbon stocks are theoretically worth $1000 to $3000 per hectare per year in terms of global warming injuries prevented[17]—yielding a far higher rate of return than any alternative form of current land use in the forests.

These cost estimates are preliminary and exploratory. They urgently need to be firmed up, as do the many other benefits inherent in forests and amenable to creative economic analysis. Only then will we be in a position to give "real world" regard to the immediate costs of saving forests.

An alternative approach to tackling the asymmetry of evaluation is to shift the burden of proof as it concerns forest exploitation. The once-and-for-all exploiter can generally go ahead with little hindrance. This leaves the conservationist to argue the case for sustainable forms of forest use—a challenge that, in light of the many incommensurable and intangible values at stake, can be taxing indeed. What about requiring an exploiter to demonstrate that his form of forest use will generate economic returns of a sustainable sort exceeding those of any other option?

Fifth, the promotion of forests as global commons resources. By virtue of their many outputs that indivisibly benefit not just forest nations but the world community as well, forests constitute a type of global commons resource. This raises the issue of national rights and international responsibilities on the part of forest nations. Forests lie within the sovereign jurisdiction of individual nations and are subject to the policy discretion of individual governments. At the same time, the environmental services of forests extend far beyond national boundaries by virtue of their watershed basins, atmospheric processes, and climate systems ("the winds carry no passports").

We need to reconcile national prerogatives with international interests, and in a manner that recognizes the environmental interdependencies of the planetary ecosystem. The new commission should foster a coalition of interests as a basis for an eventual international instrument or set of instruments. The more the commission can establish a consensus about the world's forests and their value for all, the greater the chance that individual governments will engage in enlightened forest policies as an authoritative expectation of the community of nations. Instituting many of these policy measures will be difficult—but not as difficult as living in a world that has lost many of its forests.

## References and Notes

1. N. Myers, *The Primary Source: Tropical Forests and Our Future* (Norton, New York,1992); G.M. Woodwell, in *World Forests for the Future*, K. Ramakrishna and G. M. Woodwell, Eds. (Yale Univ. Press, New Haven, CT, 1993), pp.1–20.
2. K. Ramakrishna and G.M. Woodwell, Eds., *World Forests for the Future* (Yale Univ. Press, New Haven, CT, 1993). The policy purposes can also be promoted by the new Intergovernmental Panel on Forests under the United Nations.
3. N. Myers, in *The Causes of Tropical Deforestation*, K. Brown and D.W. Pearce, Eds. (University College London Press, London, 1994), pp.27–40. See also Food and Agriculture Organization, *Forest Resources Assessment 1990* (Food and Agriculture Organization, Rome, 1993).
4. R. Bilsborrow and D. Hogan, Eds., *Population and Tropical Deforestation* (Oxford Univ. Press, New York, in press); W.J. Peters and L. F. Neuenschwander, *Slash and Burn Farming in Third World Forests* (Univ. of Idaho Press, Moscow, ID, 1988).
5. V. Alexeyev, *Human and Natural Impacts on the Health of Russian Forests* (Institute of Forest and Timber Research, Moscow, 1991); A. Shvidenko and S. Nilsson, *Ambio* **23** (no. 7), 396 (1994).
6. A.Rosencrantz and A. Scott, *Nature* **355**, 29 (1992).
7. S. Nilsson, Ed., *European Forest Decline: The Effects of Air Pollutants and Suggested Remedial Policies* (Royal Swedish Academy of Agriculture and Forestry, Stockholm, 1991).
8. N. Myers, *The Primary Source: Tropical Forests and Our Future* (Norton, New York, 1992), pp. 263–265.
9. J. MacNeill, in *Tropical Forests and Climate,* N. Myers, Ed. (Kluwer, Dordrecht, Netherlands, 1992).
10. World Bank, *Costa Rica Forestry Sector Review* (World Bank, Washington, DC, 1992).
11. W. Devall Ed., *Clear Cut: The Tragedy of Industrial Forestry* (Island Press, Washington, DC, 1994).
12. R. Repetto, *Sci Am.* **262**, 36 (April 1990).
13. N. Myers, in *Scarcity or Abundance: A Debate on the Environment,* N. Myers and J. Simon (Norton, New York, 1994), p. 174.
14. P.P. Principe, in *Tropical Forest Medical Resources and the Conservation of Biodiversity,* M. J. Balick *et al.*, Eds. (Columbia Univ. Press, New York, 1993).
15. G.M. Woodwell, Ed., *The Earth in Transition: Patterns and Processes of Biotic Impoverishment* (Cambridge Univ. Press, New York, 1990).
16. Centre for Science and Environment, *State of India's Environment 1982* (Centre for Science and Environment, New Delhi, 1982).
17. D.W. Pearce, *Global Environmental Value and the Tropical Forests* (University College London, London,1994). See also T. Panayotou and P.S. Ashton, *Not by Timber Alone* (Island Press, Washington, DC, 1992).
18. For their constructive comments on early drafts, I thank J. Kent, J. MacNeill, J. Maini, R. Schmidt, Spears, O. Ullsten, and G. Woodwell.

❑

## Questions

1. Why should forests be protected?

2. Why are forests in decline?

3. Name five possible policy options needed to protect forests.

*Answers are at the back of the book.*

*Much pollution is being disposed of in our oceans, affecting many marine species. Since the sixties, the Steller sea lion population has decreased by approximately 94 percent. There are many different reasons for this, including pollution, climatic changes, marine debris and disease, and commercial fishing. When commercial fishing is done on a large scale, the entire aquatic ecosystem is affected. For example, when a key prey species is overharvested, the organisms that depend on that species find the search for food more difficult. This initiates a vicious cycle within the food chain. This is the case with pollock, where overfishing has caused the decrease of the Steller sea lion population.*

# The Mystery of the Steller Sea Lion
## David Holthouse

*National Wildlife*, December/January 1995

*The Steller sea lion is vanishing from Alaskan waters, and biological detectives are searching to find out why.*

A serial killer is running amok in Alaska's marine ecosystem, finding its victims among the seabird and marine-mammal species that populate the waters of the North Pacific. The killer strikes in secret, its identity unknown, and leaves a massive body count in it's wake. Ninety percent of the harbor seals in parts of the Gulf of Alaska have mysteriously disappeared since 1970. Pup production has declined among northern fur seals throughout the region. Bering Sea red-legged and black-legged kittiwake populations number only half as many as they did in 1976, and common and thick-billed murres have suffered a similar fate.

The killer's favorite target, though, is the Steller sea lion. The 94 percent die-off that the pinniped species has suffered in parts of its core habitat area since the late 1960s, despite the protection it has received as a federally listed threatened species for the past four years, is the most damning evidence that something foul is afoot in the North Pacific.

Biologists seeking to unmask the murderer have treated the North Pacific declines as an ecological whodunit, investigating an array of suspects—in-cluding pollution, climatic changes, marine debris and disease—so far to no avail. The threatened Steller sea lion is the primary focus of the sleuthing effort. "We haven't found a smoking gun," says Lloyd Lowry, Marine Mammal coordinator for the Alaska Department of Fish and Game's Division of Wildlife Conservation. "All we can say on solid scientific ground is that this is not a natural pattern."

The Steller, or northern, sea lion is named after George Wilhelm Steller, the German naturalist who first documented the species in 1742 during a voyage around Alaska. Males often exceed 10 feet in length and weigh more than 2,000 pounds. The Steller's diet is a bouillabaisse of fish and invertebrates, including squid, eels, cod, herring, sculpins and salmon. Its principle prey is walleye pollock, a small codfish that makes up more than half of the Steller's diet.

The Steller inhabits Pacific coastal waters from Southern California north to the Bering Strait and as far west as northern Japan. The species is relatively scarce at the ends of its range and most abundant in the core, which lies around the Aleutian Islands, Gulf of Alaska and Bering Sea.

Historically, the core range has supported more than three-fourths of the Steller's total population. There in late spring mature males and females gather on islands where the females give birth and the males fight among themselves to establish territories and access to females. Females give birth about three days after their arrival and mate within two weeks after giving birth. About 87 percent of females aged 8 to 20 are pregnant yearly. Females live to about 30, while males, with their more violent lives, usually die before they reach 18.

In the late 1960s, more than 140,000 Steller sea lions roamed Alaskan seas, but by 1989, when the last rangewide survey was taken, only about 65,000 survived. The worst decline has occurred in the eastern Aleutian islands, site of the 94 percent reduction in numbers that began in the 1970s. Lowry says that's a strong indication that something unnatural is going on. "In a normal fluctuation, a marine mammal population will slowly contract from the edges of its range, not vanish in the middle," he says. "And on a more intuitive level, when you're walking around the beaches that used to have thousands of sea lions on them that are now empty, you just feel in your gut that something is way out of balance—something most likely anthropogenic in origin." In other words, people may be at the root of the problem.

Federal and state scientists have moved steadily through a list of suspects, investigating each thoroughly. Only one viable suspect remains: commercial fishing, which many researchers believe may be altering the abundance of key prey species in ways that make foraging more difficult for the Steller sea lion and the other declining North Pacific species.

Alaska's commercial fishing industry first came under scrutiny in relation to the sea lion decline in 1986, when the Alaska Department of Fish and Game released a two-year study which showed that sea lions around Kodiak Island weighed less during recent periods of heavy commercial catch of groundfish, specifically pollock. Blood samples also suggested that the animals suffered from lack of food. "The animals were anemic, which indicates to me that they were severely nutritionally stressed," says Don Calkins, the marine biologist who conducted the study.

Pollock, common in Alaskan seas, makes the commercial fishing industry a lot of money. Last year, Alaskan waters yielded more than 3 billion pounds of pollock with a market value in excess of $350 million. Scientists consider pollock an important clue in the North Pacific mystery for two reasons: All the species in decline depend on pollock as a primary food source, and these species have dwindled as the commercial pollock catch has increased during the past decade. "We can't say for certain that fishing is taking away their food," says Lowry. "However, the fisheries are removing a lot of fish from the ocean, and there is evidence of food stress."

Commercial fisheries in Alaska have typically developed in a series of destructive boom and bust cycles in which a species is overexploited until it is too depleted to be a viable commercial target. Then fishermen switch to catching more abundant species. The industry unfurled its nets on pollock after Alaskan stocks of herring, yellowfin sole and Pacific Ocean perch crashed in the early 1970s because of overfishing.

Traditionally, pollock was used in a variety of cheap, processed fish products such as frozen fish sticks, but the recent popularity of imitation crab and lobster meat has made the fish a commercial phenomenon. Now, the majority of pollock caught in Alaska is turned into surimi, a fish paste used to make imitation shellfish products. Creating 100 pounds of surimi requires more than 650 pounds of compressed pollock, creating a heavy demand for the fish. That demand is most easily met with the use of factory trawlers, ocean behemoths often more than 300 feet long. The ships tow massive, funnel-shaped nets that scoop up everything in their paths.

Trawlers may pull in 350,000 pounds of sea life in a single haul. Not all of the catch goes to market, however. Fish that are too small or that are not the day's target species—even though they may be otherwise commercially useful fish—are simply thrown back, and since sorting is usually done at the end of the work day, they are thrown back dead. Records suggest that bycatch totals at least 500 million pounds of wasted fish yearly, a substantial fraction of which is pollock. In 1991, for example, 320 million pounds of pollock were discarded in Alaskan fisheries. Because groundfish discard is often underreported and, until recently, was not counted toward legal catch quotas, the total amount of fish taken by the trawlers often has been well above the established biological limit.

The North Pacific U.S. factory trawler fleet has increased from 12 to 65 vessels since 1986, at a cost of $40 million to $75 million per ship. The combination of heavy capital investment and ever-increasing competition has prompted the pollock industry to urge the North Pacific Fishery Management Council to keep raising the annual commercial catch limit on Alaskan pollock.

The management council is one of eight regional councils charged under the Magnuson Fishery and Conservation Act of 1976 with oversight of commercial fishing in American waters. Each council is made up of a regional director of the National Marine Fisheries Service (NMFS) and a maximum of 19 other members appointed by the secretary of commerce. All eight of the fishery councils are composed primarily of people with direct ties to the fishing industry.

Because the Magnuson Act has no provisions for nonindustry representation, other than that offered by federal bureaucrats, voting members often have a direct financial interest in the fisheries they oversee. On the North Pacific council, seven of eleven voting members are commercial fishing representatives (the other four are from NMFS and other government agencies). Conservationists are not surprised that even after scientists revealed the decline of pollock-eating species, the council voted several times to raise the legal catch limit.

NMFS has final say on all council recommendations, but by law the agency can only accept or reject a fishery plan, though it can request modifications. For example, in 1991, NMFS sent back a plan calling for a 66-percent boost in the Gulf of Alaska pollock catch, then quickly approved a new plan with a 41-percent increase. With that one exception, all pollock increases have borne the traditional rubber stamp of approval, at least in part because NMFS prefers to accept a plan rather than risk being without one at a crucial time.

Now the pollock population itself shows signs of decline. NMFS surveys taken since 1991 have shown a marked drop of pollock in several regions. In the Bering Sea, for examples, pollock biomass was gauged at 6.5 million tons, down from 12.2 million tons in 1988.

Of the seven North Pacific marine species in population tailspins, only the Steller sea lion is listed under the Endangered Species Act. But this protection has not kept it from a persistent slide toward extinction in the North Pacific.

Meanwhile, though NMFS has initiated seasonal no-trawl zones around five of the Bering Sea's most severely depleted sea lion rookeries, the agency has refused to upgrade the sea lion from threatened to endangered status, an action that could bring a series of restriction on commercial pollock fishing. At this writing, the agency has postponed a decision on the species' status until after a range-wide population survey is completed. Even if NMFS then determines to upgrade the sea lion to endangered, the process for doing so probably would take another year.

"We're not dragging our feet on this," says Sue Mello, a NMFS ecologist and Steller recovery specialist. "We are expecting the survey will show a continued decline, and we expect the species to eventually be listed as endangered. But we have to have the data to back this up because we've got people coming at us from both sides on this one. The environmentalists say we've waited too long, and the fishing industry says an endangered listing is ludicrous, that the regulations will gut their business."

Endangered listing for Steller sea lions indeed seems all but assured to set the stage for an ideological and economic controversy. "People are saying, 'Oh, it's fisheries, they're the problem, let's go after them,' without realizing the consequences of that," says Joe Blum, executive director of the American Factory Trawlers Association. "We're talking about taking away 65 percent of our harvest if there's a ban on pollock fishing." ❑

## Questions

1. How many pounds of sea life may be brought in by trawlers in a single haul?

2. Since 1970, what percentage of harbor seals have disappeared?

3. What happens in normal marine mammal fluctuations, and in what way is the disappearance of the sea lion abnormal?

*Answers are at the back of the book.*

**21** *The judicial system faces the serious dilemma of how to protect wild animals and private property rights at the same time. When property is affected, most Americans see the Endangered Species Act (ESA) as an irrational restriction. The law states that one may not harm or threaten an endangered species, including the removal of the species from its habitat. However, over half of the 956 endangered species inhabit private land in the United States. Even ESA proponents admit the law has flaws. The National Academy of Sciences suggested the creation of temporary "survival habitats," which are now being planned. These "survival habitats" are zones for threatened species. Regulations must be developed that simultaneously protect species while respecting private property rights.*

# Nature, Nurture and Property Rights

*The Economist,* July 8, 1995

Back in 1920, in a Supreme Court ruling about migratory wildlife, Justice Oliver Wendell Holmes pronounced that the protection of geese and ducks "is a national interest of very nearly the first magnitude." Two years later he conceded that "the general rule is that while property may be regulated to a certain extent, if regulation goes too far it will be recognized as a taking."

These paradoxical statements, from one of America's best jurists, sum up a quandary of the modern world: how to protect wild animals and private property rights at the same time. Last week the Supreme Court gave the nod to nature. By a 6-3 vote, the court ruled that the federal Fish and Wildlife Service may use the Endangered Species Act (ESA) of 1973 to protect natural life on private land. The government, for example, can forbid a landowner to cut a tree on his land because its presence is necessary for an animal or a plant of a kind close to extinction.

America has a solid record of protecting wild animals in general. With few exceptions—the passenger pigeon and the heath hen among them—endangered creatures get the government's protection, whatever it costs. DDT was banned, at great expense to farmers, because this insecticide threatened the brown pelican and the peregrine falcon. A prohibition on shooting egrets once cost some companies dearly.

The battle starts when the right to property is affected. The fifth amendment to the constitution says that no private property shall "be taken for public use without just compensation." Some intrusions on property rights—zoning laws, for example—are usually accepted without much argument. But not the ESA. Despite countless polls showing that Americans value wildlife, most of them see this law as an unreasonable restriction.

The Supreme Court's new decision focuses on the work "harm." The law says you may not harm a threatened or endangered species. The Fish and Wildlife agency interpreted this to include damaging or changing the places where such creatures live. Its opponents, paper and timber companies, contended that the law applied only to the animal itself. The court disagreed, citing the almost universal opinion of scientists that an endangered species cannot work its way off the list of doom if its habitat is at risk.

The matter now goes back to Congress. Politicians have in the past, tended to do as they pleased, regardless of what science or the courts say. In 1978, the lowly snail darter—an endangered fish the size of a stick of gum—held up completion of the $110m Tellico dam in Tennessee. The fight went to the Supreme Court, which said that the ESA was enacted to "halt and reverse the trend toward species extinction, whatever the cost." Not to be thwarted, Congressman John Duncan of Tennessee casually dropped an amendment into an energy-and-water bill stating that the dam would be built, no matter what any law said. It was.

The ESA will not stay unchanged. Even its keenest advocates admit it has flaws. The Tellico dam provides an example. Its completion, the Cassandras predicted, would seal the fate of the snail darter. A year later, the fish was discovered living 60 miles downstream from the dam. Anyway, say hard-nosed evolutionists, perfect diversity is impossible. Evolution dictates that species should disappear. Nine-tenths of them already have. So is the law really necessary?

Absolutely, replies the National Academy of Sciences. It issued a report in May which, while admitting that changes to the law are needed, advocated the creation of temporary "survival habitats," zones demarcated by scientists while a recovery plan for the endangered species is being drawn up. This is needed because, according to a Harvard entomologist, Edward Wilson, "the rate of extinction is now about 400 times that recorded through recent geological time and is accelerating rapidly. If we continue on this path, the reduction of diversity seems destined to approach that of the great natural catastrophes at the end of the Paleozoic and Mesozoic era—in other words, the most extreme in 65m years." That ought to make even this Congress flinch.

The trouble is that most endangered species neither soar majestically on the wing nor display themselves to admiring tourists in Yellowstone National Park. Of the 10m species in the world, most are insects, plants and fungi. They live in backyards and irrigation ditches. Two-thirds of the United States is privately owned; more than half the 956 endangered species occupy private land.

Congress has already trimmed the edges of the ESA. Now a bill has been introduced by Senator Slade Gorton, a Republican from Washington state, with backing from industry, which would give the secretary of the interior the power to order a case-by-case review of threatened species. This would then permit a decision that some species are less important than others and, accordingly, may be allotted less protection.

Environmentalists back a milder bill to be submitted by Wayne Gilchrest of Maryland and Gerry Studds of Massachusetts. These Democrats hope to fine-tune the ESA, to the benefit of the small landowner. But it is industry that the law affects most. The National Endangered Species Act Reform Coalition represents 185 utilities, energy firms and water companies, mostly in the west, which want to see big changes. They suspect that Oliver Houck, a law professors at Tulane University, is right when he calls the ESA "a surrogate law for ecosystems." Such talk freezes the blood of mining firms and utilities. Ore extraction and power lines require large tracts of land. The more land you need, the higher the chance that you will run into an endangered species. Timber companies stand to lose millions.

Still, defenders of the ESA, encouraged by the Supreme Court's ruling, fight on. Steven Meyer, of the Massachusetts Institute of Technology, produced a study last year showing that states with the most endangered-species listings were also the ones with the strongest economies. He adds that a quarter of a percentage point change in the interest rate has more effect on the economy than any hardship caused by the ESA. ❏

**Questions**

1. In protecting endangered species, when does the battle start?

2. Most Americans value wildlife, but how do they view the zoning laws?

3. What are most of the 10 million species in the world?

*Answers are at the back of the book.*

22   *Dams have caused enormous ecological damage to rivers throughout the world. In fact, aquatic freshwater species are the most endangered group in North America. A new approach to rehabilitate a river system seeks to stabilize all of the natural physical processes that form a river ecosystem, not just on reviving a particular fish species, and tries to simulate the variability of seasonal water flow. The purpose of this approach is to transform the rivers back into smaller versions of what they were before they were dammed. This is controversial because it may take water away from agriculture and human consumption. But proponents believe that this approach will improve the river's ecology, produce more healthy fish, and ultimately save taxpayer dollars.*

# A Recipe for River Recovery?

## Marcia Barinaga

*Science*, September 20, 1996

*River ecologists are advocating a broader approach to rescuing damaged rivers, betting that restoring the physical processes that shape a river's habitats will bring back ailing fisheries.*

Look at the Trinity River sa it flows through the heavily forested hills of Northern California's Trinity County, and at many spots you will see what appears to be an idyllic natural scene: flashing water coursing between wooded banks. But to the trained eye of a river ecologist, the sight is not so pretty. Those willows and alders along the riverbanks confine the river to a fixed, rectangular channel—a far cry from the shallow and shifting banks typical of a healthy river. And that is only the most outward sign of the transformation that has occurred on the Trinity since a dam completed in 1963 robbed the river of the winter and spring floods that could send as much as 3000 cubic meters of water per second (m³/s) churning through the channel. For 20 years after the dam was built, the Trinity lived year-round on a comparative trickle, an unvarying 4 m³/s released from the dam.

Without those annual floodwaters to move sediments down the channel, sweep away encroaching plants, and shift the river's banks, the Trinity's ecol-ogy changed dramatically and rapidly. In the mid-1960s biologists with California's Department of Fish and Game already noted vegetation encroaching on the riverbanks. Habitats for frogs, turtles, aquatic insects, and fish that favor the river's warm, shallow edge waters disappeared. Gravel spawning beds used by salmon filled with sand, and the local Hoopa Valley Indian tribe saw a precipitous decline in its traditional salmon fishery.

The Trinity's plight is all too common. Countless rivers and streams in the waterpoor West have suffered intense damage from dam projects built in the first half of this century. Fisheries were devastated, and several species of salmon and other commercially important fish hit the endangered list. "The way the dams were built was at best incredibly naïve," says San Francisco-based consulting hydrologist Philip Williams. "[They] were planned ignoring ecologic impacts."

But the Trinity is more than an example of a damaged river. It has become a test case for a new, albeit controversial, approach to river restoration that takes a broader perspective than has been previously taken, focusing not on single fish species but on the whole river system. The approach reflects a growing awareness that habitat modification efforts must take into account all the varied processes that shape an ecosystem (*Science*, 13 September, pp. 1518, 1555, and 1558).

Until recently, restoration efforts on rivers like the Trinity were typically led by fisheries biologists, who generally leaned heavily on a physical habitat simulation model, which goes by the catchy acronym PHABSIM. Developed by the Fish and Wildlife Service in the 1970s, the model focuses on optimizing habitats for a single important species of fish, such as salmon. Now, says Williams, "there is another group of ecologists who see restoring natural processes as a key."

Williams is referring to the natural physical processes that help a river shape its banks and bottom. The processes are best restored, according to river morphologist Luna Leopold of the University of California, Berkeley, by mimicking the seasonal variability in water flow, including occasional torrential floods like the experimental flood released last year on the Colorado River (*Science*, 19 April, p. 344). The effect is to make the rivers smaller versions of what they were before they were dammed. That "doesn't mean you can't use the water," says Leopold—indeed, half or even more of a river's natural flow may be diverted. But the remaining water must be used "to keep the river in some kind of equilibrium which depends on both high and low flows."

## A Hot Political Issue

Like all water issues in the parched West, however, this approach is fiercely controversial because higher flows would take water away from agriculture and from slaking the thirst of cities like Los Angeles. And even ecologists are not in total accord on the idea. Proponents of restoring more natural river processes believe, for example, that the approach is not only better for river ecology in general but will also produce the greatest numbers of healthy fish. But they don't yet have the numbers to prove that true, and critics argue that the impact on fisheries is far from certain. "It will make a great river," says Andrew Hamilton, a biologist with the Fish and Wildlife Service. But how much it will improve fish numbers, he says, is "just a wild guess."

These arguments will be played out publicly over the next year, in two cases. At the end of this month, the Fish and Wildlife Service will release its proposal for restoring the Trinity River, and a similar restoration plan released last February for the streams that feed Mono Lake on the east side of California's Sierra Nevada—which were dried up in 1941 by water diversions to Los Angeles—will undergo public hearings sometime within the next year.

What happens in these cases is being closely watched by river experts concerned with the conflict between water demands and efforts to maintain or restore healthy rivers. "There is a full court press to get all the [restoration] done that we can," says Kirk Rodgers, deputy regional director at the Bureau of Reclamation for the mid-Pacific region, "because many people are visionary enough to see that other [water] demands are picking up. They are trying to re-establish what [habitats] they can and put a protective cloak around them."

In an early effort to provide guidance for trying to improve prospects of river fisheries, in the 1970s the Fish and Wildlife Service developed a system of models for predicting how water-flow changes in a river would influence the capacity of the river to produce fish. At the core of this approach was PHABSIM, which predicts the depths and speeds of water that correspond to different levels of flow in a river and matches them with the known habitat preferences of fish. Water flows can then be adjusted to maximize those preferred habitats.

But many fisheries biologists say that PHABSIM presents a distorted view of what is best for a river, because it focuses too narrowly on the needs of one species of fish, and generally on just one critical life phase. For example, it might focus on ideal conditions for the rearing of juvenile Chinook salmon, which typically prefer "slow, relatively shallow water," says Sam Williamson, a research ecologist with the National Biological Service in Fort Collins, Colorado. If you only take that information into account, he notes, it might lead to a recommendation that a lot of water can be diverted with no harm to the fish. But it would ignore other needs of the salmon, such as for faster, deeper water to bring them food and keep the water temperature cool, and would also disregard the effects of such low flows on the shape of the river channel.

Williamson and others maintain that the model is not supposed to be applied that way; a complete analysis should also include factors such as how different water flows would alter the river channels. But many ecologists complain that these more complex aspects tend to get overlooked by agencies and consultants who are seduced by the numbers generated by PHABSIM and who often recommend low water flows as a result. "Whether [PHABSIM] is science or not...boy, it looks great," says Gary Smith, a fisheries biologist with the California Department of Fish and Game.

That was the case, for example, in the late 1970s, when the Fish and Wildlife Service applied the analysis to the Trinity River. It recommended that the river's water allotment be roughly doubled to tripled, depending on the wetness of the year. Cecil Andrus, secretary of the interior at the time, implemented that increase, but also called for a 12-year study of the Trinity to determine whether other changes in its management were needed.

## PHABSIM Falls Short

That study began in 1984, but by 1990 Robert Franklin, chief of the water division of the Hoopa Valley Tribe's fisheries department, was unhappy with how it was progressing. He felt the analysis relied too heavily on a narrow PHABSIM approach that would not recommend the variation in flows necessary to restore the natural processes of the river: "The tribe's position is that a healthy river is what you are striving for, and it will produce fish."

Franklin hired Arcata, California-based river-ecology consultants William Trush and Scott McBain to study the processes that create and maintain the river channel, including high flows. The need for these flows, known in the business as channel-maintenance flows, comes from a growing consensus about what is necessary for the health of an alluvial river—a river that has the potential to move its banks and bottom. One key standard, says Trush, is the ability to move the so-called "bed"—the full complement of sediments, from fine sands to boulders—down the river channel. This is essential for many river processes, such as the formation of transient gravel bars that provide river habitats, and maintenance of the gravel beds that fish use for spawning. "If you don't mobilize the bed, the fine particles intrude into the bed, fill up the interstitial areas, remove the habitat for invertebrates, and it destroys the spawning quality," Trush says.

To determine how much the bed needs to move, and how much water it takes to move the larger rocks in the bed, river morphologists study streams that haven't been altered or dammed, mark rocks, and see how often and at what flow level they move. They have even devised elaborate trapdoor systems in the bottom of one Montana stream to sample rocks and sediments that are moving downriver, says Larry Schmidt of the U.S. Forest Service in Fort Collins. The conclusion from studies carried out over the past few decades: "You have to mobilize the channel bed on the average every other year," says Trush.

Since 1991, floods lasting several days each have been released each year on the Trinity. Because flows on the river must be limited to a maximum of about 170 m³/s to avoid threatening homes built on the river's banks, the torrent was not sufficient to rip out vegetation that had been growing there for more than 30 years. But prior to the floods the study group had created several experimental sites, removing the invading vegetation with bulldozers and restoring the banks to a more natural shape.

Those physical changes, combined with the experimental flows, produced encouraging results. "The sites where they skimmed off the banks are narrowing on themselves," says Trush. "They are creating a morphology that is typical of alluvial rivers," such as shifting gravel bars in the river channel. Moreover, the researchers could see that fish preferred some of the renewed habitats. Some sites, especially those that had shallow banks, slow water, and gravel and cobble bottoms, had "extremely good use by [salmon] fry," says fisheries biologist Mark Hampton, who worked with the Fish and Wildlife Service on the Trinity project.

A modeling study the team did to analyze the effects of water levels on river temperatures also argued in favor of floods. In the spring, when the young Chinook salmon are migrating to the sea, they are very sensitive to water temperature. A river that doesn't get its normal allotment of snow melt will flow slowly, warming up more than the fish can tolerate. But the temperature model showed that flows of about 55 m$^3$/s could carry the young fish downstream quickly in a surge of hospitably cold water.

Buoyed by results such as these, the flow study group will recommend in its report, due out on 30 September, that the Trinity's water allotments should be increased. In the driest years, they would be only a little higher than the present allotment, but in wetter years when there is more water available, the annual volume of water coursing down the river would more than double. The majority of the extra water would surge down the river in the spring, when high flows are important not only to keep the temperature cool for migrating fish, but to move sand and gravel downstream and prevent seedlings from germinating and taking hold on the riverbanks. Those high flows would be punctuated with floods once every year or so to help maintain the river channel.

The flow study on the Trinity represents one of the most intensive studies of any U.S. river. "There is certainly a lot of science in the data collected that the recommendation is based on," says Hampton. But while the data suggest that fish will do better in the renewed habitats, it is impossible to quantify the expected improvement in terms of numbers of fish. "The underlying assumption…is that you have to believe that restoring those natural processes will be good for the fishery."

But before Trinity recommendations are implemented, the Bureau of Reclamation will take comments from water-user groups who may not be so willing to accept that assumption. "The whole channel-maintenance approach will come under intense scrutiny by water users," predicts Berkeley-based river ecologist Frank Ligon. Diverted Trinity river water travels through several power-generating stations on its way to the Sacramento River, and meeting the flow-study requirements would mean a reduction in power equivalent to what could sustain a community of 100,000 people, says Rodgers of the Bureau of Reclamation: "The power community is very concerned already." Likewise, the potential reduction has raised concern among municipal and agricultural users, says Jason Peltier, manager of the Central Valley Project Water Association, a consortium of water users.

Water users have become more environmentally enlightened, says Peltier, and recognize that to guarantee a stable future water supply they must "address and resolve" fishery problems. But nevertheless they will want to know what their sacrifice will produce in terms of fish. The users can "tell you in dollars and cents how it is going to affect them," says Rodgers, but "you cannot [tell] them what they are going to get in terms of pounds of fish or quantity of fish."

"The biggest challenge for the policy folks is how do you assess this now?" says Serg Birk, a biologist who worked on the Trinity project for the Bureau of Reclamation. "Do you assess it by how many fish return, or by how much habitat you create, or by measuring the parameters that the geomorphologists say indicate a healthy system because it mimics historic flows?" The assessment must consider more than just numbers of fish, says Hampton. "There are many ways to restore a fishery," he says. "You could build a hatchery and restore the fishery. But the Fish and Wildlife Service is in charge of protecting the fish and wildlife resources of the country for the benefit of the public trust. And building a hatchery doesn't necessarily do that."

Even the way that flow management will restore the overall environment requires more study, and the way to do that, says Trush, is through an approach called "adaptive management." This turns the management of a stream or river into an experiment in itself: Hypotheses are formulated, flows are manipulated to answer them, and the management of the river is adjusted accordingly. But to be done properly, adaptive management requires enough water to enable researchers to set up experiments, carry them out, and then alter the program based on their results. And researchers studying the river worry that the amount of water necessary for high-quality adaptive management may not be allotted to the Trinity in the end.

One ideal candidate for adaptive management is another project that Trush has been involved in, the restoration of the five feeder streams for Mono Lake. The lake's volume had been halved and salinity doubled as a result of the water diversions to Los Angeles. Various lawsuits in the 1980s resulted in a requirement that the city reduce by more the 90% the amount of water it takes from those streams until Mono Lake is returned to a healthier level. And in 1990 a Court of Appeals decision added the requirement that the streams be restored to a condition that can maintain fish. It will take at least 20 years for the lake to reach the required level, during which time the increased flows can be used to answer countless questions about what it takes to restore and maintain a stream and its fish population.

While Mono Lake and the Trinity may be two of the most visible cases of the new approach to river restoration, "you will see the same thing on some other rivers in California too," says hydrologist Williams, "as these ideas of ecosystem management permeate the agencies and there is a push to incorporated them into standard operations."

But while channel-maintaining flows may be catching on in California, their future seems less certain in other states. In Colorado, the U.S. Forest Service recently failed to convince a judge to limit future water diversions and guarantee the Forest Service the water necessary for maintenance flows on the South Platte River. Another important case, involving water-rights assignment for the Snake River and all of its tributaries, a water system that covers 80% of the state of Idaho, has yet to be decided. But the Forest Service hopes to learn from its setback in Colorado, as well as from the work going on in California, and present a case for the importance of high flows, channel maintenance, and adaptive management in the Snake River system, says K. Jack Haugrud, an attorney working on the case for the U.S. Department of Justice. "High flows are very important for maintaining stream channels," says Haugrud. "We intend, if we have to, to prove that in court."

It could be a tough sell. "We are in the water-poor portion of the world here," says Williamson of the National Biological Service. "It is easier to say what the minimum flow should be on a stream and divert everything else than it is to spend time trying to figure out what a stream really needs." Adaptive management, says Peltier of the Central Valley Project Water Association, "is a good concept." But it requires not only good science, he adds, but also "risk-taking, which government agencies are totally averse to doing." It will soon be seen whether the public and the water users can be convinced to take a risk on rivers like the Trinity. ❑

---

**Questions**

1. What does the PHABSIM approach predict?

2. What is adaptive management?

3. What is very important for maintaining stream channels?

*Answers are at the back of the book.*

---

**23** *The marine environment is in serious jeopardy. In addition to toxic chemicals in the ocean and climatic change that could alter fish migration and breeding, factory fishing has decimated approximately 70 percent of the world's marine fish. Depending on the location, the marine environment is being overexploited, has been exhausted, or is now slowly recovering. If the current rate of fishing continues, researchers predict that by the year 2000 there will be approximately 30 million fewer tons of fish available for people to eat. To prevent this, there must be cooperation between fisheries and within and between nations. Also, there must be better enforcement of sustainable fishing practices. The National Marine Fisheries Service recently encouraged fishing for "underutilized species," which had unexpected repercussions: Prey species declined at an alarming rate, which in turn starved other fish that depended on these species for food. If current trends continue, marine life will be severely devastated for centuries to come.*

# Vacuuming the Seas
## Dick Russell

*E Magazine,* July/August 1996

*Unprecedented factory fishing operations have created a global crisis, as species dwindle and catches decline.*

At sea 200 miles southwest of Iceland last summer, the crew of a super-trawler big enough to contain a dozen Boeing 747 jumbo jets unloaded a staggering 50 tons of oceanic redfish into flash-freezers down below, as the Icelandic ship's captain began manuevering against nearby Russian and Japanese vessels for the next set. Emotions were running high, as there was a lot at stake. Each ship was trawling nets with opening circumferences of almost two miles; that's the equivalent of 10 New York City blocks wide by two Empire State Buildings high. Soon the Russian boat steamed over the Icelander's net, and the Japanese trawler ripped loose the Russian's lines.

Such conflicts are now commonplace on the high seas, says Dan Middlemiss, a professor of military and strategic studies at Nova Scotia's Dalhousie University. "An important food source is being decimated [and] fish have become something seen as worth fighting for," he says. The global industrial fishing fleet has doubled in size since 1970, now comprising about one million large-scale vessels. Fisheries scientists consider this number to be twice the capacity that can maintain future fish populations.

"About 70 percent of the world's marine fish stocks are heavily exploited, overexploited, depleted or slowly recovering," according to a 1995 report by the United Nations' Food and Agriculture Organization (FAO). "This situation is globally non-sustainable and major ecological and economic damage is already visible." Indeed, nine of the world's 17 major fishing grounds are in serious decline, and four have been commercially "fished out." If this trend continues, the FAO foresees a shortfall of some 30 million tons of fish for human diets by the year 2000—at a time when the planet's population is rising by about 100 million people annually.

**The World Wakes Up**
Yet the out-of-control, high-tech slaughter occurring in every ocean and sea has only recently begun receiving widespread attention from politicians, the media and environmental organizations. Last December, a United Nations treaty calling for fisheries to be managed under an enforceable framework of

international law was finally signed by the United States and 27 other countries and territories. In a reversal of the Republican-controlled Congress' efforts to undermine nearly every other environmental law, the House of Representatives has voted overwhelmingly to strengthen existing U.S. fisheries regulations and the Senate is expected to follow suit. Somewhat belatedly, groups such as the World Wildlife Fund (WWF), Greenpeace, the National Audubon Society and the Natural Resources Defense Council (NRDC) have put the devastation of the oceans high on their agendas—and were heavily involved in lobbying for both mandates.

With strict controls on fishing pressure, a research study published last year in the prestigious journal *Science* indicates that nearly all of the depleted commercial species could, in fact, bounce back. The scientists' goal was to ascertain whether fish populations that have been reduced to very low levels become significantly less successful at reproduction. Of 128 fish stocks evaluated, only three were determined to have been overfished to permanent commercial extinction. There are numerous examples of recoveries once strong management was put in place, including the striped bass along America's Eastern seaboard, Atlantic herring in Iceland and Norwegian cod.

The question is whether the will exists to turn around a looming catastrophe, for solving the fishing crisis is going to require unprecedented cooperation among fishers, and within and between nations. It will also demand far more attention to the escalating loss of vital fish habitat (wetlands, mangrove forests, sea grasses and coral reefs) resulting from coastal development and pollution. When you add in the unknown factors, such as the potential effects of global climate change on fish migration and breeding, clearly the oceans are in a state of emergency.

### Early Warnings

The first big clue that something might be amiss was the collapse of the world's largest anchovy fishery in Peru during the early 1970s. At that time, a competitive fishing free-for-all between countries was at full throttle. In 1974, for example, New England fishermen were harvesting only 12 percent of the fish caught in their waters—the rest were taken by boats from the Soviet Union, Poland and elsewhere. In the face of this, many countries (including the U.S.) began imposing what are known as Exclusive Economic Zones extending up to 200 miles from their territorial limits. This kept the foreigners out, but was accompanied here and in Europe by large government subsidies to encourage development of home-grown fleets.

"Few controls, and unrestricted access in most fisheries, ultimately led to overcapitalization," recalls Gerry Studds, former Chairman of the House Merchant Marine and Fisheries Committee. For example, the Arctic Alaska Fisheries Corporation (since purchased by the world's largest chicken producer, Tyson Foods) received about $100 million in federal loan guarantees. The European Union increased its fisheries subsidies from $80 million in 1983 to $580 million by 1990, one-fifth of that money going to build new boats or improve old ones.

Simultaneously, fishing proficiency was booming beyond anyone's wildest expectations. Not only in vessel size, but with automatic trawl nets that electronically detect the approaches of fish schools; navigation aids including satellite positioning systems, and the use of "spotter" planes as fish-finders. Floating fish factories became commonplace, with 80 miles of submerged longlines containing thousands of baited hooks or 40-mile-long driftnets corralling everything in their path. In 1995, the Russians even announced the creation of an "Acoustic Fish Concentrator," a small torpedo-like object that snares fish in a trawler's net by using technology first developed for anti-submarine warfare.

### Bad Habits Die Hard

Despite increased awareness of the situation, practices such as "pulse fishing" (fishing area species until they dry up, then moving on to target a different species) persist. Between 1986 and 1992, distant water fleets fishing in international waters off the Grand Banks removed 16 times the quotas of cod, flounder and redfish permitted by the Northwest Atlantic Fisheries Organization. Little wonder that the Canadians, in a celebrated high-seas incident in 1995, were outraged enough to seize a Spanish ship— one whose illegal small-mesh nets had captured 350 metric tons of juvenile halibut before the fish reached reproductive age, and which maintained two sets of logbooks (one true and one false).

"The Spanish," says WWF's fisheries expert Michael Sutton, "are well known as an outlaw fishing nation and one of the most overcapitalized fleets in the world." One Spanish multinational corporation now owns a global network of some 30 companies in 18 nations of Africa, Asia and Latin America. And cash-starved underdeveloped countries, which long depended on local small-scale fisheries, are now selling permits to foreign boats to fish their waters, or cutting deals with outside investors to expand their own fleets.

Indonesia revealed its intention in 1994 to procure over 81,000 new vessels within the next five years, with most of the $4 billion investment coming from foreign sources. Spain and the U.S. are sharing a $200 million order to deliver 50 longline boats to Indonesia in kit form for deep-freezing tuna and swordfish. While the European Union officially says that it is planning to decommission 40 percent of its fishing capacity, at the same time it is providing "exit grants" to companies for relocating boats away from European waters. According to the WWF's Sutton, "Japanese money also goes to a lot of underdeveloped countries for developing fisheries, partly to buy their votes for the International Whaling Commission." (Japan is one of a few nations that still pursues whaling.)

The deep-water regions, those beyond the 200-mile sovereign national limits, are dominated by six countries—Japan, Russia, South Korea, Spain, Taiwan and Poland—which account for 90 percent of the world's high-seas catch. It is their practices that the new United Nations treaty seeks to address, in a landmark agreement that NRDC scientist Lisa Speer hopes "marks the end of untrammeled plundering of ocean fisheries." The treaty's most crucial provision is its "precautionary, risk-averse" approach, meaning basically that nations must err on the side of the resource if marine scientists are unsure whether fishing pressure is damaging a particular stock's sustainability. The accord also calls for improved enforcement, monitoring and scientific assessments, as well as protection of marine biodiversity by minimizing pollution and the needless destruction of non-target fish, also known as "bycatch."

In U.S. waters, where the National Marine Fisheries Service has classified over 82 percent of the commercial stocks as being overfished, the amended version of the Magnuson Fisheries Conservation and Management Act will require managers to reduce fishing volumes and meet specific timelines. Under the Act, first passed by Congress in 1976, eight regional councils acquired the authority to set annual catch limits within the U.S. 200-mile jurisdiction. But, explains Bill Mott of the Marine Fish Conservation Network (an alliance of 100 sportsmen's and environmental groups whose intensive lobbying to improve the Act prodded Congress), the domination of these councils by representatives of the fishing industry "is like letting the fox guard the henhouse."

The Gulf of Mexico Council, for instance, permitted red snapper to be fished down to five million pounds per year, where they'd once been so abundant as to yield 30-million-pound annual catches. The New England Council refused to put a lid on the groundfishery at Georges Banks, even after the Commerce Department declared several species at or near commercial extinction. At long last, though, the Council's attitude appears to be changing. A newly-amended New England groundfish plan, approved in late January, aims to reduce fishing levels by 80 percent through severely limiting the number of days a boat can be at sea. The plan also specifies several closures in the Gulf of Maine to protect juvenile fish. While many fishermen complain that these measures will put them out of business, council chairman and commercial fisherman Joseph Branceleone says simply, "Without fish, there will be no fishermen."

The latest groundfish protection effort, however, does not address the effects of towed gear being dragged across the ocean bottom—which scientists are increasingly viewing as gravely damaging to the fragile habitat where juvenile fish feed on smaller organisms. Mike Leach, head of a Cape Cod commercial fishing group, believes that, in order to rebuild the stocks, "Dragging should be banned and draggermen should be given assistance to switch to a more appropriate gear type." Funds to achieve this, however, are scarce. The federal government has already committed $25 million to a program for buying out a relatively small number of fishing boats and an additional $62 million in loans, grants and matching funds to the beleaguered New England fishing industry.

## Making the Regulations Work

Certainly, better enforcement is one key to improving the situation and, in April, federal regulators sent a strong message in seeking a record $5.8 million fine against two Massachusetts brothers and their 12 employees. Their five boats were charged with illegally taking millions of scallops, cod and other groundfish in 1995, breaking the law 300 times and filing false reports to cover up their violations.

But other recent "solutions" to the crisis—such as the National Marine Fisheries Service's (NMFS) encouragement to fishermen to begin focusing on so-called "under-utilized species"—can have unanticipated consequences for marine ecosystems. Take the little squid, for example, which as a food source is crucial to the survival of tuna, billfish and sharks, as well as marine mammals and many smaller fish. From a "trash fish" of scant interest to the American consumer a decade ago, squid have become popular as pan-fried calamari. With advances in refrigeration technology, their value (and their harvesting) has skyrocketed. Back in 1964, less than 1,000 metric tons of the Atlantic long-finned and short-finned squid were being caught. By 1994, that figure had soared to more than 40,000 tons.

At the same time, marine experts have noted an alarming trend. With far fewer schools of squid as bait in coastal waters, according to Robert Pride of the Atlantic Coast Conservation Association of Virginia, "many species of game fish are caught, even in late summer and in the fall, with empty bellies and a gaunt appearance." Bob Schoelkopf, founding director of the Marine Mammal Stranding Center in New Jersey, has similarly observed increasing numbers of emaciated harbor porpoises and seals ending up beached or entangled in near-shore nets. "We are seeing another canary in the mine, which could be the starvation of many marine species," Schoelkopf says.

An idea favored by many in government, with the ostensible aim of reducing the number of fisheries participants and thereby curbing overfishing, is

known as Individual Transferrable Quotas (ITQs). Under this scheme, and elsewhere, quota "shares" are allotted based on catch records and fishermen then buy, sell or lease these shares on the open market. That way, the thinking goes, you weed out the inefficient fishermen and replace them with professionals.

But turning fish resources into "private property" has come under fire from Greenpeace, which has forged alliances with many smaller-scale commercial fishermen. The fundamental problems with ITQs, as Russell Cleary of The Massachusetts' Commercial Anglers Association puts it, is that they "presage a corporate takeover" and threaten the very existence of fisheries-based coastal communities. The notion has merit. Since New Zealand introduced ITQs in 1986, its three largest fishing corporations have snapped up half the awarded quotas. Two of the largest holders in America's ITQ-based Atlantic surf clam/ocean quahog fishery are now the National Westminster Bank of New Jersey and a U.S. subsidiary of the world's biggest accounting firm, Holland-based KMPG. Another big ITQ purchaser is the Caterpillar Corporation.

None of this bodes well for the environment, since ITQs encourage the over-exploitation of "higher yield" fishing grounds. Enough pressure against ITQs has been generated—Greenpeace activists seized a factory trawler in a Washington port last summer to dramatize the situation—that the Senate Commerce Committee voted in March for a five-year moratorium on such privatization while the effects on coastal communities and small-boat fleets are studied.

## Making It Sustainable

What then are the best approaches to the fisheries crisis? Last February, Greenpeace released a preliminary series of "Principles for Ecologically Responsible Fisheries," which the organization is urging fish buyers to use as benchmarks for seafood purchases. These include a shift from large-scale intensive fisheries to smaller, community-based ones with sound practices. Fishing gear and methods damaging to fish populations or habitats should be phased out. No fishery ought to open or expand until "a verifiable, scientifically-based, dynamic management procedure has been established."

At a recent conference, fisheries economist Francis Christy urged a "limited entry" policy on managers, pointing out that restrictions on the number of licenses issued to fish have proven effective in revitalizing the Maryland blue crab industry.

Fishermen themselves can and should play a greater role in ensuring their own survival. A 1995 survey by a British magazine, *The Ecologist,* cites numerous examples of coastal communities around the world evolving often-unwritten rules to regulate their fisheries. The Cocamilla people in the Peruvian Amazon, observing that their lake was being overfished by commercials from other regions, ruled that only subsistence fishermen be allowed to fish there. In Newfoundland and Japan, some communities hold annual lotteries for the best fishing areas. Among the Cree people of St. James Bay, Canada, and in Donegal, Ireland, fishermen competing for particularly good spots agree to fish in turns. The Boston-based Conservation Law Foundation is currently working with fishermen in "developing economic structures for them to take on greater responsibility as ecosystem managers," says its program director Peter Shelley.

All this, of course, supports a small-scale emphasis but does not address the industrialized fleet problem. But what about a tonnage fee imposed by governments on the massive hauls of the big boat operations? The more fish you bring in, the more you pay. And the funds could be earmarked not only for fisheries research and management, but for job retraining. A federal pilot program for the failing Pacific Northwest salmon fishery already funds jobs in the restoration of river habitats. The limited dollars available in the government's Fishing Industry Grants program are currently going to fishermen with inventive ideas for reducing waste by modifying fishing gear, and to commercial vessels helping conduct surveys of Atlantic herring spawning stocks.

There is no reason why fishing captains and crews couldn't stay on the water and plant shellfish beds, help the Coast Guard with harbor oil spill cleanups, conduct fish counts, aid in public education, take water samples and serve on enforcement teams. But this will take a commitment where commercial lobbying interests like the National Fisheries Institute worry less about allocation and more about Congress' current plans to gut the NMFS budget and to remove from protection almost 70 percent of the remaining American wetlands.

## Miraculous Recovery?

When concerned citizens wake up to the ramifications of a dying ocean ecosystem, miracles can happen. It was the outcry of sports fishermen that forced managers to impose drastic sanctions on the commercial striped bass harvest a decade ago—and the fish that enabled the Pilgrims to survive has made an unparalleled comeback. In both Louisiana and Florida, successful ballot referenda spurred by sportsmen's groups have recently brought an end to the indiscriminate use of inshore entanglement gillnets. And in India, protesting fish workers have brought a halt to the registry of any new fishing boats in Indian waters.

There is little time to lose. Without greater mobilization against the rapaciousness and greed that are devastating the world's oceans, we are looking at a future where the wonders and sustenance of the sea are, if not gone altogether, confined to fish-farming pens. And that would be an unthinkable tragedy.

## Contacts

American Oceans Campaign, 201 Massachusetts Avenue NE, Washington, DC 20002/(202) 544-3526

American Sportfishing Association, 1033 North Fairfax Street, Alexandria, VA 22314/(703) 519-9691

Center for Marine Conservation, 1725 DeSalles Street NW, Washington, DC 20036/(202) 429-5609

Marine Fish Conservation Network, 408 C Street NE, Washington, DC 20002/(202) 548-0707

National Coalition for Marine Conservation, 3 West Market Street, Leesburg, VA 22075/(703) 777-0037

Ocean Wildlife Campaign, 666 Pennsylvania Avenue SE, Washington, DC 20003/(202) 547-9009

❏

## Questions

1. How many major fishing grounds are in serious decline?

2. What is meant by the term *pulse fishing*?

3. What is the "precautionary, risk-averse" approach?

*Answers are at the back of the book.*

## 24

*Beavers, the largest rodent in North America, are making an astonishing comeback. Until recently, they were trapped for fur and eradicated as "pests" to the point of extinction in many areas of the United States. But their protection by law, their rapid reproduction, and the extinction of wolves and other major predators have led to a dramatic increase in beaver abundance. They are not only numerically more common, but beavers are geographically expanding into areas where they have not been found for centuries. By some estimates, more than 12 million beavers now live in the United States. But this rapid increase has led to a classic and increasingly common dilemma in conservation biology: What should we do about native species that become too common because their predators have been exterminated by humans? This is especially problematic with beavers because of their drastic impact on ecosystems. By building dams, beavers alter the course of streams, create wetlands, and cause flooding. These activities not only cause many millions of dollars in damage each year, but they can threaten other species.*

# Back to Stay
## Jon R. Luoma

*Audubon*, January/February 1996

*Once nearly wiped out by trapping, beavers are booming across the country—and land managers must cope with the only creatures that can alter an ecosystem nearly as efficiently as humans themselves.*

Dick Foster's little corner of retirement heaven lies down a narrow lane near a sweeping oxbow of the Oswegatchie River, so far north in the state of New York that the nearest metropolis is the Canadian capital, Ottawa. On a sunny day last summer, I pulled up to the place he calls the End-of-the-Road Farm just as Foster, a retired gym teacher and coach, was coming out the door of his 19th-century stone farmhouse.

The place hasn't been a farm for decades. Like much of the rest of the former agricultural land here in New York's North Country, Foster's 300 acres reverted to forest decades ago. And that's just how he and his wife, Sandra, like it. The "farm" is now a place to hike, to bird, to canoe and garden and cross-country ski, and to log out a few of the valuable northern hardwoods, like sugar maple and hard cherry.

Of course, the view from the house used to be prettier, with a row of fat old black oaks hanging their boughs over the Oswegatchie. There is also the matter of a little bog, once located on state-owned land a few yards beyond the property, where Foster used to take grade-school kids to look at insect-eating flora like sundews and pitcher plants. The oaks, it seems, were girdled by busy teeth and died of thirst; the bog was inundated into oblivion. In fact, if the Fosters allowed nature to take its course, much of their stream-laced forest and meadow—a third of their land—would soon be under water.

And that's part of the story of why Dick Foster, nature lover, finds himself at war, not with the usual suspects—polluters, drainers, ditchers, and developers—but with booming populations of beavers, the only living creatures with enough engineering skill to alter ecosystems nearly as efficiently as humans themselves.

Foster is not the only one in conflict with these, the largest of North America's rodents. Farmers, woodlot managers, and homeowners are being driven to distraction by the result of an environmental success story. Once fantastically abundant, beavers had by the end of the 19th century, been pushed to the brink of extinction by trapping. Now they are back. And with their major natural predator, the wolf, largely absent, it looks as if they are back to stay.

In fact, they are breeding prodigiously in some regions, accomplishing with busy efficiency precisely what they evolved to do: cutting down trees, incessantly gnawing on bark to keep their chisellike teeth razor-sharp, stopping running water from running, and flooding dry land into ponds in which to feed and shelter and breed.

As a species, the creatures are simply attempting to follow a biological imperative that leads them to manipulate large swaths of the American landscape back to what it once was: a great patchwork of beaver-made ponds and wetlands, rich with related species. The rub is that, in the interim between their near extinction in the late 1800s and their present recovery, we humans have taken over, bringing with us our roads, basements, backyards, wells, septic tanks, woodlots, and golf courses—artifices that respond poorly to, say, a sudden inundation by thousands of gallons of water.

Massachusetts Department of Fisheries and Wildlife biologist Tom Decker says that in the past five years alone his state, with perhaps 29,000 of the animals, has seen a doubling of beaver-related complaints. The good news, he says, is that "beavers are now found throughout almost all of their traditional range in Massachusetts." The bad news: "They're trying to share that landscape with 6.2 million people."

Mike DonCarlos, a wildlife-management specialist with the Minnesota Department of Natural Resources, says, "It's reached the point where there are too many beavers to avoid conflict with people." In Minnesota there are, in fact, too many of them to count. Instead, the state samples a series of standard reference areas, which, DonCarlos says, show "dramatic increases since the late 1980s," with a population peak in 1992 three times as high as that of the early 1970s. Extrapolating from those surveys, he believes that there could be as many as 1 million of the animals in the state. In fact, he says, the population has boomed so much in the past half-decade

that "we've pretty much lost control of it."

In northern New York's St. Lawrence River valley, where Foster's home lies, the number of beaver families—which average seven animals each—has doubled in 10 years, to the point where the animals now occupy about 40 percent of all potential habitat. State wildlife biologist Joe Lamandola says that with the population boom has come a boom in complaints: about 500 each year in the valley. "I try to tell people that beavers have value," he says. "But when a guy bought a young woodlot twenty years ago to provide for his retirement and he finds that it's now up to his nose in water and all the trees are dying, it's hard to tell him to appreciate them."

No one knows precisely how many beavers now thrive across the United States, but estimates run to 12 million and beyond. Nor does anyone know precisely why the numbers have soared so dramatically in so many places. One theory is that the phenomenon follows a principle of biology, that populations grow or recover gradually until breeding-age adults reach critical mass, and then the numbers begin to soar exponentially. At least as important is the fact that trapping, which once limited population growth, has declined across North America as fur has fallen out of favor and pelt prices have plummeted.

Foster says the booming beaver population on his land has compelled him to trap the animals. "I was thrilled the first time I saw beavers on this property," he says. His retirement haven, like many present-day dairy farms and villages here-abouts, probably spent much of its presettlement history under the waters of beaver ponds. He took me back along rutted roads and woodland trails to a pair of stick-and-mud dams for a look at how beavers here are attempting to establish their domain once again.

For Foster, the conflicts are evident. "I don't think trapping's wrong or immoral," he says. In fact, he markets the pelts from the animals he traps, so that at least some use is made of them. "But I don't happen to like killing these animals. I don't like it one bit. I got so tired of it that I got my family together and asked whether we should just give the place over completely to the beaver. I got a resounding no."

According to the New York Department of Environmental Conservation (DEC), in 1994 beavers caused about $6.2 million in damage to crops, commercial trees, and human structures in the state. Minnesota's DonCarlos says his state doesn't compile such figures, but he suggests that the numbers there also run into the millions—money spent to repair roads or to cover the costs of preventing even more damage.

Comprehending the efficiency and energy with which beavers can build and dam, particularly in the autumn as they prepare for winter, takes direct observation. During a year when I lived in the St. Lawrence River valley, not many miles from Foster's house, I marveled at how, in a matter of days, a solitary beaver had mowed down and hauled into a culvert virtually all the alder shrubs in a seasonally damp wetland behind our house. At the other end of the culver—an extremely long one that ran perhaps 75 yards under an adjoining yard and diagonally across a road—another neighbor was more distressed than amazed. In a matter of a few more days, the creature had logged out about a third of a windbreak of aspen trees. Still, the animal was doomed: There would be virtually no autumn or winter water in which it could submerge the food cache it would need to survive the frozen months. Water would come, but only with the spring snowmelt—too late to save the beaver, but just in time to inundate the neighbor's yard and cellar.

Of course, there's another side to this animal's story. "Beavers," says Ray "Bucky" Owen, Maine's commissioner of inland fisheries and wildlife, "are the number one wetland managers in the state." Surveys show that about half of that state's inland ospreys nest and feed in beaver flowages. Similar studies in Massachusetts show that about two-thirds of its great blue heron nesting sites are in the flowages. Beaver ponds also provide habitat for scores of other species, from muskrats to ducks. During their clear, unsedimented early years, the ponds support brook trout. They help buffer flooding and erosion on stream courses and recharge groundwater. Beavers are, in fact, so effective at this sort of ecological good work that experiments by ranchers and scientists in some arid western states have proven beaver damming can restore eroded, damaged stream courses and adjoining parched and livestock-beaten lands, with benefits ranging from newly abundant songbird habitat to a burst of vegetation for cattle and wildlife.

When the first white settlers arrived on this continent, North America was up to its ecological keister in the creatures the Ojibwa called *amik* and taxonomists have come to call *Castor canadensis*. From Maine to Oregon, from the Arctic tundra to the Sonoran Desert, there were once 60 to 400 million beavers across the North American landscape—meaning that there were beavers on nearly every suitable pond, lake, stream, and rivulet. Their effect on the landscape was often profound: Early explorers in Oregon reported having to make their way only along ridgetops, so flooded and swamped were the valley floors—now farmland and towns—by beaver activity. Biologists Robert Naiman, Carol Johnston, and James Kelley concluded in a 1988 article in *BioScience* that lands so blessed with beavers become a "shifting mosaic" of habitats, with flooding, more flooding, and the expansion of forest openings as trees are beaver-cut or pond-drowned. Wetlands transition back to young forest and then older forest as one pond site is abandoned for another. The biologists reported that between 1834 and 1988, the United States lost perhaps 100,000 square miles of wetlands, much of that former beaver pond.

Plants and animals generally live in habitats to which they have adapted. Beavers, on the other hand, adapt habitats to suit their needs. In fact, says Thomas Eveland, a biologist from Pennsylvania's Luzerne College who has served as an adviser to several states struggling to manage human-wildlife conflicts, "Next to man, the beaver probably does the most of any animal to manipulate its own environment."

That environmental manipulation occurs mainly through the construction of spectacularly engineered dams of sticks, logs, and mud, resolutely knit together on a foundation of logs braced against rocks or trees, or forced into bottom sediments at angles that impel the current to wedge them even deeper. Ponds, and sometimes virtual lakes, swell into existence behind the dams, leaving waters deep enough for a submerged entrance to a beaver lodge, safe from predators, and for a winter food cache of sticks; beavers eat the cambium, the nutritious, sapfilled inner bark.

The animals use their famous flat tails not only to flail upon the water, warning of danger with a great wet kaboom, but also to prop themselves upright while eating or working. Their hind legs, huge and powerful, are webbed for propulsion. Their front paws, by contrast, are surprisingly delicate—almost tiny hands, with which they can pick at food or pack mud into crevices.

Perhaps the beaver's most remarkable feature, though, is its chisellike teeth. To keep them sharp, the animals gnaw on trees even when they're not hungry. The gnawing peels off a layer of fast-growing dentin on the back of the teeth and sharpens the bright-orange enamel on the front. (It also means that a pondful of beavers, by debarking living trees, can kill acres of trees beyond those they drown or cut down.)

Although revered by Native Americans, the beaver was valued by early white settlers not for its ecological good works but rather, as Eveland puts it, only as "living gold"—for its valuable pelt, the "mining" of which reached extraordinary levels. Between just 1630 and 1640, for instance, some 80,000 beavers were trapped annually from the Hudson River and what is today western New York.

Tom Decker, the Massachusetts biologist, worries that increasing conflicts will cause an overreaction. "People's tolerance can rapidly change from a sense that it's a value to have these animals around to a sense that they're just pests, like cockroaches," he says. "If their main experience with these animals is property damage, that their basement is flooded, or that they can't use their septic system, they're going to start seeing them as vermin. So our ability to keep beavers and their wetlands around depends on our ability to control beavers."

By way of example, Decker tells the story of the township of Chelmsford, now a suburb of Boston but once a pioneer fur-trading community. In 1988 Chelmsford residents, at the urging of animal rights activists, voted to ban trapping on the wetlands and streams that lace the area. Four years later, after two public wells had been flooded and homeowner complaints about beaver damage had soared from an average of about 1 per year to 30, voters rescinded the ban. "Four years before," Decker says, "trappers had been portrayed as evil people. But trapping was the only thing that was controlling the beaver population. After they lifted the trapping ban, people were literally inviting the trappers into their homes, saying, 'Please come through our yard and set your traps back there by the stream.'"

Indeed, in 1994 Massachusetts liberalized its trapping rules, doubling the take of beaver pelts. In North Carolina, where beavers were a rare sight as recently as 1950, the legislature two years ago set up a trapping season to help suppress a population now estimated to be causing more than $1 million in damage each year.

But trapping as a management tool raises plenty of hackles. In New York, a 1995 attempt to change trapping laws, intended to suppress beaver populations by as much as one-third in some areas, ran into a wall or opposition not only from animal rights groups but also from mainstream conservationists, including both the Sierra Club and the state's Audubon Council. "Beavers are the only source of new wetlands in the state," says council president Andrew Mason. "If the population is cut by a third, that's going to have an effect on the number of wetlands." On the other hand, Mason says, his group does not oppose changes in the law that would make it easier for a local official or a homeowner faced with a beaver nuisance to obtain a permit to have the animal trapped or shot.

But even some traditionally trained wildlife managers question whether trapping can again be the management tool it once was. Europe, for example, is the greatest (albeit declining) market for pelts; however, the European Union may soon act to ban the importation of pelts from countries that use methods it defines as inhumane. As the market collapses, dragging prices with it, the number of knowledgeable trappers is falling. Thus, purely practical questions remain as to how to increase trapping.

In the face of what he calls his state's "out-of-control" beaver population, Minnesota's DonCarlos has begun to promote the use of Clemson Beaver Pond Levelers, drainage pipes developed at Clemson University. Enclosed in wire mesh and filled with holes, the gadgets are designed to eliminate any sound of running water or trace of suction, so the ever-vigilant beavers won't bury them in sticks and mud. The devices allow wildlife managers to target areas where the animals present problems and either to drain a pond completely or to maintain one deep enough for beavers but small enough to prevent conflicts with people.

New York's DEC has criticized similar gadgets as too costly and prone to failure. But DonCarlos says that experiments with more than 100 of the Clemson levelers in his state show that they almost always work. Although similar devices have been used successfully in Maine and Massachusetts, they hardly solve all the problems. They don't work in shallow, low-flow streams. And they wouldn't have prevented the loss of Dick Foster's oaks, girdled by "bank beavers," which live in lodges along the sides of deeper rivers like the Oswegatchie.

As conflicts between beavers and humans accelerate, the dilemma goes to the heart of our relationship with nature. There may be some merit in the practice of sticking sewer pipes into beaver dams in order to out-engineer these natural engineers. But there is hardly aesthetic merit, or even great environmental merit. Unlike beaver dams, polyvinyl-chloride pipes do not degrade. Similarly, plastic-based fake fur or synthetic clothing stuffed with sheets of fossil fuel-based polyester insulators might keep us warm and feeling virtuous. But it's possible we'd do well to learn from the native people who once lived in harmony with this creature. They saw no contradiction between reverence for the beaver and a warm fur hat on a winter day. ❏

**Questions**

1. Why do beavers build dams?

2. When was the beaver population in the United States at its lowest? What was the original North American population size?

3. What do beavers use their tails for?

*Answers are at the back of the book.*

**25** *Farmers, environmentalists, and anti-hunger activists are working together to change the way food is raised and distributed to the inner cities. These groups, however, envision much more than just providing food for people. They visualize a food system that nourishes the environment and local economies. By supplying locally grown food, communities help themselves economically. They also conserve energy and lessen pollution by not having to transport food from across the country. Organic and sustainable agriculture reduces the amount of chemicals on food and chemical seepage into groundwater. Some programs concentrate on the garden itself as a basis for employment and education. Program tutors instruct the youths in basic science, math, and economic development. Most important, these groups are learning that through group action and organization they have power.*

# Common Ground
## Barbara Ruben

*Environmental Action, Summer 1995*

*Farmers, environmentalists and anti-hunger activists join forces to redefine the way food is grown and distributed.*

Fourteen miles beyond the White House and ten miles from the dilapidated rowhouses of Washington's poorest neighborhoods, Pennsylvania Avenue gives way to exurbia's newest pastel housing developments, interspersed with rolling fields. A blue heron spreads its wings against the sky above a seven-acre organic farm plot, where fledgling sprouts of broccoli, carrots, collard greens and beets push through the soil in the late-April sun.

Alesia Dickerson strides down the neat rows, straightening the cloth batting covering the cabbage and broccoli to help protect the crops from an invasion of maggots. Last summer, she worked as a volunteer on the farm, lived in a Washington homeless shelter and could barely distinguish between kale and Swiss chard. Today, she makes $5 an hour at the farm, lives with her mother and aerates compost like an expert.

"I didn't know anything about farming before," she says. "I do now. I like to watch things grow."

The farm is tended by employees and volunteers of From the Ground Up, a project of the Capital Area Community Food Bank that links sustainable agriculture with low-cost produce for inner city residents. The program also employs two other people living in shelters.

From the Ground Up is one of a growing number of programs that join the environment, access to nutritious food and the inner-city poor under the idea of "community food security." Whether through farmers' markets in low-income areas, community gardens at public housing or community supported agriculture—in which consumers directly pay farmers for a share of the crop—anti-hunger groups, farmers and environmentalists are sowing the seeds for changing the way food is raised and distributed.

It's a coalition of groups that has rarely joined forces in the past. "It's as if the environment is one box here, welfare and hunger in a box there," says Robert Gottlieb, coordinator of environmental analysis and policy in the Department of Urban Planning at UCLA, whose students did one of the first studies of community food security in the wake of the Los Angeles riots. "Food security is the kind of issue that builds bridges and sets agendas for environmental and environmental justice groups, which have touched on pesticides or farmworkers, but not in conjunction with access to the actual food produced."

Kate Fitzgerald, executive director of Austin's Sustainable Food Center, says that she has worked

**Reprinted with permission from *Environmental Action*, Summer 1995, pp. 26–28.**

smoothly with local and national environmental groups, but that, "Historically there's been a tension between sustainable agriculture and hunger groups. Agribusiness put forth myths saying that sustainable grown food would be more expensive," she says. "It prevented a dialog between farm groups and anti-hunger groups."

But that may be changing. The key, says Mark Winne, executive director of the Hartford Food System, is to change traditional views of agriculture as merely a money-making business. "I get the sense sometimes that if agriculture wasn't producing food, it wouldn't make a difference to the [Connecticut] Department of Agriculture. If farmers in the state stuck to high-end stuff like oysters or mushrooms—multi-million dollar enterprises—people would still say you have farming going on.

• • •

As grocery stores flee from what owners consider unsafe and unprofitable inner-city locations, residents are often left with less nutritious and more expensive food. In such cities as New York, Los Angeles and Hartford, low-income residents pay 10 to 40 percent more for groceries than those with high-incomes and access to large supermarkets, according to a study by the Community Food Access Resource Center in New York. A national study by the Second Harvest Food Bank in 1994 found that one in every 10 Americans has used an emergency food pantry.

But more than just providing food for people, community food security advocates envision a food system that also nourishes the environment and local economies. For example, the average food item travels 1,400 miles before it reaches a consumer, says Andy Fisher, coordinator of the Community Food Security Coalition, which formed last year and includes a number of sustainable agriculture, hunger and environmental groups. At that rate, it takes about 10 energy calories to deliver one food calorie to the dinner plate. By providing locally grown food, communities not only get an economic boost, but save the energy—and resulting pollution—from trucking food in from across the country.

In addition, the organic and sustainable agriculture practices advocated by community food security proponents reduce the amount of chemicals on food and washed into groundwater. Urban gardening and farmers' markets can also brighten the often bleak landscape of the inner city.

"Some people use our farmer's markets as a way to escape the Bronx or Brooklyn," says Tony Mannetta, assistant director of New York City's Greenmarkets, which organizes markets in 20 locations, many of them in lower-income areas. "I've seen elderly people just taking a walk through them, smelling a mound of basil here, admiring the bunches of flowers there."

Although only a portion of the produce in the markets is organic, Mannetta says once farmers get into the program they start using fewer chemical pesticides and fertilizers. Cosmetic perfection isn't required. Customers will tolerate an apple that's misshapen, or even one that has a worm hole," he says. "We've found the chemical salesmen even start complaining about the change."

The farmers' market run by the Ecology Center in Berkeley, California, at three locations, including one low-income neighborhood, boasts 70 percent of its produce as certified organic, the highest rate in California and perhaps the country, according to its co-manager Kirk Lumpkin. The Ecology Center also forbids any produce grown in soil using the biocide methyl bromide, which has been shown to destroy the ozone layer.

Produce not sold at the Ecology Center and some other markets is donated to local food banks and shelters. Seattle's community gardening program donates more than two tons of produce a year through a program called Lettuce Link.

Although farmers' markets around the country are traditionally found in upscale neighborhoods, groups like the Ecology Center and Greenmarkets say they are committed to bringing them to lower-income sections of the city. In Austin, for instance, the only farmers' market was located an hour and 25 minutes by bus from a low-income, mainly Latino community. Last year, the non-profit Sustainable Food Center organized a farmers' market for the east side, in which more than 40 percent of the population lives below the poverty level.

In addition to the farmers' market, the Sustainable Food Center runs a community garden at the site and a food school. "Some of the people will initially look at an eggplant and say, 'I won't eat that. I don't know how to cook it,'" says Nessa Richman, who started the farmers' market. The center's education efforts extend to fliers posted at the gardens to inform residents that, for instance, the cilantro has purposely been left to grow unwieldy to attract lady bugs that will eat the aphids preying on other vegetables.

The farmers' market accepts both food stamps and special Women's Infants and Children's (WIC) farmers' market coupons that are available, in addition to the regular benefits. Interest in using food stamps was so high that in the two weeks after the center put out a pamphlet on the subject, the office was deluged with 7,000 calls for more information.

But it can be difficult persuading farmers to accept the food stamps and coupons—or to even set up a stand in a lower-income neighborhood.

At a farmers' market organized by the Ecology Center, farmers have had their cash boxes stolen and once a man confronted two women with a knife. The Ecology Center then provided a cellular phone for emergencies, but no one so far has had to use it. "The market creates its own positive atmosphere," says Lumpkin.

Greenmarkets in New York offers a $100 credit to farmers toward renting stall space if they will accept food stamps. But in many states, including New York, food stamp transactions have entered the high-tech age. Benefits are accessed through an electronic card, much like an automatic teller machine card. But since most farmers' markets have no electricity or even access to a phone to confirm food stamp eligibility, the few farmers who would accept food stamps many times aren't able to adapt to the new system.

"We're looking at cellular phone links for EBT (electronic benefits transfer), but all I keep thinking is there would be a $5 call for a $2 purchase," says Manetta.

• • •

Some programs focus on the garden itself as a source of employment and education. The Seattle Youth Garden Works, started this year, will employ five to 10 homeless youth in organic gardens to raise produce for a farmers' market. In addition to teaching about sustainable agriculture and environmental issues, the program tutors the youth in basic science and math and provides a forum to learn about economic development.

"It seems sometimes that recycling and conservation and environmental righteousness are for the rich, and that the poor are people who litter and eat junk food and don't buy recycled because it costs more. And I think that's wrong," says Margaret Hauptman, who began the program. Hauptman says she joined her love of gardening and working with children in planning the program. "I experience a lot of joy and healing working in the soil. It's a kind of transcendent experience, and I wanted to share that."

The Homeless Garden Project in Santa Cruz, California employs about 20 homeless people part-time in its 5-acre organic garden. Food is sold at a farmers' market and directly from a community supported agriculture (CSA) program. Since the project began in 1989, more than 100 homeless have worked at the garden.

The Hartford Food System has run low-income community gardens as well as a CSA farm since 1978. The farm provides produce for both middle-income residents and low-income groups, which distributes the food to about 900 of their clients. Food recipients help out at the farm.

"Hartford is radically divided between rich white suburbs and a poor inner city made up largely of Latinos and African Americans. Our biggest education effort is on the local food supply," executive director Mark Winne says. "We have teen mothers who have never seen a carrot growing before. They can't get over that they can eat it right there and make lunch out of what they've harvested."

Winne's group is now studying the feasibility of the Hartford School System purchasing more locally grown food. About 25,000 children are enrolled in the schools, 80 percent of whom qualify for the subsidized school lunch program. Almost no food used now is locally grown, and none of it is organic.

• • •

Back at From the Ground Up's farm in suburban Washington, director Leigh Hauter talks about weeding with the Civilian Conservation Corps and Americorps. The acres the program tills are part of a larger sustainable agriculture center owned by the environmental group the Chesapeake Bay Foundation. Farmed primarily for tobacco and corn for 200 years, the land hasn't yet recovered from centuries of monoculture, but Hauter is still expecting a fair crop.

Part of the 45,000 pounds of produce he estimates will be raised will be sold for half price to community groups and churches, which in turn sell the food to their members. When Hauter talked to parishioners at a church in Washington's impoverished Anacostia, several members told him they had been share croppers in North Carolina decades before and recalled spreading ashes on the soil to serve as fertilizer, a practice Hauter emulates using lime today.

"I think we have a lot to learn from each other," he says. "We teach people that by group action they have power. That lesson is what we're trying to get across everywhere—organize to make your life better. Maybe that can translate beyond buying vegetables." ❑

---

## Questions

1. What do community food advocates envision?

2. What does the Seattle Youth Garden Works focus on, and what are other areas of learning that they include in their program?

3. How does the concept of food security bring diverse groups together?

*Answers are at the back of the book.*

---

**26** *Deforestation has many affects: extinction of animal species, global warming, and soil erosion, to name a few. Because of this, the international tropical timber trade has come under close scrutiny. However, implementing a ban against forestry could increase deforestation and would affect forestry projects that are trying to promote sustainable forestry. A growing consensus is to promote tropical timber produced from sustainable sources. This would require that wood products purchased from well-managed forests be labeled for consumers. This creates incentives for producers to assume sustainable forest management practices and maintain the well-being of the forest ecosystem. The need for certified timber presently exceeds the ability of both the United States and the United Kingdom to produce it.*

# Labeling Wood
## Cheri Sugal

*World Watch*, September/October 1996

### How timber certification may reduce deforestation.

A series of landmark developments, including satellite photography revealing massive burning of the Amazon and scientific findings confirming a link between deforestation and climate change, has greatly heightened public awareness about the loss of tropical forests in the past decade. The loss now amounts to more the 14 million hectares of tropical forest—equivalent to the entire state of Florida—every year.

As a result, the international tropical timber trade has become a target of public campaigns to curb deforestation, the argument being that consumers can "save" the rainforest if they refuse to buy tropical timber products. In the United Kingdom, for example, more than 30 local authorities have ceased use of tropical hardwoods. Since 1992, approximately 200 city councils in Germany and 51 percent of Dutch municipalities have banned use of tropical timber. And in the United States, a growing number of cities and states (including New York, California, Arizona, and Minneapolis), have banned or are considering prohibiting the use of tropical timber in public construction project.

Applied indiscriminately to tropical timber, however, such prohibitions could boomerang by making forestry less competitive with agriculture, which causes far more deforestation than cutting trees for timber does. Prohibitions may also undermine the few incentives that fledging forestry projects have to promote sustainable management. Many such promising projects would quickly wither away without demand and capital from the North. Bans also face an uphill battle to the extent that they conflict with international rules of free trade.

Given these drawbacks, there is a growing movement to use the market to *promote* tropical timber produced from *sustainable* sources, through labeling of wood products, rather than ban all tropical timber indiscriminately. The intent is to assure consumers that the wood products they purchase originate from wwll-managed forests, thereby helping to develop a market for these products, and ultimately to provide sufficient incentives for producers to adopt sustainable forest management practices. The organizations that have undertaken to provide independent certification ("third-party" certifiers) operate on the principle that good forest stewardship must mean more than sustained timber supply; it also means maintaining the health and integrity of the forest ecosystem, and ensuring that all pertinent stakeholders share in the benefits. Stakeholders include both people and wildlife that live in the forest, indigenous cultures that have traditional land use rights, and landowners and loggers that have legitimate economic needs. Most certifiers strive to achieve this balance by requiring adherence to a long-term management plan, minimum-impact harvesting methods, efficient utilization of all forest products including non-timber forest products, and third-party audits.

All third-party certifiers also trace and track products throughout the "chain of custody" to ensure that the product originally evaluated and certified has been used at each step in processing, manufacturing, and distribution.

• • •

The effect of certification on tropical deforestation has been questioned, however, on the grounds that logging constitutes only a small portion of deforestation in the tropics. According to the United Nations Food and Agriculture Organization (FAO), an estimated 90 percent of all deforestation is done for agricultural purposes, with only 10 percent owing to logging.

Detractors also argue that only 14 percent (about 240 million cubic meters) of the tropical trees cut each year is used for industrial "roundwood" (the logs that get cut into boards for construction or wood products) while the remaining 86 percent (or nearly one-and-a-half billion cubic meters) is used for fuelwood and charcoal. Finally, of the wood harvested, only 28 percent enters international trade in the form of logs, sawnwood, or wood-based panels—the kinds of products to which eco-labeling might apply. Combined, these numbers suggest that international trade accounts for less than 1 percent of tropical deforestation.

This conclusion, however, is misleading—and too quick. It sweeps over what happens in particular countries, and overlooks the role of logging in opening up previously intact forests for *other* causes of deforestation. In Southeast Asia's dipterocarp forests, for example, logging operations generally penetrate previously inaccessible primary forest, and loggers may remove up to 40 percent of the standing timber volume and leave between 15 and 40 percent of the ground with no forest cover.

Moreover, logging opens large areas of primary forest to penetration and clearing for other uses—

including the massively destructive uses of agriculture and cattle ranching. This is true even in South America, where timber volumes are much lower. According to the FAO, deforestation rates are eight times higher in logged-over areas than in non-logged areas.

Blanket claims that commercial logging exacts only a small toll on tropical forests may also be based on a misinterpretation of data, as much as what really happens on the ground. The FAO statistics are based on the presumption that deforestation means the *complete removal of tree cover*. Since most logging in the tropics involves selective cutting that leaves a ragged residual cover, a logged-over area may not be counted as a deforested area. Yet, many such areas are undoubtedly deforested in an ecological sense. Careless logging can destroy or fatally injure residual trees and lead to further forest loss. In Brazil's eastern Amazon, for example, in efforts to extract a mere 2 percent of the trees, over 26 percent of all remaining trees greater than 10 centimeters (four inches) in diameter were destroyed or seriously damaged. In Malaysia, to remove only 3 percent of the trees in a selective harvest of dipterocarps, 48 percent of the remaining trees were destroyed. And the damage continues after the loggers have left, as the remaining trees are more likely to fall in a violent storm than are the trees in an unlogged forest.

Logged-over forests, where leaf litter and woody debris dry out, are also more vulnerable to forest fires. The 1982-83 fire in the East Kalimantan, for example, burned 3.5 million hectares of logged-over forest, and spread to an additional 800,000 hectares of unlogged forest.

Statistics can also be misleading in reflecting the portion of logging used for timber, as opposed to the portion either wasted or used for other purposes. To begin with, the figures for timber production represent only that portion of "stemwood" (the tree's trunk) that is actually used, and do not include roughly half of the wood mass of each tree felled that is left behind in the forest to rot. They also do not include wood produced as a by-product of road building, or wood that is cut but not removed from the forest because it has been damaged or because it turns out to be too costly to haul out. In fact, the actual amount of felled timber is much greater than documented.

Then, these figures fail to take into account differences in the relative contribution of industrial production and fuelwood extraction within the tropics. The demand for fuelwood is a problem that afflicts primarily the dry tropics. In Mali and Burkino Faso, for example, fuelwood extraction accounts for about 95 percent of all tree cutting. In the moist tropics, however, cutting of fuelwood is only a serious threat in the immediate vicinity of large cities, and cutting for furniture or veneer is a much bigger threat. In Gabon, for example, the share of wood going to timber is 32 percent; in Congo, it is 36 percent; and in Malaysia, it is a devastating 82 percent.

Furthermore, there are some tropical countries that rely heavily on tropical timber exports, where there can be little doubt that international trade has played an important role in fueling deforestation. In Malaysia, for example, where 15 million hectares (almost 50 percent) of original forests have already been lost, exports in the form of logs, sawnwood and wood-based panels in 1992 accounted for 45 percent of all timber production.

Finally, and perhaps most significantly, in questioning the potential value of forest products certification by claiming that the timber industry's role in tropical deforestation is small, the critics of certification have ignored the very different situation prevailing in the world's great temperate and boreal forests, in which 75 percent of all logging—some 1.4 billion cubic meters per year—is for production of industrial roundwood. Only 25 percent is used for fuelwood and charcoal production. These forests account for 89 percent of the total global trade in forest products, including 83 percent of the total volume of industrial roundwood. According to a World Wildlife Fund publication the timber trade is undoubtedly the *primary* cause of forest loss in temperate and boreal countries still possessing substantial old-growth forests. So, demanding that products from such forests be certified is likely to have a significant overall impact in those regions.

• • •

Since the US-based Rainforest Alliance's "Smart Wood" Program (the first and largest forestry certification program) certified its first "well-managed" forest in 1990, certification efforts have sky-rocketed. By the spring of 1996, nearly 2.4 million hectares of natural forest, an area approximately the size of Belize, had been certified by four third-party certifying organizations. And reflecting the role of temperate forests in international trade, 88 percent of the certified area consists of forests located in the United States, United Kingdom, and Poland. A quick perusal of the world suggests how much unmet potential exists for extending reliable certification into the boreal forests of Russia and Canada.

In addition to third-party certification, national certification initiatives have been proliferating. The Brazilian forestry sector has been developing a methodology to define the origin of raw materials used by the forest industry, which has resulted in what is called a "Certificate of Origin of Forest Raw Material" (CERFLOR). In Indonesia, Lambaga Ekolabel Indonesia (LEI) was formed in 1993 to develop a certification and labeling scheme for Indonesian forest products.

The explosion of certification initiatives can easily lead to confusion in the marketplace over the credibility of certain labels. Conflicts have already arisen as some less scrupulous timber sources establish self-certification schemes that amount to little more than a greenwashing of unsustainable practices. Claims of "sustained yield," "produced from farmed plantations," "we have never used tropical rainforest trees," or "one tree is planted for each one felled," even if true, do not provide assurance of environmental sustainability.

The establishment of the Forest Stewardship Council (FSC) should reduce some of the confusion in the market place created by the abundance of claims. The FSC was established in 1993 to set global standards whereby those organizations certifying the sustainability of a productive forest could themselves be accredited. The FSC was created through a consultative process involving environmentalists, representatives of local peoples, and industry. It has developed and registered an accreditation mark which will soon appear alone or alongside the logos of its accredited certifiers.

To date, the FSC has accredited four third-party certifiers: the Rainforest Alliance Smart Wood Program and Scientific Certification Systems Forest Conservation Program, the SGS Forestry Qualifor

Programme, and the Soil Association Responsible Forestry Programme. It is working in close cooperation with national governments (such as Switzerland) to accredit their certification schemes.

Other initiatives are simultaneously underway. The International Standards Organization (ISO), a non-profit, *industry-supported* federation, has supported the development of "environmental management systems" (EMS) guidelines. These EMS standards, known as the 14000 series and scheduled for implementation in 1997, are being developed under the leadership of the Canadian Standards Association.

The ISO 14000 series, in contrast to the FSC's approach which seeks to ascertain whether *forests themselves* are maintained in a sustainable manner, assesses only a company's *internal management processes*. The limitations of ISO 14000 certification are that it requires only the existence of environmental management systems, it does not require any specific levels of environmental performance, and it does not guarantee that firms have actually complied with environmental regulations.

• • •

The effect that certification will have on changing forest management practices in the near term remains unclear. Today, demand for certified wood currently exceeds the supply in the United States and United Kingdom. The volume of certified timber or industrial roundwood, including sawlogs, veneer logs, and pulpwood (about 1.5 million cubic meters) is less than 0.1 percent of total production of industrial roundwood (about 1.7 billion cubic meters). Thus, consumer action alone—demanding that all wood purchases come from certified sources—is presently unlikely to slow the current rates of deforestation. A greater number of timber producers will need to recognize the potential economic gain associated with certification. This could be accomplished by two mechanisms: forest products from sustainably managed sources could attract a "green premium;" and producers could avoid the loss of market access where certification is required, or could gain market share where consumer awareness is high.

Can timber sales attract a "green premium"—whereby certified timber is sold at a higher price than uncertified timber? Credible surveys say it can.

A 1992 Gallup survey of citizens in 24 nations found that 63 percent of citizens in high income nations, 55 percent in middle income nations, and 45 percent in low income nations would be willing to pay higher prices to protect the environment. According to a Purdue University study conducted in 1992, 68 percent of US household earning $50,000 per year said that they "would be willing to pay more for furniture whose construction materials originated from a sustainably well managed North American forest."

Whether this willingness materializes into actual purchasing decisions remains to be seen. According to Mark Eisen, Manager of Environmental Marketing for the North American retail chain Home Depot, the actual purchasing behavior of consumers at his stores is currently based more on "price-quality" relationships than on environmental considerations. Only when all other criteria are relatively equal will the "greenness" of a product make a difference. If a price premium cannot be expected for sustainable production, the costs (of inspection, external monitoring, chain of custody verification, and foregone export earnings) associated with certification may put certified suppliers at a short-term disadvantage compared to their non-certified competitors.

Nevertheless, long term benefits will accrue as consumer awareness increases and certified producers gain market share in countries developing either laws or voluntary initiatives to exclude non-certified timber. Austria, for example, attempted in 1992 to regulate imports of tropical timber through mandatory labeling of tropical timber products, along with a voluntary "quality mark" for timber from sustainably managed tropical forests. After protests from Malaysia and Indonesia over "legality" under the General Agreement on Tariffs and Trade (GATT), the legislation was amended in 1993 so that labeling would be introduced on a voluntary basis to mark timber from *all* types of forests.

The "UK 1995 Plus Group," a partnership between the World Wide Fund for Nature-UK and 54 companies in the United Kingdom (including many retailers), has pledged to purchase and sell only certified wood and wood products by December 31, 1999. The group as a whole accounts for 10 percent of the 20 million cubic meters of wood (including roundwood, sawnwood, wood-based panels, pulp, paper, and paperboard) imported into the UK (a value of over U.S. $2 billion per year). A similar "North American Buyers Group for Certified Timber" is still being designed by the New York-based Environmental Advantage.

Finally, the International Tropical Timber Organization (ITTO), a commodity organization of the United Nations with 42 industrial and tropical timber-producing member countries, set the year 2000 as a goal beyond which only sustainably produced wood products would be used in international tropical timber trade.

The financial impact is likely to be greatest when consumer demand is high. Retailers are themselves beginning to raise consumer awareness in the United States and Europe. Home Depot, with 340 stores and $15.5 billion in sales, of which 10 percent is comprised of wood and wood products, accounts for 13 percent of the North American retail home building industry. Since 1991, Home Depot has required that its more than 5,000 vendors have their environmental claims for products or packages evaluated by Scientific Certification Systems—one of the FSC's four accredited labels. Of the several hundred products evaluated, approximately 25 are now certified. Colonial Craft, for example, a well-known manufacturer of hardwood moldings, door and window grilles, and picture frames, is aiming to make 50 percent of its total production certified in the next three years, and 100 percent within five years.

Rainforest Alliance has been concentrating on high visibility products to further raise consumer awareness. Gibson guitars, for example, recently produced its first production-line guitar made entirely of Smart Wood.

Combined, these efforts could be both the carrot and the stick for adoption of sustainable forest management. Right now, their effectiveness may be greatest in temperate and boreal forests—the sources of the majority of forest products sold in markets in the European Union and United States. Their effectiveness in the tropics will be most pronounced in those countries—mostly in Africa—that have a large share of their exports destined for Europe and the United States. Congo and Gabon, for example, export 88 percent and 69 percent of their tropical timber, respectively, to the European Union.

For countries like Malaysia, which export most of their timber to Asia or Japan, US and European demand for certified products is likely to be ineffective. In fact, the United States and Europe import only 7.5 percent and 20.1 percent, respectively, of all tropical wood. Over half of *all* tropical timber products are imported by Japan, South Korea, China and Singapore. Japan alone imports over 28 percent of the world's tropical timber. And, by far, the largest share (85 percent) of tropical timber is consumed by domestic markets where so far little or no consumer demand for certified timber exists. In those countries—and in most of the world, perhaps—the first need is to increase public awareness of what is at stake in the consumption of wood, beyond its immediate cost to the purchaser. ❑

## Questions

1. Over the past decade, how much of the tropical forests have we lost?

2. The FAO statistics regarding deforestation are based on what presumption?

3. What two mechanisms are needed for timber producers to recognize the potential economic gain associated with certification?

*Answers are at the back of the book.*

## 27

*Air, soil, water, and rice and beans have for thousands of years been accessible to almost everyone. Recently, advances in biotechnology have made issues of ownership and control of commercial and wild germplasm very important. Biotechnologists can create plants to tolerate herbicides, counter insects, or thrive in drought or heat. The companies they work for are claiming certain types of cotton, soybeans, and vegetables as their own. Some are succeeding in patenting concepts that could hinder corporate research. However, efforts are being made to reward farmers and indigenous communities for their contributions to biological diversity. Biotechnology has made genetic resources even more valuable to future generations.*

# Who Owns Rice and Beans?
## Fred Powledge

*BioScience*, July/August 1995

***The Patent Office's seeming shift on broad biotechnology patents still leaves unanswered questions about plant germplasm.***

For thousands of years, the fundamental elements of agriculture have been dirt cheap. Everybody knew seeds were important, but hardly anybody claimed to own them. The plants that a researcher produced were usually available to other scientists for experimentation and research. Rice and beans, wheat and soybeans were part of the global commons, along with air, soil, and water.

The promises of biotechnology have made ownership and control of commercial varieties and of wild germplasm—even that with no proven agricultural and medicinal potential—increasingly important. Legal battles, often involving multinational companies, are being fought over proprietary claims to certain forms of cotton, soybeans, other vegetables, and their progeny. At the same time, farmers, government officials, and nongovernmental organizations in many cash-poor, germplasm-rich countries are demanding a place at the international bargaining table. They say they have a legitimate claim to the germplasm that serves as the raw materials of biotechnology. Representatives of these countries want control of, or at least compensation for, commodities that traditionally have been there for the taking.

Classical breeders have always been able to produce new plants by patiently crossing related varieties in experimental fields. But the genetic manipulation possible with biotechnology allows researchers to freely traverse species lines, to insert just one desired quality into a new plant rather than an uncontrolled number of traits, and to create plants that will do just what their designers want them to do—tolerate herbicides, resist insects, or prosper in drought or heat.

Until biotechnology came along, seeds and plant tissue were covered by a set of laws and international conventions that were considerably less strict than the utility patents that apply to mechanical inventions. Protected germplasm could be used freely by researchers other than the original breeder to stimulate further innovation, and there was at least rhetorical recognition of the contribution of farmers to the preservation and improvement of plant varieties.

But as government-sponsored basic research on food crops declines and industrial research grows, control of plant breeding is passing rather quickly into the hands of multinational chemical companies. These companies insist that genetically manipulated

**Reprinted from *BioScience*, Vol. 45, pp. 440–444. © 1995 American Institute of Biological Sciences.**

germplasm be fully covered under the utility patent system, just like a new kind of light bulb or automobile starter. As intellectual property, rice and beans are big business for corporate lawyers and international trade negotiators who never need go near a wheat field or research station. This enormous change, which can profoundly affect the staple foods enjoyed by consumers around the world, is taking place with little notice by the general public.

One recent event captured the attention of the plant breeding community and advocates of Third World rights, if not of the general public. It is the Agracetus case.

In 1991 and 1992, Agracetus, a Middleton, Wisconsin-based subsidiary of the multinational specialty chemicals company W.R. Grace, was granted two patents on all cotton created in the United States through any technique of genetic engineering. The company had asked the US Patent and Trademark Office (PTO) for the patents in 1986. In the words of an Agracetus background sheet, the more comprehensive of the claims "covers all cotton seeds and plants which contain a recombinant gene construction (i.e., are genetically engineered)." Utility patents do not automatically give other scientists the right to use patented material for research purposes or as a basis for newer varieties. In this case, Agracetus has said it would make free research licenses available "to all academic or governmental researchers upon request."

News of the amazingly broad patents, which run for 17 years, shook fellow members of the biotechnology community and outraged advocates of farmers from the Southern Hemisphere. Five requests were made to PTO to reexamine and negate the claims. The first step on the established route for challenging patent grants is a review by the patent examiner.

Two entities requested a reexamination of Agracetus's broadest claim. One is an anonymous requester represented by a law firm. The other is the plant patent arm of the US Department of Agriculture (USDA), which claimed that the method described by Agracetus for transforming cotton was not new, having been previously described in several papers. (To be granted, a request for a utility patent must he novel, or not anticipated by what

patent experts call "prior art"; it must have utility; and it must be nonobvious to someone with "ordinary skill in the art.")

Some of Agracetus's critics raised other objections that had little to do with the mechanics of patenting. It is "morally unacceptable," said one of them, to control the manipulation of life on such a magnificent scale. Furthermore, the patent would give a single multinational corporation unprecedented control over one of the world's staple crops. But the opponents knew it is not the patent office's job to consider such arguments, and they framed their objections in technical terms.

When the examiner announced, last December, that she had reviewed the claims and was now rejecting them, there was considerable speculation in the industry that PTO had not realized how broad the patent was and now was attempting to backpedal. *The New York Times* noted that it was the third time since Bruce A. Lehman became Commissioner of Patents and Trademarks that PTO "had retroactively rejected the claims made on behalf of a highly visible, controversial patent after it had been issued." Both previous rejections are now under appeal.

While opponents of broad species patents celebrated and *The Wall Street Journal* proclaimed "a potentially crippling blow" to the broad patents, Agracetus's parent company, W.R. Grace, dismissed the decision as a mere "office action," which it referred to as "a routine preliminary step in a lengthy reexamination process." The company also reminded competitors that its patents "continue to be valid" pending the outcome of the process.

Russell Smestad, Agracetus's vice president for finance and commercial development, said in an interview in April that "rejection," in the language of the patent office, does not mean the same thing as "rejection" in lay language. "What it means, basically," he said, "is that they cannot permit or allow or issue the claims without more information. They use the word 'rejection,' which sounds drastic, but that is a normal part of the patent process."

The PTO's "Office Action in Reexamination" in the Agracetus patents uses the phrase, "Claims 1–16 [or 1–7, or 13–15] are rejected under 35 U.S.C. 103 as being unpatentable. . ." or ". . . as being anticipated" by what the office calls "prior art references."

And: "Patentee believes that his is the 'first biochemically verifiable genetically engineered' cotton plant. This is not persuasive because being first is an indication of diligence, not of obviousness."

Smestad said the company had filed a response to the PTO action. "Certainly at this point in time we think we would have a valid case to proceed further," he said.

Patent experts say it is not at all unusual for reexaminations to end in rejection, because it may not be until the claim is issued that challengers can marshal their opposition. More than 90% of such rejections remain rejected, according to a PTO spokesperson. What sometimes happens is a rejection will result in a revision of the application so the patent will be accepted; applicants naturally seek the broadest possible coverage and are not surprised when they must tone down their claims.

Far fewer rejected patents—approximately 1%—enter the formal appeal process, which starts with a PTO review and can extend to the US Circuit Court of Appeals. Of that 1%, says PTO, patents are reissued in approximately half the cases.

In 1994, Agracetus obtained a similar cotton patent from the European Patent Office. A challenge was filed to the patent during Europe's nine-month opposition period, and the company is awaiting a decision by the patent examiner there. Agracetus has also received a patent on genetically modified soybean in Europe. The multinational company is conducting research on transgenic rice, maize, peanuts, and beans. Smestad said his company was "not currently pursuing commercial opportunities ourselves" in those crops.

**Industry Wants Patents**

Although biotechnology companies are in favor of patents for plants, some elements of industry were clearly disturbed at the granting of broad species patents to Agracetus/Grace. Simon G. Best is the chief executive officer and managing director of Zeneca Plant Science of Wilmington, Delaware, a part of the British-owned multinational Zeneca group of pharmaceuticals, agrochemicals, and specialty chemicals. "Broad patents for broad and pioneering inventions can be legitimate," he said in an interview. "But that doesn't mean necessarily that patents like those granted to Agracetus have met or did meet those standards" required by the US patenting system. The Monsanto Company, which has invested heavily in agricultural biotechnology, has filed opposition papers to Grace's European patent on transgenic soybean, arguing that the patent will stifle research and, in the words of a spokesperson, is "simply too broad."

Others, however, say, if they had filed first, they would feel entitled to the patent and its rewards. William Tucker is manager for technology transfer at DNA Plant Technology of Oakland, California, which includes in its repertoire techniques for making transgenic tomatoes that ripen properly even when picked early. As for broad patents on food crops such as Agracetus's, he said recently, "The view is from where you sit. If we'd got something as broad as that on a patent, then we'd be very happy. But coming from the other side, it's clearly hard to deal with a patent as broad as that."

Tucker says PTO's initial granting of the cotton claim may have been a fluke. "I don't think those things will be issued any more," he said. "It's one of those quirks of the Patent Office [from] back in the days when they really didn't know much about biotechnology." As patent examiners become more familiar with the prior art that is around, he added, it is going to get harder for applicants to secure broad patents.

Like others in the industry, Tucker sees no moral or ethical problem with the protection of genetically manipulated plants under the utility patent system, as opposed to the less restrictive plant breeders' rights that have prevailed for the last few decades. "A plant variety has been created because of the inventiveness of a set of people," he said. "And it has certain properties that have certain commercial utility. I think you need to be able to protect that invention.... Just because it's biological and self-reproducing doesn't to me make it any different from a piece of machinery that you manufacture from nuts and bolts and screws."

Spokesmen for industry associations agree with this position. "Patenting plants is no different than patenting any other kind of product," said David R. Lambert, executive director of the American Seed Trade Association, which represents approximately

600 active members. Richard Godown, senior vice president of the Biotechnology Industry Organization, another Washington group, which has 585 members, sees the cotton case as an example of a smoothly functioning system of protection: "Agracetus was granted these two broad-range patents, and the industry recognized it, and so the industry is dealing with Agracetus."

## Patents on Concepts?

The university research community, which has become closely affiliated with the biotechnology industry itself, has been relatively quiet in discussions about the broadness of patent claims. One exception is Peter J. Day, the director of the Rutgers, New Jersey, Center for Agricultural Molecular Biology and chair of the National Research Council's committee on managing global agricultural genetic resources. Before going to Rutgers, Day was director of the Plant Breeding Institute in Cambridge, England.

"I think it's perfectly legitimate to patent a particular method of producing transgenic plants," said Day in a recent interview. "What I object to in the Agracetus patent is that it patents any genetically engineered cotton produced by any means whatever. So that means that if someone develops a novel method for genetically engineering plants, including cotton, and they apply it to cotton, say, next year, they are unable to market that genetically engineered cotton without an agreement with Agracetus, because Agracetus have patented the concept of genetically engineered cotton. That, I think, is absurd." Such a patent, he added, would certainly stifle corporate research.

John Barton, a professor at the Stanford University law school and recognized expert on global intellectual property rights, is also concerned about patents of the sort claimed by Agracetus. Barton said in an interview: "I think that kind of patent is a mistake. At the same time, I think that the fact that there are some errors in the way the patent system has been implemented doesn't mean it isn't going to be useful. I do think it's going to be important to build some international arrangements such that patents don't become too powerful as tools of monopolization for the existing major companies."

## More Seats at the Table

Industry tends to think of patents as a matter between the company holding the patent and its competition. Others argue that the discussion about ownership of germplasm actually should involve many more people, including those farmers whose stewardship has kept the plants alive for centuries. Under the utility patent system, farmers and indigenous communities have no formal role unless they can successfully argue that they perfected germplasm that is novel, has utility, and is nonobvious—a most unlikely possibility.

The biotechnology industry considers genes from undomesticated plants, animals, and microorganisms the strategic raw materials for the creation of new agricultural, pharmaceutical, and industrial products. The great majority of these genetic materials exist now in the tropics and other parts of the nonindustrial world. "But these genes are seldom 'raw materials' in the traditional sense because they have been selected, nurtured, and improved by untold numbers of farmers and indigenous peoples over thousands of years," said Hope Shand at the 1994 National Agricultural Biotechnology Council conference "Agricultural Biotechnology and the Public Good." Shand is the research director of the Rural Advancement Foundation International (RAFI) in Pittsboro, North Carolina. RAFI has formally challenged the issuance of broad species patents, including Agracetus's 1994 transgenic soybean patent in Europe.

Organizations in the Southern Hemisphere frequently accuse northern industries of collecting seeds and other germplasm from the traditional centers of genetic diversity (which are concentrated in the South), changing them a bit through plant breeding, and then selling them back to their original curators at an unconscionable markup. Norah Olembo, of the Kenyan Ministry of Science and Technology, put it this way: "What went freely now comes back with a price tag." This objection is widely made whether the collected germplasm comes from farmers' fields, weedy wild relatives of the agricultural crops, foods and medicinal products from forests, or collecting forays into tiny village markets.

Suman Sahai, head of the Gene Campaign, an organization based in New Delhi and dedicated to protecting the genetic resources of the Third World and the rights of its farmers, says: "God didn't give us 'rice' or 'wheat' or 'potato.' There were wild plants in the forests, which forests happened to be located in the tropical countries in the South today. But it was a very concerted effort to convert, refine, breed, select, cross, and create economically valuable crops—food crops, cash crops, everything. Who did all of that work?"

Demands have increased in recent years for greater recognition for the native stewards of germplasm—not only for the varieties they have developed but also for the job they have been doing of conserving it in the face of rapid global overdevelopment and population growth. These demands contributed to the adoption, as part of the 1992 United Nations Conference on Environment and Development, of a Convention on Biological Diversity. The convention is a binding treaty affirming that "the conservation of biological diversity is a common concern of humankind," but it lacks real teeth to support the efforts of farmers and indigenous communities. There are ongoing efforts by nongovernmental organizations and developing countries to counter the treaty's weaknesses (which were largely imposed by the United States and some other industrialized nations) and to make it a force in ensuring intellectual property rights for the less-affluent world.

The point that is frequently made by these advocates is that wild or indigenously cultivated germplasm is just as valuable as finished seed that is used in commercial agriculture. Breeding programs must continue because farmers need ever-new varieties to stand up against changing insect or fungal populations and as farmland spreads to more marginal areas. And those programs, whether they involve classical plant breeding or sophisticated biotechnology, draw constantly upon the unfinished seeds of the Andean slopes, the African savannas, and the tropical peasant's backyard garden. The stewards of this germplasm deserve recompense, say the advocates.

For many in the northern biotechnology community, the arguments for southern compensation are not persuasive. They see a vast difference between finished and wild germplasm. Simon Best, of Zeneca, says: "By and large, wild material historically was

perhaps a small portion of the finished genome of a hybrid family or a varietal family that took 20 or 30 years to develop: hundreds or thousands of man-years.... My view, and I think most people's view, is in reality that the value of the wild material is much less than most people think—and that sort of discrepancy is artificially inflaming the debate right now."

Henry L. Shands, who oversees the USDA's genetic resources program, tends to agree, and he adds that the "ownership" of wild and indigenous germplasm is difficult to pin down. "In the case of agricultural plants," he said in an interview, "there is no country that is not dependent on at least one other country for the genetic resources it grows....

"If you say, 'Well, I own this and you own that,' then I could say, 'Well, you own that but I own this.' We're interdependent. We need to exchange material for our own benefit. It's an 'I win, you win' situation then."

Furthermore, said Shands, "There's nothing that says that [southern farmers] have to buy this material. But farmers are going to buy what yields well."

Meanwhile, to insulate its holdings from potential ownership claims on germplasm, last fall the Consultative Group on International Agricultural Research (CGIAR) placed its enormous genebank collections under the control of the Food and Agriculture Organization (FAO) of the United Nations. CGIAR, which took the action to protect what it often calls "the common heritage of humankind," is a collection of 17 research centers that are situated in the South but receive most of their funding from northern governments and organizations such as the World Bank. Currently, any researcher can request and get seeds from its genebanks.

Now, partly with John Barton's help, the CGIAR centers are exploring the possible use of material transfer agreements to control the use of their germplasm by other interests. Such agreements, which are currently used by many commercial groups, set the rules for transferring genetic material. The US National Cancer Institute (NCI), which annually obtains samples of approximately 6000 plants and marine organisms, has drafted such an agreement that, according to the Institute, "recognizes the need to compensate source country organizations and peoples in the event of commercialization or a drug derived from the organism collected." NCI has signed such agreements with approximately a dozen nations, including Madagascar, Indonesia, Belize, and the Philippines, and with a foundation representing indigenous people who live predominantly in Ecuador. Even in those areas where an agreement has not yet been signed, NCI's four plant and one marine collectors do their work under the terms of the agreement, said an official in NCI's Natural Products Division, and leave copies of the agreement behind.

## A Reward System

Despite industry views on ownership, there is an effort under way to devise a system to reward farmers and indigenous communities for their ongoing contributions to biological diversity. The trick, all agree, lies in ensuring that the rewards actually get to the people who deserve them and do not get filtered out by bureaucracies. There is an even more basic problem of deciding who really made the contributions and deserves the credit. Even agricultural plants in the rich centers of biological diversity have ancestors from foreign lands.

The World Resources Institute (WRI), a Washington policy and research organization, has been studying the problem, particularly in connection with germplasm from tropical countries that is desired by northern pharmaceutical firms. Walter V. Reid, a WRI vice president, says he thinks the "most realistic mechanism" would be to collect royalties. Otherwise, says Reid, "you're going to rely on the good will of governments to return these benefits locally. And that's a big 'if.'" The royalties from germplasm would go to a fund, which would be used to encourage biological conservation by distributing it through networks of nongovernmental organizations that work with local communities.

The framework for such a fund already exists through the Fund for Plant Genetic Resources, which was established in 1987 by the FAO's Commission on Plant Genetic Resources. But contributions to it are voluntary, and they have been minimal.

Another way for the biologically rich nations to take advantage of what they have, thinks Sahai, is to take control of biotechnology itself. "The raw material for biotechnology is in the South," she said during an interview in New Delhi. "The technological expertise is there." (Indeed, research institutions in the southern India city of Bangalore have been hailed as hotbeds of technological brainpower. Both homegrown firms and branches of US corporations have established what many call the Silicon Valley of India.)

"And, most of all, for us there is a very important factor: Unlike all the other technologies so far, this is not a capital-intensive technology. It's a skill-intensive technology. The fact that we have the skilled manpower at very, very competitive costing makes India a potential player in the field of biotechnology. And therefore it becomes even more important for us—and it's always important as an environmental goal— to preserve the resources....

"Because of the advent of biotechnology, the fact is that the most lucrative resource on Earth right now is genetic resources. There are big bucks out there," says Sahai. "Any one who gets control of genetic resources is going to dominate the world economy." ❑

---

## Questions

1. What does genetic manipulation with biotechnology allow researchers to do?

2. How does industry tend to think of patents?

3. What is the single most important factor that has made genetic resources the most lucrative resource on Earth right now?

*Answers are at the back of the book.*

---

# Section Three

# Problems of Environmental Degradation

**28** *The decline of many long-lived species due to the exposure of man-made chemicals is a very serious and alarming problem. Researchers once looked at environmental pollutants only as a carcinogenic threat. Now they are looking at these pollutants as a cause of damage to the reproduction, immunity, behavior, and growth systems of the body. In the mid-seventies, exposure to the chemical DDT seemed to be correlated with an abnormally low number of males in a California gull population. In the early nineties, there were similar findings in alligators at Florida's Lake Apopka. The populations of certain animal species are in decline, but how does this affect the human population? In 1991, an analysis was done of many smaller studies of global human sperm counts over the past 50 years. The sperm count had declined by half between 1940 and 1990. Studies show endometriosis, testicular cancer, and possibly other types of cancers are increasing due to environmental pollutants.*

# The Alarming Language of Pollution
## Daniel Glick

*National Wildlife*, April/May 1995

On California's Channel Islands in the mid-1970s, an ecologist found an abnormally high ratio of female gulls to male gulls. In Florida in the early 1990s, a team of endocrinologists discovered abnormally small penises in alligators near a former Superfund site. And in Great Britain, biochemists have noticed in the last few years that something in wastewater effluent appears to be creating hermaphroditic fish.

Sound like bizarre episodes of *Wild Kingdom?* Actually, these observations are all clues to a far-flung scientific sleuthing saga. Over the last few years, experts from a dozen disciplines have been piecing together field and laboratory evidence that environmental pollutants may be doing far more damage to wildlife and humans than previously suspected, in ways no one had imagined possible. For starters, by sending various false signals to endocrine (or hormonal) systems in the body, pollutants could be harming vertebrate reproduction worldwide. All of this evidence could comprise one of the most alarming messages wildlife has ever sent our way. "If we don't believe that animals in the wild are sentinels for us humans, we're burying our heads in the sand,"

says Linda Birnbaum, director of the environmental toxics division of the Environmental Protection Agency (EPA).

Endocrine-disrupting chemicals are associated with problems ranging from developmental deficiencies in children, to smaller penises in pubescent boys, to infertility. "Every day, I get more concerned," says John McLachlan, chief of the laboratory of reproductive and developmental toxicology at the National Institute of Environmental Health and Science (NIEHS).

Implicated are huge numbers of products—including some pesticides, industrial solvents, adhesives and plastics. A very few, such as PCBs and the pesticide DDT, have been banned or are more heavily regulated in this country than in the past—though they persist in the environment. But thousands have never been regulated. Much of the stuff is deposited worldwide by the atmosphere and has been found in both the Arctic and Antarctica.

Until the last few years, the biggest question for regulators has been: Does a given chemical cause cancer, and if so, at what exposure level? (And very few chemicals have even been tested for carcinogenicity.) Now some researchers are also asking: Does a chemical harm reproduction, immunity, behavior or growth?

Also, regulators have long assumed each chemical to be innocent until proven guilty. But researchers are growing increasingly concerned at evidence that related chemicals may be able to harm the body in similar ways. For example, DDT and dioxins (often commonly referred to in the singular) are members of a group of similar chemicals called organochlorines. They are not to be confused with the chlorine we safely use to disinfect swimming-pool water and bleach our clothes. While DDT is a deliberate product, dioxins are unwanted byproducts of industrial high-temperature use of chlorine.

A 1994 National Wildlife Federation report, *Fertility on the Brink: The Legacy of the Chemical Age*, concluded that there is enough evidence to warrant phaseouts, at the very least, of certain chemicals released into the environment. The list includes dioxins, some pesticides and hexachlorobenzene. Federation counsel Elise Hoerath argues that the problem has become "a significant public health threat."

Others warn that hormonal activity is so complicated and poorly understood that costly action to ban certain chemicals is uncalled for until we know more. "As a citizen, I would like to see some of these chemicals banned," says Carlos Sonneschein, professor of cellular biology at Tufts University School of Medicine. "As a scientist, I would like to have more data."

Still, the data have been steadily adding up, thanks largely to the work of zoologist Theo Colborn, a senior scientist at the World Wildlife Fund and director of its wildlife and contaminants program. In late 1987, Colborn began sifting through studies of declining wildlife populations in the Great Lakes region. On the left side of a piece of paper, she listed species with steep population drops: bald eagle, Forster's tern, double crested cormorant, mink and river otter, among others. On the right, she listed their health problems, including organ damage, eggshell thinning, hormonal changes and low birth survival rates.

Each of the animals depended on a fish diet. Fish in the notoriously polluted Great Lakes were known to contain high concentrations of various synthetic chemicals, especially in fatty tissue, and Colborn wondered if the pollutants were causing the disorders. Were toxics tinkering with the immunity, behavior, growth or behavior of fish eaters? Colborn began searching the scientific literature. "I was really concerned," she recalls. "It was very obvious that these chemicals were developmental toxicants." Yet for the most part, testing had only looked for cancer. "We've been blinded," she says. "We never tested for developmental effects."

Even so, some studies did find those effects. Researchers had found in the mid-1970s that exposure to DDT seemed to be correlated with an abnormally low number of males in a California gull population. In the late 1970s, toxicologist Michael Fry of the University of California at Davis was able to cause "feminization" of male gull embryos (they developed abnormal testes containing ovarian tissue) in his lab by injecting uncontaminated eggs with DDT.

Many years later, in the early 1990s, University of Florida comparative endocrinologist Louis Guillette started finding similar problems in alligators at Florida's Lake Apopka. The area was a former Superfund site that had been contaminated in 1980 with the chemical dicofol, an organochlorine that also contained some DDT. The lake also contained a mix of agricultural chemicals from farm runoff.

Working with colleague Timothy Gross and other researchers, Guillette found that alligator eggs were barely hatching, teenage males had abnormally small penises and the level of the male hormone testosterone was far below normal. Later, Guillette conferred with a researcher who had produced remarkably similar results in lab rats by exposing them to a compound similar to DDE, a breakdown product of DDT. "Oh my God," Guillette said after seeing the data. "I think we have a major problem here."

As Colborn compiled evidence from wildlife biologists, toxicologists and the medical literature, she realized that other scientists were asking some of the same questions. So, in 1991, she helped bring a group of them together to compare notes for the first time. After another meeting last year in Washington, D.C., 23 wildlife biologists agreed that "populations of many long-lived species are declaring.... Some of these declines are related to exposure to man-made chemicals and their effects on the development of embryos."

Their reasoning is based on the knowledge that sex differentiation is determined by tiny amounts of male and female hormones interacting in the developing fetus. Contrary to what we've all been taught in introductory biology classes, animals do not exhibit male or female traits simply because they possess or lack a Y chromosome. If a hormone impostor shows up during fetal development, sexual function can go akimbo. "Very, very low levels of contaminants can have an effect on developing embryos," says the University of Florida's Guillette. "A dose that wouldn't bother an adult can be catastrophic to an embryo."

Soon after Fry's discovery that DDT injections could "feminize" gull eggs, biologist David Crews of the University of Texas discovered in 1984 that he could control the gender of slider turtles with minute quantities of the female hormone estradiol. For many turtles, the temperature of the eggs' environment determines gender. Heat produces a female; cold yields a male. But in the lab, Crews could coax embryos incubating at a male-producing temperature to become female with just a drop of estradiol on the eggs.

Estradiol is an estrogen, and Crews' study fits a scary pattern. A number of synthetic substances are so-called "environmental estrogens," acting like the hormone Crews used to bend the turtles gender. In recent work, he and colleagues have found they can create sexually mixed-up turtles with "cocktail" mixtures of certain PCB compounds. Some of the turtles have testes and oviducts. Others have ovaries but no oviduct. Most alarming, these effects occurred at extremely low doses. Somehow, the combination of several PCBs is far more disrupting than one PCB compound alone.

Of course, not all estrogens are bad; when they occur naturally, they play critical roles in the body. Deliberate therapeutic doses even help women through and beyond menopause, in part by protecting bone density and cardiac health. Environmental estrogens, however, are a different story. NIEHS researcher McLachlan, who calls estrogen the "Earth Mother of hormones," has shown that certain chemicals can bind to or block estrogen receptors, which may in turn cause developmental deviations.

Think of the estrogen receptor as a lock on a cell, and natural estrogen as a perfect key. Scientists believe that literally hundreds of compounds have a chemical structure that also fits the lock—and which could produce similar responses. But then, these chemicals may "fit" into estrogen receptors without producing the cascade of cellular events that follow exposure to actual estrogen—and no harm may be done. Still, even if that's so, when the impostor key is in the lock, the real key may not be able to enter.

Since the number of chemicals that fit into the estrogen lock, or receptor, are so numerous, no one can clarify all the effects of these multiple exposures. "If there are so many estrogens out there, how can anybody figure out which one is doing what?" asks Thomas Goldsworthy of the Chemical Industries Institute of Toxicology. "Some of the mechanisms aren't clear yet."

Some of the effects, however, are becoming clearer. Toxicologists Earl Gray and Bill Kelce of the EPA reported last year that the common fungicide vinclozolin, used on many fruits and vegetables, can block receptors for the male hormone androgen and cause sexual damage in male rats. At certain doses, rats exposed to vinclozolin do not develop normal male traits even though they do produce testosterone. At high exposures, male rats develop severely abnormal genitalia. Gray thinks fruit treated with the fungicide does not contain enough residue to harm humans, but he is looking into the question. And he is sure of one thing: "There are clearly other environmental anti-androgens we haven't discovered yet," he says.

The findings of field work like Guillette's and laboratory analysis like Gray's have been bolstered by studies of inadvertent human exposures to endocrine-disrupting compounds. In 1979, women in Taiwan who ate rice oil contaminated with polychlorinated biphenyls (PCBs) and polychlorinated dibenzofurans (PCDFs) offered an ideal if tragic laboratory to track long-term effects in humans. Researchers have followed 118 children of the women and an identically sized control group. Members of the exposed group have suffered developmental delays, growth retardation and slightly lower IQs. Many of the boys, who are now reaching puberty, have abnormally small penises.

Between the 1940s and 1970s, diesthylstilbestrol, or DES, was given to an estimated two million to six million women during pregnancy to help prevent miscarriage. In children of DES mothers, the drug caused a range of developmental and health problems, some of which only surfaced in the process of creating the next generation. Among males, researchers have noted abnormalities in scrotums, an unusually high prevalence of undescended testicles and decreased sperm counts. Among DES daughters, clinical problems include organ dysfunction, reduction in fertility, immune-system disorders and other difficulties.

The DES example leads to an alarming hypothesis: If some endocrine-disrupting pollutants act like DES, which had effects long after birth, perhaps we won't see the consequences until exposed offspring themselves begin trying to have kids. And that raises the question: What actual harm to humans have scientists found from exposure to the sea of chemicals released into the environment over the past 50 years?

Enter Niels Skakkebaek, a Danish researcher in Copenhagen. In 1991, he published a meta-analysis of many smaller studies of global human sperm counts over the past half century and found that the counts declined by half between 1940 and 1990. Other more recent European studies sought to disprove Skakkebaek's results, but ended up corroborating them. If sperm counts have indeed dropped, one clue to the reason may come from lab tests in which estrogen-mimicking compounds have affected the Sertoli cell, which is related to sperm production.

Research has also implicated environmental toxics in the rise of endometriosis, testicular cancer and possibly other cancers as well in recent decades. In one study that went on for 15 years, 79 percent of a rhesus monkey colony exposed to dioxin developed endometriosis (the development of endometrial tissue in females in places it is not normally present).

Dioxin is not thought to imitate estrogen, but is clearly an endocrine disrupter in at least some animals. In the monkeys, the endometriosis increased in severity in proportion to the amount of dioxin exposure.

What should the rest of society do while the researchers compare notes? "The tough call isn't for the scientists now," says Devra Lee Davis, a top scientific advisor at the U.S. Department of Health and Human Services. "It's for the regulators." There are signs that the federal government is beginning to pay heed. In the EPA draft dioxin reassessment report, now under review, dioxin is characterized as a potent toxic "producing a wide range of effects at very low levels when compared to other environmental contaminants."

The International Joint Commission, a bilateral organization that advises on environmental issues along the U.S.-Canada border, has repeatedly called for virtual elimination of toxic substances in the Great Lakes region. And a little-noticed amendment to the Clean Water Act proposed by the Clinton administration (the reauthorization died in the last Congress) would have required regulators to look at "impairments to reproductive, endocrine and immune systems as a result of water pollution." Even skeptic Goldsworthy of the Chemical Industries Institute of Toxicology says, "We are changing our environment. There's no question about that."

The World Wildlife Fund's Colborn says she welcomes scientific skepticism and even has days when she hopes she is imagining the whole thing. "We admit there are weaknesses, because we are never going to be able to show simple cause-and-effect relationships," she says of the complicated theory. Still, she adds, "The research has reached a point where you can't ignore it any more, and new evidence is coming in every week." For visitors to her Washington, D.C., office, Colborn lets a pesticide manufacturer have the last word: On the wall hangs a 1950s label from a one-pound package of a substance called DuraDust, 50 percent of which was pure DDT. The label promises, "Its killing power endures." ❏

## Questions

1. How might pollutants be harming vertebrate reproduction?

2. What determines gender in turtles?

3. What potent toxic does the EPA characterize as "producing a wide range of effects at very low levels"?

*Answers are at the back of the book.*

**29** *People like to live by the water, but they seldom stop to consider the negative environmental effects modern technology can have on the natural landscape. The Chesapeake Bay is an example of an overpopulated shoreline. There are too many people, cars, houses, and farms competing for the disappearing resources. Both scientists and the state and federal governments are working on a plan called "Sustainable Chesapeake." One of the designated tasks will be to estimate the carrying capacity of the Chesapeake Bay area. They will also assess what will be needed to maintain healthy forests, duck populations, and crab and oyster stocks. Policy options for the area will be explored. If the Chesapeake Bay can be recovered, the largest estuary in the country could also become the most productive.*

# Holding the World at Bay
## Susan Pollack

*Sierra*, May/June 1996

*A fisherman and a scientist struggle to save America's largest estuary.*

Larry Simns anchors his white workboat and re-baits his fishing lines. Now that the diesel engines are shut off, the upper Chesapeake is quiet this late October afternoon. A flock of honking Canada geese breaks the silence as it darkens the sky, then descends to a nearby salt marsh. The low sun paints water and sky a creamy red. Were it not for a view of the sleek twin-spanned bridge that carries thousands of people to Maryland's Eastern Shore each day, you might think that you were seeing the same Chesapeake celebrated by 17th-century explorers.

An intense, wiry man with weathered good looks, Simns has an Eastern Shore accent derived from the region's first English settlers. "Arstering, clamming, fishing, that's all I ever done or wanted to do," he tells me. He lifts a fishing rod from its metal holder at the stern and plucks the line with his forefinger, feeling for a bite. There is none. Simns ducks behind the wheelhouse to put a bluefish on ice in the cooler. He moves about the boat with the assurance he learned as a child working with his great-grandfather. He would row while the old man tonged for oysters and scooped squirming crabs into the boat

with a dip net. That was a half century ago—when no one worried about how many people could live in the Chesapeake's 64,000-square-mile drainage basin without suffocating and poisoning the bay and depleting its oysters, crabs, and other natural resources.

A fish tugs at Simns' line. He knows from the quick jerk that it's a striped bass. The powerful fish corkscrews as Simns reels it out of the water to the side of the boat.

Not long ago, Simns' hook would have come up empty. The East Coast's biggest striped bass population was nearly wiped out here in the late 1970s and early 1980s. It took a fishing ban and baywide cleanup to begin to restore the popular sport and commercial species, known locally as rockfish.

But the cleanup has not kept pace with the impacts of human population growth. Stocks of many other fish and shellfish in the bay have dwindled or collapsed and the estuary itself is in deep trouble. The Chesapeake's celebrated oyster crop has been ravaged by disease, pollution, and overfishing. This single fishery once provided a quarter of America's oysters, but may soon become a memory, as may the skipjacks, 100-year-old wooden boats that dredge for oysters under sail.

Years ago, shad swarmed here, but they, too, are almost gone, victims of overharvesting and dams that block their migration to spawning grounds on Chesapeake tributaries. Herring stocks have ebbed. Soft-shelled clams are scarce. Deep-water areas of the bay are oxygen-starved in the summer, and the bay's bottom grasses, so vital to marine life, have all but disappeared. With them have vanished many of the estuary's wildfowl—the redheads and American wigeons that nested here when Simns was growing up. The world's major source of blue crabs could be at risk if fishing pressure here increases.

For Simns, the dwindling of the once fecund Chesapeake is a bitter disappointment. He has spent the past 35 years battling to protect the interests of the watermen (the local term for the fishing community), and has successfully fought off harmful sewer projects, the dumping of contaminated dredge spoils, and the siting of a nuclear-power plant on rockfish spawning grounds. He also helped establish Maryland's first wetlands protection act. The 58-year-old Simns is a pragmatic, conservative Democrat, and an upholder of the small-town American values espoused by the Methodist Church, the backbone of Eastern Shore towns like his native Rock Hall. He also knows how to play the political game. As president of the Maryland Watermen's Association, he shares crab cakes with the governor at summer festivals and he's groomed younger watermen to follow him into state politics.

Simns is an optimist, committed to seeing things improve. Yet he confides that he is worried. "It's getting harder and harder to make a living on the bay," he says. "Younger people are moving away, leaving the communities they grew up in." Instead of earning a living oystering as he normally does each fall, Simns has been reduced to guiding parties of recreational anglers.

As the bay's resources shrink, watermen themselves have come under attack for overfishing species such as oysters and shad. But Simns insists that they are the bay's best defense against pollution. "Without watermen, who navigate every river, creek, and marsh, there won't be anyone who knows or cares enough to save the bay," he says.

It's easy for watermen to point the finger at Baltimore's belching smokestacks across the bay.

Although steel mills, chemical plants, and paint factories are some of the culprits, responsibility for the bay's decline is more widespread. Watermen like Simns learned from firsthand observation what scientists are now confirming: the Chesapeake is sinking under the pressure of too much human activity. There are too many cars, too many houses, too many farms, and too many people vying for diminishing resources.

Simns' commercial perspective almost mirrors that of the ecologists: "With his increasing population and wasteful practices, man is destroying the habitat that the bay's seafood depends on."

• • •

The Chesapeake's British discoverer, John Smith, marveled in 1612: "Heaven and earth have never agreed better to frame a place." Nearly 300 years later, journalist H.L. Mencken called the Chesapeake an "immense protein factory." America's largest estuary, it could also be our most productive, given half a chance. Although the Chesapeake is long—200 miles from its head in Maryland at Havre de Grace, north of Rock Hall, to its mouth near Norfolk, Virginia—its average depth is only 20 feet. Life for many marine species begins in its salt marshes, where microscopic organisms feed tiny fish and shellfish. These wetlands attract ducks, geese, and swans, making them a haven for birders and hunters. Even more important, wetlands are working to clean up the bay; they purify the water as they soak up both sediment and contaminants.

But the nutrients that feed the bay can also destroy it. Right now the estuary is fighting a losing battle against nitrogen and phosphorus, which come mostly from sewage, manure, farm and lawn fertilizer runoff, auto exhaust, and power plant emissions. Excessive quantities of these nutrients are encouraging too much algae to bloom, which depletes the bay's oxygen. The algae also prevents the sun from reaching valuable bottom grasses. Low oxygen and traces of toxic chemicals may have made the bay's oysters more vulnerable to MSX and Dermo, two diseases that are reducing the already diminished oyster crop. (See "The Oyster Is Our World," *Sierra,* September/October 1995.) A slight increase in the estuary's salinity since 1981 caused by unusually dry spring and summer weather ignited these diseases, which are now as severe as the blights that devastated America's chestnut and elm trees.

As the oysters die, the bay is losing a critical natural filter. Oysters remove silt and plankton as they pump water through their systems. An adult can filter 50 gallons of water a day. A century ago, when Mencken was young, the bay's oyster population was so large that it was able to filter the equivalent of nearly all the water in the bay in a matter of days. Now, with the population reduced to one percent of what it was in its heyday, it takes a year to filter the same amount. Harvests of Chesapeake oysters, which peaked at 15 million bushels a year in the 1880s, held steady at 2 million all through Simns' early fishing years, but have since dropped to fewer than 100,000 bushels, causing some scientists to call for a harvest ban to protect what's left of the diminishing brood stock.

What happens along the bay's shores in Maryland and Virginia is not the whole Chesapeake story. Some of the problems occur hundreds of miles away. The watershed that feeds the Chesapeake starts as far north as New York's Cooperstown of baseball fame; it follows the Susquehanna River, the bay's major freshwater source, and includes Baltimore, Washington, D.C., and Richmond, which together form one of the nation's most heavily developed urban corridors. Like a big sponge, the Chesapeake absorbs pollutants from hundreds of miles of land connecting the bay and its many tributaries. Manure from dairy, pig, and poultry farms in Lancaster County, Pennsylvania, sewage from a leaky pipe in upstate New York, lawn fertilizers from the Philadelphia suburbs, road runoff from Baltimore, and auto exhaust from Washington, D.C., all end up in the bay.

The Chesapeake story is not unique. Around the United States, other estuaries suffer from the strains of too many people. Once-bountiful Long Island Sound has been choked by New York City and Westchester County sewage effluent. In Puget Sound, flatfish like English sole are afflicted with liver tumors possibly caused by chronic exposure to hydrocarbons used in industrial manufacturing. Salmon, once abundant in San Francisco Bay, have been severely depleted by the diversion of huge volumes of fresh water to irrigate San Joaquin Valley farms and supply water to the Los Angeles basin.

Nevertheless, the American population continues to flock to the coasts. Today, half of the people of the United States live along the Atlantic or Pacific, the Gulf of Mexico, or the Great Lakes. That number is expected to increase to 75 percent in the next 25 years. Worldwide, two-thirds of the population live along coastlines. By the year 2025, the United Nations predicts that more than 6 billion people will be coastal dwellers, 300 billion more than the current world population. The impacts could be devastating, not only on fish and shellfish, but on forests, air, and water.

Simns has watched as the population in the Chesapeake watershed has mushroomed from 8 million in the 1950s to nearly 15 million people. By the year 2020, that population is predicted to increase by another 2.6 million.

Simns' hometown of Rock Hall is beginning to suffer from a development boom that is sweeping the Annapolis side of the bay. Waterfront condominiums and vacation and retirement homes are driving up real-estate prices, squeezing out the younger generation. The cheapest single-family house available in a new subdivision is $99,000, more than ten times what Larry Simns paid for his first home. Simns' son, Robert, 28, moved out of town to find work and affordable housing elsewhere.

The morning after our fishing trip, I climb into Simns' pickup for a brief tour. We drive along the windswept harbor road past condominiums and restaurants. Simns stops longest to point out a place that's no longer there. Hubbard's Pier was razed a few years ago to make way for a new 75-boat marina. People once came there to get news of the bay. Watermen in knee-high rubber boots drank coffee from white porcelain mugs as they exchanged weather reports and news about rockfish prices. Some sold the oysters and rockfish they'd caught, while anglers from Washington, D.C., and Philadelphia cradled six-packs and fishing rods and booked charters. On winter days, as spray crashed over the breakwater, the talk got livelier, the tales taller. But when the bay's natural resources began to collapse, Hubbard's owner sold out. So did the two fish businesses next door. A crab processing operation was replaced by a restaurant, and the harbor's only ice plant shut down. Today only one seafood processing plant survives.

Simns' pickup whizzes past the farm fields and salt marshes where he once worked as a duck hunting guide. Much of the marshland is now protected as the Eastern Neck Island National Wildlife Refuge. Eastern Shore farmers have cut back fertilizer use. Even so, their picture-postcard farms are still polluting the bay. And the building boom continues. A new sewer connection will allow over a hundred additional houses to be built on fields stretching from the Chester River to the bay. Gesturing at fields of soybeans, corn, and jewel-green alfalfa, Simns says, "You won't recognize this place in another decade."

Simns knows that more people mean trouble. But, while he supports laws such as Maryland's decade-old Critical Areas Act (which restricts development within 1,000 feet of the shore), he sees no way to curb population growth in the watershed. "You can't stop population," he says. "Only the good lord can stop population."

• • •

But some people think the good lord needs a helping hand. "Scratch any environmental problem and you'll find it has something to do with population," says Ed DeBellevue of the University of Maryland's Chesapeake Biological Laboratory as we hike along the hilly western shore. The sweet smell of leaf mold fills the woods that an October rain has washed clean. We pass brilliant red oak, sycamores, and sweet gum with its star-shaped leaves. DeBellevue spots a red-bellied woodpecker in a tulip poplar and pauses to listen to the trill of a Carolina wren. But the 46-year-old, white-haired ecologist has more on his mind than trees and birds. A longtime Audubon Society activist, DeBellevue is now working with the Sierra Club to rescue the Chesapeake from strangling population growth.

Birding was DeBellevue's pathway to environmental activism. Over the years he's seen many of his favorite birding spots fall to development. His activism is also driven by a childhood experience: in Florida at age eight he watched bulldozers destroy a pond where he had listened to bullfrogs and collected turtles and snakes. Years later, he successfully fought another plan to pave over a wildlife sanctuary at the University of Florida for a traffic circle. *The Population Bomb* by Paul Ehrlich gave him a global view of what he had seen firsthand during Florida's development boom. It raised the specter of the world's population outstripping the ability of natural resources to support it. "Had we started taking the population threat seriously when Ehrlich published his book in 1968," DeBellevue says, "we'd have less damage to undo today, both globally and locally. The longer we wait the more dire the situation becomes."

"We still act as if the earth's resources are inexhaustible," DeBellevue points out. "Or that we can just move on. When the potato famine struck Ireland in the 1840s, the Irish came to America. Under Dust Bowl conditions in the 1930s, farmers moved west. But today there are no new frontiers. We can't settle in the desert, because there's no water. Alaska costs an arm and a leg to heat. We can't continue clearcutting the rainforest because we'll lose valuable genetic information that's found nowhere else."

Few people realize how what happens on land affects the water. "Just as wetlands filter out toxic substances, trees absorb carbon dioxide and give off fresh oxygen," DeBellevue says. "For every acre of forest we develop, we lose oxygen, clean water, timber, and animals that lived in the forest." Yet forests, wetlands, and farmland in the Chesapeake watershed are being gobbled up at a rate of 140 square miles a year, an area five times the size of Baltimore. Per-capita use of land in the watershed is four times greater today than in 1950.

"There may be no such thing as a doomsday," DeBellevue says. "It's more likely there's a doomscentury, a dooms-era, where life gradually becomes intolerable. With overpopulation, we may be starting to face such a dooms-century on the Chesapeake now."

Some bay observers are more sanguine. "Population per se is not a threat if we can keep pushing technology," argues Bill Matuszeski, director of the U.S. Environmental Protection Agency's Chesapeake office, which is coordinating a cooperative federal/state restoration effort. A key goal is reducing nitrogen and phosphorus discharges into the bay 40 percent by the year 2000. Currently phosphorus reductions are on schedule due largely to a baywide ban on phosphate detergents, but nitrogen reductions are behind, partly because only a handful of communities in the watershed have installed nitrogen removal equipment. The trouble is, such technological fixes tend to be very expensive.

"Encouraging developers to curb suburban sprawl by clustering new housing and commercial building will help mitigate the impacts of population growth," DeBellevue says. "So will recycling, reducing the amount of sewage we put in the water, and reducing the fishery take. But none of these remedies will completely solve the problem. The only foreseeable solution is to reduce population growth."

DeBellevue does not go so far as to advocate government-imposed limits on population or family size, although he strongly supports efforts to make birth control and family planning available to all Americans. He would like to see Congress amend the tax laws so that they no longer encourage Americans to have large families. But, like most people in his community, he does not advocate barring newcomers.

After all, DeBellevue himself is a transplant. Six years ago he moved to suburban Calvert County, one of the fastest-growing counties in the United States. He believes "Americans should be able to live wherever they choose, provided they pay the full environmental costs of living in that region." Right now, he says, Chesapeake residents "are not paying these full costs. They are deferring them onto the future."

DeBellevue's solution to the population growth dilemma is rooted in ecological economics. The key is environmental-impact fees. For example, developers could shoulder their environmental costs by paying a fee for the water and air pollution problems they cause, giving them an economic incentive to lessen the damages. Individuals could be charged for the number of bags they bring to the dump, rather than paying an across-the-board dump fee as part of a local property tax. "The idea is to provide an incentive to reduce trash and to recycle," DeBellevue says. On another front, the manufacturers of mer-

cury thermometers could be required to pay the full costs of disposing of that toxic element. This fee would be passed on to the consumer, possibly making the mercury thermometer more expensive than a digital one, and encouraging more environmentally sound technology. Meanwhile, residents could pay a higher impact fee for purchasing an item such as lawn fertilizer based on the cost of its damage to the ecosystem.

DeBellevue is now helping to coordinate research for a new Sierra Club project aimed at determining how to keep the Chesapeake watershed in good ecological health. He'll be working with a team of scientists from academia and the state and federal governments to develop a "Sustainable Chesapeake" research agenda. Already on the list of tasks is determining the region's carrying capacity—that is, how many people can live in the Chesapeake region over a long period of time without depleting the ecosystem. "We need to be able to calculate the costs of adding more people to an already stressed watershed," DeBellevue says. Researchers will estimate harvest levels needed to maintain healthy forests, duck populations, and crab and oyster stocks. They will also study the costs of cleanup and how to conserve clean air and water. Later Sustainable Chesapeake's coordinators will invite planners, civic leaders, business people, and other residents to help explore and promote those policy options—whether clustered development, family planning, or impact fees—that hold the most promise for Chesapeake renewal.

• • •

In Calvert County, former State Senator Bernie Fowler wades up to his waist in the Patuxent River every June to test whether he can see down to his toes as he did when he was a young man in the 1950s. Fowler has been doing this nearly 20 years— ever since the first alerts were sounded about the Chesapeake—and he plans to continue his ritual until the bay is clean once again. Last year, DeBellevue accompanied the senator and a hundred other people. The water was so cloudy they could not see their toes. But DeBellevue does not give up hope. "If everyone who lives in the watershed takes responsibility for achieving sustainable communities, then in our lifetime we'll be able to see our toes again," he says.

It is unlikely we'll ever again know the bountiful bay that John Smith praised in the early 1600s or that H. L. Mencken applauded almost 300 years later. But the Chesapeake could be restored to the health that both Larry Simns and Bernie Fowler knew as children.

Walking on the edge of a lush marsh that Saturday afternoon, where the land meets the sea, DeBellevue reflects: "We need to reduce total consumption and total population. There are only so many trees, so many fish, so many molecules of oxygen, droplets of fresh water, only so much land. Every time another person is born, the slices of the pie get smaller." ❑

---

**Questions**

1. What is considered the natural filter of the Chesapeake Bay?

2. How do wetlands clean the bay?

3. How does the Chesapeake act as a sponge?

*Answers are at the back of the book.*

---

*It has taken centuries for the planet to become overwhelmed with pollution. Unfortunately, most of the pollution winds up in the ocean. Up until the sixties, experts thought that the only way to control pollution was to harness its expansion, treat polluted areas chemically, or remove the contaminated material and place it elsewhere. Removing contaminated material from the ocean is impractical. However, microbiologists have discovered that some microorganisms can degrade petroleum pollutants. The capacity of microbes to break down, eliminate, or isolate pollutants from the environment is called bioremediation. Perhaps it will be the tool of the future for solving the world's pollution problems.*

# Sorcerers of the Sea
## Elizabeth Pennisi

*BioScience*, April 1996

*Making microbes do our dirty work.*

The dream of any company saddled with pollution control regulations and of any environmentalist overwhelmed by present levels of contamination would be to wake up and find that nature had magically taken care of tidying up the damage. Such is the promise of bioremediation, the use of the metabolic and concentrating capabilities of microbes to break down, remove, or sequester pollutants from the environment.

Until 30 years ago, most experts thought that the best they could do was contain the spread of pollution, physically remove contaminated material, or treat it chemically. Then microbiologists began realizing that microorganisms can degrade petroleum pollutants. They noted that some bacteria could take chlorine off chlorinated hydrocarbon compounds so those too could "disappear." Other species, including some plants, took up and concentrated heavy metals, making it possible to remove these from the environment. Some microorganisms are so diverse and adaptable they seem capable of evolving abilities to deal with almost any toxic substance. Like invisible sorcerers, they work their magic, cleaning up oil spills and ridding mud of the worst poisons.

Because of these microbial talents, bioremediation promises environmentally friendly, energy-efficient, and cost-effective cleanup. This potential has set off a worldwide search by both academic and entrepreneurs for atypical microbial consumers—those that can metabolize organic pollutants, process toxic substances, or concentrate heavy metals. The hope is that even if the organisms themselves do not make their way into commercial application, then perhaps their genes will. Some innovative researchers plan to combine genetic material from several organisms to customize bacteria for particular jobs. "Everybody's promising a magic bullet," says Kenneth Nealson of the University of Wisconsin in Milwaukee.

### Pressing Need for Marine Bioremediators
For much of bioremediation's 25-year history, most US researchers in the field have been scouring contaminated soils, and to a lesser extent polluted fresh water, for bioremediation candidates. "We know so much about [soil bacteria]," says Nealson. But with three-quarters of Earth's surface as ocean, and parts of it extremely dirty, an enterprising few microbiologists (many of them supported in part by the US Navy) have begun tapping the degradation potential of saltwater species.

The need for bioremediation in marine environments is critical because the oceans are the ultimate sink for most pollution. Toxic materials settle into them from the atmosphere, or they flow into coastal bays and estuaries from ground and surface waterways.

Nutrient overload, sewage, metals, and synthetic organic compounds are viewed as some of the worst threats to the marine environment, says Sabine E. Apitz at the Remediation Research Laboratory in the Marine Environment Division at the Naval Command, Control and Ocean Surveillance Center in San Diego, California. Pesticides, polycyclic aromatic hydrocarbons (PAHs), and polychlorinated biphenyls (PCBs) are among the most worrisome because they persist and have accumulated on the ocean floor.

"One of the biggest [pollution] problems is marine sediments," explains Bradley M. Tebo of the Scripps Institution of Oceanography in San Diego, California. "They are inherently different from [terrestrial] soils." Undersea "soils" are less amenable to study, and they have different properties and different flora and fauna. Yet from these muds, pollutants gain access to the food chain, gradually working up the chain and concentrating in whales and dolphins and in seafoods that humans consume either directly or indirectly. Even pollution that was once buried can become hazardous again because of dredging or other disturbances.

But terrestrial microbes are not adapted to marine conditions and so cannot be used readily to clean up this environment. What is needed are salt water-adapted marine species, with enzyme systems that can process toxic compounds or concentrate metals even in anaerobic environments. Furthermore, ocean species may possess a range of useful capabilities not found in terrestrial species. Genetic engineers envision adding some of those capabilities to improve on terrestrial microbial workhorses.

### Searching for Seagoing Bioremediators

Scientists already know that some bacteria, fungi, and algae can break down certain pollutants, particularly in environments where oxygen is present (*BioScience* 45: 332-338). But marine sediments often lack oxygen, making anaerobic processing necessary. So the hunt is on for anaerobes that can do what bioremediating aerobes do, but through chemical pathways that do not require the use of oxygen.

Scientists are using sophisticated genetic probes to try to find the anaerobic microbes they need. For example, Kevin R. Sowers, of the Center of Marine Biotechnology (COMB) in Baltimore, Maryland, is using polymerase chain reaction technology to probe PCB-laced sediment samples from coastal regions near Maryland, South Carolina, and California for signs of bacteria capable of breaking down the contaminant. (PCBs, because of their hydrophobic nature, tend to be ensconced in oxygen-free sediments and are sometimes degraded, but no one knows how or by what.)

If any PCB degraders are discovered, Sowers hopes to isolate them and study how they process these contaminants. Then, as these molecular mechanisms become known, genetic engineers can begin to tinker with the genes involved to improve on nature's work, creating living "scrubbers" that can break down PCBs more efficiently and under a wider variety of conditions.

Russell T. Hill, also of COMB, is searching for a different type of microorganism. He has been surveying a groups of filamentous bacteria called Actinomycetes. Most Actinomycetes are found on land; they are known for their ability to make antibiotics and other biologically active compounds. But Hill has found some marine Actinomycetes in Baltimore's Inner Harbor that have evolved ways to survive in the presence of toxic heavy metals such as cadmium, cobalt, copper, and mercury. Hill is working to understand the molecular basis for this tolerance, with the ultimate goal of possibly transferring it genetically to other microorganisms that must survive in the presence of these metals as they degrade other contaminants.

At Scripps, Tebo looks for microbes that tolerate toxic heavy metals and are capable of consolidating these toxins. Several non-marine examples are in use already. In sewage treatment, microorganisms help detoxify activated sludge by gathering up heavy metals. These "sludge-scrubbing" microbes make extracellular polymers whose charged surfaces attract and trap metal particles, which can then be filtered from the sludge. Other types of bacteria take in metals and then, through intracellular chemical reactions, make them volatile—as in the case of mercury. And still others accumulate metals in different parts of their cells. In each instance, the microbes immobilize the metal and concentrate it enough that it can be separated from other material, Tebo says.

Tebo finds that sulfate-reducing anaerobes are showing the most promise for the metal-immobilizing task in marine environments. *Desulfovibrio desulfuricans*, for instance, can make a variety of metal sulfides. Thus, dissolved ions of silver, mercury, tin, manganese, iron, nickel, or aluminum become insoluble metal sulfides. The metal-laden bacterial become paramagnetic or ferromagnetic, which makes it easy to separate them from the remaining bacteria and sediments by a process called high-gradient magnetic separation, Tebo explains. He is working with a company that has commercialized this approach. This technology has been used to remove mercury from contaminated industrial effluent and to remove radioactive sediments located near a nuclear reprocessing plant on the Irish Sea. Tests in the Irish Sea indicate that this approach could remove up to 90% of the radioactivity released into seawater, Tebo reports.

Another marine bacterium, the *Bacillus* species strain SG-1, makes spores that oxidize manganese, Tebo says. These spores also can bind to several other metals, including cobalt, zinc, iron, and cadmium, even when these metals exist in low concentrations. Because spores are resistant to heat, sunlight, toxic chemicals, detergents, and other substances, they may prove useful in a variety of environments and may even be recyclable, he suggests. Thus, Tebo envisions that the spores could be dumped into a polluted site and collected when they are laden with metal oxides: The metals would then be recovered from the spores and the spores reused again.

Studies indicate, too, that a protein on the spore surface catalyzes the precipitation of these metals. By altering this protein genetically, researchers may be able to enhance or customize the spore's bioremediating properties.

### No Superbugs
These discoveries have barely tapped the diversity of marine organisms. And the potential of improving on nature using molecular biology has excited many researchers interested in using bioremediation to solve the world's pollution problems.

But similar quests for cures for cancer, AIDS, and other diseases have shown that magic bullets are hard to come by. For one, laboratory results do not really tell how well the bioremediation will work in nature. Moreover, regulations still preclude widespread use of genetically engineered microorganisms.

"It isn't going to be one bacterium that's going to work against everything. Each one will have its little narrow place," Nealson predicts.

"Any search for a 'super' bug is missing a key point," adds Ronald M. Atlas from the University of Louisville in Kentucky. "In most cases, you're usually using a mixture of organisms."

### Suitable Working Conditions
Atlas believes that to carry out a particular cleanup operation, the microorganisms doing the job probably should be sought in the polluted site. That is where the microbes are most likely to have already evolved the ability to handle a particular toxin. For example, branched hydrocarbons typically are broken down more slowly than unbranched alkanes. Yet in Prince William Sound, the branched molecules called pristane and phytane disappear quickly. Apparently millions of years of terpene-loaded pine sap dripping into this sound have helped select for bacteria well equipped to digest these complex hydrocarbons, says Atlas.

To Atlas, bioremediation means creating the right conditions for the residents to do their job effectively—basically "modifying an environment to favor individual microorganisms," he explains. Consider petroleum, which includes a mix of hydrocarbons of varying complexities. The properties of each mixture and the makeup of the local ecosystem affect how fast degradation occurs, he notes. For example, microorganisms capable of degrading petroleum are ubiquitous in the ocean, but their productivity is often limited by the amounts of fixed nitrogen, phosphorous, and oxygen available.

Spills off of Brittany, France, degrade quickly, not only because exposure to ballast has selected for organisms with oil-eating abilities, but also because waves keep the water well aerated, and agricultural fertilizer runoff provides other nutrients. Thus, even though many companies have begun commercializing cultures for seeding polluted sites, it may often make more sense to fertilize or aerate contaminated waters than to inoculate them with new microorganisms, Atlas points out.

Indeed, in bioremediation's most visible success story, the whitening of rocks darkened after the *Exxon Valdez* spill was achieved in part by applying fertilizer to these areas. Scientists were able to speed up biodegradation three to five times.

But it remains hard to extrapolate results of laboratory experiments to the much more complicated and variable real world. Apitz calls for more long-term field studies that will help scientists understand how pollutants move through marine ecosystems and become available to organisms.

Just how toxic and persistent are these contaminating substances? Many factors—temperature, salinity, pH, toxicity, the types and density of organisms present, even the amount of current or type of sediment—can affect degradation, Apitz says. Interactions on a microscopic level also matter. Thus, no one is really able to predict the rate of decontamination at a particular site or even how well a certain remediation approach will work. Bioremediation efforts need to incorporate advances being made in basic sediment biogeochemistry, she argues.

### Science of Marine Bioremediation

Yet there is hope, Apitz adds. For years, chemical oceanographers, geochemists, and marine ecologists have been studying the cycling of carbon, phosphorus, and other substances through the environment. Their knowledge can help environmental engineers understand what is happening chemically in contaminated sediments.

In her experiments, Apitz has begun to assess bioremediation in settings that resemble real world conditions. She recently evaluated bioremediation in soils created to mimic the real thing. They were two years in the making. Typically, such experiments use clean, synthetic sediments. But actually pollutants and the clay, sand, and organic components of real soils interact: Over time, some organic compounds will change—sometimes adhering to particles surrounding them, sometimes changing their own physical structures. Thus, a toxic substance that might be readily accessible to microbial processing shortly after contamination may become less—or more—amenable to cleanup as time passes.

To assess the changes that might occur and how microbes handle pollutants over time, Apitz placed sand or clay in vials with specific pollutants, then let those vials sit to enable their contents to "age." This aging affected microbial cleansing activity. For example, microbes able to remove the pollutants from the aged sands were much less capable of cleaning up the aged clays. These results suggest that the type of soil and duration of contamination could affect the cost-effectiveness of bioremediation. Also, because some bacteria are better at accessing organic pollutants than others, she says that her results emphasize the need to factor in these conditions whenever microbial intervention is being considered.

But one may not need to know everything about the degradation process to enable microbes to work effectively, Derek R. Lovley, a microbiologist at the University of Massachusetts at Amherst, points out. Some microbes are proving quite versatile. He and his colleagues have found that bacteria that reduce sulfate in sediments from San Diego Bay also quite readily break down PAHs. "Self-purification is greater than we thought," he notes. The microbes now found capable of chowing down on PAHs had been in sediments where PAHs had been around for a long time. He suggests that, given enough time, bacteria will eventually evolve a way to consume almost any petroleum-related compound. But what is key is that the rate at which PAHs are added to these sediments not exceed the rate at which they degrade.

Each of these observations helps build the scientific foundation that will lead to a realistic picture of what bioremediation can do for the marine environment. The microbes may not work magic, but they can help. "One needs to have some patience with this stuff," Nealson reminds himself and others. Even with tapping all nature's help, he adds, it is going to take a long time to undo the damage that has been centuries in the making. ❑

## Questions

1. Why is bioremediation critical for marine environments?

2. Why aren't terrestrial microbes used in marine environments?

3. What are considered the four worst threats to the marine environment?

*Answers are at the back of the book.*

*Many urban areas have used up most of the available water resources. New sources of drinking water need to be found. Communities nationwide are now studying the safety, economics, and feasibility of inserting treated sewer water into the ground to supply decreasing aquifers. This also includes those tapped for drinking water. This is known as artificial groundwater recharge, a process that involves injecting treated city wastewater directly into aquifers or leaching it into the ground. Two methods for returning the treated wastewater to the aquifer are the use of absorption layers of soil and percolation to filter viruses and contaminants from the water, and direct injection into the aquifer after being treated thoroughly. It is likely that recycled wastewater will be increasingly relied upon in coming years.*

# Drinking Recycled Wastewater
## Ginger Pinholster

*Environmental Science & Technology*, **April 1995**

***Can groundwater recharge safely address the drinking-water needs of rapidly growing urban areas?***

As the 21st century approaches, communities around the world, faced with population growth and increased urbanization, scramble to find new sources of drinking water. "Most cities have already fully exploited the readily available water resources," EPA warns.[1] The California Department of Water Resources braces for annual water shortages ranging from 3.7 million to 5.7 million acre-feet (1.2 million to 1.8 million gallons, or 4.6 billion to 7 billion cubic meters) by 2020.[2] To meet growing population needs, U.S. planners traditionally have built new dams, levees, and canals. But public willingness to pay for new water facilities "has declined dramatically from the dam-building heyday of the 1950s and 1960s," according to a recent report by the National Research Council.[3]

Consequently, communities throughout the United States are studying the safety, economics, and feasibility of directing treated sewer water into the ground to replenish dwindling aquifers—even those tapped for drinking water. The practice, known as artificial groundwater recharge, typically involves injecting treated city wastewater directly into aquifers or spread-ing it onto the ground to infiltrate the surface. It is unclear exactly how many regions practice groundwater recharge, but James Crook, director of water reuse at Black & Veatch (Cambridge, MA), estimates that "hundreds" of U.S. cities are recycling wastewater for nonpotable purposes from crop irrigation in arid western states to landscaping at Florida's Walt Disney World. A half-dozen cities, including El Paso, TX, and Los Angeles are recharging potable aquifers; a dozen more communities are considering similar projects, says Crook.

Though reclaimed wastewater has been used to augment drinking-water supplies in Los Angeles County since 1962, mounting public concern about the safety of recycled water is sparking renewed debate among the scientific community. Debate has focused on whether treated wastewater can be clean enough to drink and is free from viruses and hazardous substances. But economics also is a concern: Is it cheaper to treat wastewater to replenish aquifers or "import" water from other sources?

A National Research Council (NRC) report titled "Ground Water Recharge: Using Waters of Impaired Quality," released in September 1994, offers a promising, though qualified, endorsement of groundwater recharge practices. Treated city wastewater can be used to boost potable aquifers under certain conditions, when no "better quality" water exists, according to the report. The committee was careful to add, however, that recharge technologies are "especially well-suited to nonpotable uses such as landscape irrigation."

For water managers facing public opposition to recharge projects using treated wastewater, the report provides new ammunition. Coincidentally, it was released the same week that the Miller Brewing Company filed a lawsuit to block a $25 million recharge effort in Upper San Gabriel Valley, CA. If successful, the lawsuit "would really give water reuse a black eye," says Crook, who served on the NRC groundwater recharge committee.

Miller's lawsuit charges that use of treated wastewater "will irreversibly pollute the basin," possibly damaging its product. Cass Luke, a spokeswoman for the Upper San Gabriel Valley Water District, says Miller's objections are based solely on public relations concerns, rather than scientific evidence of a health hazard.

The brewery supports the principle of groundwater recharge, but the company has a problem with this specific case, says Miller spokesman Victor Franco. The spreading ground for the treated wastewater, adjacent to the brewery, is a very porous soil, according to Franco, and the filtering effect as water percolates through the soil would not occur because the water would "cascade through."

The lawsuit underscores recurring questions about the safety of treated wastewater. Given proper treatment, reclaimed wastewater can be as safe or safer than traditional drinking-water sources, according to Herman Bouwer, chief engineer for the U.S. Department of Agriculture's Water Conservation Laboratory in Phoenix, AZ. After all, he says, wastewater slated for use in aquifers typically is subjected to primary, secondary, and sometimes advanced cleanup procedures—from settling of solids to biological oxidation of organics to salt extraction via reverse osmosis and adsorption of synthetic organics by granular activated carbon.

"About half the people in our country use groundwater [for drinking]," says Bouwer, an NRC committee member, "but not all groundwaters are pure and pristine." Surface water supplies from rivers, streams, and lakes frequently are polluted by sewage effluent upstream. Runoff from cattle farms can contaminate surface waters with potentially deadly parasites such as *Cryptosporidium,* which can resist disinfection.

But other researchers insist that uncertainties related to the chemical composition of reclaimed wastewater could jeopardize public health. "Human sewage is a mish-mash of complex organic materials, only some of which have been identified," says Henry Ongerth, former sanitary engineer for California's Department of Public Health. "Of the substances that have been identified, only a fraction have been studied for their toxicity.... Why add to the risks we already face?"

**Is It Safe to Drink?**
Nonpotable aquifers frequently are recharged without fuss or fanfare. "For car washes, street sweeping, and golf-course irrigation, no one is opposed to this type of recycling," says Forest Tennant, a physician in West Covina, CA, who is head of the grassroots group Citizens for Clean Water. Yet Tennant and others staunchly oppose refilling potable aquifers with treated wastewater. Tennant hopes to thwart the recharge project in Upper San Gabriel Valley.

When it comes to groundwater recharge, the controversy most often hinges on whether treated city wastewater is safe to drink. Questions focus mainly on two constituents of treated wastewater: viruses and disinfection byproducts.

According to a 1993 analysis of virus-monitoring data collected over a 10-year period from six California wastewater treatment plants, secondary-level treatment effectively removes 99.8% of detectable viruses.[4] Large quantities of treated wastewater, averaging 275 gallons per sample, were collected monthly. Only one of 590 samples tested positive for enteric viruses, reports study author William A. Yanko, a laboratory supervisor for the Los Angeles County Sanitation District (LACSD). Yanko says his data show that California's existing treatment requirements ensure "essentially virus risk-free effluents" for recharge projects.

But another 1993 study of viral risks was less conclusive.[5] In that report, author David K. Powelson of the University of Arizona at Tucson notes that although soil can strip remaining viruses from treated wastewater as the water infiltrates an aquifer, studies have shown that "virus removal is dependent on virus type and environmental conditions." Removal or inactivation of two types of viruses (MS2 and PRD1) from treated effluent directed into test basins composed primarily of sand and gravel varied depending on sample depths. At a depth of 4.3 meters, for example, virus removal ranged from 37% to 99.7%.

Earle Hartling, water recycling coordinator for the LACSD, says viruses require a host and therefore are inactivated quickly in underground aquifers. "All a virus does is invade a cell, take over the DNA-replicating machinery of the cell, and cause disease. It does not survive long periods [in an aquifer] because it has no opportunity to replicate itself," says Hartling, who has been known to delight news photographers by chugging vials of treated wastewater. As proof that viruses pose no threat in recharged aquifers, Hartling and others frequently cite a landmark 1984 health effects study prepared by Margaret H. Nellor and colleagues.[6] Over a 5-year period, the authors say, "No viruses were detected in groundwater or chlorinated reclaimed water samples" collected from three sites in California.

Bob Hultquist, senior sanitary engineer for the California Department of Health Services, counters that "viruses don't live very long, but it's all relative because they can live in excess of a year." Therefore proper pretreatment of recycled wastewater is critical, he adds.

## Disinfection Hazards

To eliminate viruses, wastewater usually is disinfected with chlorine and less frequently with alternative disinfectants such as ozone, monochlo-ramine, or ultraviolet radiation. Unfortunately, a host of chlorine disinfection byproducts (DBPs) are thought to be hazardous to human health, Philip C. Singer, professor of environmental science and engineering at the University of North Carolina–Chapel Hill, notes in a 1994 study.[7] In 1976, for example, the National Cancer Institute deemed chloroform, a trihalomethane (THM), to be carcinogenic. Hundreds of other DBPs have been found since in drinking water, including dichloroacetic acid, which "is believed to be a more potent carcinogen than any of the THMs, based on animal studies," says Singer.

"There's very clear evidence that these compounds are carcinogenic, but the doses must be very high," says Richard J. Bull of Washington State University in Pullman, author of a major study on DBP health effects.[8] "Now, whether they're dangerous at the concentrations you would find in drinking water is a question."

Nellor's data indicate "no increased rates of infectious diseases, congenital malformations . . . or all cancers combined," and thus don't link DBPs to cancer, the National Research Council report notes. However, cancers may remain latent for more than 15 years—longer than the period of Nellor's study, it adds. Chlorine DBPs in reclaimed water could be minimized by expanding the use of alternative disinfection processes, the report notes. But it cautions that little is known about the byproducts of ozone, monochloramine, and ultraviolet disinfection.

Potential problems associated with alternative disinfectants were discussed in a recent one-year study of DBPs at Jefferson Parish, LA.[9] A treatment strategy of preozonation and postchlora-mination produced the lowest levels of 18 halogenated DBPs, based on total organic carbon and total organic halide. Author Benjamin W. Lykins, Jr., points out that ozonation results in increased assimilable carbon, which must be controlled to prevent microbial regrowth. Ozonation byproducts such as aldehydes, ketones, and acids also are a concern, says Lykins, chief of the EPA's Systems and Field Evaluation Branch in Cincinnati, OH.

In general, the National Research Council report says the body of existing health effects studies "do not suggest a health concern" associated with treated wastewater. For example, in a 20-year study in Denver, 344 rats showed no toxicologic, carcinogenic, or reproductive effects after drinking samples of treated water, even when concentration levels were amplified 500 times.[10] But study author William C. Lauer notes that "as little as 10% of the measurable total organic carbon [in treated wastewater] has been estimated to be amenable to identification."

## Entering the Aquifer

Two recharge methods, surface infiltration and direct-well injection, are available to water managers when importing water is not an option. These methods can also be used to prevent seawater from contaminating a coastal fresh water aquifer.

The Montebello Forebay Groundwater Recharge Project in south-central Los Angeles County, CA, established in 1962, is an off-channel surface infiltration-type system. Wastewater at Montebello Forebay is subjected to advanced treatment, including chemical coagulation, dual-media filtration, and chlorine disinfection, Hartling explains. Then it is combined with other sources, such as storm water runoff and surface waters from northern California and Colorado. Spreading basins are flooded and dried alternately to prevent clogging and mosquito breeding and to promote aerobic soil conditions. Reclaimed water currently represents 20–30% of the inflow to the Montebello Forebay aquifer.

The other groundwater recharge method, direct-well injection, has been practiced at Water Factory 21 in Orange County, CA, since 1976. Construction of the facility began in 1972 to prevent seawater intrusion into four overtapped groundwater aquifers, says Mike Wehner, health and regulatory director for the Orange County Water District. Today, highly treated wastewater is mixed with deep well water and injected into threatened aquifers through a series of 23 multiple-casing wells located about 3.5 miles from the shore.

The direct-well approach enables Orange County to penetrate aquifers through a thick layer of clay. The same method lets the city of El Paso recharge a 350-foot-deep aquifer. At both locations, wastewater is extensively treated prior to injection. Pretreatment of activated sludge secondary effluent at Water Factory 21 begins with lime clarification, which removes suspended solids, heavy metals, dissolved minerals, and many viruses by elevating the water's pH level. Recarbonation then normalizes the pH, and mixed-media filtration removes more suspended solids. In a final step, some water is fed through an activated carbon adsorption system where organic molecules latch onto complex carbon pores before the remaining flow is rechlorinated. Another stream is forced under high pressure through a reverse-osmosis membrane, which removes salt and organics.

Soil infiltration recharge systems may offer the advantage of scrubbing additional contaminants from treated wastewater. According to Hartling, the soil infiltration system at Montebello Forebay reduces total organic carbon by as much as 90% (though this could be either by removal or dilution) and removes 50% of all nitrogen. Soil infiltration also can remove parasites that tend to be resistant to disinfection. Given the right soil conditions, "parasites like *Cryptosporidium* and *Giardia* can be filtered out mechanically by nature," says Herman Bouwer of the USDA's Water Conservation Lab.

**Recharge Price Tags**
Recharge may be an increasingly attractive option as competition for water grows and public funding for new water facilities shrinks, says Henry Vaux, Jr., professor of resource economics at the University of California–Riverside. Costs associated with artificial recharge "are going to be quite variable," he says, but reclaimed water can be less expensive than imported water.

When the Orange County Water District completed an internal economic feasibility study in 1993, Vaux says, the price tag for nearby surface water was $600 per acre-foot.[3] Transporting this surface water to spreading grounds would have cost the district an additional $82.40 per acre-foot, for a total of $682.40 per acre-foot. Conversely, reclaimed water is readily available for recharge purposes and the cost of advanced treatment ranges from $251 to $387 per acre-foot.

Upper San Gabriel Valley has proposed building a new nine-mile pipeline to funnel treated wastewater from the San Jose Creek Water Reclamation Plant to nearby spreading grounds. Water District Manager Bob Berlien says the project would be cost-effective over the long term because the region currently imports water for $235 per acre-foot, whereas reclaimed water would cost just $200 per acre-foot.

Groundwater recharge costs also are affected dramatically by the level of pre- and post-treatment required to ensure compliance with drinking-water standards. At Lake Buena Vista, FL, where the Reedy Creek Improvement District is studying the feasibility of discharging treated wastewater into a recreational lake, researchers predicted the costs of four treatment options.[11] Estimated capital costs ranged from $11.3 million for a treatment system based on biological "deep bed" denitrification (rather than reverse osmosis) to more than $23 million for a system that includes a full suite of treatment technologies. Because direct-well injection recharge provides no soil-aquifer treatment, reclaimed water tends to require more advanced, and more costly, pretreatment, Vaux notes.

## Regulatory Issues

Water drawn from recharged U.S. groundwater aquifers must comply with maximum part-per-million type standards set by the Safe Drinking Water Act. Aside from that, however, no federal regulations directly govern recharge practices such as the level of monitoring or pre- and post-treatment needed to ensure water quality.[1]

Many states have regulations governing recharge. According to a 1993 survey, 36 states have regulations or guidelines related to water recycling, but only 10 directly address the use of reclaimed water for purposes other than irrigation.[12] In states without regulations, EPA's *Guidelines for Water Reuse* manual serves as a blueprint for water reuse projects, says James Crook, a principal author of the publication.

"There's no formal agency position saying that we're strongly encouraging or discouraging [recharge]" said Robert Bastian, an environmental scientist with EPA's Office of Wastewater Management, but EPA typically has been "very positive toward water reuse practices," he adds. Michael Cook, director of EPA's Office of Wastewater Management, recently offered a qualified endorsement of the proposed recharge project in Upper San Gabriel Valley. In a letter accompanying an Environmental Impact Report commissioned by the water district, Cook says that "comprehensive research and demonstration projects as well as monitoring of existing operating systems have documented the environmental safety and lack of public health hazards associated with well-run water reclamation and reuse practices in the United States, including projects

involving the recharge of potable surface water reservoirs and groundwater aquifers." He softens his support, however, by adding, "concerns are often raised when new reuse projects [such as the San Gabriel project] are proposed." Public concerns may be based on a "lack of knowledge," a fear of plummeting property values, or "the negative consumer image of drinking reclaimed water," Cook says.

California and Florida are revising their recharge regulations. Title 22 of the California Administrative Code defines a minimum treatment level for reclaimed water slated for nonpotable reuse (a cycle of coagulation, flocculation, sedimentation, filtration, and disinfection). A brief 1978 amendment to Title 22 (Article 5.1) notes that requirements for potable reuse will be established "on an individual case basis." A committee directed by the California Department of Health Services is refining a more specific set of regulations that include minimum performance standards, based on water quality analysis, for potable recharge systems. The proposed regulations also would require that reclaimed water be held underground for at least six months prior to reuse— "long enough to get a high percentage of [virus] die-off," says Bob Hultquist. He expects the draft regulations to be approved in early 1995. Florida is revising Chapter 62-610 of its Administrative Code, which deals mainly with nonpotable water reuse systems. The state Environmental Regulation Commission will review revised regulations in May, reports Dave York, reuse coordinator with the Florida Department of Environmental Protection. The draft regulations would set maximum contaminant levels for groundwater recharge.

While dealing with more stringent maximum contaminant levels in the future, recharge managers also will have to comply with new EPA limits on DBPs, according to Philip Singer.[7] EPA's revised rules probably will include requirements for collecting data on raw water quality, tougher treatment safeguards against *Giardia* and *Cryptosporidium,* and maximum contaminant levels for total THMs and other DBPs, Singer says.

Russell Christman, professor of environmental sciences at the University of North Carolina–Chapel Hill, fears that existing federal regulations may not ensure public safety when potable aquifers are recharged. "When you have a [water] source that can't be entirely characterized—if only 10 or 20% of its organic content can be identified—of what comfort is the fact that the water meets existing drinking water standards?" asks Christman.

## A Critical Test Case

Concerns about public safety are driving the San Gabriel Valley lawsuit, according to Miller Brewing Company. To prove its case, attorneys for the company have collected expert declarations from researchers including Daniel A. Okun, Kenan professor of environmental engineering, emeritus, at the University of North Carolina–Chapel Hill. No long-term health hazards have been linked to the 32-year-old Montebello Forebay recharge project, Okun notes. But he also claims that "San Gabriel doesn't have quite the same aquifer situation [because] the soil there is more permeable and less likely to remove trace organics." Planners have proposed tertiary treatment based on conventional granular filtration. More advanced technologies, such as reverse osmosis, would be needed to remove organics, Okun says.

Recharge into San Gabriel aquifers might disturb a Superfund site containing a plume of industrial contamination, groundwater activist Tennant charges. But the contamination is located well upstream from the proposed recharge sites, countered the water district's Cass Luke.

In an August 9, 1994, letter to water district manager Bob Berlien, a representative of the California Regional Water Quality Control Board wrote that questions about water quality were "satisfactorily addressed" by a draft 1993 Environmental Impact Report.[13] "We believe the District's project will have positive regional and statewide benefits," wrote Robert P. Ghirelli, an executive officer for the Control Board.

U.S. water managers are following the Miller lawsuit closely. "We are worried that it might have negative impacts because public perception of water reuse is very, very important," says Bahman Sheikh, water resources and reuse policy specialist for the West Basin Municipal District. Already there have

been two delays in getting to court, and the first hearings were delayed until February, Victor Franco said.

In Los Angeles County, Earle Harding began receiving calls from concerned citizens shortly after the Miller lawsuit was filed. "The reverberations and repercussions are starting already," he says. "This is scary, given the fact that reclaimed water will be critical to compensate for impending water shortages."

## References

1. "Guidelines for Water Reuse"; U.S. Environmental Protection Agency: Washington, DC, 1992; EPA/625/R-92/004.
2. "California Water Balance: California Water Plan Update"; California Department of Water Resources, 1994; Bulletin 160-93.
3. "Ground Water Recharge: Using Waters of Impaired Quality"; National Research Council: Washington, DC, 1994.
4. Yanko, W.A. *Water Environ. Res.* **1993,** 65, 221–26.
5. Powelson, D.K.; Gerba, C.P; Yahya, M.T. *Water Res.* **1993**, 27(4), 583–90.
6. "Summary: Health Effects Study Final Report"; Nellor, M.H.; Baird, R.B.; Smyth, J.R. County Sanitation Districts of Los Angeles County: Los Angeles, CA, 1984.
7. Singer, P. C. *J. Environ. Eng.* **1994**, 120(4), 727–44.
8. "Health Effects of Disinfectants and Disinfection By-products"; Bull, R.J.; Kopfler, F.C. American Water Works Association Research Foundation: Denver, CO, 1991.
9. Lykins, B.W.; Koffskey, W.E.; Patterson, K.S. *J. Environ. Eng.* 1994,120(4), 745–58.
10. Lauer, W.C.; Wolfe, G.W.; Condie, L.W. *Toxicol. Chem. Mixtures* **1994**, 63–81.
11. "Advanced Wastewater Reclamation Program Final Report"; CH2M Hill: Gainesville, FL, 1993; prepared for the Reedy Creek Improvement District, Lake Buena Vista, FL.
12. Payne, J.F. et al. *Proceedings of the Water Environment Federation 66th Annual Conference.* **1993**, 9, 137.

13. "Draft Environmental Impact Report"; CH2M Hill: Santa Ana, CA, 1993; prepared for the Upper San Gabriel Valley Municipal Water District, El Monte, CA.

14. Lauer, W.C. et al.; "Denver's Direct Potable Water Demonstration Project: Final Report"; Denver Water Department: Denver, CO, 1993.

## Questions

1. Name two recharge methods used when importing water is not an option.

2. What have U.S. planners traditionally done to meet the growing need for water?

3. With what substances is wastewater usually treated to eliminate viruses?

*Answers are at the back of the book.*

**32** *Future growth opportunities in the pollution control industry are predicted for companies and individuals seeking employment. Air pollution control systems markets are expected to expand around the world as developing nations industrialize. In the United States, the Clean Air Act (CAA) of 1990 will continue to create new technologies. A considerable near-term market is anticipated in retrofitting city solid waste combustor plants. The pollution control industry in Canada and Mexico may increase by 50 percent or more in the near future. These opportunities illustrate once again how the marketplace, jobs, and the environment do not have to be in conflict.*

# Particulate Control
## The Next Air Pollution Control Growth Segment
### Robert W. McIlvaine

*Environmental Manager*, April 1995

*Where should environmental firms direct their research, money, and work force? Where will the next growth spurt in the industry occur? How should firms prepare for the next decade? In what direction should environmental professionals take their careers as they search for the field's next market boom?*

**Summary**
Expect markets for air pollution control systems to balloon, thanks to a resurgence of heavy industry in the United States. The Clean Air Act (CAA) of 1990 will also have a major impact in forcing the creation of new technologies, such as cleanable HEPA filters and other novel devices. A substantial near-term market in retrofitting municipal solid waste combustor plants is anticipated, and the market for thermal gas treatment will rise substantially. In addition, although the Canadian-Mexican market is relatively small compared to the United States, the pollution control industry in each country will expand by 50% or more within five years.

The recent documentation of health risks associated with small particle inhalation forms the basis for tighter particulate control regulations. This is
likely to result in rapid growth in sales of particulate control equipment.

## Hello Mr. Greenfield

There is a new face in the neighborhood. In fact, Mr. Greenfield has not put in many appearances over the last fifteen years so his name may be unfamiliar to some readers. But back in the '70s when basic industry was expanding in the United States and lots of new plants were being built on what were formerly green fields, the term "greenfield project" was quite familiar. Now industrial America is making a big comeback and this will have an incredibly large effect on the air pollution industry in the United States and therefore the world. More than $600 million of air pollution control projects have been started in just six weeks as part of tens of billions of dollars in new plants committed by manufacturers of steel, castings, semiconductors, chemicals, pharmaceuticals, automobiles, engines, pulp mills, refineries, and municipal wastewater treatment plants.

The U.S. philosophy of focusing on the bottom line for next month, rather than looking at the long-term has proven a weakness in the country's industrial outlook generally and a major detriment to the air pollution industry. This had resulted in continuous downsizing. The steel industry output has shrunk by 33%. There were twice as many foundries some years ago as there are today. Five years ago, the United States was running far behind Japan in the race to dominate the semiconductor industry.

Today the picture has been dramatically transformed. The United States leads the world in supplying semiconductors and has become a low-cost producer of steel. Demand is soaring for both products. As proof, the automobile companies just negotiated purchases of steel at prices 8% higher than their last contracts. Industrial America has been running at an unprecedented capacity rate and there is no way to increase output except by building new plants. A secondary effect can be expected from these expansions. The power industry and the municipal wastewater treatment plants have not anticipated this kind of expansion for industrial America. The Gross National Product (GNP) is headed for a 3% increase this year. Because electricity demand follows GNP, expect a need for 21,000 MW of power plants just to accommodate the burgeoning market. And this brings us to the next question.

## What about the Power Industry?

The increase in demand for electricity is just one of the factors that will impact air pollution control expenditures. Utilities in the United States are receiving confusing signals on which direction to take in complying with both future and present regulations not only for air pollution control, but for transmission of power. The next two years could be a watershed period of overwhelming change for the North American electric power industry. The changes might include open access transmission and premature closure of nuclear power plants.

Competition through open access transmission could result early on in overcapacity. Areas that are short of electricity will receive power from those that have sufficient reserves. This could have a negative impact on air pollution control expenditures over the next year or two. The long-term effect, however, could be a huge increase in air pollution control expenditures as part of a massive construction program for mine mouth, coal-fired power plants. The CRSS/Philips mine mouth power plant in Mississippi represents an indicator of the future. The newly announced power plant will supply electricity to several states in the Southeast and can be expected to compete or cooperate with local utilities. Mine mouth power plants in Wyoming and Montana could supply the West Coast with coal-fired electricity. Nuclear power plants face a competitive disadvantage in this new environment. The California Public Utilities Commission expects full retail wheeling of electricity by 2002.

The March and August 1994 issues of the *Journal of the Air & Waste Management Association* provided extensive coverage of the controversy relative to particulate emissions from utility boilers. Recent studies strengthen the contention that utility emissions are both greater in quantity and more harmful than previously thought.

The emphasis on fine particulate control is opening the door for suppliers of wet precipitators. Research-Cottrell, Joy, and Lurgi have enjoyed success in the mining industry. Beltran, Sonic, and Belco have a number of units on industrial applications such as incinerators. One of the most significant advances is the application to coal-fired boilers. Southern Environmental is completing installation of a counterflow, two-field wet precipitator with four-point suspension on each field for one of the boilers at the Sherburne Station of Northern States Power. Presently, only the FGD scrubber on this plant exists. In the new arrangement, the FGD scrubber will be followed by the wet precipitator making it unique in the United States, where typically a dry precipitator is followed by a wet FGD system.

Southern Environmental, EPRI, Southern Services, and Southern Research have embarked on a project to analyze particulate removal at a 1 MW pilot combustor installed at Southern Research. In addition to determining particulate and air toxics removal performance, investigators will examine the use of additives for mercury control and the ability to operate in an unsaturated state.

Several new developments are directed at fine particulate. Wahlco Environmental Systems has a patented, new in-duct flue gas conditioning system.

The system simplifies the conditioning process by generating sulfur trioxide directly from the sulfur dioxide existing in the flue gas stream. Externally supplied feedstock (either sulfur or sulfur dioxide) is no longer needed, nor are auxiliary process heaters, which were formerly required. The new in-duct system precisely controls the generation of $SO_3$ by controlling the exposure of catalyst blocks positioned in the duct to the gas flow. Deflectors placed over the catalyst blocks adjust the contact between the gas flow and the catalyst surface, controlling the catalyzation of $SO_2$ in the gas flow to $SO_3$.

### Other Markets Are Strong as Well

Delays in implementing Title I and Title III of the Clean Air Act have also resulted in increased potential for air pollution control equipment. McIlvaine is in the midst of an extensive analysis of the post-combustion nitrogen oxide ($NO_x$) market for power plants, municipal incinerators, and other applications. Close to $10 billion will be spent on $NO_x$ control over the next decade. Nonattainment areas in the East will be particularly active.

The continuous emissions monitoring market has continued at a high level because of $NO_x$ nonattainment continuous emissions monitors (CEMS). There will also be a positive impact on the market from the enhanced monitoring rule. The rule, slated for April 1995, will require enhanced monitoring at some 18,000 sources, where an individual emission point has the potential to emit 30 tons per year of a regulated pollutant. This drops to 15 tons per year in serious nonattainment areas and 7.5 tons per year in severe nonattainment areas, and only 3 tons per year in extreme areas. The operators must collect sufficient data to demonstrate continuous compliance. Continuous emissions monitors are the most accurate and also the most expensive. A plant faces fines and other sanctions if it cannot demonstrate compliance.

The mass particulate emissions monitoring offers the fastest potential growth. This is a market waiting for the technology. The beta gauge tape sampler available from F.A.G. and Environment is one option. The micro balance is another. The biggest hurdle is getting a representative sample out of the duct work and providing a transport system which allows consistent results. Graseby Andersen has developments in all three areas including a micro balance mass determination system, a sophisticated software program to calculate any losses in the transport system, and a new shrouded probe which is shown in the attached photograph. This unit operates at a fixed flow rate and collects a representative particulate sample even with changes in free-stream velocity. The shrouded probe was originally developed to provide continuous representative sampling of radionuclide particles at U.S. Department of Energy facilities. More recently, the shrouded probe has demonstrated the capability to provide continuous single-point aerosol samples from industrial sources.

Another particulate measurement technique has been overlooked in the United States, but has been used extensively in Europe. The typical transmissometer application in Germany, for example, is installed and individually calibrated as a particulate monitor. Operators collect stack measurement data simultaneously with a manual method for dust density and with a transmissometer setup to measure optical density. When a regression line is established to define this relationship between optical density and dust density, the instrument output can be linearly translated into dust density. In Germany most stacks are regulated in dust density established from such transmissometer measurements, or more recently from optical side scattering instruments. Monitor Labs LS541 transmissometer, which is normally used to monitor opacity in the United States, can be set up with the slope and offset of the above regression line entered into the control unit, in which case an output is available to provide dust density directly in $mg/nM^3$. As long as some degree of consistency exists in the particle size distribution and composition, which is typical after a baghouse or electrostatic precipitator, the optical measurement proves a reasonably accurate measure of dust density.

Expect substantial business for air pollution control companies in dealing with Department of Defense cleanup. A $450 million incinerator system is under construction at the Tooele Army Depot and is designed to destroy mustard and nerve gas. Incinerators are planned in seven other states, including Alabama, Arkansas, Colorado, Indiana, Kentucky, Maryland, and Oregon.

Cleanable HEPA filters have been a boon for industries handling hazardous fine dusts. The first cleanable absolute filters introduced by several companies in Europe three years ago had similar designs comprising a box-shaped cartridge of glass media cleaned by an indexing tube delivering reverse pulse air. Since that time, MAC Environmental has redesigned the cleanable HEPA filter into the Miasmactic™ which incorporates a cylindrical cartridge made of reinforced HEPA media. Cleaning is accomplished off-line with medium pressure pulsing. This cleanable HEPA has found a waiting market in manufacturing processes for computer circuit boards, television tubes, inorganic paint pigments, and pharmaceuticals. In the making of television tubes, lead powder is sprayed on the inside of the screen to prevent radiation emissions. A closed Miasmactic filter system captures overspray powder and pulses it from the cartridges directly into a recycle system for return to the spraying process. Problems with hazardous dust and cartridge disposal are avoided.

## Big Incinerator Retrofit Program

A massive investment in air pollution control equipment will be required at existing municipal waste combustor sites around the country. The U.S. Environmental Protection Agency (EPA) has proposed rules and must, under a statutory deadline, finalize standards by September 1995. The proposal would require these combustors to reduce acid gas emissions, including sulfur oxides and hydrogen chloride. It would also require substantial reductions in particulate matter and heavy metals including mercury. A very low limit would be set on dioxins and furans, and $NO_x$ would also be reduced.

The proposal calls for most plants to add additional CEM equipment and increase intermittent stack testing, particularly for the various heavy metal emissions. Emission requirements are more stringent for one hundred nineteen large municipal waste combustor plants with two hundred thirty-five individual combustor units than they are for the sixty smaller plants with one hundred thirty-seven units.

## $1.7 Billion Thermal Treatment Market

Volatile organic compounds (VOCs) and odors are effectively removed by either thermal oxidation or adsorption. Regulations to reduce ozone and air toxics are rapidly expanding the market for pollution control systems. In 1991, the annual purchases of thermal gas treatment and adsorption systems in the United States totaled just over $700 million. By the year 2000, the annual purchases are projected to increase $1.7 billion, resulting in an incremental increase of over $1 billion per year.

There are several types of thermal treatment equipment. One type is recuperative thermal treatment, which uses heat exchangers to capture heat generated by the incineration of the organic pollutants and the extra fuel necessary to ensure combustion. Another category, catalytic thermal treatment, involves the use of a catalyst to accomplish the oxidation at lower temperatures thereby using less fuel.

A third technology is called regenerative thermal oxidation (RTO). It treats the gas in multiple combustion chambers filled with ceramic packing. Because these units are capable of operating at high temperature and utilize low quantities of outside fuel, they have been the most popular segment of the market.

Whereas only a handful of companies offered RTOs in 1987, presently more than thirty companies in the United States manufacture these devices. Of the four largest companies, one was started as an environmental company offering conventional thermal oxidizers, and another was the original developer of the RTO. The other two largest suppliers are companies furnishing complete surface finishing systems. Large Fortune 500 companies are entering this field. One is primarily a catalyst supplier offering the RTO as an alternative technology. Another is a major chemical company with a pollution control division and a number of plants which will utilize the RTO technology. Oriented strandboard VOC reduction has the largest present application for these systems. Another large purchasing segment has been the automobile industry, which is using the RTO technology for automobile paint facilities.

Semiconductor plants have become major RTO purchasers. The chemical industry and wastewater treatment plants are major longer-term markets. Market growth will not be limited to industrial applications. Bakeries and other small emitters in nonattainment areas will be installing this equipment.

## 50 Percent Growth for NAFTA Air Pollution Control Market

Canada, Mexico, and the United States will experience air pollution control industry growth of 50% or more over the next five years. Orders for air pollution control systems in Canada are expected to rise from $285 million in 1994 to $460 million in 1998. Mexican air pollution control system sales will rise from $60 million in 1994 to $90 million in 1998.

The 1994 total North American Free Trade Agreement (NAFTA) air pollution control market including hardware, testing, and services was just under $4 billion. The United States accounts for over 91% of the present NAFTA market with Canada and Mexico accounting for 7% and 2%, respectively. In contrast, the Mexican market compares to that of an average U.S. state. The Canadian market is equivalent to larger U.S. states, such as Ohio and California.

The types of equipment being sold in the three markets differ. In the United States, measurement and reduction of nitrogen oxides represents a major potential. In Mexico, the largest potential can be found in dust control in basic industries. In Canada, pulp mills and mining are much more important than in the United States. In all three countries, enforcement responsibilities are shared between federal and state/provincial governments.

## Conclusions

Future markets will be greatly affected by new plant expansions with opportunities in Mexico, Canada, and more importantly in the developing Asian nations. New advances in technology will both change and increase the market. ❏

---

**Questions**

1. By what methods are volatile organic compounds removed?

2. What two changes could the North American electric power industry see in the next two years?

3. What is the expected growth in the pollution control industry in Canada and Mexico?

*Answers are at the back of the book.*

---

**33** *The Scripps Institution of Oceanography in California plans a new way to assess global warming. They will measure temperature below the surface of the Pacific Ocean by using low-frequency sound waves. Such data is crucial because the ocean stores most of the heat that powers the climate. However, marine mammal experts and environmentalists are concerned for the underwater inhabitants. Sound waves may harm whales and other creatures. A test is planned to determine if sound sources harm marine mammals.*

# The Sound of Global Warming
## Stuart F. Brown

*Popular Science,* July 1995

*Cold War spy technology could become the world's largest ocean thermometer to measure global warming. But will the residents object?*

A program that uses sound waves to measure ocean temperatures could improve global climate models but may be scrapped if whales and sea lions don't like it.

The Scripps Institution of Oceanography in La Jolla, Calif., hopes to inaugurate a $35 million program to measure temperatures beneath the surface of the Pacific Ocean. Knowing whether ocean temperatures are rising or falling over time would greatly increase the accuracy of computer models designed to predict climate change.

But the Scripps program—called the acoustic thermometry of ocean climate (ATOC)—uses low-frequency sound waves to determine ocean temperature. This has some marine mammal experts and environmentalists concerned because sea creatures such as blue whales, elephant seals, and sea lions either have hearing ranges that can detect ATOC sound waves or occasionally dive to depths where the sound-generating devices would operate. "This sound will travel through more than a quarter of the whole Pacific," says whale biologist Linda Weilgart of Dalhousie University in Nova Scotia, who triggered the controversy in a flurry of Internet ex-

changes last year. "You've got to be sure you're not affecting the long-term welfare of marine mammals, such as fertility rates, growth, and mortality" before going ahead with the program, she says.

The controversy over the Scripps ATOC program is especially ironic, since it pits animal-protection advocates such as the Sierra Club and the Natural Resources Defense Council against scientists who believe the program could help us learn more about one of the biggest mysteries of the environment—global warming. The ocean plays a bigger part in global climate than most people realize. "Most of the heat that powers the climate is stored in the seas," says oceanographer Walter Munk, the project's principle investigator. "You won't get the atmospheric climate prediction straight unless you get the ocean climate prediction straight."

Measurements of ocean-surface temperatures can be made by satellites, but their radar or infrared instruments are only capable of sensing the top few millimeters of water. Deep waters, which contain most of the ocean's heat, can also be sampled by oceanographic research ships dispensing sensing instruments. This process is expensive, however, for the amount of data gathered. ATOC's proponents argue that acoustic thermography's ability to sense the average temperature of an immense volume of water makes it the most practical method.

Using sound waves to measure water temperature has its origins in a 1944 experiment by Maurice Ewing of Columbia University, who discovered a natural "channel" in the sea that could carry sound waves across vast distances. This sound channel, at a depth of about 2,800 feet, is a seam of medium-temperature water that's isolated by a layer of warmer surface water above, and a layer of cooler, deep water below. The thermal and pressure barriers on either side of the middle-depth layer act as a wave guide, keeping certain sound frequencies bouncing between its two "walls." Ewing's original experiment proved this when an underwater explosion was detected 900 miles away.

The U.S. Navy was quick to realize the implications of Ewing's work. It developed sound fixing and ranging (SOFAR), a method that uses hydrophones, or submerged microphones, to pick up noises underwater. For example, the noise of vibrating machinery aboard Soviet submarines was detected from one thousand miles away by SOFAR monitoring of the oceanic sound channel. "SOFAR was a mainstay of U.S. security during the Cold War," says Munk. "This method was our main source of information about one of Russia's most threatening activities."

Curiously, a Soviet scientist had independently discovered the sound channel in a 1946 experiment, but for some reason the Soviet navy didn't capitalize on the findings. Soviet strategy changed abruptly in the 1970s, when spies revealed the success of SOFAR. Much quieter Soviet submarines were soon in service.

By the late 1970s, Munk was pioneering the techniques that would lead to acoustic thermography. He performed acoustic tomography experiments, using multiple sound emitters and receivers to produce three-dimensional temperature maps of areas of the sea. The method exploited a natural phenomenon: Sound travels faster in warm water than it does in cold water. Therefore, the average temperature of the water can be determined by clocking the travel time of low-frequency sound from its source to a receiver. For example, water warmer by a mere five one-thousandths of a degree decreases sound travel time across a 6,000-mile path by 150 milliseconds.

In 1991, Munk led a test program which showed that an underwater sound source exploiting the sound channel could be broadcast over great distances. A signal transmitted underwater from Heard Island in the southern Indian Ocean near Antarctica was detected by sensors 11,000 miles away. This experiment opened the door for ATOC, which uses a pair of sound emitters and an array of sensors to measure temperatures across vast areas of the Pacific.

ATOC sound emitters produce low grumbles of 75 hertz that are transmitted in coded 27-second sequences and are repeated 43 times for a total of about 20 minutes. The coding identifies the signal, which weakens and becomes buried in the ocean's random noise before it arrives at a receiver. Repetition provides replacements for individual signals that may be canceled out by background noise en route. Each chunk is tagged with its exact departure time. Computers then correlate clearly received chunks of different sequences into a precise measurement of sound travel time.

"Actually detecting climate change in the oceans will take at least a decade, and 20 years would be even better," says ATOC program manager Andrew Forbes. "If you only measure for five years, you may find yourself tracking a trend that is just riding on the back of an El Niño," Forbes says. "So you have to get beyond those known periodicities in the ocean and atmosphere and measure at least a couple of normal cycles."

The mission plan calls for one sound source to be anchored in the waters at Pioneer Seamount off central California, and another to be placed eight miles off the north shore of Kauai, Hawaii. An assortment of acoustic receiving devices located 3,000 to 6,000 miles distant will collect sound waves and convert them into average temperature measurements along 18 paths through the Pacific. The Navy has agreed to allow researchers access to part of its once-secret network of submarine-detecting hydrophones.

Once the ATOC network is established in the Pacific, the equipment will gather temperature measurements for 24 months. Forbes hopes the early insights gained into the thermal characteristics of the Pacific will lead to the development of a long-term acoustic thermometry network monitoring large ocean areas, particularly in the Atlantic, where major flows of cold, polar bottom water enter the global ocean.

But the entire program hinges on the outcome of a six-month test aimed at determining if ATOC sound sources harm marine mammals. If federal and state permits are issues—perhaps as early as this summer—researchers will gradually bring the omnidirectional sound emitters up to full power for 20-minute transmissions for four-day periods, alternating with week-long periods of silence. Time-depth recorders will be attached to marine mammals in the neighborhood, and their swimming speeds and patterns, along with heart and respiratory rates, will be monitored.

Sound intensity from the ATOC microphones, which at 195 decibels roughly equals the noise of a large container ship at close range, diminishes rapidly as it radiates. At 2,700 feet from the source, the sound level decreases to 136 decibels, the equivalent of breaking waves, according to program officials. "We don't expect to see distress in these animals," says Daniel Costa, a marine biologist at University of California, Santa Cruz, who is heading the $2.9 million study on the effects of ATOC sound waves on sea mammals. "What we expect to see, if anything, is that the animals would express annoyance and avoid the site."

Program managers at Scripps have given the marine mammal group control of the sound emitters and the authority to modify or halt the entire program if they detect harm to sea life. Ocean temperature measurements will begin only if the system is found to be safe. Still, marine biologist Christopher Clark, head of the ATOC marine mammals study, is embittered by the controversy. He feels that opposition to the program is grounded in emotion rather than scientific fact. "This is environmental activism gone completely astray," Clark says. "They should be focusing on the real acoustic pollution in the sea, which is the barrage of noise from supertankers and other shipping traffic."

If ATOC clears regulatory hurdles, Walter Munk and his acoustic oceanographers will transform a Cold War submarine snooping technique into the biggest thermometer in the sea. Scripps scientists plan to share data with researchers at NASA's Jet Propulsion Laboratory, who are now receiving ocean surface-height measurements from the orbiting *Topex-Poseidon* spacecraft. "The satellite altimetry gives you the temperature of the upper oceans, because when they are warmer the water level is higher," Walter Munk explains. "With ATOC, we get the temperature structure of the interior ocean. We will use these two views to help produce a good climate-prediction model, which we think does not now exist." ❑

## Questions

1. Why is there a controversy between animal-protection advocates and scientists?

2. How can the average temperature of water be determined?

3. Where is most of the heat that powers the climate stored?

*Answers are at the back of the book.*

**34** *Within the last century, the Earth has warmed by approximately one degree Fahrenheit. It is reasonable to assume that increasing population, more advanced technology, and rising pollution levels are contributing to changing the Earth's climate. However, climatic change could also be attributed to natural phenomenon—such as volcanic eruption or the sun. In a concerted effort to resolve the debate, two teams of scientists developed computer models. These models were programmed to take into account that we are able to both warm and cool large portions of the earth simultaneously. Both teams agreed that human-made global warming is most likely occurring. Even though there are weaknesses to the study, it is probably accurate to assume that human influences are affecting climatic change.*

# Verdict (Almost) In
## Carl Zimmer

*Discover*,  January 1996

Police detectives aren't the only people who look for fingerprints. Climatologists do, too: they've been looking for the collective fingerprint of humanity on Earth's climate. Most of them suspect that the 6 billion tons of carbon we pump into the atmosphere each year, in the form of carbon dioxide, could warm the planet through the greenhouse effect. In the coming century the warming could be dramatic; but is it detectable already? This past year two teams of climate modelers said yes: man-made global warming is happening—almost certainly, anyway, and it's getting more certain every year.

Certainty would be easier if it were just a matter of looking at the thermometer. "We know that Earth has warmed by roughly a degree Fahrenheit in the past century," says Benjamin Santer, an atmospheric scientist at Lawrence Livermore National Laboratory in California, "but you could have many different combinations of factors—volcanoes, the sun, carbon dioxide—that give you the identical temperature change." To exclude the natural suspects, researchers have been looking not just at the average global temperature but at the geographic pattern. The idea is that if we are warming the planet by polluting it, we'd produce a different temperature pattern than the sun would.

The two teams that said in 1995 that they'd found our geographic fingerprints (Santer's at Livermore and a group at the British Meteorological Office) both used computer models. No other method is possible: you can't put the planet in a laboratory and run experiments on it. And though they used different methods, they were successful for the same basic reason: they took into account that we are able not only to warm the planet but also to cool large regions of it.

That's because each year we release not just 6 billion tons of carbon but 23 million tons of sulfur, mostly from fossil fuels and mostly in the form of sulfur dioxide. This gas turns into sulfate aerosols that reflect sunlight back into space even as carbon dioxide is trapping heat near Earth. The cooling effect of the sulfates is more regional—they tend to stay close to their sources, mainly in the Northern Hemisphere, while $CO_2$ spreads around the globe—but in just the past few years it has become clear that they have a big impact on the geographic temperature pattern. The Livermore and British teams were the first to include the effect in supercomputer climate models.

The Livermore researchers first simulated the atmosphere with preindustrial levels of $CO_2$ and measured the natural variability it might experience over the course of a few centuries. Then they added today's levels of $CO_2$ and sulfur. Overall, the combined gases did warm the planet, although not as much as $CO_2$ would alone. But the more striking result came when the researchers compared the geographic temperature pattern predicted by their model for today's polluted world with year-by-year records of the real world's climate over the past 50 years. They found that with each passing year the real-world pattern grew more like the model—which makes sense, because the real-world levels of sulfates and greenhouse gases were climbing toward today's levels. Santer and his colleague calculate that the chances of this trend's being a coincidence caused purely by natural climate variability—and unrelated to air pollution—are slim at best.

The British team reached essentially the same conclusion by a different approach; you have to simplify something to model climate even on a supercomputer, and the two teams chose different things. The British used a more realistic ocean than the Livermore group did, one that could transport heat to and from it depths, but a less realistic atmosphere: rather than re-creating the complicated chemistry of sulfate aerosols, they simply estimated how much sunlight Earth would reflect for a given level of sulfur emissions. Then they put in the actual measured increases of atmospheric carbon dioxide year by year since 1860 and tracked the response of the model. After 1950, the real world temperature pattern conformed increasingly to the one predicted by the model—suggesting, just as the Livermore study did, that $CO_2$ and sulfates were taking increasing control of climate. The chance of natural variability's producing the pattern was less than 10 percent.

The British team let their model run into the future. As sulfur emissions rise and $CO_2$ rises faster, they found, global temperature should rise 2.3 degrees Fahrenheit by the year 2050. Without sulfates, it would rise 3.3 degrees. (North America would get a bigger break—it would warm only 3 degrees instead of 4.5.)

Other climatologists have been praising these studies, but the two teams themselves are quick to point out weaknesses. The Livermore correlations between model temperature pattern and reality are much looser in winter and spring than in summer and fall. The British correlations work on the global scale, but when the researchers analyze a region like Europe or North America in detail, the correlations fall apart. And though both models now include sulfates, neither includes soot or other haze-producing hydrocarbons, which can either cool the planet or warm it. No one understands these effects well enough yet to put them in a computer model.

Yet the fact that both teams found the same strengthening pattern may nevertheless hint that our influence on climate is making itself felt. "We've found emerging evidence that we're beginning to see a fingerprint, but we're not quite there yet" is the cautious conclusion of John Mitchell, who led the British team. "As far as understanding climate change goes, this is the end of the beginning, not the beginning of the end." ❑

---

## Questions

1. When evaluating the change in the earth's temperature, what are researchers looking at to help them rule out natural phenomena?

2. What chemicals do we release into the atmosphere each year, and in what quantities?

3. The cooling effect of sulfates is regional, but how far does carbon dioxide spread?

*Answers are at the back of the book.*

---

## 35

*Since the discovery of the Antarctic ozone hole, the atmospheric science community has increased its understanding of stratospheric ozone. Through a series of field observations, laboratory experiments, and computer modeling. During this time, countries from around the world have joined the Montreal Protocol on Substances That Deplete the Ozone Layer to phase out chlorofluorocarbons and halons. Over time, evidence has accumulated that the Arctic winter stratosphere has the same chlorine species as the Antarctic ozone hole. Scientists believe that an unusually long Arctic winter could initiate severe ozone destruction. When Arctic stratospheric temperatures hit new lows in 1995, reports indicated that the ozone had diminished dramatically. For the ozone layer to recover, nations must abide by the Montreal protocol.*

# Complexities of Ozone Loss Continue to Challenge Scientists

## Pamela S. Zurer

### *Chemical & Engineering News*, June 12, 1995

*Severe Arctic depletion verified, but intricacies of polar stratospheric clouds, midlatitude loss still puzzle researchers.*

This past winter brought record ozone loss to the Arctic polar regions, scientists at an international conference confirmed last month. While reluctant to call the severe ozone destruction a "hole" like the one that develops each year over Antarctica, European researchers presented a convincing case that the depletion in the far north resulted from the same halogen-catalyzed chemistry that triggers the Antarctic phenomenon.

But few other issues addressed at the weeklong International Conference on Ozone in the Lower Stratosphere, held in Halkidiki, Greece, could be resolved with as much certainty. Atmospheric scientists are still struggling to grasp the exact nature of the polar stratospheric clouds that are so crucial to the fate of ozone in the polar regions. The dynamics of the stratosphere remain imperfectly understood. And questions persist about the mechanism of the gradual ozone-thinning trend over the midlatitude regions of North America, Asia, and Europe, where most of the world's people live.

Without a doubt, a broad outline of the complex behavior of stratospheric ozone is in focus. And—as the research presented at the conference attests—scientists are working diligently to fill in the details. Until the remaining uncertainties are clarified, however, the ability to quantitatively predict the condition of the ozone layer will remain elusive, especially as chlorine levels are expected to peak over the next few years and then slowly decline over several decades.

The goal of the recent meeting was to bring together U.S. and European scientists to share their results. "It is vital [that] information is exchanged as widely as possible within the world scientific community," said University of Cambridge chemist John L. Pyle, one of the organizers. Designed to provoke discussion, the conference featured a handful of invited talks and more than 200 poster presentations. Its sponsors included the European Union (EU), the World Meteorological Organization (WMO), the National Aeronautics & Space Administration (NASA), and the National Oceanic & Atmospheric Administration (NOAA).

For some of the 300 scientists from 40 nations who attended, the meeting marked a return trip to the lush Halkidiki Peninsula in northern Greece. Eleven years ago they had gathered to discuss ozone depletion at the very same beach resort.

Back then, depletion of stratospheric ozone by chlorine and bromine from man-made chemicals was only a hypothesis. But the discovery of the Antarctic ozone hole the following year brought theory to life, kindling a surge of research and political activity. In the decade since, the atmospheric science community has greatly improved its understanding of stratospheric ozone through a combination of field observations, laboratory experiments, and computer modeling. Meanwhile, the nations of the world have joined in the Montreal Protocol on Substances That Deplete the Ozone Layer to phase out production of chlorofluorocarbons (CFCs) and halons, the major sources of ozone-depleting halogen compounds in the stratosphere.

On the minds of many researchers as they arrived at the conference was the question of Arctic ozone depletion during the winter just past. For some years, evidence has accumulated that the Arctic winter stratosphere is loaded with the same destructive chlorine species believed to cause the Antarctic ozone hole. Only the normally milder northern winters have prevented massive ozone loss.

Atmospheric scientists have been predicting that a prolonged cold Arctic winter—more like those usually experienced in Antarctica—could unleash severe ozone destruction. Arctic stratospheric temperatures hit new lows in the early months of 1995, and preliminary reports indicated that ozone had decreased dramatically (C&EN, April 10, page 8).

Indeed, WMO's network of ground-based ozone-monitoring instruments observed record low ozone over a huge part of the Northern Hemisphere, averaging 20% less than the long-term mean, Rumen D. Bojkov told the conference. Bojkov, special adviser to the WMO secretary general, said the period of extreme low ozone began in January and extended through March.

"In some areas over Siberia, the deficiency was as much as 40%," he said. "It's only because of normally high ozone in that region that we do not have what you would call an ozone hole."

Measurements from ground-based instruments alone are not enough to prove that Arctic ozone has been destroyed chemically, however. Changes in ozone could also result from the constant motion of the atmosphere transporting air with different ozone concentrations from one place to another.

"It's difficult to tell if the variations are chemical or dynamical," mused NASA atmospheric scientist James F. Gleason. "Could an ozone high over Alaska have been balancing the low over Siberia?" Unfortunately, there have been no daily high-resolution satellite maps of global ozone to help answer that question since NASA's Total Ozone Mapping Spectrometer (TOMS) aboard Russia's Meteor-3 satellite failed in December.

Even if TOMS data were available, it would be extraordinarily difficult to untangle chemical destruction of ozone from dynamical fluctuations. The exception is the evolution of the Antarctic ozone hole each September. The stratosphere over Antarctica in winter is isolated by a circle of strong winds called the polar vortex, so ozone concentrations there are normally at a stable minimum before the ozone hole begins to form. The dramatic ozone depletion that occurs as the sun rises in early spring is unmistakable.

The Arctic polar vortex, in contrast, is usually much weaker, and ozone concentrations in the north polar regions are constantly changing. They normally increase in late winter and early spring, bolstered by waves of ozone-rich air from the tropics. So even if ozone amounts hold steady or increase somewhat in the Arctic, ozone still may have been destroyed: The concentrations may be significantly less than they would have been had there been no chemical depletion. Researchers have resorted to ingenious methods of calculating Arctic ozone loss indirectly—for example, by studying the changing ratio of the amount of ozone to the amount of the relatively inert "tracer" gas nitrous oxide in a given parcel of air.

This past winter, however, the Second European Stratospheric Arctic and Midlatitude Experiment (SESAME) generated a wealth of data that is helping to overcome the complications posed by ozone's tremendous natural variability. The 1994–95 EU-sponsored research campaign employed aircraft, balloons, and ground-based instruments to study the stratosphere. European scientists eagerly presented their latest findings at the Halkidiki conference—all of which point to widespread chemical destruction of Arctic ozone.

One elegant experiment used coordinated balloon launches to measure ozone loss directly during the Arctic winter. The trick is to measure the amount of ozone in a particular parcel of the air, track the air mass as it travels around the Arctic polar vortex, and then measure its ozone content again some days later. The approach was described by physicist Markus Rex, a doctoral student at Alfred Wegener Institute for Polar & Marine Research (AWI) in Potsdam, Germany.

In a previous experiment, Rex and his coworkers used wind and temperature data from the European Center for Medium-Range Weather Forecasts to identify which of some 1,200 ozonesondes—small balloons carrying electrochemical ozone sensors—launched during the winter of 1991–92 intercepted the same air mass at two different times. From the matches they identified, they estimate over 30% of the ozone at 20 km within the Arctic polar vortex was destroyed during January and February of 1992 [*Nature,* **375**, 131 (1995); C&EN, May 15, page 28].

Rather than again rely on chance matches as they had in 1991–92, the researchers coordinated releases of more than 1,000 ozonesondes from 35 stations during this past winter's SESAME campaign. After launching a balloon, the scientists used meteorological data to forecast its path. "As the air parcel approached another station, we asked that station to launch a second sonde," Rex said.

The scientists observed that ozone was decreasing throughout January, February, and March 1995. And they found the decline in a given air parcel was proportional to the time it had spent in sunlight, consistent with photochemical ozone depletion catalyzed by halogens.

Rex and his coworkers calculate that ozone was being lost at a rate of about 2% per day at the end of January and even faster by mid-March, when the sun was flooding a wider area. Those depletion rates are as fast as those within the Antarctic ozone hole.

"The chemical ozone loss coincides with, and slightly lags, the occurrence of temperatures low enough for polar stratospheric clouds," Rex said. Such clouds provide surfaces for reactions that convert chlorine compounds from relatively inert forms to reactive species that can chew up ozone in sunlight.

The results of other SESAME experiments add to the conclusion that the Arctic suffered severe ozone loss last winter. For example:

- Temperatures in the Arctic stratosphere in winter 1994–95 reached the lowest observed during the past 30 years, reported Barbara Naujokat of the Free University of Berlin's Meteorological Institute. The north polar vortex was unusually strong and stable, breaking up only at the end of April.

- Profiles of the vertical distribution of ozone within the polar vortex revealed as much as half of the ozone missing at certain altitudes compared with earlier years, reported AWI's Peter von der Gathen.

- An instrument carried by balloon into the stratosphere above Kiruna, Sweden, recorded high concentrations of chlorine monoxide (ClO) in February, said Darin W. Toohey, assistant professor of earth systems science at the University of California, Irvine. Chlorine monoxide, the "smoking gun" of ozone depletion, forms when chlorine atoms attack ozone. Simultaneous ozone measurements showed substantial amounts missing.

These and many other findings coalesce into an "incredibly consistent" picture of Arctic ozone depletion, said Cambridge chemist Neil Harris. But was there actually an Arctic ozone hole this year?

"I wouldn't call it a hole," said Lucien Froidevaux of California Institute of Technology's Jet Propulsion Laboratory (JPL).

"At most we've got half a hole," said Cambridge's Pyle.

"We don't have to be so hesitant," said NOAA research chemist Susan Solomon. "The data show ozone was not simply not delivered but actually removed. This is exciting confirmation of substantial Arctic ozone depletion. It's never going to look exactly like an Antarctic ozone hole, but so what?"

Whatever one chooses to call what happened in the Arctic earlier this year—one wag suggested "Arctic ozone dent"—key questions remain unanswered.

Will the severe depletion return in subsequent winters, intensify, or increase in area? How are the dramatic ozone losses in the polar regions affecting stratospheric ozone over the rest of the globe?

"Yes, I believe there have been statistically significant changes in Arctic winter ozone that we can observe," said NOAA chemist David Fahey. "But where do we go from here? Can we predict future changes?"

One issue hampering atmospheric scientists' ability to make qualitative predictions of future ozone changes is the difficulty in understanding the exact nature of polar stratospheric clouds (PSCs). For several years after their critical importance to the Antarctic ozone hole was discovered, researchers thought they had a good grasp of the situation. But reality has turned out not to be so neat, said Thomas Peter of Max Planck Institute for Chemistry, Mainz, Germany.

It is the presence of PSCs that makes ozone in the polar regions so much more vulnerable than it is in more temperate regions. The total amount of chlorine and bromine compounds is roughly uniform throughout the stratosphere. The halogens are carried there by CFCs and haloes, which break down when exposed to intense ultraviolet light in the upper stratosphere.

In most seasons and regions, the halogen atoms are tied up in so-called reservoir molecules that do not react with ozone—hydrogen chloride and chlorine nitrate ($ClONO_2$), for example. However, PSCs—which condense in the frigid cold of the stratospheric polar vortices—provide heterogeneous surfaces for reactions that convert the reservoir species to more reactive ones.

The most important reaction is between the two chlorine reservoirs:

$$ClONO_2 + HCl \rightarrow Cl_2 + HNO_3$$

The molecular chlorine produced flies off into the gas phase, where it is photolyzed easily by even weak sunlight to give chlorine radicals—active chlorine—that can catalyze ozone destruction.

Equally important is the fate of the nitric acid ($HNO_3$) produced by the heterogeneous chemistry. It remains within the PSCs, effectively sequestering the nitrogen family of compounds that would otherwise react with active chlorine to reform chlorine nitrate. That process, called denitrification, allows the photochemical chain reactions that destroy ozone to run efficiently for a long time without termination.

Laboratory and field experiments have confirmed the importance of heterogeneous reactions in the winter polar stratosphere. What is at question now is the actual composition of the PSCs, how they nucleate and grow, their surface area, and their chemical reactivity. All those factors affect the interconversion of halogen compounds between their active and inactive forms, and thus the rate and amount of ozone depletion.

Peter described the "happy period" in the late 1980s when scientists were confident they understood just what PSCs are. Type I PSCs were thought to be crystals of nitric acid trihydrate (NAT) that condensed on small sulfate aerosol particles once temperatures cooled below about 195 K. Frozen water ice (type II) appears once stratospheric temperatures plunge lower than about 187 K, which generally happens only in Antarctica.

Now it appears type I PSCs are not so simple. "Say 'bye bye' to the notion PSCs must be solid," Peter said. "They can be liquid. Both types of particles are up there."

Margaret A. Tolbert, associate professor of chemistry and biochemistry at the University of Colorado, Boulder, explained that "Everybody assumed type I PSCs were NAT, which condenses about 195 K. But observations show nothing actually condenses until about 193 K. That doesn't prove the particles aren't NAT. But they may instead be supercooled ternary solutions" of water, sulfuric acid, and nitric acid.

Such supercooled solutions could develop from small sulfate aerosol particles. (The stratosphere contains a permanent veil of sulfate aerosol droplets, which form when sulfur dioxide from volcanic eruptions and carbonyl sulfide emitted by living creatures are oxidized to sulfuric acid.) As the stratosphere cools in winter, the sulfate aerosols could take up water and nitric acid, growing larger but remaining liquid.

Whether type I PSCs are solid or liquid can make a significant difference, said NOAA chemist A.J. Ravishankara. He noted that chemistry could occur not just on the surface of supercooled solutions, but also in the interior of the droplet, which he likened to a little beaker. That implies scientists would have to consider not just the surface area of the particles but their volume in calculating the rates of chemical processes involving PSCs.

Furthermore, he said, the supercooled solutions may persist over a larger temperature range than solid NAT particles. That would allow transformation of halogens to their active forms to take place over a wider temperature range than previously recognized.

The implications of chemical processing taking place on and in supercooled ternary solutions extend beyond the polar regions, where PSCs appear, to more temperate regions of the globe. Although changes in ozone in the midlatitude stratosphere are nowhere near as dramatic as in the polar regions, they are real and substantial. The latest United Nations Environment Program study "Scientific Assessment of Ozone Depletion," concludes that ozone in the midnorthern regions, for example, has been decreasing at a rate of about 4% per decade since 1979.

Atmospheric scientists have been struggling to quantitatively explain that decrease, which is predominantly in the lower stratosphere. Chlorine and bromine radicals are clearly implicated, but in the absence of PSCs they destroy ozone most voraciously at much higher altitudes where there simply isn't all that much ozone to begin with. Modelers have been plugging every known ozone destruction cycle into their calculations but still have not been able to account for all of the ozone loss observed below about 20 km.

Roderic L. Jones, of Cambridge's chemistry department, noted that chemistry involving supercooled ternary solutions could have significant effects on ozone trends at midlatitudes. "Look at areas in the Northern Hemisphere that are exposed to temperatures just above the NAT [condensation] point, about 197 or 199 K," he said. "It's a big area, extending as far south as 50° N."

Supercooled solutions may turn out to play an important role in explaining what's going on at midlatitudes. But JPL modeler Ross J. Salawitch said he thinks the problem may arise from the way scientists approximate the dynamics of the stratosphere in their models.

Two-dimensional models treat ozone as if it diffused out uniformly from the tropical stratosphere where it is produced. "The real world is more like the 'tropical pipe'" paradigm, Salawitch said, in which air rises high into the stratosphere in the tropics and moves downward again at higher latitudes, like a sort of fountain.

"The issue of whether the global diffusion or the tropical pipe model better represents reality is not just an academic discussion," Salawitch said. "The question of a midlatitude deficit may disappear when the models handle dynamics better."

Answers to some of the issues that continue to bedevil atmospheric researchers may become clear as more data accumulate. Participants in the SESAME campaign have barely had time to think about what they observed. And NASA has just begun its new three-year Stratospheric Transport of Atmospheric Tracers mission.

But the stratospheric ozone layer may reveal even further complexities in the coming years. As Christos S. Zerefos, local organizer of the conference from the laboratory of atmospheric physics at Aristotle University of Thessaloníki, Greece, pointed out in his closing remarks, the ozone layer will only begin to recover if the nations of the world continue to comply with the Montreal protocol. If not, atmospheric scientists may have even greater puzzles to contend with. ❑

## Questions

1. What are the major sources of ozone-depleting halogen compounds in the stratosphere?

2. What has prevented massive ozone loss?

3. What was used to study the stratosphere, and what were the results?

*Answers are at the back of the book.*

**36**

*Depletion of the atmospheric ozone layer is generally considered one of the major environmental threats facing humanity and indeed all life on earth. The ozone layer shields the earth from high levels of ultraviolet and other dangerous solar radiation so that the loss of even a few percent of the ozone layer would lead to increased mutation rates, skin cancer, blindness, and many other health hazards. Harmful effects on plant and animal life, including plankton in the ocean, would also occur, with potentially widespread impacts on many ecosystems. Because of these threats, many nations signed the Montreal Protocol of 1987, agreeing to phase out production and use of chlorine-containing chemicals, such as CFCs, which deplete the ozone layer. Recent evidence suggests that the protocol has been successful in slowing the rate of CFC production. However, developing nations have, for economic reasons, been less effective in reducing production.*

# Ozone-Destroying Chlorine Tops Out
## Richard A. Kerr

*Science*, January 1996

The title of the session at the American Geophysical Union's fall meeting last month was "The Montreal Protocol to Protect the Ozone Layer: Has It Worked?" The answer was "yes, so far at least." The prime evidence for the success of the 1987 international agreement to restrict the use of ozone-destroying chemicals—most of which contain chlorine—is that atmospheric chlorine has peaked and is on the way down.

The chlorine decline, reported by atmospheric chemist Stephen Montzka of the National Oceanic and Atmospheric Administration in Boulder, Colorado, bodes well for the stratospheric ozone layer. One computer model of ozone destruction presented at the meeting predicts that the chlorine controls imposed by the recently strengthened protocol should allow the ozone layer to begin recovering before the end of this decade. But some new observations suggest that the recovery may be delayed. Losses to another ozone-killer, bromine, may be temporarily offsetting the gains from the chlorine reduction.

The good news on chlorine comes after decades when the annual release of one million tons or more of chlorofluorocarbons (CFCs), used for refrigeration, blowing foams, and cleaning electronics, drove chlorine concentrations up several percent each year. If no controls had been adopted until 2010, calculates Michael Prather of the University of California, Irvine, stratospheric chlorine would have topped out at levels more than three times higher than today's, the Antarctic ozone hole would appear well into the 22nd century, and springtime ozone losses over middle northern latitudes would soar above today's 8%, possibly to well above 30%.

Instead, by 1990 the Montreal Protocol restrictions began to slow the rise in chlorine noticeably (*Science*, January 1, 1993, p.28). By the end of 1994, as production of CFCs plummeted, chlorine peaked, reported Montzka, at least in the lower atmosphere where it can be readily monitored. And now the amount of chlorine in CFCs and other halocarbons seems to be headed down, Montzka said. Using a computer model, Charles Jackman in Greenbelt, Maryland, found that if the chlorine controls hold, ozone should begin recovering by 2000 and return to 1979 levels—the year the Antarctic ozone hole became obvious—by around 2050.

Recent atmospheric data reported by Ronald Prinn of the Massachusetts Institute of Technology suggested, however, that potential gaps in the existing protocol could slow the recovery. Although chlorine—the major ozone destroyer—seems to have peaked, says Prinn, the total ozone-destroying power of humanmade chemicals in the atmosphere has "perhaps reached a plateau, but certainly is not decreasing." This measure also includes bromine, an ozone destroyer that is scarcer than chlorine but at least 40 times more potent on an atom-for-atom basis. Prinn finds that the increasing concentrations of halons—bromine-containing compounds released from fire-protection systems—have for the moment sustained the ozone-destroying power of the atmosphere.

Production of halons was halted in 1994 under the protocol, but halons in existing firefighting systems are a continuing source of emissions. And because replacements for some halons have not yet been identified, users may be tempted to go on consuming existing industrial stocks. Methyl bromide, a soil and stored-grain fumigant, could also contribute to a future bromine increase. Meeting in Vienna last month, the parties to the protocol decided to phases out use of methyl bromide by 2010, but as yet unspecified exemptions may be granted.

Even chlorine, although under control, is far from eliminated as a threat. Rich, technologically sophisticated countries have found it relatively easy to move away from CFC use, notes Prather, but developing countries, which have laxer schedules to meet under the protocol, have yet to follow suit. Even in wealthy countries, the hydrogenated CFCs used in place of traditional CFCs are still weak ozone destroyers. Clearly, the Montreal Protocol has some more milestones to reach. ❏

---

## Questions

1. According to the model by Charles Jackman, when should the ozone layer return to its 1979 levels, if current controls hold?

2. Is bromine more destructive than chlorine? If so, how much more destructive? Where does bromine come from?

3. What are halogenated CFCs? Do they destroy ozone?

*Answers are at the back of the book.*

---

## 37

*According to a 1994 report by an Environmental Protection Agency work group, animal factories are the largest contributors to polluted rivers and streams. This includes storm sewers and all industrial sources combined. Most of the two billion tons of manure produced by farm animals each year comes from factory farms. Super-wastes that come from these factories have devastating impacts on the local environment. The enormous waste problems that these factory farms have created have not been solved, and some states are campaigning to keep animal farms out.*

# Fowling the Waters
## Jim Mason

*E Magazine*, September/October 1995

*Animal factories are the biggest contributors to polluted rivers and streams—bigger than storm sewers, bigger than all industrial sources combined.*

Roger Brown joined Citizens Against Corporate Hog Factories (CACHF) because he believes his rural Missouri community is turning—literally—to manure.

Brown ought to know. The former manager of a poultry complex for Arkansas-based Hudson Foods parted ways with the company in a dispute over how to safely get rid of the manure-soaked litter from the company's turkey "growout" buildings, or "factories," as he and the locals call them. Brown and other Missourians are fighting a half-dozen agribusiness corporations that want to bring in hog factories. "If they come in, we'll have one big stink around here," he says.

"Factory" farming is a billion-dollar industry in America. Over 90 percent of the chicken and eggs we eat get produced in crowded, windowless buildings, each holding as many as 100,000 animals. Beef cattle are raised not in bucolic fields, but in huge, dusty feedlots. Farmers slaughter more than one million veal calves—raised in tightly confining crates—every year. Seven-hundred-pound hogs stand

crowded together in spaces barely larger than their own bodies.

People in North Carolina, Iowa, northern Missouri, Illinois, Tennessee, and almost a dozen other states want to keep factory farms out. These states are becoming battlegrounds as the corporate takeover of poultry and hog farming is rapidly changing the face of animal agriculture. Where once farm animals were dispersed among the nation's grainfields and pasturelands, allowing their wastes to go back to the soil slowly and evenly, today the mobility of corporate money and technology allows Tyson, Hudson, Conagra, Cargill, Continental Grain, Premium Standard Farms, Murphy Farms, and other agribusiness firms to out-compete traditional farmers.

Brown and other critics feel that big agribusiness wants to cash in on the public's seemingly insatiable demand for cheap meat. The corporations go to regions that have poor environmental laws, an anti-regulatory culture, low wages and a docile, anti-union labor pool. There they set up huge factories in which most caretaking chores are mechanized, and any manual labor is so routinized that workers are easily trained and replaced.

The trouble is, such schemes have created huge waste problems, which corporations have been neither quick nor eager to solve. A 60,000-bird egg factory full of "1ayer" hens jammed into rows of cages stacked four-high, for example, produces 82 tons of manure every week. In the same week, 50,000 hogs in a megafactory can produce over 3,000 tons of manure. In all, America's farm animals produce about two billion tons of manure each year—about 10 times that of the human population—and most of it now comes from factory farms. The environmental hazards of animal manure were brought dramatically home last June 24 when 25 million gallons of hog waste spilled into the New River in Haw Branch, North Carolina, causing serious pollution and killing countless fish.

What's worse, factory manure is more polluting than the old-fashioned kind. When on pasture, animals get a high-fiber, low-cal diet of grasses and roughage, plenty of vitamins and minerals, and traces of micronutrients like copper, zinc and selenium. When animals are confined, these elements have to be added to the feed—often in excessive amounts. And, to speed growth, factory animals get a steady diet of ground grain and other rich feedstuffs loaded with protein and energy—so loaded, in fact, that the animals can absorb only about 20 percent of all the nutrients. The rest become a very rich manure—rich not only with protein and the usual organic matter, but also with nitrogen, phosphorous, heavy metals, feed additives and other potential pollutants.

Factory super-wastes, if not carefully handled, can create havoc in the local environment. Full of organic matter, decaying animal waste uses up oxygen in fresh water. Rich in nitrates, phosphorous, and other minerals, it encourages algae to grow, which takes up even more oxygen. This can kill streams and the fish and other life in them.

The 550 million chickens in factories surrounding the Chesapeake Bay contribute heavily to nitrate pollution of the area's soils and waters. Manure from New York state dairies pollutes the watershed for cities' drinking water. And in Wisconsin, "the dairy state," cow manure carried the microorganism cryptosporidium that wound up in Milwaukee's water supply, causing death and widespread dysentery in 1993. According to a 1994 report by an Environmental Protection Agency (EPA) workgroup, animal factories are the biggest contributors to polluted rivers and streams—bigger than storm sewers, bigger than all industrial sources combined.

There's a final cost behind the much-touted "efficiency" of the factory farm: Even the best factories convert no more than 23 percent of the energy and protein fed to animals into energy and protein in the form of meat, milk, or eggs.

Contact: United Poultry Concerns, P.O. Box 59367, Potomac, MD 20859/(301)948-2406. ❏

---

## Questions

1. What percentage of the chicken and eggs that we consume comes from factory farming?

2. What types of areas do corporations choose in order to set up animal factories?

3. How can factory super-wastes destroy streams and the life contained in them?

*Answers are at the back of the book.*

---

**38**    *Germany perceives that eliminating pollution can strengthen the nation's economy. The Germans believe that efforts to decrease pollution by increasing efficiency will reduce operating expenses. In turn, this will increase employment opportunities and boost income. Having the world's most rigid environmental regulations encourages the development of "green" technologies that Germany can market globally. Recycling in Germany has numeric requirements. For example, 90 percent of discarded glass and metals and 80 percent of paper, board, plastics, and laminates must be recycled. Recycled plastic increased from 41,000 tons in 1992 to ten times that in 1993. Germany also has an environmental labeling program in which the government gives a brief description of the product's qualities, such as "low-noise" or "100-percent recycled." This label has a figure in blue with outstretched arms encircled by the laurel wreath of the United Nations. It is aptly named the Blue Angel environmental labeling program. Germany is looking to the future through innovation. With long-term stringent environmental laws benefiting the economy and employment, Germany has become a model for the world.*

# Green Revolution in the Making
## Curtis Moore

*Sierra*, January/February 1995

---

*Nations like Germany that mandate clean technologies are poised to profit. It's an economic lesson the U.S. has yet to grasp.*

All in all, it's been a pretty tough 14 years for Americans seeking to make a buck by protecting the environment, and this factory in the heart of Germany says it all. As wide ribbons of heavy, brown kraft paper unspool from massive rolls onto a production line, a coverall-clad worker stands with his beefy left hand gripping a switch. At his elbow, a constant stream of cream-colored gypsum paste squirts between the kraft sheets, forming an endless plaster sandwich that disappears into a flat, shimmering oven where it is baked to rock hardness. With his back arched and his head cocked, the worker peers down the production line as mile after mile of what Americans call "Sheetrock" or "wallboard" thunders through the factory, bound for building sites in Germany and across Europe to form the walls and ceilings of offices and bedrooms, closets and boardrooms.

Just another factory making one of the thousands of products so common that they are scarcely worth noting, a casual observer might say—but not

so. This factory represents the leading edge of a new technological revolution, one that could transform the industrial world from a cauldron of pollution to a relatively safe haven. For this wallboard is made from—are you ready?—air pollution.

This process of making wallboard, mortar, and other construction materials—and from them, homes and offices—out of the residues of air pollution is emblematic of the innovations that have sprung up as Germany, propelled by a fierce environmental ethic, has leapt to the forefront of the global environmental movement.

The German passion for environmental protection was fueled initially in the late 1970s and early '80s by reports of *Waldsterben,* or "forest death"— the widespread damage to the country's forests caused by air pollution. After that, the meltdown at Chernobyl and mounting fears of stratospheric-ozone depletion and global warming established a firm ecological consciousness, leading the *Los Angeles Times* to comment that in Germany, "environmental correctness has come to rival tidiness and punctuality as a national obsession." As ethically committed as Germany's citizens and government are to protecting the earth, they also perceive the process of

**Reprinted with permission from the January/February 1995 issue of *Sierra*.**

eliminating pollution as an opportunity to further strengthen their nation's economy.

Already running a close race with the United States as the world's leading exporter of merchandise, Germany is convinced that its environmental regulations, easily the world's most stringent, will stimulate the development of a wide range of new "green" technologies that can be marketed globally just as demand for them is beginning to increase sharply. The Germans also believe that new efforts to curb pollution by boosting efficiency will further reduce operating expenses in their already efficient economy, providing them with a competitive edge over Japan and (especially) the United States.

The homes-from-pollution process illustrates how environmental concerns have stimulated German innovation, causing many of the country's firms not only to launch their own research programs, but to raid the workshops of less-alert competitors—including the United States, where many of these new technologies were developed. Like any number of other emerging technologies, ranging from super-efficient electrical generators to add-on pollution-control systems, the homes-from-pollution process is a product of Yankee ingenuity. It was originally installed in 1973 at the Cholla I power plant in Arizona during the first wave of air-pollution regulation in the United States, but the process was exported to Germany in 1980, where it has thrived and been perfected. This is how it works:

When coal is burned to generate electricity, prodigious amounts of pollutants pour into the air, including sulfur dioxide, which causes acid rain. Some nations, though not many, require modest controls over these emissions. If the regulations are stringent, scrubbers are usually installed to remove the sulfur dioxide by spraying the exhaust with a watery mist containing limestone. The pollution/limestone reaction produces a sludge that is usually dumped on the ground or into pits or waterways.

But in Germany, where all power plants are equipped with pollution controls, the sludge can't be dumped because the law prohibits it. Such waste must be put to some use, leaving German power plants with two options: develop a means other than scrubbers to eliminate the air pollution, or find a way to use the scrubber sludge. German industry has done both, yielding two simultaneous streams of innovation, one aimed at developing pollution-control systems superior to scrubbers, the other at devising better ways to use scrubber waste. Both streams not only help make the German economy itself more efficient, but create products that can be sold on the world market, boosting employment and income at home.

When the homes-from-pollution system was exported to Germany in 1980, it was initially marketed by Knauf-Research Cotrell (KRC), a subsidiary of its U.S. developer and Knauf Gypsum. Rapidly improved there in response to the German air-pollution and waste requirements, the technology was acquired in October 1986 by the Salzgitter Group, which now sells the system globally.

One place where the technology has been installed is New Brunswick, Canada, where the 450-megawatt, coal-fired Belledune power station went into operation in 1993. The production of market-grade gypsum was "a fundamental requirement" contained in the specifications for the Belledune plant, in the words of an executive of New Brunswick Power, because it not only solved waste-disposal problems, but was less expensive than competing systems. Thus, a North American innovation traveled to Europe and back again in the space of 20 years (though the profits are being made by Germans) and is selling globally because it is, quite simply, better than the alternatives.

Sadly, the U.S. market for the homes-from-pollution process was destroyed in the 1970s when the federal government allowed utilities to build "tall stacks" for dispersing sulfur dioxide over wide areas—thus creating a new acid-rain problem—rather than requiring them to eliminate it. Even if strict controls on power plants had remained in effect, however, lax waste-disposal regulations might have had the same ultimate impact. In Germany, though, the process has proved so effective and profitable that in 1990 Knauf Gypsum opened a British plant at Sittingborne-on-Thames, where German air-pollution residues are made into building materials for homes and factories. Flowing in the opposite direction, of course, is profit that can be plowed back into the German economy—perhaps to acquire still more products of U.S. origin.

There are other examples of remarkable innovation stimulated by Germany's tough attitudes toward pollution:

• The Ford auto plant in Cologne complied with new requirements by modernizing its paint-spray line, cutting pollution by 70 percent and the cost of painting a car by about $60—a savings that makes German-built cars marginally more salable.

• The "4P" plastic-film manufacturing and printing plant in Forchheim, where plastic bags for frozen french fries and other foods are printed and stamped by the millions, was forced to cut pollution by 70 percent. The company installed a recycling system that reclaims up to 90 percent of the plant's solvents, saving so much money that the 4P pollution controls will not only pay for themselves, but actually start saving the company money by reducing the cost of solvents. A sister plant with a similar system already recaptures solvents—once again lowering its overhead while increasing profit.

Little wonder that Edda Müller, former chief aide to Germany's minister for the environment, declares emphatically that "what we are doing here is economic policy, not environmental policy."

She is not alone in this view of the future, nor is Germany. For example, Takefumi Fukumizu, U.S. representative of Japan's powerful Ministry of International Trade and Industry, says that industrialists in his country see "an inescapable economic necessity to improve energy efficiency and environmental technologies, which they believe would reduce costs and create a profitable world market."

With virtually no coal, oil, or natural gas, and limited mineral resources, Japan has historically been forced to do more with less than its principal industrial competitors, the United States and Germany. As a result, it makes steel, automobiles, and a wide range of other goods with greater efficiency and less pollution than any other nation. That national thrift and the technologies it has spawned are now global commodities as other nations increasingly search for cleaner, more efficient manufacturing methods and energy use. "The potential profit in such a market," explains Fukumizu, "is limitless."

In the United States, however, governments and businesses alike remain so focused on short-term profits and quarterly earnings that they overlook the true source of long-term wealth: innovation. Necessity breeds invention, and during the 1970s, when protecting the environment and saving energy were seen as essential elements of national policy, the United States brought hundreds of new products and processes to the verge of commercial reality.

These ranged from systems to generate electricity from wind and sunlight with zero pollution to little-known devices such as fuel cells that can power everything from homes to locomotives with zero or near-zero pollution and noise, while requiring minimal space. Yet these and thousands of other born-in-the-U.S.A. environmental products were abandoned during the 1980s as the Reagan and Bush administrations, the Congress, and many state officials turned their backs on environmental protection, orphaning technologies that now stand to generate billions, perhaps trillions, of dollars for their new proponents.

Solar photovoltaics, for example, were originally developed to generate electricity for space satellites, then modified for ground-based uses, making the United States the world's leading producer. But when Ronald Reagan took office, he slashed federal funding for the program from more than $150 million to zero. Then he rejected the "energy independence" policies of presidents Nixon, Ford, and Carter, substituting a "cheap oil" strategy expressly designed to increase U.S. reliance on Persian Gulf oil by driving prices down through secret negotiations with Saudi Arabia. As oil prices plummeted, they destroyed the U.S. market for solar and other forms of renewable energy, allowing the Japanese, Germans, and others to buy companies, patents, and production licenses for pennies on the dollar. Now Japan is the world's leading producer of solar cells. The United States is second, but the nation's largest factory is owned by the German conglomerate Siemens. If its production were assigned to Germany instead of the United States, America's photovoltaic sector would drop to a level on par with those of developing nations like Brazil.

A similar fate befell fuel cells, compact and virtually silent devices that chemically convert fuel to electricity. When run on hydrogen, fuel cells produce zero pollution or, if a hydrogen "carrier" such as natural gas is used, almost zero. First developed for the space program, they still meet all of the electrical needs of NASA's space shuttles. But in the 1980s, U.S. companies such as General Electric and Englehard turned their backs on fuel-cell technology. As a result, the world's first fuel-cell assembly line was Japanese, and the first zero-polluting, fuel-cell-powered bus is Canadian. Both employ technologies that were developed with hundreds of millions of U.S. tax dollars. The governments of both Canada and Japan helped their nation's companies acquire and develop the fuel-cell technology.

The list goes on and on, and includes technologies ranging from high-efficiency light bulbs to new ways of burning coal, all developed in large part, with U.S. capital, but now wholly or partially in the hands of others. In the United States, the cheap-oil strategy remains in place, energy taxes have been rejected by Congress, and environmental laws continue to fall further and further behind those of Germany, Japan, Sweden, the Netherlands, and other industrialized nations. Once the world's environmental leader, the United States is now a laggard, its political landscape hostile to those seeking to pioneer in what many regard as a new industrial revolution greening the global economy.

Germany, meanwhile, has been restructuring the technological basis of its economy to make it sustainable over the long run, leading to a profusion of new environmental products and processes spurred by the world's most aggressive protection programs. Consider, for example, the following:

• It is retrofitting all power plants. While politicians in North America were arguing about whether acid rain was real, Germany listened to its scientists and adopted rules requiring every power plant within its borders to slash the air pollutants that cause acid rain by 90 percent. By 1989 the German retrofit was complete. Today, seven years before the U.S. control program will take full effect in 2002, Germans are selling Americans and the rest of the world anti-pollution technology and know-how.

• It is aggressively phasing out chemicals that destroy the ozone layer and cause global warming. In 1989 Germany mandated a ban by 1995—five years before the rest of the world—on chlorofluorocarbon (CFC) gases, the primary culprits in the destruction of the ozone layer that protects Earth from solar radiation. It had also committed to reducing emissions of carbon dioxide, the principal cause of global warming, by 25 percent by the year 2010. These are the swiftest and toughest phase-downs in the world, and they required German industries to respond quickly, creating new products and processes that can be marketed globally as other nations begin to follow suit.

• It is revolutionizing the trash business. Aiming not only to reduce the volume of trash swelling landfills and clogging incinerators, Germany has also fostered a new industry by adopting a "take back" program that requires everything from cameras to yogurt cartons—and the scrubber sludge from which Knauf Gypsum makes wallboard—to be collected by manufacturers and recycled. The program was so fabulously successful that the volume of trash quickly outstripped the nation's recycling capacity, thus creating even further pressure for industry to minimize packaging and other waste. Although the program was originally meant to include cars as well, German manufacturers staved off formal government action by agreeing to mount voluntary take-back programs, thus starting a global movement among car makers to develop vehicles that can be recycled. Some are already rolling off the assembly line with bar-coded parts and instructions for dismantling an auto in 20 minutes.

Like most of Germany's environmental laws, the take-back rule imposes explicit, numeric requirements: as of this year, 90 percent of all discarded glass and metals must be recycled, as well as 80 percent of all paper, board, plastics, and laminates. Incineration, even if used to generate power, has been ruled out as a solid-waste-disposal method because the burning of materials pollutes the air, especially with highly toxic dioxins and furans.

Because the take-back law sweeps virtually every form of waste into its ambit, its results were almost immediate: 400 German companies randomly surveyed less than 18 months after the law took effect on December 1, 1991, said they had completely abandoned use of polyvinyl packaging, plastic foams, and 117 other types of packaging.

All but one of 146 companies had stopped using "blister" packs, which are both tough to recycle and yield dioxins when burned. One of every four companies was using packaging made at least in part from recycled materials. Companies were running full-page newspaper advertisements touting the recyclability of their products. And with good reason, as almost two-thirds of Germany's consumers shop for environmentally friendly products. Indeed, public insistence on recycling has become so widespread in Germany that the amount of recycled plastic rocketed from 41,000 tons in 1992 to ten times that amount a year later. Now, the nation has become a favorite testing ground for products to be marketed as environmentally safe. When in 1991, for example, Procter & Gamble introduced Vidal Sassoon "Airspray" hair spray in the United States, it did so only after testing in Germany. Similarly, two years earlier, P&G launched its "Enviro-pak" containers for laundry detergents in the United States only after testing in Germany.

Companies such as P&G have no choice but to develop such products if they wish to do business in Germany. One reason for this is the government's Blue Angel environmental labeling program. Introduced in 1977, Blue Angel is a symbol owned by Germany's environment ministry, which describes it as "a market-oriented instrument of government" that informs and motivates environmentally conscious thinking and acting among manufacturers and consumers. The ministry licenses the label's use for about 3,500 products selected on a case-by-case basis by the independent, nine-member Environmental Label Jury. The label depicts a blue figure with outstretched arms encircled by the laurel wreath of the United Nations. Inscribed in the border for each product is a brief explanation of the product's qualities, such as "low-polluting," "low-noise," or "100-percent recycled." Although there are imitators in other countries—the Green Cross of Canada, for example—Germany's Blue Angel remains far and away the most famous and successful environmental-labeling program.

In the United States, efforts to establish such a government-sponsored labeling system have foundered on industry opposition. A private effort, Green Seal, is struggling to establish itself, but is hampered by high testing costs and a lack of publicity. In Germany, however, the Blue Angel offers its bearers the prospect of winning an edge over competing brands and products in the environmentally conscious German marketplace. The prospect of its award—and attendant profits—has made it possible for a wide variety of environmentally friendly products ranging from low-pollution paints to mercury-free batteries to establish themselves. Public recognition of and enthusiasm for the Blue Angel program has boosted the market share of many products. For instance, before water-soluble lacquers were awarded a Blue Angel in 1981, these products commanded a meager one-percent market share. Today, 40 percent of Germany's do-it-yourself wood finishers and 20 percent of its professionals buy the less-toxic coatings. Similarly, biodegradable chainsaw lubricants are in high demand by the foresters who manage virtually every acre of Germany's woodlands. First introduced in 1987, the formula eliminates up to 7,000 tons a year of highly toxic oil otherwise absorbed by forest floors and nearby streams. After receiving a Blue Angel, these oils achieved a dominating position in the market.

Having deployed these weapons in their battle against pollution of air, water, and soil, some German officials believe they have all but exhausted the reductions that can be achieved through conventional cleanup means such as wastewater-treatment plants and scrubbers. Nevertheless, pressured by voters to cut pollution further, the government is imposing a wide range of increasingly tough requirements designed to reduce pollution by further increasing efficiency both in factories and on the highways.

Regulations now being implemented, for example, will force drivers out of gas-guzzling cars and onto energy-efficient public transit. Inner cities are being systematically closed to auto traffic, while highway, bridge, and other tolls are being raised, and long-term "green passes" for public transportation are sold in all of Germany's major cities. A Berlin green pass costs about $40 a month, and is valid for an unlimited number of rides. A comparable pass in Washington, D.C., costs roughly twice as much. Germany also intends to increase bicycle ridership by providing specially marked lanes on sidewalks and at intersections.

Systematically shifting people and goods in this fashion not only reduces pollution, but boosts the overall efficiency of Germany's economy by cutting transportation costs. Commuting by train, for example, slashes both fuel consumption and air pollution by up to 75 percent compared with cars, and 90 percent compared with planes. Traffic congestion and the pollution it generates, as cars creep through crowded roadways or idle at stoplights, is also cut, because trains occupy only a quarter of the road space required by buses and 1/13th that needed by cars. Because trains run on electricity generated by Germany's domestic coal, oil imports required to fuel diesel buses or gasoline cars are likewise reduced.

The nation's self-imposed target of reducing carbon dioxide emissions from the former West Germany by 25 percent and from the former East Germany by 30 percent—both by the year 2010—requires the economy to become even more efficient. One way the country intends to achieve this is to put energy that is now being wasted to some useful purpose.

In most power plants and factories, only about one-third of the energy in coal, oil, or gas is actually used. The rest escapes as waste heat. The German government has prepared regulations that will require large- and medium-size industries and utilities to market this waste energy. It can be used to heat homes and factories (or, by running CFC-free "absorption chillers," to cool them), operate paper mills and chemical plants, and even generate a few more kilowatts with super-efficient technology. Officials estimate that use of this waste heat will boost efficiency to roughly 90 percent and that air pollution—already at the world's lowest levels—will be chopped by at least half.

Because of the immense cost of bringing the former East Germany into compliance with the environmental requirements of the former West Germany, the waste-heat law has been delayed while officials turn to more pressing needs. Work is already under way, for example, on shutting down 80 percent of the former East Germany's power plants while retrofitting the remaining facilities that generate 10,000 megawatts—that's slightly more than Thailand's entire electricity consumption—with state-of-the-art pollution controls.

The cumulative effect of all these programs is to place Germany in a commanding position as nations beset with environmental problems search for ways to reduce pollution quickly and inexpensively. Thailand, for example, decided to install scrubbers on its coal-fired power plants after a single episode of air pollution in Mae Mo District sent more than 4,000 of its citizens to doctors and hospitals. Smog-bound Mexico City has been forced to implement emissions controls on cars and factories. Taiwan is even going so far as to require catalytic converters for motorcycles. Such mandates will almost inevitably benefit Germany because, as Harvard Business School economist Michael Porter explains, "Germany has had perhaps the world's tightest regulations in stationary air-pollution control, and German companies appear to hold a wide lead in patenting—and exporting—air pollution and other environmental technologies."

In the United States, however, where environmental standards were relaxed by a succession of Reagan/Bush appointees, often in the name of competitiveness, "as much as 70 percent of the air pollution control equipment sold . . . is produced by foreign companies," according to Porter, whose 855-page study of industrial economies, *The Competitive Advantage of Nations,* examines the impact of environmental regulations on competitiveness.

Germany's actions continue to contrast sharply with those of the United States, even under President Clinton, whom most environmentalists supported as the green answer to George Bush. Germany's emissions limits on power plants and incinerators are 4 to 300 times more stringent than those of the United States. German companies that generate electricity from wind, solar, or other renewable forms of power are reimbursed at twice to three times U.S. levels. German recycling is mandatory, while American programs are usually voluntary where they exist at all.

Still, support for Germany's environmental initiatives is by no means unanimous. Wolfgang Hilger, for example, the chairman of Hoechst, Germany's largest chemical company, complained bitterly in 1991 that the government had lost all sense of proportion. He claimed that regulations had jeopardized 250 jobs at his company, and threatened it with a $100-million loss. But Hilger represents a minority view. Most German citizens and businesses remain convinced both that environmental protection is essential and that the technological innovation stimulated by stringent environmental requirements will, over the long term, strengthen their national productivity and competitiveness.

Tragically, U.S. political leaders continue to embrace the outmoded and false view that the environment can be protected only at the expense of the economy, when the truth is precisely the opposite. Meanwhile, products of American genius continue to depart for Japan, Germany, and other nations, only to be sold back to U.S. industry sometime in the future. So far, the homes-from-pollution process hasn't traveled full circle back to its place of invention in the United States. But don't be surprised if sometime soon you see a piece of wallboard being nailed into a new of office or a remodeled home only to find it boldly emblazoned: "Made in Germany." ❑

---

## Questions

1. What is the Blue Angel environmental labeling program?

2. How will waste heat be marketed, and what will be its effect on efficiency and air pollution?

3. How much more stringent are Germany's emissions limits on power plants and incinerators than those of United States?

*Answers are at the back of the book.*

---

**39** *The use of herbicides and pesticides is becoming a concern, especially for the segment of the population exposed daily to these chemicals. These fears were intensified in Boone, North Carolina, when the community realized that the chemicals used on their Fraser firs contributed to the high rate of childhood leukemia in the area. They found that the chemicals were leaching down into the water supplies. This discovery initiated a change in local farming practices. As farmers turned to natural biological-control methods instead of using harmful chemicals, groundwater supplies improved and more wildlife appeared in the area. Most important, there has not been a new case of childhood leukemia in four years. The case of Boone, North Carolina, illustrates ecologically sound and healthful ways to grow crops.*

# Growing a Healthy Crop for Christmas
## Nan Chase

*National Wildlife*, December/January 1996

*Concerned about leukemia rates in their community, these North Carolina Christmas-tree growers voluntarily reduced pesticide use.*

Six years ago, Christmas-tree farmers in and around the peaceful Appalachian Mountain community of Boone, North Carolina, faced up to a horrible possibility: That their heavy use of chemicals to control insect pests and weeds in their fields of Fraser firs might be contributing to the community's high incidence of childhood leukemia—a rate 9.2 times higher than the number expected for a population of 36,000, according to federal cancer statistics. Local doctors were also concerned that the chemicals might be seeping into water supplies throughout Watauga County. They turned to the North Carolina Central Cancer Registry for help.

The farmers later made an impression on the registry's field staff. "Their feeling was, 'We drink the water too. If you're concerned, we're concerned,'" says Tim Aldrich, director of the registry. Aldrich and other North Carolina authorities were indeed concerned. Though no evidence existed that conclusively linked local chemical-pesticide use to the cancer rate, the possibility of such a link was enough to spark a revolution in Watauga County's Christmas-tree industry.

Today, after coordinated educational efforts between state agricultural officials and tree growers, hundreds of Watauga County farmers have cut back drastically on the number and amounts of toxic chemicals they use. Their new farming practices are also producing more habitat for wildlife. "We've simply substituted knowledge for chemical application," says Gene Brewer, county agricultural director for the North Carolina Cooperative Extension Service.

At tree farms throughout the area, growers have completely eliminated some chemicals from their standard rotation. They are applying other pesticides as sparsely as one-tenth the amount recommended by manufacturers, turning instead to natural biological-control methods to rid their fields of insect pests. The results of this revolution are heartening.

The plump, glossy Fraser firs are selling as well as ever—Watauga County alone produced 542,000 trees worth $12.2 million last year—and markets for the trees continue to expand throughout the country. "They go in every direction: north, south, east and west," says a longtime Boone tree farmer Kenneth Dotson. "We're planting more and more every year."

Whether or not the chemicals used on the Christmas-tree farms contributed to the area's excessive leukemia rate, growers say they are pleased to be taking steps to improve groundwater supplies for communities downstream. And they're happy to see wildlife flourishing in their fields and in nearby streams and woodlands. "We've seen more wildlife in the last five years than we saw 30 years ago," says Dotson, whose land now provides habitat for a range of songbirds, water-fowl, wild turkeys, foxes and deer.

Dotson's two sons, Jerry and Tom, who now run the family's farm operation, were just schoolboys when their parents began planting Christmas trees in 1962 to halt severe erosion caused by hillside vegetable farming. Growing corn, beans and potatoes on steep slopes near Boone, says Kenneth Dotson, "was washing our land away."

Like other area farmers, the Dotsons began planting fast-growing white pines. But the family soon switched to more profitable Fraser firs. The firs sell for higher prices than pines because of their attractive, long-lasting needles. However, the firs also require more care to grow, including frequent shaping and fertilizing. A Fraser fir takes as long as nine years to reach a marketable 6-foot height.

From the beginning, the tree farmers applied chemicals liberally. "We thought that if a little was good, a lot would be better," recalls Kenneth Dotson's wife, Pauline. The farmers also preferred to keep their field neat by mowing closely between the rows of Christmas trees.

Farmers used blanket sprayings of toxic diazinon or Chlordane to kill the grubs that feed on the firs' roots, and they sprayed heavily with herbicides to eliminate weeds. The woolly aphid, which attacks the bark and kills trees, was doused with another potent chemical.

Such tactics continued throughout the county until 1989, when residents received bad news: three reported cases of childhood leukemia within 1 square mile, and three more scattered nearby—an unusually high number. Local doctors who diagnosed the cases noticed that the sick children all lived in an area where Christmas trees and tobacco were grown. The doctors called the North Carolina Cancer Registry, which could not find a conclusive link between local chemical use and the leukemia.

"The link of pesticides with cancer risk is generally accepted," says Registry Director Aldrich. However, he adds, the source of the health problems may be found beyond local groundwater contamination.

At the National Cancer Institute in Maryland, Director of Occupational Studies Aaron Blair agrees that a link between pesticide use and elevated cancer rates seems strong. But he cautions that farmers are exposed to many suspected carcinogens, including diesel exhaust, fuel oil and airborne microtoxics that could come from sources outside the immediate area.

Rather than wait for researchers to better pinpoint the source of the leukemia, Watauga County tree farmers decided to take matters into their own hands. They turned to county Agricultural Extension Director Brewer, who developed a series of workshops to teach new techniques for dealing with tree-farm pests.

Previously, the Watauga tree growers had started their planting cycle in late winter with what one farmer called "killing the earth"—a field treatment of "pre-emergence" herbicide to control weeds before they even sprouted. Growers mowed grass regularly, even though grubs prefer short grass for laying eggs. To compensate, the growers had to use more chemicals to kill the grubs. Today, many farmers are skipping the pre-emergence herbicide treatment and letting the grass grow taller. As a result, grubs no longer pose a serious problem at most farms.

After the trees are shaped in summer and harvested in fall, growers are allowing a cover crop of rye to mature and die back naturally. The cover crop provides nutrients for the soil and food for wildlife. "The appearance of the farm is not as good. It's not picture perfect," says local grower Carroll E. Garland. "But we do not have soil washing away, and we do not have the effects of chemicals." The first time Garland planted a field without chemicals, he noticed ducks returning to a nearby pond. That field recently produced his biggest harvest of trees.

Farmers like Garland and the Dotsons now rely on North Carolina agriculture officials to help them determine fertilizer application doses for each of their fields. Throughout the county, use of chemicals has declined from an average of 192 ounces per acre per year to 45 ounces.

Pediatrician Bill Horn, one of the Boone doctors

who first noticed the cancer cluster in Watauga County six years ago, now voices cautious optimism that the unusual rate of leukemia has dropped since the Christmas tree growers adopted new horticultural practices. Horn notes that there has not been a new case of childhood leukemia in the original cluster area in four years.

Meanwhile, growers themselves are seeing other benefits from the changes. "It used to be in the nursery business that your neighbor was your competitor," says Jerry Dotson. "Now they're our allies. Our only competitor in Christmas trees today is the artificial tree." ❑

## Questions

1. What is meant by the term *pre-emergence*?

2. What does the cover crop of rye provide?

3. What type of method did the farmers eventually use to rid their fields of insect pests?

*Answers are at the back of the book.*

# Section Four

# Social Solutions

**40**

*China is employing economic incentives to improve environmental compliance. These incentives include pollution levies, discharge permits, environmental achievement rewards for officials and managers, price reform, security deposits, environmental taxes and tariffs, environmental labels, and fines. But China's pollution problems remain significant. Approximately 75 percent of China's energy needs depend on coal consumption. This contributes enormously to air pollution. Pollutant levels in most of the large cities exceed World Health Organization standards. The 1979 Environmental Protection Law (EPL) set guidelines to emphasize pollution prevention. Also included was a "polluter-pays" principle that forces an enterprise to pay a fee if it discharges pollutants exceeding state standards. In 1989, a new EPL was introduced. It addressed weaknesses in the 1979 law and laid the groundwork for new pollution control policies. The development of environmental laws, regulations, and infrastructure has greatly slowed environmental degradation in China. With economic reforms decreasing the central government's control, the promotion of economic development over environmental protection is becoming evident.*

# China Strives to Make the Polluter Pay

## H. Keith Florig, Walter O. Spofford, Jr., Xiaoying Ma, Zhong Ma

*Environmental Science & Technology*, June 1995

*Are China's market-based incentives for improved environmental compliance working?*

Following the birth of the People's Republic of China in 1949, an emphasis on the development of state-owned heavy industry in urban areas left a legacy of large point sources of air and water pollution. Economic reforms introduced in 1978 have sparked rapid growth in industrial output accompanied by increasing pollution discharges into urban airsheds and water courses. Residential waste has intensified the industrial pollution problem. Consumption increases caused by growth in household incomes are propelling concomitant growth in per capita solid waste generation. As millions of unemployed farmers migrate to urban areas, pollution problems are exacerbated by untreated sewage and the burning of coal for domestic heating and cooking. A rapidly expanding transportation sector threatens to become a significant source of air pollution in China's larger cities.

Since the enactment of its first trial environmental legislation in 1979, China has moved aggressively to develop ambient and emission-effluent standards, establish an infrastructure for ambient environmental monitoring, and experiment with new programs for pollution reduction. Although these programs depend in part on central planning and moral suasion, the Chinese are harnessing economic incentives as environmental protection instruments.[1] As China moves toward a full market economy, these incentives become more attractive. Economic instruments that are in use or being tested include pollution levies, discharge permits, environmental achievement rewards for officials and managers, price reform, security deposits, environmental taxes and tariffs, environmental labels, and fines.[2]

Although China has made notable progress in environmental protection, her pollution problems remain serious. China depends on coal for about 75% of primary energy needs, including residential heating and cooking and industrial process heating. This use contributes heavily to air pollution in urban areas, particularly in winter. Air pollutant levels in most large cities exceed World Health Organization guidelines. High levels of airborne particulates are thought to be largely responsible for a death rate from chronic obstructive pulmonary disease five times that of Western industrialized countries. In many urban areas, surface waters are polluted by sewage and industrial wastewater. In 1993 only 55% of all industrial wastewater discharges met discharge standards.[3]

**Evolving Environmental Regulations**

After three decades of central planning and isolation from the Western world, China in the late 1970s moved quickly to address the environmental legacy of the past and stave off the environmental effects of rapid economic growth sparked by economic reforms. China's first modern environmental legislation was passed for trial implementation in 1979. The 1979 Environmental Protection Law (EPL) described goals and principles of environmental protection and authorized a system of environmental regulation, monitoring, and enforcement. The law emphasized pollution prevention by prohibiting the siting of facilities with noxious emissions in residential areas; exhorting enterprises to control pollution or face closure, relocation, merger, or mandatory process or product changes; requiring environmental impact assessments for new or upgraded industrial facilities; requiring new or expanded facilities to include pollution prevention and control in design, construction, and operation (dubbed the "Three Simultaneous Steps" policy); requiring new facilities to meet discharge standards; and promoting development of an indigenous environmental technology industry. The law also embraced the "polluter pays" principle by collecting fees from enterprises that discharge pollutants in amounts exceeding state standards. China's State Council issued rules clarifying the discharge fee system in 1982.

In 1989 a new EPL was passed that superseded the 1979 trial law. It reaffirmed existing policies on siting restrictions, environmental impact assessments, the Three Simultaneous Steps, and discharge fees. The 1989 law also addressed some shortcomings of the 1979 law and paved the way for new policies on pollution control. A system was established to reward factory managers and government officials for meeting environmental goals and to punish those failing to meet the goals within a specified time.

Greater attention was devoted to gaining economies of scale by the centralized treatment of industrial wastes. Incentives to recycle wastes were instituted, and a system was developed to quantitatively rank urban environmental quality and services, thus harnessing the power of publicity to encourage environmental improvements.

To implement the 1979 EPL, environmental protection units at the state, provincial, city, and county levels were formed. The 1989 EPL required individual enterprises to set up environmental units to collect and report effluent and emissions data. China's environmental bureaucracy grew rapidly through the 1980s and currently employs more than 200,000 people nationwide, including about 60,000 in industrial environmental protection offices and 80,000 in provincial, city, and county environmental protection bureaus. In 1984 China's State Council formed the Environmental Protection Commission to oversee China's institutional environmental protection structure. Composed of all relevant ministry and agency heads, it sets broad policy directives and resolves interagency disputes. In 1988 the Environmental Protection Commission elevated the Environment Office in the Ministry of Urban and Rural Construction and Environmental Protection to full agency status, forming the National Environmental Protection Agency (NEPA) to take responsibility for environmental policy.[4]

China's first environmental quality standards were developed in the early 1970s. During the 1980s more comprehensive standards were developed for ambient air and water quality, and new standards were introduced for industrial pollutant emissions, vehicle emissions, and environmental monitoring.[5] The standards are stringent enough to require significant pollution reductions without being unrealistic given China's economic base.[6] In general, Chinese discharge standards are somewhat weaker than those of Western industrialized countries.[7]

China's environmental policies are being developed and tested in a rapidly changing economic system. Since the beginning of economic reform in 1978, China has liberalized or freed prices on many commodities. Many state-owned enterprises may sell a portion of their products in markets outside the standard quota system and exercise autonomy in choosing suppliers and customers. Taxes and accounting rules for state-owned enterprises now encourage more cost reduction. Collective and private enterprises, operating in largely free markets, are growing in number and now comprise more than half the economy. Despite these changes, substantial remnants of the planned economy remain, particularly in heavy industry, energy and transportation.

## Pollution Levy System

Article 18 of China's 1979 EPL specifies that "in cases where the discharge of pollutants exceeds the limit set by the state, a fee shall be charged according to the quantities and concentration of the pollutants released." Although local environmental protection bureaus (EPBs) began collecting fees in 1979, formal procedures interpreting the 1979 law were not issued until 1982. These measures required that a pollution levy be paid by any enterprise that discharged pollutants above relevant standards. A state fee schedule came with the regulation, but provincial and local governments could charge higher rates with approval from the central government. For industrial wastewater discharges, the fee for any given pollutant was based on the multiple by which the pollutant concentration exceeded the standard. For air emissions, fees were based on multiples by which standards were exceeded, but air emissions standards included a mix of concentration-based and mass-based limits. "Overstandard" fees were assessed only on the pollutant most in violation in a waste stream.

As established in 1982, the discharge fee system provided incentive to reduce discharges only to levels specified in standards. No incentive existed to further reduce discharges, even if the marginal cost of control was small. To provide incentive for further pollutant discharge reductions, a volume-based industrial wastewater discharge fee was introduced in 1993.[8] This fee is charged on the total quantity of wastewater discharged. (.05 yuan per ton; 8.5 yuan = $1). However, a factory is not required to pay both an overstandard pollution fee and a wastewater discharge fee. The overstandard fee supersedes the wastewater discharge fee if the effluent standards are violated. In 1993 collections of this "within standard" fee amounted to about 10% of the collec-

tions of the overstandard fee.[9]

The 1982 and subsequent procedures defining the pollution levy system specify four additional categories of penalty. Following a three-year grace period, effluent fees increase 5% per year for enterprises that fail to meet effluent and emission standards. Double fees are assessed both for facilities built after passage of the 1979 EPL that exceed standards and for old facilities that fail to operate their treatment equipment. A fine of 0.1% per day is specified for delays of more than 20 days in paying discharge fees. Penalties for false effluent and emission reports or for interfering with EPB inspections are mandated. These four penalties are referred to as the "four small pieces" component of the pollution levy system.

Fees and fines collected support EPB operations and subsidize pollution control projects for enterprises that have paid into the system. Local EPBs may use 20% of the fees and 100% of the fines to fund their operations. Up to 80% of the fees are allocated for pollution control loans to enterprises that have paid into the pollution levy system.

Thus, as established in 1982, the pollution levy system was intended to provide both "stick" and "carrot" pollution control incentives. However, the system turned out to be more of an EPB funding source than an incentive for reducing industrial emissions

## Design Limitations

A number of observers have noted that the pollution control incentive provided by the levy system is low because fees are small relative to pollution control costs. Fees are not indexed for inflation, and, for state-owned enterprises, they can be included under costs and later compensated through price increases or tax deductions.[6,7,10,11] Thus, many enterprises choose to pay the fees rather than incur pollution control costs, which often require significant capital investment. Because the fees and fines can be lower than operating and maintenance costs, enterprises that install pollution control equipment have little incentive to operate it.[10]

Nationwide, collections of pollution fees have grown steadily over the past decade but recently have fallen behind inflation in most provinces.

Most of the growth resulted from increases in the number of enterprises assessed rather than fee rate increases.[9,10] In 1993 about 2.7 billion yuan were collected in discharge fees and penalties from 254,000 enterprises. This represents an average annual fee per paying enterprise of only 10,500 yuan ($1200-$1700 depending on the exchange rates). The average annual gross output value for a state-owned industrial enterprise is about 15 million yuan. For firms that pay discharge fees, the fees typically make up less than 0.1% of the firm's total output value. By comparison, U.S. industry environmental compliance costs are estimated to be a little more than 1% of total manufacturing costs.

Since the pollution levy system was established in 1979, about 60% of the total amount collected has gone to pollution abatement grants and loans for existing (old) enterprises.[8] Nationwide, grants and loans from pollution discharge fees contribute about 8% of China's total capital investment in pollution control and about 20% of China's pollution reduction investment in existing factories.[12] Thus, although the discharge fee system provides a significant fraction of China's pollution control spending, the amount are small compared to the 12 billion yuan per year NEPA estimates is needed to meet industrial effluent and emissions standards by the year 2000.

Industrial wastewater effluent standards currently are specified in terms of allowable concentrations rather than mass flow rates. In the past, some enterprises could meet discharge standards and avoid fees by diluting their waste stream with fresh water. Therefore some local governments imposed fines for diluting waste streams.[5]

Although the discharge fee system provides significant operating revenues for local EPBs, it provides little incentive for enterprises to invest in pollution prevention or control. Because the policy is applied uniformly, it does not account for regional differences or the assimilative capacity of local environments. To address these two concerns, a discharge permit system was introduced to control pollution from large enterprises. Water pollution permitting was implemented on a trial basis in 17 cities in 1987 and now is operating in 391 cities.[9,13] Trial air pollution permitting was begun in 16 cities in 1991 and has expanded to 57 cities.[9] The discharge licenses specify both the maximum pollutant concentrations and a factory's maximum annual wastewater discharge volume. Criteria for setting limits vary from city to city. Some call for apportioning total allowable loads within a region to achieve ambient environmental quality standards; others are based on the emissions status quo or on the capabilities of available and affordable technology.[10,13] Fines are levied for failure to meet permit conditions.

To effectively negotiate a permit, EPB personnel need technical knowledge of industrial processes, but few of them have had the opportunity to gain such information. Therefore, the EPBs are susceptible to industry-biased claims.

In many regions, the pollution levy and discharge permit systems operate simultaneously. Enterprises thus can face conflicting or discontinuous incentives from a concentration-based fine applied to behavior out of compliance with discharge standards and a mass-based fine for exceeding permit limits. Conflicting incentives also have arisen between the levy and the tax systems. In earlier years, some enterprises shielded profits from taxes by paying into the levy system and then recovering 80% of their payments under a rebate program.

### Local Resistance

In the early 1980s some enterprises resisted fee collection by local environmental protection units.[14] The collectors often were turned away when they appealed to higher local officials. Because of the threat to the economic welfare of vital local enterprises, local officials often preferred to waive the fees, particularly for unprofitable enterprises. This problem still exists in many rural areas but has improved substantially in urban areas.

Enforcement of the pollution levy system is weak for China's 8 million township and village industrial enterprises (TVIEs), which are significant sources of rural pollution. Because most TVIEs are small, local EPB revenues from fee collection are less than those from larger state-owned enterprises. Therefore, because they have limited personnel, EPBs concentrate on the largest polluters first. The TVIE sector is growing rapidly and contributes about half of China's industrial output.

Low collections per unit output can reflect either high compliance rates, such as in Beijing, or weak enforcement, such as in Liaoning where many large and bankrupt heavy industries are excused regularly from making payments.

In December 1994 NEPA began a two-year study of the pollution levy system. The objective is to correct deficiencies and propose changes to improve effectiveness and efficiency consistent with a market economy and with ongoing economic and institutional reform. NEPA's Department of Supervision and Management is conducting the study with a World Bank technical assistance loan. The technical portion of the study is being conducted by the Chinese Research Academy of Environment Sciences in Beijing with the assistance of foreign consultants.

Intended to be both comprehensive and specific, the study will address four main areas: designing mass-flow levy formulas for pollutants with fee schedules based on the marginal costs of pollution control; designing a pollution levy fund to include institutional arrangements, technical assessment of loans, and priorities for the use of the fund; designing an information management system for calculating fees and maintaining billing and receipt records; and practical issues of implementation. The latter includes emissions and effluent monitoring, calculating fees, fee collection, and fund management. The goal of the study is to develop a pollution levy system for China that reduces emissions and effluents, achieves environmental goals with the least cost, and imposes minimal administrative burdens on local EPBs and regulated enterprises.

## Other Incentives

The 1989 EPL specified that government at all levels should be responsible for environmental quality in their jurisdiction. In 1990 this was formalized as a contract system in which officials from mayors to enterprise managers agree to work toward environmental goals. Depending on the organization, goals can include objectives for environmental quality, pollution control, facility construction, and environmental administration. Although there is no penalty for failing to meet contract goals, rewards for doing so can include grants, bonuses, or special status that offers tax breaks and control of foreign exchange.

In the autonomous regions Inner Mongolia and Guangxi Zhuang and in Fujian Province, a compensation fee is being imposed on sales of products made outside the province by highly polluting industries.[15] The levy, approved by the State Council, is applied to commercial coal, steel, crude oil, and electricity. Revenues will be used for the region's pollution prevention and control and recycling projects.

Recognizing that the growing demand for environmental products would otherwise be filled by foreign firms, China is encouraging the growth of an indigenous environmental products industry. Now more than 4000 enterprises in China make pollution control, monitoring, and recycling products.[9] These enterprises have fixed assets of about 3 billion yuan and an output of roughly 6 billion yuan per year. The Chinese government encouraged the growth of such firms in several ways. In Ningbo, a port city in Zhejiang Province, China established its first environmental products market. Elsewhere, special industrial parks for environmental protection industries are being established to take advantage of synergies and economies of scale.

The inefficiencies of materials use associated with China's centrally planned economy prompted the government to advocate "comprehensive utilization of materials" in the 1970s. Incentives such as tax breaks on recycled materials sales, subsidies for recycled materials sold at a loss, reduced prices for recycled materials, and low-interest loans for recycling projects were introduced.[11] This is one of several programs managed by a new NEPA division concerned with clean production.

## Monitoring and Enforcement Problems

China's environmental policy is comprehensive, complex, rapidly developing, and contains a mix of command and control, moral suasion, and economic incentive. The development of environmental laws, regulations, and infrastructure has greatly improved, but monitoring and enforcement still are major problems. Compliance has been best for large new facilities because abatement equipment was incorporated in the early design stages. But many medium- and small-scale enterprises, particularly rural ones, feel little or no pressure to comply, and larger enterprises operating at a loss can maneuver for exemptions.

With economic reforms diminishing the central government's control, a strong bias favoring economic development over environmental protection, and no support from an independent environmental movement, environmental protection in China faces an uphill battle.[11,16] Until the Chinese legal system is strengthened, it may be necessary to employ short-term means such as taxes on inputs that do not rely heavily on monitoring and enforcement.

A number of macroeconomic incentives drive environmental protection in China. Price reform for raw materials and profit retention for state enterprises induced manufacturers to be more efficient, resulting in less waste per unit of output. Price reform still has a long way to go, however. For instance, water still is priced below its scarcity value in most areas.

The most important accomplishment of the discharge fee system has been to provide operating revenue for local EPBs, whose collection activities contributed significantly to enhanced public and official awareness of environmental problems.[11,14] But this arrangement can distort incentives within the collection bureaus, which might focus on the largest industrial facilities where payoffs are greatest or tolerate continuous violations to maintain an income stream. However, linking fee collection to EPB revenue does provide incentive for the agency to do its job.

As in most industrialized countries, command and control is the principal instrument of Chinese environmental policy. The 1979 and 1989 EPLs both require all enterprises to meet discharge standards established by NEPA. But this "legal" requirement is enforced weakly through low-level fines targeted at the largest and most egregious polluters. The discharge permit system will attempt to address this problem by collecting enough in permit fees to finance enforcement. But this probably will not extend to the smallest rural enterprises.

Although local EPBs are receptive to citizens' environmental complaints, the Chinese government is reluctant to allow formation of independent activist environmental groups. If allowed to flourish, such organizations could ease the government's enforcement burden by bringing additional pressure to bear on noxious facilities.

The Environment and Resources Protection Committee of China's National People's Congress expects to approve 14 new or revised environmental laws in the next few years.[17] These should address gaps in existing legislation such as controlling disposal of solid and hazardous waste, bring China into compliance with its international commitments, and improve existing pollution control measures.

## Acknowledgments

This paper was supported in part by a grant from the United Nations Environment Programme through the Organization for Economic Cooperation and Development. Views expressed do not necessarily reflect those of UNEP, OECD, or any of their member countries. The authors thank Xia Kunbao and participants at the OECD/UNEP Paris Workshop on the Application of Economic Instruments for Environmental Management, May 1994, for helpful comments.

## References

1. Ross, L. Environmental Policy in China; Indiana University Press: Bloomington, IN, 1988.
2. Zhang, K M. "Apply Economic Measures to Strengthen Environmental Protection Work, Promote Sustained, Stable, and Coordinated Development of the National Economy"; Zhongguo Huanjing Bao [China Environment News], July 23, 1991; English translation in JPRS-TEN-92-005, U.S. Joint Publications Research Service, March 3, 1992.
3. "Zhongguo Tongji Nianjian [China Statistical Yearbook]"; State Statistical Bureau, distributed by China Statistical Information and Consultancy Service Center: Beijing [various years].
4. "Introductions to the Environmental Protection Organizations in China"; National Environmental Protection Agency: Beijing, 1992.
5. "Huanjing Baohu Zhengce Fagui Biaozhun Shiyong Shouce [Handbook of Environmental Protection Laws, Regulations, and Standards]"; Beijing Municipal Environmental Protection Bureau; Jilin People's Publishing House: Changchun, 1987.

6. "China Environmental Strategy Paper"; World Bank: Washington, DC, 1992.

7. Krupnick, A. Incentive Policies for Industrial Pollution Control in China; presented at the annual meeting of the American Economics Association: New Orleans, LA; January 2–5, 1992.

8. Ma, X Y. Effectiveness of Environmental Policies for the Control of Industrial Water Pollution in China; working paper, Civil Engineering Department, Stanford University; March 1994.

9. Zhongguo Huanjing Nianjian [China Environment Yearbook]" National Environmental Protection Agency; China Environment Yearbook Publishing House: Beijing [various years].

10. Sinkule, B. Implementation of Industrial Water Pollution Control Policies in the Pearl River Delta Region of China; Ph.D. dissertation, Department of Civil Engineering, Stanford University, August 1993.

11. Vermeer, E.B. China Information 1990, 5(1), 1–32.

12. Qu, G.P. Basic Analysis and Assessment of China's Environmental Protection Investments and Policies; published in three parts in Huanjing Baohu [Environmental Protection], Nos. 3-5, March 25, April 25, and May 25, 1991. English translation in JPRS-TEN-91-014, July 9, 1991, and JPRS-TEN-91-016, August 22, 1991, U.S. Joint Publications Research Service.

13. Rozelle, S. et al. Natural Resources Modeling 1993, 7, 353-78.

14. Jahiel, A.R. The Deng Reforms and Local Environmental Protection: Implementation of the Discharge Fee System, 1979–1991; presented at the 46th Annual Meeting of the Association for Asian Studies: Boston, MA; March 1994.

15. Xia, K.B. "Fines: Forcing Polluters to Listen"; China Environment News (English ed.), January 1993, 42,6.

16. Ross, L. Policy Studies Journal 1992, 20(4), 628–42.

17. Ross, L. China Business Review 1994, 21, 30–33. ❑

## Questions

1. Why is the enforcement of the pollution levy system weak for China's 8 million township and village industrial enterprises?

2. What is the objective of the two-year study of the pollution levy system that NEPA began in 1994?

3. What is the goal of this study?

*Answers are at the back of the book.*

**41**

*Microenterprises are businesses employing only a few people. They are more flexible than larger businesses and provide a large share of jobs. Microenterprises may soon provide support to a substantial portion of the world's smallest businesses. Factors shaping microenterprises include shared liability, peer support, and low overhead. Inner cities of the United States as well as developing countries are benefiting from microenterprise. Industrial countries are now implementing this proven formula for success, which has become the backbone of rural economies and poor nations. Microenterprise is proving to be not only productive, but perhaps vital for the sustainability of human economies. This will help create important ties to the local community and ecology, which are essential for a healthy global economy.*

# Microenterprise
## Hal Kane

*World Watch*, March/April 1996

*It is not big corporate or government employers, but millions of tiny one- or two- or five-person businesses, that will have to provide a large share of the jobs—and the critical ties to local community and ecology—that are so vital to the global economy.*

The room did not look at all like the inside of a bank. There were no inch-thick security windows, no polished desks for the officers, or plush chairs for the clients, and no guards. Nor did the clients look much like the kind of people who apply for business start-up loans these days—no tailored suits or $200 briefcases. And they didn't sit in discreet anonymity, waiting their turns for confidential appointments with the loan officer. Instead, they gathered casually around a large table.

There were six clients: all mothers and Spanish-speaking immigrants to the United States. The loan officer, a 24-year-old administrator for a nonprofit group called the Foundation for International Community Assistance (FINCA), did not exhibit the smooth self-assurance of an experienced banker. She had never done this before, and it wasn't even her office—it was the cluttered, borrowed office of a local tenant's union. On the table, a plastic cover incongruously paraded a children's cartoon charac-

ter. It was a Sunday afternoon in Alexandria, Virginia, and all the regular banks in the city were closed.

The "officer" invited the applicants to present their plans. The first, a woman named Rosa, explained that she had been running a child care business for five years, taking care of five children, 40 hours a week, for $100 per child. She needed $1,500 to buy toys, books, chairs, a table, and diapers so that she could expand her clientele. Another applicant, Sandra, explained that since most of the borrowers sold products like clothes, cosmetics, and business cards, it was important for them to receive loans before Christmas, so that they could buy more stock to sell during the rush season.

The paperwork had been done earlier. None of the applicants would have qualified for a loan from a conventional lender, but FINCA was not operating by conventional rules. Now, after each applicant agreed to assume a share of responsibility for the others, all six loans were approved. The meeting eventually ended with a celebration: food and drink and rounds of applause as each check was signed. With that, four new one- or two-person businesses—"microenterprises"—expanded, and two were born.

Outside the building, drivers passed by in their Toyotas and Buicks, unaware of the unusual transaction within. To a public accustomed to the idea that business ownership is something increasing beyond the reach of ordinary working people, the chance of securing a startup loan without substantial collateral may be inconceivable. Yet such a chance—the chance to break the vicious circle in which poverty denies aspiring entrepreneurs the creditworthiness to work their way *out* of poverty—may be an essential tool for reaching people who otherwise benefit little from the global economy.

What the fledging loan officer was doing was part of a growing movement to extend business credit to the poor—whether in the villages of the developing world or the inner cities of the United States. FINCA's mission, which began 12 years ago in Bolivia, is to provide financial assistance to people who would be unable to get it through conventional channels—and to provide it in a way that lets new microenterprises get off the ground without either excessive risk of default or heavy reliance on charity.

These tiny enterprises contrast starkly, of course, with the companies most citizens of industrialized countries think of when we refer to "business." It is the large corporations that dominate much of our attention—in their omnipresent advertising, their lobbying and dealing with governments, and their performances on the New York or Tokyo stock exchanges. The world's 500 largest corporations, for example, control 25 percent of the world's economic output. Yet, they employ only one-twentieth of one percent of the world's population. It is with much smaller enterprises that most people make their livelihoods—many of them so small that even their own governments pay little attention to them.

By some measures, the real backbone of world commerce and global employment is made up of the millions of unsung small enterprises that farm small plots of land, cook food, provide daycare for children, make clay pots or straw mats by hand, do piecework for apparel makers, and carry out the countless other tasks that larger business don't do. In the cities of developing countries, for example, a growing percentage of the working population— sometimes estimated as high as 50 percent—is engaged in microenterprise activity. In the seven countries of southern Africa, there is evidence that small, unregistered enterprises provide work for substan-

tially more people than the "regular," legal ones do. In Latin America and the Caribbean, more than 50 million microenterprises employ more than 150 million workers. Even in a wealthy country like the United States, more than a quarter of all employees work for establishments of fewer than 20 people, and those businesses constitute 87 percent of all U.S. business establishments.

The tasks these businesses perform cover the whole range of human activity, from the basics of housing and farming to the luxuries of entertainment and tourism. In many parts of the world, microenterprises frequently have only one employee—who is also the owner—or they benefit from the work of family members who are not really employees at all. In wealthy countries, many microenterprises may be larger, up to 10 to 20 people, for example, but still small in comparison to many of their competitors. But throughout the world, what most of these businesses do have in common is a lack of access to resources. They get little help from lawyers or accountants; often they are not able to afford retail space; many of them are not even legally registered as businesses.

As a result, many of these enterprises also lack the protections against excessively long hours, exhaustion, and injury or illness that larger or more officially regulated businesses are likely to provide. And much of the work is tedious and drab. In 1983, for example, Nobel prize winner Rigoberta Menchu described some part-time work done by her family and their village neighbors during her childhood in Guatemala. "We grow little beans but we don't eat them," she wrote. "They all go to market…for us it's almost a day's walk to the town and…we have to carry our beans on our backs. I used to carry 40 or 50 pounds of beans or maize from our house to the town. We'd sell maize too when there was something we needed to buy….When my mother goes to town, she shouts very loud to all the neighbors: 'I'm going to market,' and they say: 'Buy us soap, buy us salt, buy us chile,' and tell her how much she should buy….This is how we sell things as well. Most people in our village make straw plaits for hats, or they make mats, or weave cloth, so at the weekend they get it all together for one person to sell."

Meanwhile, the large corporations that have

brought wealth to many parts of the world have failed to take that wealth to other parts—most notably to most of Africa and to large parts of South and Southeast Asia. These companies will have to be complemented by another form of business, one that can succeed in the poorest nations. Microenterprises have been able to do this.

In part, this is because microenterprises are more flexible and mobile than most larger, more complex and building-bound businesses. They provide part-time work to women and men who also have to take care of families, and seasonal work in places where crops have to be harvested. They require little capital, office space, or startup time. They can thrive in rural areas, thereby slowing the rush to urbanization. Jobs in microenterprises are accessible to immigrants and disenfranchised people who need to moonlight or share jobs. And they are run by women at least as often as men, helping to reverse a pervasive global inequity.

Microenterprises also offer an alternative to the conventional strategy for bringing development to poor nations—making large loans to governments for massive power or infrastructure projects. Such project-oriented development has come under growing criticism from grassroots activists, who say the projects often benefit large contractors and central governments more than they help local people. More investment in smaller, local industries, they argue, could bring economic and social benefits at far less cost. Their view is reflected in an old Chinese saying, "many little things done in many little places by many little people will change the face of the world."

**Credit Without Collateral**

In recent years, some socially concerned lenders have begun to demonstrate that for people facing economic disaster, the need to feed one's family can be at least as strong an assurance of reliability as the fear of losing property.

An incident recalled by Ela Bhatt, the Chair of an Indian microcredit organization called Women's World Banking, demonstrates the point. "In 1975, when the bank was not taking many risks, a vegetable vendor came who was under such economic pressure that she was absolutely desperate. Her husband was an unemployed textile worker, and he

would somehow roam about and fill his belly each day, but it was a very difficult situation for her and her children. The bank decided to extend her a loan of Rs.50 (about $5.50 in 1975 dollars), and someone went with her to buy green masalas like coriander, mint, ginger, garlic, and chilies. That day SEWA (the Self-Employed Women's Association) cared for her children, who were sick and hungry. She earned Rs.6 profit selling the masalas that day, and she took home food that night. She continued building her business day by day, and the next week she repaid Rs.51. It was hardly any risk for the bank and it literally meant life or death for that woman. After that we started extending those Rs.50 loans to many women."

The first major demonstration of this kind of lending came in Bangladesh, a country whose name was virtually synonymous with poverty, around 1978. A professor of economics at Chittagong University, Mohammad Yunus, began an experiment aimed at helping impoverished villagers. Defying the usual rules, he lent them unsecured money to start up small enterprises such as rice processing, rickshaw driving, and weaving. Instead of collateral, the borrowers would form small groups and agree to a pact of mutual liability—if one defaulted, the others would have to pay from their own profits. The participants in a pact often knew each other, which created peer pressure for successful repayment, and along with the compelling need for an income source in a place with few other opportunities, it produced a surprising result. After the first two years, Yunus found he was getting a payback rate of 99 percent. The experiment, by then officially the Grameen Bank, was expanded and has become legendary in the development world.

The Grameen prototype was widely watched, and by the mid-1980s, similar programs had been established by nonprofit aid organizations around the world. In Latin America, a nongovernmental organization called Prodem had been serving as a traditional charity, receiving grants and donations which it had then parcelled out as loans to poor borrowers who started microenterprises. But in 1990, Prodem was changed into Bancosol—an institution that functions like a commercial bank insofar as it does not lose money on its loans and is even able to raise its own funds by borrowing on commercial markets and through the interest collected on past loans.

As it became clear that loans from organizations like Bancosol to small enterprises were getting successfully repaid, more charitable organizations followed suit—metamorphosing from grant-dependent bodies into independent financial institutions that do not rely (or rely as heavily) on outside aid. In Paraguay, for example, a nonprofit group called the Foundation for Cooperative Development has lent $18 million to more than 15,000 microentrepreneurs during the past decade, creating nearly 20,000 jobs. One day last year, the Foundation offered $150,000 worth of bonds on the securities exchange to finance a new portfolio of loans to microentrepreneurs. The offering was sold out in less than 10 minutes.

Meanwhile, the Grameen Bank, with its two-decade track record to inspire investor confidence, recently sold $163 million in bonds to six Bangladeshi commercial banks at annual interest rates between 4 and 6 percent—the first time the Grameen Bank had moved away from reliance on grants and soft loans from the International Fund for Agricultural Development and donor governments. In addition to the money from those bonds, Grameen officials, like the officials of other microcredit institutions, are reinvesting the money earned from past loans—a substantial sum, since interest rates paid by microentrepreneurs are commonly around 20 percent and payback rates frequently above 98 percent. Low-income people who would never have been offered loans by ordinary banks are now generating substantial profits for the Grameen Bank and other microcredit institutions.

Since the late 1970s, our understanding of what makes micro-lending succeed has improved to the point that the practice may now be on the verge of supporting a substantial portion of the world's smallest businesses. Two decades of experience have solidly confirmed the reliability of the high payback rates found by Dr. Yunus, which were eventually credited not only to the effectiveness of mutual liability, but to two other techniques he had used—externalizing credit-check costs, and offering support services to applicants along with the funding.

Externalizing credit-checks eliminated what had been considered a serious barrier to microenterprise lending by conventional banks—the expectation that the administrative costs of managing tiny loans could exceed the entire value of the loan. Community development banks found an ingenious solution: making the clients themselves do the legwork. When Yunus formed the Grameen Bank, he required each borrower to share responsibility for the loans of others within groups of five of six borrowers, in addition to the responsibility taken by the creditors. As a result, the loans had remarkably little overhead.

The support services include advice, technical assistance, and sometimes even the donated labor or equipment needed to make a venture succeed—all provided both by fellow members of a borrower's group and by representatives of the creditor. Some observers have come to believe that these services account for much of the success of microcredit—perhaps even more than the money itself. In the case of the Alexandria, Virginia group, for example, the borrowers did not speak English. A FINCA representative quietly coached one of the borrowers on how to spell s-e-v-e-n-t-y, so that she could write a check. (In other countries, many of the borrowers are illiterate and sign documents with thumb prints, since they cannot write their names). And the members of the group often send each other clients, buy each other's products, and coach each other on how to take care of their money.

Moreover, much of the corruption that can be rampant in the underground economy of the informal sector is curbed by this lending structure. In the Grameen Bank, all transactions occur in the presence of group representatives and other colleagues. This transparency, coupled with an annual rotation of leadership positions at the center, reduces the opportunities for abuse of power.

With a now proven formula—shared liability, peer support, and low overhead all contributing to high payback rates—one microcredit institution now states in its promotional literature, "Collectively, these banks are rapidly evolving into a World Bank for the poor." Mohammed Yunus seems to agree; last fall, he met with representatives of other microenterprise groups to plan a microcredit summit to take place in Washington, D.C., in early 1997. The declared goal of the summit, he said, is to reach 100 million of the world's poorest families, especially the women of those families, by the year 2005.

## Reaching the Out-of-Reach

In addition to reaching the disenfranchised poor of the developing world, these small enterprises offer a growing value to the industrialized world. Many of the "inner cities" of the United States, for example, emerged from the 1970s scarred by riot damage and gutted by extensive middle-class flight to the suburbs—leaving the blighted core labeled off-limits by conventional banks. Aid to inner cities has been limited largely to such programs as food stamps, subsidies, and welfare, which may be essential but which some experts—including Harvard Business Professor Michael Porter—believe do not build a long-term base for economic well-being or growth. Inner cities may be fertile ground for microenterprise, however; Porter notes that inner city markets remain poorly served, especially in retailing, financial services, and personal services—leaving abundant opportunities for new entrepreneurs.

In Seattle, Washington, a microcredit group called the Cascadia Revolving Loan Fund has confirmed Porter's assessment by offering microcredit loans along with strong support services; it has given borrowers technical assistance on subjects ranging from accounting and employee benefit plans to marketing. In eight years, it has loaned nearly $2 million and lost less than 1 percent of it. "That's competitive with traditional banks on a portfolio they wouldn't touch," says Cascadia's executive director, Patty Grossman.

It is not just unemployment, however, but a more pervasive change in the corporate jobs market, that is pointing the way to a stronger role for microenterprise. The change can be seen in several concurrent trends: greater reliance on temporary or contract work; the trends toward telecommuting and job-sharing; and a widely noted retreat from the old understanding that a job was a stable, long-term relationship like a marriage. Even in Japan, job security is no longer the almost inviolable bond between employer and employee it once was.

As industrial countries proceed down the path, in a sense they are following the job strategies of the developing countries, rather than the other way around. The industrial countries are developing more of the small, micro, and individual enterprises that have long formed the backbone of rural economies and poor nations—except that in the industrial countries, these small businesses are often consulting firms and independent contractors. As corporate mergers and consolidations shed traditional employees, much of the work they did is being done by these contractors or consultants.

These trends have been labeled "de-jobbing," and according to writer Walter Truett Anderson, the process is proceeding at such a pace that many economists, management experts, and futurists are now talking freely about the "end of the job." Instead of possessing a "job," people will simply do work. The job, in fact, is a relatively recent social invention. As William Bridges notes in his book, *Jobshift*, "Before 1800—and long afterward in many cases—'job' always referred to some particular task or undertaking, never to role or a position in an organization." You might *do* a job, but you don't *have* one.

The effects of this shift are intensified by the growing mobility of the global labor force. In more affluent societies, people with marketable skills move freely from place to place. In the past, their work might have dictated where they lived, or vice-versa. Now, many people choose both. A chemical engineer who once might have had to live near Secaucus, New Jersey, or Metairie, Louisiana, may now decide she wishes to live in the mountains of Colorado, while still working as an engineer. With a good modem and a nearby airport, she can.

Meanwhile, in more troubled parts of the world, the mobility driven by civil upheavals and environmental or economic disruption is producing a very different, though not unrelated, kind of reliance on independent enterprise. Immigrants, for example, may not be quickly welcomed into jobs in their host countries—and are forced to create places for themselves by being flexible and resourceful. Many resort to moonlighting, working part-time, and sharing jobs. In Eastern Europe, writes Anderson, such people become "hustlers, traders, independent manufacturers, freelance deal-makers."

## Bigger Is Not Always Better

Though microenterprises offer an opportunity to provide employment for groups of people not reached by large corporations, they are not suitable substitutes for all the functions performed by big companies. They cannot make medical equipment or aluminum, build large aircraft, or distribute fresh food to thousands of retail stores every few hours. They do not have the capital for large, long-term investments, so they usually can't conduct research and development for new products, and they can't exploit economies of scale.

On the other hand, it would be a mistake to continue regarding microenterprises as the poor cousins of the corporate world. For many tasks, small businesses may be better suited; they have the inherent advantages of high flexibility, lack of bureaucracy, and speed of decisionmaking. Very small businesses may also find more success in certain cultural settings than big companies do.

Some analysts argue, for example, that China is better suited to family businesses than to giant corporations. And in the late 1980s, when Chinese peasants were migrating to the cities in numbers large enough to alarm the government, Deng Xiaoping encouraged small towns and villages to start their own enterprises, creating jobs in the countryside so villagers could stay there. Owned by the local governments, these businesses usually employed fewer than 100 people, making anything from metal pails to silk rugs. Some of these undertakings were too large to be considered microenterprises, but were far from being big companies. Others employed just a few people. Yet by 1991, they were reportedly contributing about 30 percent of China's GNP. The number of these countryside enterprises had soared from 1.5 million in 1978 to 19 million in 1991, creating about 112 million new jobs—and slowing the migration into cities.

In most countries, however, microenterprises have been neglected. They have not been rewarded with the subsidies, tax breaks, and other benefits often received by major industries as political spoils; rarely can they afford to participate in financing political campaigns, lobbying for favorable legislation, or, in some countries, establishing profitable relationships with corrupt governments.

In the developing countries, the major flows of funding support have been historically oriented to large projects—hydroelectric dams, highways, pipelines, and mines. Only more recently has attention begun to shift to the development of "human capital"—the nurturing of educated and healthy people who can contribute to sustainable economic growth. But little official attention has focused on the kind of small-scale entrepreneurship that could help to give such people more opportunities to *use* their growing capabilities.

Even so, some analysts believe that it would be a mistake to shift public assistance toward microenterprises; they argue that without first investing adequately in electricity and roads, few businesses of any size will thrive. These analysts, such as Richard Rosenberg of the World Bank, also claim that the benefits to society that come from human capital investments like educating children are larger than those that will accrue from assistance to tiny companies, and that without growing investments in education, even microenterprises will suffer. Rosenberg strongly supports finance for microenterprise when funds are available, but argues that the funds should not come from spending on other more urgent programs, such as developing higher levels of literacy.

Critics also note that even where small businesses have received strong support, they have had a mixed history of success and failure during the past quarter-century. Many microenterprise development schemes emphasized supplementary, part-time income instead of full businesses, and not enough income was earned to support families or to give women more say about how money would be spent in their households. As a result, they did not improve women's status in the labor market, or expand their opportunities.

A key to making microenterprises a legitimate path for development in the future will come with the kinds of changes—in financing, support services, and public policy—that allow these activities to operate as full-fledged personal, family, or small-group businesses rather than just supplementary crafts grafted onto existing livelihoods. In this regard, the pioneer microcredit banks have made an important breakthrough. More recently, both the World Bank and the Inter-American Development Bank have decided to allocate funds for microcredit. The World Bank pledge has been set at $200 million.

In an era when governments are financially strapped all over the globe, the prospect of securing much stronger public support for microenterprise development might seem remote. But the big development bank decisions illustrate a unique quality of this kind of development that could give it a critical boost. Microenterprises have a strong potential appeal to both conservative and liberal politicians.

For liberals, there is the opportunity to help disenfranchised people—women and the poor—to thrive. There is the appeal of enabling people to work in ways that give expression to their individuality, rather than as cogs in a large industrial machine. And, perhaps most appealing, there is the thought that microenterprises give the worker a closer look at the meaning of his work. If he is a farmer, for example, he is likely to be closer to the land than if he is an employee of a large agribusiness firm; he is more likely to have to work personally with the complexities of local soil, weather, and water, and to be more knowledgeable about what practices are sustainable.

For conservatives, there is the opportunity for disenfranchised people to make their way out of poverty by virtue of hard work instead of charity. There is the claim of some analysts that development loans would produce better results if, instead of being directed to governments, they went straight to private industry, including small industry. And, finally, there is the possibility of taking moral pressure off corporations that are laying off large numbers of employees, if it can be said that those ex-employees now have ample opportunities to live their own lives as independent small businesses or contractors. The World Bank and IAD Bank decisions may reflect the influence of such thinking.

Whatever their origin, the development banks' entry into finance for microenterprises can be seen as a momentous endorsement—not of microenterprise as a substitute for infrastructure projects or for children's education or public health, but as an important complement to those needs. No longer stigmatized as a "backward" kind of business, to be rolled over by the juggernaut of large-scale modern development, microenterprise has the potential to be not only a very productive, up-to-date kind of business, but one that may well prove vital to the long-term sustainability of human economics. ❑

---

**Questions**

1. Instead of collateral, what are the terms of agreement in microenterprise?

2. What are some trends that can be seen in the United States that make microenterprise a more viable option?

3. What are some advantages that microenterprise has over big companies?

*Answers are at the back of the book.*

---

**42** *There is always tension between advocates of economic productivity and advocates of stricter environmental regulations. Although most people want a clean environment and economic prosperity, the general attitude of society seems to suggest that economics is the dominant priority. Current global development is rooted in economic solutions that are not ecologically or socially plausible. However, there are factors that can make sustainable development paths more attainable in the future. One is the growing understanding that prior ways of development are not practical for the planet or for people. A second is the awareness that society has failed to incorporate environmental costs in economic calculations. Society's inclination is to judge all activities economically, without regard to their environmental impact. There is now a movement toward a more holistic worldview.*

# Reassessing the Economic Assumption
## Willis W. Harman

*The Futurist*, July/August 1996

*Our goals of a clean environment and a good quality of life for all cannot possibly be met by a world system bent on unlimited economic growth.*

Is it rational for the economy to be the paramount institution in modern society? And for social decisions to be influenced predominantly by economic logic and economic values?

During the twentieth century, the scientific world view increasingly challenged the tenets of the Judeo-Christian tradition. Meanings, values, and goals stemming from that tradition grew weaker, and the market became increasingly recognized as an efficient decision maker.

As materialistic, economic values and goals came to replace more-transcendentally based values, market-oriented decision makers made increasingly poorer decisions. For example, tremendous pressures are placed on corporate CEOs by the markets to make decisions that are smart in terms of short-run financial return but socially and ecologically ill-advised in the long run.

There is now a growing disparity between the values of modern society and the goals it purports to accept. Consider these widely accepted goals: to meet basic human needs of all people; to have a healthful environment; to guarantee liberty, fairness, equity, and the rule of law throughout the world; and to eliminate poverty.

Now consider what our behaviors and policies imply about our basic assumptions: that the economy is and should be the dominant institution in modern society, that sustained economic growth is necessary to provide jobs and to provide the resources to clean up the environment, that steady increase in productivity is necessary for continued gains in standards of living, that technological advance and competition are essential for progress, and that free, unregulated markets generally result in the most efficient and socially optimal allocation of resources.

These underlying assumptions are now completely incompatible with our goals, even if they seemed to work well in the past. For example, there is a strong correlation between economic product and environmental deterioration, as evidenced by pollution, toxic chemical concentration, forest depletion, desertification, thinning ozone layer, global warming, and so on.

Diversity of plant and animal species in an ecosystem leads to resilience, while an ecosystem consisting primarily of one species is fragile, susceptible to being wiped out by disease or invader. But the modern economy is steadily reducing biodiversity. The species that survive will be those that are useful in terms of the economy. We can be reasonably certain that this will prove to be an inadequate criterion for a healthy ecosystem.

An example can be seen in agriculture. Unlike other industries, which extract, use, and discard resources—agriculture replenishes resources—it takes, uses, and returns. But modern agriculture is treated like other industries. It is extremely productive in terms of output per person-hour or per acre of land, but it is also extremely expensive in terms of soil loss, water and soil pollution, alienation of farmers, decay of rural communities, and increasing vulnerability of the food-supply system due to reliance on single crops. The market is unable to assign a value to many factors vital to sound agriculture, such as topsoil, ecosystem, family, and community. And the excessive emphasis on productivity causes overproduction, which leads to low prices and economic ruin.

**More! More! More!**
Ever-increasing productivity is seen as essential to economic health, with competition as the main driving force. But increased productivity is failing to meet the goal of improving the quality of life for the average citizen. This is partly because so much of the productivity increase is eaten up by the peripheral support structure. As the service sector becomes larger and larger, it dilutes the productivity increases of the sector that is producing tangible goods. In addition, a large part of the increased productivity goes into servicing corporate debt.

In an economy-dominated value system there is a pervasive belief that quality of life is to be measured in technological terms, that technological advance equals societal progress.

Some technological advance does indeed add to quality of life. But new technology is often developed and applied without being guided by a strong moral sense and social vision. Technological advance often replaces high-paid, low-tech workers with low-cost automated processes and low-wage foreign labor. It pushes those formerly high-paid production workers into low-paying service jobs and shifts wealth from displaced workers to those who own or control the technology.

Progress is the driving force behind all the assumptions at the heart of our economy-dominated society. Material progress assumes that what we have is never enough. We must continue to accumulate and consume forever, with no upper limit. But the idea of progress loses all meaning if progress no longer implies the democratization of affluence— improving the quality of life *for all*. It was the prospect of universal abundance that made progress a morally compelling ideology in the past.

In a modern industrial democracy, the tendency for power to accumulate in the hands of a mighty few is held in check by a variety of regulating measures, such as antitrust laws, fair trade agreements, graduated income tax, collective bargaining, regulatory commissions, and so forth. But these mechanisms have proven inadequate to combat the forces bringing about an increasingly inequitable distribution.

This failure is partly due to the growth of giant transnational corporations with enormous economic power and geographic spread. But more fundamentally, the mechanisms fail because the basic materialistic paradigm itself contains no rationale or incentive for more equitable distribution of power and resources—a rationale that was once provided by society's altruistic, religious ethic.

It is obvious that extending Western consumption patterns to the rest of the world would have a staggering impact on the earth. But continuing the present patterns of the enormous and growing disparity between the world's rich and poor peoples will lay the groundwork for worldwide conflict and eventual social carnage. On no grounds are the industrial paradigm and late-twentieth-century capitalism more bitterly challenged.

**The Global Development Dilemma**
There is perhaps no more misused word in the English language than "development." We speak of land development and typically mean stripping the land of vegetation and paving it over with asphalt.

We speak of human development and typically mean destroying traditional community and conditioning people to survive in an urban environment. We speak of economic development or improving well-being, but typically we mean increasing economic production and consumption.

Clearly these concepts of development do not lead to a long-term viable global future, or to shared well-being even in the medium term. There is, indeed, a development dilemma of global proportions.

The dilemma is that the global system in its present form is incompatible with an ecologically sustainable global society; it is incapable of resolving the plight of the poorest countries. The possible paths of global development that seem to be economically feasible are not ecologically or socially plausible, and those that are ecologically feasible and humanistically desirable are not economically or politically feasible.

To illustrate this dilemma, let us imagine three possible futures.

**Scenario 1:** All developing countries succeed in following the example of the industrialized and newly industrialized countries. The result: The planet is hard-pressed to accommodate six or eight billion people living high-consumption lifestyles; intense political battles arise over environmental and quality-of-life issues.

**Scenario 2:** The high-consumption societies continue to be high-consumption, while the poorer countries remain low-consumption (i.e., poor), with low per capita demand on resources and the environment. The result: a global system with such persisting disparity of income and wealth that vicious "wars of redistribution" (with terrorism as the main weapon) are unavoidable.

**Scenario 3:** High-consumption societies voluntarily cut consumption to ameliorate some of the problems. The result: severe unemployment problems in the formerly high-consumption societies.

The fact is, all past assumptions about the future of the planet are being challenged by the present reality. There is no consensus on what constitutes a viable pattern of global development, but it is increasingly clear that present trends do not: The present domination of economic values is incompatible with

a wise relationship to the earth and its resources; the materialistic paradigm systematically marginalizes people who have no meaningful roles in the society—i.e., with no jobs; it results in a society that habitually confuses means (e.g., economic and technological achievement) with goals; and it persistently endangers the future of the human species with arms races that appear to be endemic to the system.

What has led to this global dilemma? We treat knowledge and an ever-increasing fraction of overall human activity as commodities in the mainstream economy. We assume that an individual's primary relationship to society is through a job. Our social thinking is dominated by concepts of competition, commercial secrecy, money exchange, and scarcity, when in fact one of our main "problems" for the future is our capacity to overproduce.

## What Is Our Purpose?

The key issue as we look ahead is not how we can stimulate more demand for goods and services and information. It is not about creating more jobs in the mainstream economy. The key question is much more fundamental: *What is the central purpose of highly industrialized societies?*

The answer becomes apparent from the emerging values and beliefs about the nature of human beings. *The central purpose of highly industrialized societies is to advance human growth and development to the fullest extent, to promote human learning in the broadest possible definition.* The key task is to find our deepest meaning in the quality of all our relationships, with one another and with nature.

Granted, up to now it has been extremely difficult for a society or a nation to pursue a development path different from the path dictated by the mainstream world economic system. However, several factors will make diverse development paths more feasible in the future.

One of these factors is the growing realization that the past ways of development are, in the end, not good for the planet and not even good for people. The highly industrialized countries are going to have to find some development path for themselves that, without unduly sacrificing quality of life, does not make such voracious demands upon the resource base and effect such gross insults to the ecological and life-support systems of the planet.

A second important factor is the growing crisis in meaning in the developed world. Just as individual riches are not always found to produce a happy life, so the allurements of affluent industrial society fail to provide the kind of shared meanings that make a society cohesive and inspire mutual loyalty.

The penchant of the modern world to judge all things in terms of economics, with its inherent short-term focus, is rooted in the materialism of the present scientific world view. In that picture, higher values have little force, since they are not judged to be reality based. Fortunately, there is now a movement toward a more transcendental world view. As that movement continues to gain force, the legitimacy of the old order will be increasingly withdrawn.

There is nothing more crucial to this time of transition than sharing with one another our interpretations of why the transformation is necessary or seems to be happening. There is no conversation more critical today than that around these questions: Growth—in what sense, and to what end? Development—for what? What is the right development for this society? What is viable global development? What is a "world that works for everyone"? What are the requisites for achieving that goal? What are the costs of not achieving it? ❑

## Questions

1. List six examples showing a strong correlation between economic product and environmental deterioration.

2. What is the belief of an economy-dominated value system?

3. What is the driving force behind the assumptions of an economy-dominated society?

*Answers are at the back of the book.*

**43** *In an age of increasing population and decreasing resources, compromises must be reached to create a more sustainable society. Environmental concerns must be addressed, and solutions must focus on the future, not on profits. For example, forests are worth more standing than when logged for timber, and they contribute a range of products that people use worldwide. The greatest value of many forests is their capacity to act as a reservoir for carbon that would otherwise be discharged into the atmosphere, accelerating climatic change. Today, the use of paper and wood is increasing, and alternatives must be found. This will require major alterations in the way the world does business.*

# What Good Is a Forest?
## Bill McKibben

*Audubon*, May/June 1996

*Economists now agree with ecologists: forests are worth more standing than logged.*

Let's assume, for the duration of this article, that to you trees are vertical stalks of fiber, that a forest carries no more spiritual or aesthetic value than a parking lot, that woodland creatures are uninteresting sacks of calories, and that the smell of sunbaked pine needles on a breezy June afternoon merely matches the scent that comes from those conifer-shaped air fresheners that dangle from your rearview mirror.

Let's assume, in other words, that you've done something rotten and God has turned you into an economist.

Now you have an assignment: What should be done with the one-third of the earth's dry land that is covered by forest? You can cut it all down, save it all, or do anything in between—but only if you can defend your decisions without appeal to sentiment. Bottom line only, please.

At the moment, much of that land is turning from green to brown; forests are falling across Asia, Africa, South America, and North America. Some of the changes are permanent: woods turned into subdivision or shopping mall. Some of them are temporary, as when ancient forest is converted to second growth, and then to third, and so on, in order to supply paper. Except for those places where desperate peasants are clearing out small holes to grow food, all this activity is justified by the profit motive. People are making money. But are they making the best use of the land? Are their economic decisions good or bad? What is a forest really worth?

For a long time environmentalists tried to side-step this debate. "In the eighties, industry began demanding economic quantification," says Sandra Neily, a policy analyst at the Maine Audubon Society. Neily, who has just completed a survey that attempts to calculate the values of the state's forests, says, "We were afraid that if you weighed an industrial park against a wetland, we'd always lose. We didn't have the data." But now the data are coming in. Biologists, chemists, ecological economists, and others have begun compiling figures that show just what the natural world is worth. From prairie to desert to reef to river, they're showing how woefully uneconomical many of our decisions have been. But for now, we'll stick to forests.

"If you've been out in a rainstorm under a major canopy tree, you know how long you can stay there before you get wet," says Leslie Sauer, a principal of the ecological-design firm Andropogon Associates. "The water passes through a lot of obstacles, which reduce its impact along the way." Hence, when it finally reaches the forest floor, it seeps in instead of bouncing off. But if you cut down the trees for fields, or for roads, or for houses, or for anything else that's not as permeable, more of that water rolls straight into a stream, cutting channels, carrying silt, causing floods.

And that leaves no water in the ground to seep out come the hot days of summer. We've known this a long time; the Adirondack Park, the first large experiment in conservation in the eastern United States, was created in part by downstate business interests fearful that mountain logging would dry up the Hudson River and the Erie Canal. But now we understand the systems in more detail. Once 10 percent of an upland watershed is compacted or paved over, says Sauer, the river system becomes progressively less useful. Channels are cut deeper and deeper, flooding becomes more frequent, water quality degrades. Soon you have to build levees, water-treatment plants, the works. "Nature used to do all these things for free," Sauer points out. "We can't afford to maintain the infrastructure we have now—and we certainly can't afford any more."

New York City recently agreed to pay upstate counties more than $1 billion to protect the watersheds around its reservoirs. Not because it liked the trees, but because a treatment plant to replace the work the trees were doing for free would have cost $8 to $9 billion. If we restore forests, says Sauer, we can avoid some of the same costs in other places.

Forests provide a whole host of minor products—from bark to shrubs to berries to fruit—that support people worldwide. Acre for acre, living forests are often more valuable than the sum of their timber, especially because they grow back quickly. Alan Drengson, director of British Columbia's Ecoforestry Institute, says, "Many of our forests have a higher value in mushrooms and ornamental plants, like salal brush and sword ferns, than in woody materials. When I was a boy we used to go out and gather ferns and sell them. Now there are big fleets of semis picking them up."

Though ornamental ferns are not essential, a stable climate probably is. The clouds of carbon dioxide we've released since we evolved into *Homo automobilis, Homo thermostatens*, and *Homo wal-*

*martius* are now poised to raise the temperature four or five degrees Fahrenheit in the next century. Forget the way this heat will feel—forget the sweat gluing your shirt to your back—and consider only that magic bottom line. Economists have calculated, extremely conservatively, that global warming could knock 2 percent off the world's gross product over the next century by depleting resources and increasing energy use. Since forests and their soils contain immense amounts of carbon that would otherwise contribute to the greenhouse effect—perhaps one and a half times as much as in the atmosphere, according to George Woodwell, director of the Woods Hole Research Center, on Cape Cod—keeping the forests standing has a quantifiable economic impact.

Recently, a university team assessing the worth of Mexico's forests for everything from tourism to nuts found that their highest value was as a reservoir of carbon that would otherwise be released into the atmosphere, accelerating climate change. This rule holds true in many forests. "If you have a Sitka spruce stand in the Tongass [National Forest in Alaska], it might contain more than fifteen thousand grams of carbon per square meter," says Woodwell. "And if it's clear-cut, it contains very little," especially because much of the carbon is in the now unprotected soil. If new trees grow, they will slowly soak up carbon. But it will be a long time before they contain even half as much as the native forest.

Still, the fact that forests are saving the world from the greenhouse effect doesn't do much for the local economy. Maybe you're better off just cutting the trees down—or maybe not. A team of economists issued a report last December attempting to explain the "Northwest paradox." As logging declined in the Pacific Northwest during the past half-decade, the region didn't turn into a new Appalachia, as some had predicted. Instead, its economy expanded more than that of any other part of the nation. Oregon had its lowest unemployment rate in a generation, as new high-tech jobs more than replaced those lost in the partial forestry shutdown. To figure out why, economists had to factor in the silly, sentimental preferences of other Americans—the fact that, for whatever bizarre reasons, they wanted to live near some big old trees, drink some clean water, see some wildlife. "The comparative advantage, given that people care about where they live, goes to those areas that are able to hang on to more of what people consider a superior quality of life," says Thomas Power, an economist at the University of Montana. His report, signed by 60 other area economists, concluded: "The Pacific Northwest does not have to choose between jobs and the environment. Quite the opposite: A healthy environment is a major stimulus for a healthy economy." So, for instance, Sony built a plant in Springfield, an Oregon mill town set in a beautiful area, that employs 350 people starting at $9.50 an hour. "They wanted a pristine spot by the river," says the mayor.

Employment figures tell only part of the story. There's also tourism, and pharmaceuticals, and the way that large forests can moderate local climates. But perhaps it's time to address the obvious: If intact forests can produce such economic benefits, why do we most often cut them down instead? There are several answers, some of them obvious and some more obscure.

You are holding the most basic explanation in your hands. This nation uses an enormous amount of fiber, for paper and for timber, and we are using more of it all the time. It's true that we've made tremendous gains in recycling. In some parts of the domestic paper industry, says John Ruston of the Environmental Defense Fund, the majority of new mills coming on-line use recycled instead of virgin fiber. And there's more potential: If the United States could increase its recycling rate from the current 40 percent to 50 percent, that would increase the world's supply of fiber by 3 percent. But the depressing facts of exponential growth apply here as in so many places. Because the world's population keeps growing, and because that population uses greater amounts of paper and wood all the time, recycling doesn't even allow our forests to run in place. "The demand for paper products is growing so rapidly worldwide that even though we're adding lots of new fiber through recycling, we're still using more virgin fiber every year," says Reid Lifset, director of Yale University's Program on Solid Waste Policy. An international consortium of book, newspaper, and magazine publishers recently warned of upcoming paper shortages. In response, they chose not to print fewer of their products or to use smaller type or thinner paper but to demand that the World Bank "encourage extensive investment in paper production."

One of the reasons we use—and waste—so much fiber is that it's cheap, and one of the reasons it's cheap is that the economics that drive logging simply fail to reflect any of the other values of forests.

Consider the public forests first. Many of the world's forests are public, under the control of government officials. In this country, most of our national forests are in the West, in the vast domain of the U.S. Forest Service. Increasingly, their financial management is coming under scrutiny. The Forest Service has spent the past decade trying to fend off the charges of American environmentalists that its "management strategy"—which consists of paying for the construction of roads to groves of timber and then selling the logs off to the highest bidder—loses money for the taxpayer. In the vast majority of cases the agency has been forced to concede that the cost of the roads far exceeds the receipts from the sales (and to argue, therefore, that the roads and clearcuts represent recreation opportunities and wildlife-habitat improvements). But it's always insisted that because a few of the forests in the Pacific Northwest are able to sell their mammoth trees for big bucks, the system as a whole breaks even. The biggest flaw in this argument, as Tim Hermack, director of the Native Forest Council, in Eugene, Oregon, points out, is simple: The Forest Service turns a profit because it sets a value on those publicly owned trees of precisely zero dollars. It didn't cost the Forest Service anything to grow them—God and the moist fog off the ocean took care of that—so it figures them as a "free good" and whatever it clears from selling them off as profit. This is much closer to Mother Theresa than to Adam Smith. As Hermack points out, "In private industry any accountant who so drastically under-valued his company's assets would be immediately dismissed and might even go to jail."

The debate over the value of publicly owned trees has sharpened in recent months. On the one hand, more and more grassroots environmentalists are backing Hermack's call for a "zero cut" in the national forests. They want those trees valued for everything from storing carbon to supporting local economies with their sheer beauty. On the other side, Republican member of Congress—defenders, theoretically, of free enterprise—rushed through a bill last summer to increase the cut in national forests and curtail the right of citizens to protest. President Bill Clinton signed the law after saying he wouldn't; then, in the fall, he limply called it a mistake and asked for its repeal. The Congressional Research Service has already concluded that the legislation could cost taxpayers $25 million because, among other things, it overestimates the price the timber will bring.

The Clearwater National Forest, in Idaho, which was "salvage logged" a few years ago, shows what this legislative mistake will cost. According to Carl Ross of the nonprofit Save America's Forests, who ran photos of the devastation in his newsletter, "They did their so-called salvage logging on a series of slopes, and the result has been a series of mud avalanches throughout the forest this fall. Whole streams are completely destroyed, miles and miles of trout streams."

On private forestland—which means most woods in the southern and eastern United States—life is a little more logical. No one values a tree at zero. But big timber companies with large industrial forests clear-cut, spray herbicide from helicopters, grow endless stands of small trees, cut them down before they turn into a true forest, and otherwise "intensively manage" their land to produce fiber without much thought for the other values of the forest. Partly this is because no one pays big timber owners such as Georgia-Pacific to store carbon or filter water; they can make a return only by selling fiber. But even that central failing of economics doesn't explain why the big companies almost always choose to cut down small trees over and over again instead of letting them grow into big forests where each individual tree would be worth far more—and where, by happy accident, the other values of the forest would be more protected.

To understand that process, says Joachim Maier, an independent forestry consultant, you need to calculate the future value of an asset and thus determine what to do with it now. If you have a stand of trees, you can either cut it down and invest the proceeds or let it mature until the trees are very valuable. Once upon a time, says Maier, foresters figured on a rate of return on their investment of 2 or 3 percent. As a result, "they got financial rotations that were similar to the biological rotations." That is, trees and money grew at roughly the same rate, so you could afford to wait to chop them down. In the 1960s and '70s, though, foresters started basing their decisions on returns of almost 10 percent, reflecting rising interest rates. Forests started falling at a record pace so the money could buy stocks, other companies, or new forests in Indonesia. For several decades now, money has grown faster than trees. Foresters have thus been forced by the impeccable "logic" of economics to turn the trees into money as quickly as possible.

The whole picture is more complicated than that, of course. Forest-products companies also need to calculate factors like supplying their own paper mills, which also have revenue targets to meet. And property taxes, income taxes, and competitive factors also influence decisions, says Joel Swanton, a senior management forester at Champion International, which owns 1.3 million acres across the Northeast.

But the results of the various calculations have been predictably depressing. From the air, much of northern Maine resembles a dog with terminal mange, with vast clearcuts stretching off in every direction. In some spots the autumn colors turn up in early summer because the hardwoods have been killed by aerial doses of herbicide designed to produce pure stands of softwoods. Logging roads run everywhere, right to the borders of Baxter State Park, the state's big wilderness tract, which is home to Mount Katahdin. Recent federal studies of several Maine counties indicate the extent of the damage, says Mitch Lansky, author of *Beyond the Beauty Strip*, a scathing account of the state's industrial forestry. Red spruce trees—a staple of the paper and lumber mills—have been cut at 3.7 times their rate of growth. That's bad news if you're a black bear hoping to inhabit a spruce forest or if you're a logger hoping to cut trees sometime in the future.

As a result, Maine environmentalists are now challenging the state's private logging industry almost as strongly as western activists attack abuses on public lands. "Before we're done, people are going to recognize that this is as important as the Pacific Northwest," says Jonathan Carter, campaign director for a referendum that, if approved this fall, would ban clear-cutting in the core of the Maine woods. Though the timber industry began running television commercials attacking the ban before it was officially put on the ballot, Carter's troops still succeeded in collecting a record number of signatures in a one-day push. "People were standing in line all across the state," he says. "The people are angry, and they ought to be—they've seen the places destroyed, the jobs lost."

Even before the current referendum campaign, the huge timber companies that control most of Maine's forests had begun to respond to public outcries. Champion, for instance, launched a "sustainable forestry initiative" that is setting goals for everything from water quality to aesthetics. When it's done, says Swanton, all the company's land will be classified—some for high-yield management, some for ecological protection. "We think we can manage our ownership in ways that meet the needs of most people," he says. At least a few environmentalists are hopeful that he's right. Others are more skeptical. Neily, the policy analyst for Maine Audubon, which has yet to decide if it will back the referendum, sums up the dilemma: "The industry keeps looking for ways they can create the characteristics of old growth—the habitat, the water quality, and so forth—without having to grow a tree for a long time." In other words, what you need is time for a stand of trees to grow into a forest capable of doing all the other things we've discussed.

If the economics of forestry are to change dramatically (dramatically enough that you'll be able to view the results from a satellite, just as you can monitor the current deforestation), it will require major shifts in the way the world does business. We'll need to reimburse the companies and countries holding carbon-rich ancient forests. In a few isolated cases, that's started to happen on a small scale. Western utilities, for instance, have tried to compensate for new coal-fired power plants by planting or protecting trees in the tropics. Developers might have to repair upstream watersheds before they build new projects. We'll all need to pay zeal-ous attention to waste and look for alternatives to wood and paper. And we'll need a new forestry, one that manages both private woodlots and vast industrial forests for many values now ignored and that concentrates on growing high-quality older trees.

That new forestry is slowly being born on a few larger tracts, such as the quarter-million acres the Menominee Indians manage in northern Wisconsin, and in small-scale demonstration forests east and west. If you want a sense of this forestry, stop by Sam Brown's woodlot in Cambridge, Maine. "I grew up in Washington State, and my heritage was in lumbering," he says. Brown represents the fifth generation of a timber family; his father worked in the Pacific Northwest with Weyerhaeuser, the greatest industrial-forestry giant of them all. But Brown moved to Maine, bought 300 acres of land, and fell in with some "alternative foresters—local people who pecked the corn a different way. I liked their results and their attitude."

A tinkerer by nature, Brown has spent the last decade devising small-scale machinery that allows a forester to work carefully, without compacting the soil or damaging surrounding trees the way a full-size skidder—a heavy tractor that drags trees out of the woods—often does. His current model features a radio-controlled winch mounted on a trailer, so the forester can gently "tweak" logs out to the road. "The challenge for me is to develop a technology that's economically possible," he says, "with a capital cost low enough that a logger with some intelligence and drive can do good work without having to sell himself to John Deere or the big banker." (For a small logging contractor, the huge payments on an $80,000 skidder can all but require him to cut more trees, more carelessly, than he might like to.) With his low-priced system, Brown says he's more or less in control of his destiny. "I can practically live off the interest," he insists. Brown extracts just a half-cord to a cord of wood per acre each year, earning from $50 a cord for pulp to $600 a cord for veneer-quality wood. "I'm looking out the window right now at some ash trees and some rock maples," he says. "Someday I'll be able to market them for a decent price. Or someone else will—these trees will live for a hundred and fifty to two hundred years."

Drengson, the British Columbia academic who

helped found the Ecoforestry Institute because no forestry school was interested in the concept, says the new-forestry movement is "not big at all in terms of wood volume, but in terms of the number of people involved, it's grown significantly over the past five years." Many of the newcomers turn to old-time foresters who've been practicing the art for decades. It's a little like organic farming 20 years ago—and indeed, some of the same people who have been confronting agribusiness for many years are now standing up to careless forestry.

Wendell Berry, the Kentucky farmer-essayist, writes a good deal about small woodlots in his most recent collection, *Another Turn of the Crank*. "A forest makes things slowly," he writes. "A good forest economy would therefore be a patient economy. It would also be an unselfish one, for good foresters must always look toward harvests that they will not live to reap." Such injunctions imply a million pieces of subtle technique, each fitted to the particular soil and climate—how steep to build a road, where to put a culvert, when to turn your back on the woods for fear of harming muddy soils. They're the kind of techniques that David Brynn, the county forester for Addison County, Vermont, tries to teach small landowners. "It's tough—careful logging doesn't lend itself to large-scale mechanization," he says. "But on these small-scale family forests, whose primary purpose is often recreation or peace of mind, it gives an opportunity for people who consider themselves environmentalists to become more active participants in the marketplace."

As they become involved, though, they will need to make that marketplace more realistic. They'll need to consider, for instance, the example of Mel Ames, who helped put his eight kids through college off his woodlot in Atkinson, Maine. A forester by training, he's been managing the land for 50 years without ever clear-cutting. He has always depended on high-value trees, which grow slowly and have tight, narrow rings.

The result is strong, attractive wood. "Prices are going up, especially for quality wood," he says. "When you start cutting in a stand, you'd better understand which trees are going to be worth a lot in the future." As long as he avoids expensive equipment, he says, "a person can make a living"—and grow a forest with more wood per acre than it contained a half-century before. "I suppose I could have clear-cut it and put the money in the bank or the stock market," he says. If so, he might well be richer, and the land would certainly be poorer. "But I try to look at my woodlot like a stock market investment. Only there's a lot of things like hunting and fishing and canoeing and looking at moose that you don't get with any stock market."

All of us who make decisions about our own woodlots, about the national forests, or even about the vast tracts of industrial forest will need to shed some of the prejudices of the economist—the supposedly logical rigor that prevents us from thinking about real costs and real benefits, short- and long-term, local and global. We'll need to stop thinking so simplistically about forests, need to try for an understanding as rich, complex, and multifaceted as the woods themselves. We'll have to remember that money sometimes grows on trees, but so do many other things. ❑

## Questions

1. What happens when forests are cut down and replaced with fields, roads, or houses?

2. Explain the Northwest paradox.

3. When the Clearwater National Forest in Idaho was "salvage-logged," what was the result?

*Answers are at the back of the book.*

**44**

*For the environmental technology industry to work, it needs to tie its products and services to profitability. Often, regulated industries will buy environmental technologies if they increase production, save money, and clean the environment. The U.S. environmental technology market in products and services is worth roughly $135 billion per year. Traditional environmental industries dominated 1994 revenues. However, companies that handle hazardous waste have been hurt by competition and overcapacity. This is because many factories now produce less waste. Companies that are involved in producing pollution equipment had total revenues of approximately $60 billion last year and are expected to grow worldwide.*

# Selling Blue Skies, Clean Water
## Jeff Johnson

*Environmental Science & Technology*, June 1995

*Will deregulation, pollution prevention, and international competition hold promise or problems for a stagnant environmental compliance industry?*

A decade ago, the environmental compliance business—a newborn industry spawned by legislation such as Superfund, the Resource Conservation and Recovery Act (RCRA), and the Clean Air Act—was said to face a brilliant future. RCRA's ban on dumping hazardous waste on land held great promise for the incineration industry, Superfund was expected to send revenues for remediation businesses sky high, and Clean Air Act requirements were thought to provide solid revenues to many environmental technology industries.

But today, the overall market is predicted to grow at a humble 3 or 4% annually. What happened? Were projections and expectations unrealistic? Was the promise undercut by an easing of regulations? Did the regulated industry just find a cheaper way to meet compliance targets?

The dynamics that drive the environmental compliance business are complex and in flux, making it difficult but important to ferret out where the industry is headed and what it needs to prosper. Adding to the confusion is today's antiregulatory climate and the regulated industries' desire to soften if not roll back the laws and regulations that have created this industry. However, experts see a way out. Call it pollution prevention or common sense, they say the environmental technology industry has to tie its products and services to production efficiency to beat out the competition. Increasingly, regulated industries will buy environmental technologies only when they increase production and save money as well as clean the environment. Environmental technology market analysts predict a bright future for companies that combine environmental and production improvements rather than sell end-of-pipe compliance hardware.

Overall the U.S. environmental technology market in products and services is worth about $135 billion a year, according to Environmental Business International, Inc. (EBI), an environmental research, consulting, and publishing firm in San Diego. About 74% of that total is services and 26% is equipment.

Looking at estimated 1994 revenues, traditional environmental industries dominate: solid waste management ($30.6 billion, 23%); water utilities ($24.3 billion, 18%) and water equipment and chemicals ($13.8 billion, 10%); resource recovery ($16 billion, 12%); hazardous waste management ($8.6 billion,

6%); waste management equipment ($11 billion, 8%); and remediation and cleanup services ($8.9 billion, 6%).

Suffering a down market, says Grant Ferrier, head of EBI, are companies that manage hazardous waste and have been hurt by stiff competition and treatment overcapacity; the remediation industry, reeling from a stall in Superfund reauthorization and cuts in federal cleanup funding; and the air pollution control market, dragged down by delayed regulations and weak enforcement. Doing well are companies in the water sector, which he calls the "sleeping giant" of the U.S. environmental industry. Its total revenues were about $60 billion last year, nearly half those of the total environmental industry, and the sector is expected to grow in the United States and abroad.

Ferrier points to other bright spots in addition to designers and sellers of wastewater treatment systems and supplies, including solid waste handlers, the recycling industry, and engineering firms that provide companies with technical advice and engineering services.

The total environmental market will grow, Ferrier says, but not very fast. He notes that three of eight mutual funds that dealt in environmental stocks dropped those portfolios last year because of poor stock performance. But consolidation and mergers in this historically fragmented industry are taking place, and that may help buoy up survivors. Four years ago, for instance, 1400 environmental testing labs competed for about $1.5 billion in annual revenues, and today 1150 chase $1.6 billion.

Ferrier and other analysts predict a strong future for pollution prevention equipment (1994 sales of $800 million) and engineering services (1994 sales of $15 billion)—a 15% annual growth for pollution prevention and at least a 5% yearly increase for consulting and engineering services over the next five years. More important, however, is the potential these sectors hold for combining compliance with production efficiency and beginning to move past a regulation-driven marketplace.

## The Role of Regulations

"You must remember, there has been no natural market for environmental technologies, like there is for food or clothing," says Donald L. Connors, head of the International Environmental Business and Technology Institute, a Boston environmental technology research and promotion firm, and a founder of one of the first environmental business trade associations, the Environmental Business Council of Massachusetts.

"The demand for clean air and water is created by regulations, and a change in regulations has a major impact on this business. Weakening environmental laws and regulations is a negative for the million or so people who make a living in the environmental industry," Connors adds.

Although a regulatory floor of some sort is necessary to drive the environmental market, where to fix the bottom is a subject of much debate in the new Congress, the regulated community, and the environmental movement.

However, even when the floor was set high, such as under the 1990 Clean Air Act Amendments (CAAA), compliance dollars fell far short of expectations of environmental technology marketers, who too often hung their hopes on cost estimates from regulated industries.

When the CAAA were debated in Congress in the late 1980s, regulated industries and their trade associations said compliance costs would top S100 billion a year, more than what was then spent on all environmental compliance. EPA estimates were much lower, about &25 billion a year. Actual spending is now half of EPA's estimate, according to Joan B. Berkowitz, an analyst with Farkas Berkowitz & Co., who says spending is about $13.5 billion a year and only in part a result of the CAAA.

Although cost estimates from regulated industries were considered inflated, they looked pretty good to environmental compliance businesses. However, environmental industry analysts now wonder where those big compliance dollars fled.

Analysts blame EPA for the down market for air pollution controls and single out the Clinton administration's slow release of air regulations and weak enforcement resulting from the reorganization of EPA's enforcement office in 1993. Now that enforcement is back on track, the Agency has been forced to delay issuance of new regulations to avoid stirring up the antiregulatory Congress.

The mood in Congress is sure to hurt Clean Air Act-related businesses, says Jeffrey C. Smith, executive director of the Institute of Clean Air Companies. "A corporate executive would be foolish to buy new air pollution control equipment if the Act may be frozen, rewritten, or a new cost-benefit requirement tacked on," he says.

Berkowitz predicts that regulatory confusion will continue. For instance, compliance dates faced by the majority of industries covered by the CAAA's maximum achievable control technology standards remain "uncertain," she says. Even when the rules are promulgated, industries will have many routes of compliance, Berkowitz believes, such as process changes and emissions trading as well as end-of-pipe controls. "There are hundreds of technologies out there seeking market share, assuming there is a market."

### Beyond Compliance

To survive in this uncertain climate, where regulations cannot be relied on to drive the market, the challenge for environmental compliance businesses is to find ways to move beyond compliance. Or in the words of Ferrier, firms must "sell value" and find the "economic validation" for environmental investments. "Environmental companies must find economic drivers, not regulatory ones, for environmental technologies," he says.

"Most [pollution] generators view environmental expenditures as a cost and something that takes away from the bottom line, not as an investment," Ferrier says. "The trick for environmental service and technology providers is to change that mindset in customers to see expenditures as an investment in a shift to long-term efficiency and a phase-out of certain chemicals."

Ferrier points to water treatment as one sector in which economic drivers are likely to take precedent over regulations. As clean water becomes more expensive and discharge fees to sewage treatment facilities increase, he believes industrial polluters will be more likely to turn to firms that sell water treatment or water recycling systems as a way out of dependence on treatment facilities and their fees. As a result, he predicts, this business will grow.

Another example in which economic concerns are beginning to outweigh regulations is in the consulting field. Engineering firms increasingly are providing industry with long-range guidance that couples compliance with production efficiency. One business that has moved into this area and is profiting is TRC Companies, Inc., headquartered in Windsor, CT, with 900 employees and $100 million in revenues. TRC specializes in air pollution control, pollution prevention, and hazardous waste engineering, says Vincent A. Rocco, TRC chair and chief executive officer. Despite the weak national market for air pollution control equipment, Rocco says, TRC increased revenues from air pollution control engineering by 30% last year. It is the fastest growing part of TRC's business.

He describes TRC's work as a process in which company engineers examine a client's production methods and then design manufacturing improvements that lower production costs and cut pollution. In particular, the firm develops a production management plan that combines production efficiency and compliance with the CAAA's operating permit provisions. The permitting provisions, Title V, require companies to determine their air emissions and lay out a comprehensive operating plan to control them.

According to Rocco, the permit provisions provide his clients with an "opportunity to define a broad range of products and select the most cost-effective control options and ultimately to be in the position where a client doesn't have to worry about the regulatory policeman for the five-year life of the permit."

TRC is preparing operating permits for 300 factories and has coupled the requirements to a review of a company's total operations, both production and environmental strategies.

What TRC is selling is basic pollution prevention by examining a company's manufacturing process and seeing how it can be made better. This analysis, Rocco says, requires a manufacturer to closely consider what it is making, what its chemical mass balance is, and what it is going to make over the next five years. Then these components must be woven into a permit.

"Companies have to anticipate process changes and write them into the permit," Rocco says. "They must plan for flexibility, see product reformulation, controls, pollution prevention as options, and include strategic planning as part of environmental controls." He calls the CAAA's air toxics provisions simply "good housekeeping."

"Probably the biggest challenge to industry is to stop and think about where it wants to be in five years in terms of productivity," he says. "That's future shock. Nine out of 10 plants don't even have final as-built plant drawings. If it wasn't for Title V, they might not know how they make a product, how the plant is piped, or where they have leaks."

Ferrier sees a solid future for engineering consulting firms that specialize in pollution prevention and other adjustments to the manufacturing process. But he warns that many of the companies that generate pollution may have already captured much of the "low-hanging fruit"—the first 20-30% of easy emissions reduction. "The next 20% will be much tougher and more expensive," Ferrier says. "We are talking about redesigning, rebuilding a whole factory, but this is the future—a focus on process, on energy use, higher productivity, efficiency, and not only environmental compliance."

## Regulatory Rollback?
Tough regulations and strict enforcement have been the primary drivers for the environmental market, but times are changing. In recent years, many companies have significantly reduced toxic emissions in response to voluntary programs promoted by EPA as well as community and stockholder pressure that springs from the annual publication of the Toxics Release Inventory of emissions to the environment. Connors notes that many companies have incorporated an environmental ethic into how they plan production, and they are not solely driven by environmental regulations. "But," he adds, "lots of companies are not working under that model."

Despite regulations and voluntary cuts in emissions, TRI figures show U.S. companies still put 2.8 billion lbs. of pollutants into the environment each year, which signals plenty of business for environmental industries. However, as Ferrier points out, each incremental reduction will get more difficult and costly. How aggressively manufacturers pursue pollution reduction programs in the new era of deregulation may determine the environmental industry's future.

Looking at the CMA permit provisions, which have been a boon to companies like TRC, manufacturers charge that the requirements are too bureaucratic and place manufacturers in a regulatory straitjacket when they make normal product changes over the five years a permit is in force. EPA has never finalized the regulation, but states have moved ahead with their own rules based on Agency drafts and the law. Industry permit applications are due to the states by the end of this year under the Act.

Several corporations—Occidental Petroleum, Procter & Gamble Co., Intel Corp., and others—recently formed the "air implementation reform coalition" and announced their intention to change CAAA Title V. They said they doubt a federal hammer is needed and argue that most states have adequate permit programs in place without the Acts new requirements. Title V, according to the coalition, creates debilitating delay that could cripple industry's ability to react quickly to marketplace changes."

They have a strong ally in newly elected Rep. David McIntosh (R-IN), who has vowed to block the regulation, if not change the law. McIntosh first gained a reputation as a deregulator when he headed the Bush-era Council on Competitiveness and opposed the permitting provisions of the CAAA. Now he heads the House Government Reform and Oversight Subcommittee on National Economic Growth, Natural Resources, and Regulatory Affairs.

Resistance to regulations runs deep, and a bumpy road may lie ahead in the form of legislative proposals before the new Congress, according to Alan Miller, director of the University of Maryland's Center for Change and co-author of *Green Gold,* a study of international competition for environmental technologies.

In his role as researcher, Miller interviewed many officials in regulated industries, and he says, "If you turn off the tape recorder, you will find deep pent-up anger from a lot of frustrated people—even from some of the most environmentally progressive companies in America. They see themselves as victims of regulatory rigidity, and if offered a chance to get rid of all those forms and requirements in one fell swoop, they would jump at it. This is not necessarily a clear strategy, but more of a feeding frenzy. I don't think companies have thought through that they may be giving a competitive advantage to their less progressive competitors, or that they might wind up with 50 different sets of regulations."

Even officials at companies that have been held up as models of environmental compliance say they have trouble with Title V. One of them is Merck & Co., Inc., the large pharmaceutical company, which, its officers say, has voluntarily phased out air emissions of carcinogens and has set a goal of a 90% reduction of emissions of chemicals listed on the Toxics Release Inventory by year's end.

Merck Vice-President for Environmental and Safety Policy Dorothy P. Bowers says putting together a Title V plan is a "very, very major operation." She would like to see the title changed, even if it takes rewriting the Act. Meanwhile Bowers says Merck is preparing five Title V applications for its companies operating in states where the plans are required.

Generally, Merck supports regulatory standards, Bowers says, emphasizing how the company has examined its manufacturing activities to see whether process changes, reduction in toxic chemical use, or pollution controls can help cut pollution. The problem, she says, "is the bureaucracy and process of getting us to meet standards."

Although she says "very few responsible companies support a rollback of standards," she adds that it might be worthwhile to revisit "at least some Clean Air Act regulations. The United States seems to lead the world in environmental bureaucracy."

**Help in the International Market**

A way to ease the impact of today's backlash against environmental regulations in the United States may be to turn to the international market. And U.S. companies increasingly are looking to foreign shores to fill marketing voids at home. To exploit this $300 billion market, U.S. companies have begun to get a helping hand from the federal government and even states.

Trudy Coxe is not your average environmental technology booster, but last year the Massachusetts secretary of environmental affairs found herself in India trying to help sell the Bombay port authority on a satellite-based ship-tracking system to avoid environmental disasters from ship collisions and oil spills.

"There we were, saying 'Rah, Rah, Raytheon. There's no company that can do the job better than Raytheon,'" Coxe recalls, referring to the Massachusetts-based high-tech company. Having the state's top environmental official on a trade mission with the governor and some 30 business representatives may seem unusual, but for Coxe it has become almost commonplace. She has traveled with the state delegation to Brazil, Argentina, Chile, and Sardinia.

Governor William Weld, she says, has singled out sectors of the Massachusetts economy that have the potential to merit international promotion: finance, health care, biotechnology, computers, and environmental services. The promotions seem to be working. Following a visit by Coxe and other state and business people, she notes, Raytheon sold the Brazilian government a satellite system to monitor the rain forest. The system is similar to that proposed in Bombay and to one the company developed following the *Exxon Valdez* oil spill.

Over the past few years, the Clinton administration Department of Commerce has begun to help U.S. environmental technologies get a foothold in the international market, which is expected to double in size by the turn of the century (*ES&T*, January 1995). But Coxe says Massachusetts is the first state to actively promote the industry.

Market analysts predict great growth for the international sector. Connors says many nations are only now developing environmental policies and they lack an infrastructure and trained government and industry staff to comply with pollution reductions. "Many companies there are like we were 20 years ago," he says.

Ferrier also predicts more emphasis on the international marketplace for U.S. environmental technologies, in part because of a slowdown in the U.S. market. He notes, for instance, that businesses that sell environmental instruments and testing equipment are doing half their sales outside the United States, as are providers of solar and wind energy systems. U.S. water treatment systems companies are doing one-third of their business outside U.S. borders and the percentage is expected to grow, he adds.

Coxe believes support for environmental technologies will benefit the overall Massachusetts economy. She wants to roll environmental technologies firmly into the state's economy and encourage development of an "atmosphere" in which environmental technology businesses can thrive with universities and research facilities and in which jobs are the result. As an example, Coxe points to the state's decision to join California's clean vehicle demonstration program, which will lead to production of a small number of electric cars. That decision gave a boost to Massachusetts' Solectria Corp., the developer of an electric powertrain.

"Solectria may give us a chance to bring back the thousands of auto industry jobs lost when General Motors shut down a big plant in the state a decade ago," Coxe notes. "And this car would be green."

But a successful environmental business is based on a firm regulatory floor, Coxe acknowledges. She worries that a congressional attack on environmental regulations will hurt states like Massachusetts that have tried to move ahead in the environmental technology business arena.

"Rules set a standard for people to strive for and set a standard for new technologies," Coxe says. Because many of Massachusetts' environmental laws are stronger than federal ones, Coxe says, Washington events may have less impact on Massachusetts than on states where standards are not as high.

"In the longer term, though, I don't want to see the states in economic warfare with one another, and I think that is where we might end up if federal laws get weakened. The justification may be to give states and businesses more flexibility, but an overall dismantling would pit one state against another to lower standards. If that happens, I know there will be a constituency of people who will be very vocal and persuasive in seeking weaker regulations that could be very detrimental to us in the long term."

## The Next Century

What will the environmental technology market look like in the next century? Will it grow? Will it disappear and be absorbed into the nation's overall capital spending accounts? If analysts are right and pollution prevention proves to be the industry's future, will that mean more revenues?

Analysts describe a tug of war over waste, with one sector of the compliance industry wanting to handle it and another sector wanting to eliminate it. In the long run, some analysts predict pollution prevention will kill off the environmental technology industry.

"In general, producing less waste is bad for the environmental technology industry," says Jonathan Naimon, corporate program manager of Investors Responsibility Research Center Inc., a Washington, DC, firm that assesses companies' corporate environmental performance. "Process modification, better valves, and so forth lead to less waste to handle or treat, with the result that pollution prevention will harm a lot of things that [Vice President] Al Gore thinks are going to get much bigger. Ultimately, these technologies, even advanced ones, will run out of work."

Naimon says companies he tracks are producing fewer toxics per unit of revenue than they ever have before. "Pollution controls are not dying but they are slowing dawn, and the seeds of pollution prevention signal the demise of the environmental technology industry as we know it. In the future, we will have better seals and flanges and process engineers to cut waste and raise productivity."

His views are borne out by an annual pollution abatement spending survey of 17,000 companies conducted by the Commerce Department Bureau of Economic Analysis. The figures show a shift in corporate spending over the past 10 years from end-of-pipe pollution controls to what the bureau calls "integrated technologies" that combine environmental with manufacturing process changes. In 1983, integrated technology spending made up about 15% of compliance spending and controls made up the rest. The most recent figures, from 1992, show that integrated technologies reached 36%. Commerce Department officials also note that at some point the environmental compliance spending figures will have less meaning because they will be thoroughly blended into other technological production spending.

"In the long run, in the macro sense, effective

pollution prevention will eliminate the environmental technology market in the United States," Ferrier says. Today, about 90% of these revenues are focused on waste, pollution, and cleanup, he says, but if pollution is prevented and Superfund sites eliminated, there will be a peak to the curve.

"The services and equipment sectors are growing in the short term, but by the turn of the century we will see their revenues start to decline, and in the future they will be engulfed by general manufacturing, driven by production and material resource efficiency systems." ❑

## Questions

1. What is the biggest challenge to industry?

2. What have been the primary drivers for the environmental market?

3. Generally, what is bad for the environmental technology industry?

*Answers are at the back of the book.*

**45**

*Environmentalism and big business working together may seem paradoxical. Profit margins often encourage companies to contaminate the land, sea, and air. However, opponents of the green movement have found that support of the environment is sound business—either by creating new markets or by protecting existing markets against competitors. Government regulation is behind the growth of the cleanup industry. America, Japan, and Germany have the largest shares of the world environmental market, and all have strong environmental laws. In Germany, 2,500 companies earn more than half their revenues from green technology. Insurance firms and even large oil firms are rethinking their position. Even though oil demand would be hurt, the cleanup industry would help natural-gas businesses. DuPont, the world's largest producer of CFCs, backed a ban on their use and now leads the market for CFC substitutes created by the ban. These are a few examples of how the green movement and big business have come together, not only to make money but to help save the environment.*

# How to Make Lots of Money, and Save the Planet Too

*The Economist,* **June 3, 1995**

In principle, you might expect "greens" and businessfolk to be at one another's throats. A blind pursuit of profit, say environmentalists, encourages companies to foul up the land, sea and air. Likewise, few things annoy the average capitalist more than rampant tree-huggers and their ludicrous owl-protecting, business-destroying rules. Across America, businessmen are cheering the efforts of Republicans in Congress to make a bonfire of green regulations.

Or so it seems. Yet a strange love affair is growing between some firms and some parts of the green movement. In places such as Washington and Brussels a fast-growing army of business lobbyists is working for tougher laws. Many firms have discovered that green laws can be good for profits—either by creating new markets or by protecting old ones against competitors.

Whenever a green law forces a company to change its machinery, clean up some manufacturing process, decontaminate a site or even just "consider" the environmental impact of something it is doing, it adds to the clean-up industry. Defining this industry is difficult (does it, for example, include clean fuels, such as solar power, as well as technologies which reduce emissions from dirty fuels?), but one report from the Organisation for Economic Co-operation and Development put its value at $200 billion in 1990.

The OECD thinks it might grow to $300 billion by the end of the decade, and some experts are even more bullish, seeing a rising demand for clean-up services from fast-growing countries such as China, Taiwan and South Korea, and from the former Soviet Union as it undoes the pollution inflicted by communism.

The driving force behind this industry's growth is government regulation. In America, its godfather was California's Jerry Brown, who as governor pushed through clean-air rules that led indirectly to Los Angeles's "Smog Valley," where many clean-up firms started. America, Japan and Germany—the three countries with the largest share of the world environmental market—all have particularly stringent environmental laws. "It is an industry uniquely dependent on government policy," says Adrian

Wilkes, director of the Environmental Industries Commission (EIC), a new British lobby group launched last month. The EIC argues for tougher environmental standards, more rigorous enforcement, and investment subsidies. Its impressive list of supporters includes 25 green campaigners and parliamentarians. But its money comes from the clean-up firms. British firms that manufacture pollution-control equipment have been complaining that the National Rivers Authority makes it too easy to discharge pollutants into rivers, and that air-quality standards are too weak.

In America the Environmental Technology Council, which represents firms dealing with hazardous and industrial waste, has pushed for tougher regulation since 1982. In 1992, together with several big green groups such as the Sierra Club, it sued the Environmental Protection Agency (EPA) for allowing firms to dilute waste rather than treat it. It won the case, thus boosting business for its members. Last year, in another argument with the EPA, it again joined forces with mainstream green groups and won tougher regulation on the burning of hazardous waste in cement kilns.

In Germany, the 2,500 companies that earn more than half their revenues from green technology are beginning to organise themselves. The Environment Industry Association, founded in January, already has 50 members; by next year, says Helmut Kaiser, a consultant who founded the group, it will have 1,000. Environmental businessmen have been heartened by the recent success of the Green Party in regional elections. The party has long argued that green industry can create jobs. Indeed, Mr. Kaiser's group will argue that new technologies, such as the recycling of industrial waste water, save more money than they cost. And it will also lobby for more regulations—with plenty of advance notice so that polluters can ready their chequebooks.

Mr. Kaiser complains that a government decision to back away from a requirement that electronic equipment be recycled cost the green industry "millions." Even so, German waste-management companies profited hugely from a stringent law in 1991 that forced companies to recycle the packaging in which their goods were sold. Many of the firms are now lobbying East European countries such as Slovakia and Czech Republic to adopt a similar law.

Even on global environmental issues some businesses are beginning to lobby for tougher agreements. The main opponents of international targets to reduce greenhouse-gas emissions are coal producers and oil-producing countries. Yet other businesses are siding with the greens. The Business Council for a Sustainable Energy Future, a group of American clean-energy firms formed in 1992 has been calling for international targets on greenhouse gases, which would boost demand for clean energy. Earlier this year it launched a European offshoot.

Insurance firms, worried by a spate of natural disasters, have begun to campaign on climate change. Even big oil firms are thinking twice about their stance. Tough targets would hurt demand for oil, but could help their natural-gas businesses. Significantly, the Montreal Protocol on curbing the use of ozone-eating CFCs was secured with support of big business. In 1988 Du Pont, the world's largest producer of CFCs, backed a total ban on their use. Du Pont, alongside Britain's ICI, now leads the large market for CFC substitutes created by the ban.

## Protect Me, I'm Green

Environmental regulation can also raise barriers to entry in established markets. This is most stark when green rules protect domestic producers from imports. Last year the European Union complained unsuccessfully about American standards on car fuel-efficiency. Ostensibly aimed at conserving energy, these happened to protect American car makers from imports of large, upmarket European cars. Another dispute involves Germany's 1991 packaging ordinance, which forces brewers to use refillable bottles. Apart from its green merits, the rule also protects Germany's small brewers which, unlike foreign competitors, already have local distribution in place.

Green laws can split domestic industries too. American greens are urging the EPA to toughen limits on chlorine emitted by the paper-making industry. Though some big paper companies are opposing tougher standards, others, who have already invested in chlorine-free technologies, are siding with the greens.

Even firms traditionally opposed to environmental regulation are becoming more pragmatic. In recent years in America, for example, alliances of mainstream companies (including oil and chemical firms), environmental companies, and government regulators have sprung up to promote better forms of regulation. In particular, they want laws which allow polluters to choose the most economic way of reducing emissions—rather than specifying a particular green technology or product to be used.

Traditional "polluters" also want to see the same laws enforced on their competitors. In America, points out Daniel Esty, a former senior official at the EPA, the pressure for federal environmental regulations in the 1960s and 1970s came not just from green groups but from firms anxious that differing state rules were putting some of them at a competitive disadvantage. Now the same complaint is made on a global scale: many firms in countries where green rules are stringent say they will lose out unless poorer countries follow suit.

In other words, even greenery's most vigorous opponents now direct a lot of their energy towards trying to influence how laws are written rather than whether they are written at all. For the mainstream green movement, this is splendid; environmentalists now have rich allies in smart suits. Whether the emergence of the green business lobby is good news for environmental policy-making, however, is another question. Governments should forever be wary of lobbyists, even those in suits. ❑

## Questions

1. How can green laws be good for profits?

2. What is the driving force behind the cleanup industry's growth?

3. Who are the main opponents of international targets to reduce greenhouse-gas emissions?

*Answers are at the back of the book.*

**46**

*An international effort must be made to stabilize human interactions with the Earth. A global partnership will be needed to emphasize several solutions. These solutions include a new relationship between the industrial North and the developing South, a division of responsibility between different levels of government, and an active participation of citizens. So far, the world community has responded to the environmental challenges through more than 170 ecological treaties that affect roughly one-quarter of the Earth's land area. If these treaties are obeyed, humans may prevent global ecological collapse and social disintegration. The success of the Montreal Protocol is an encouraging example that we may succeed.*

# Forging a New Global Partnership to Save the Earth

## Hilary F. French

*USA Today Magazine*, May 1995

*An international effort must be made to stabilize the planet before environmental deterioration reaches a point that it becomes irreversible.*

In June 1992, more than 100 heads of state and 20,000 non-governmental representatives gathered in Rio de Janeiro for the United Nations Conference on Environment and Development (UNCED). It resulted in the adoption of Agenda 21, an ambitious 500-page blueprint for sustainable development. In addition, Rio produced treaties on climate and biological diversity, both of which could lead to domestic policy changes in all nations. Significantly, the conference pointed to the need for a global partnership if sustainable development was to be achieved.

Since Rio, a steady stream of international meetings have been held on the many issues that were on its agenda. For instance, the September 1994, International Conference on Population and Development in Cairo put the spotlight of world attention on the inexorable pace of population growth and the need to respond to it through broad-based efforts to expand access to family planning, improve women's health and literacy, and ensure child survival.

The pace of real change has not kept up with the increasingly loaded schedule of international gatherings, though. The initial burst of international momentum generated by UNCED is flagging, and the global partnership it called for is foundering due to a failure of political will. While a small, committed group of individuals in international organizations, national and local governments, and citizens' groups continues trying to keep the flame of Rio alive, business as usual largely is the order of the day in the factories, farms, villages, and cities that form the backbone of the world economy.

As a result, the relentless pace of global ecological decline shows no signs of letting up. Carbon dioxide concentrations are mounting in the atmosphere, species loss continues to accelerate, fisheries are collapsing, land degradation frustrates efforts to feed hungry people, and the Earth's forest cover keeps shrinking. Many of the development and economic issues that underpin environmental destruction are worsening. Income inequality is rising, Third World debt is mounting, human numbers continue growing at daunting rates, and the amount of poor people in the world is increasing.

The global partnership that is needed to reverse

these trends will have several distinct features. It will involve a new form of relationship between the industrialized North and the developing South. Another feature will be a division of responsibility among different levels of governance worldwide. Problems are solved best at the most decentralized level of governance that is consistent with efficient performance of the task. As they transcend boundaries, decision-making can be passed upward as necessary—from the community to the state, national, regional, and, in some rare instances, global level. A third requirement is the active participation of citizens in village, municipal, and national political life, as well as at the United Nations.

Above all, the new partnership calls for an unprecedented degree of international cooperation and coordination. The complex web of ecological, economic, communication, and other connections binding the world together means that no government can build a secure future for its citizens by acting alone.

**Protecting the Global Environment**

One of the primary ways the world community has responded to the environmental challenge is through the negotiation of treaties and other types of international accords. Nations have agreed on more than 170 ecological treaties—more than two-thirds of them since the 1972 UN Conference on the Human Environment. In 1994, the climate and biological diversity conventions as well as the long-languishing Law of the Sea treaty received enough ratifications to enter into force. In addition, governments signed a new accord on desertification and land degradation.

These agreements have led to some measurable gains. Air pollution in Europe has been reduced dramatically as a result of the 1979 treaty on transboundary air pollution. Global chlorofluorocarbon (CFC) emissions have dropped 60% from their peak in 1988 following the 1987 treaty on ozone depletion and its subsequent amendments. The killing of elephants has plummeted in Africa because of the 1990 ban on commercial trade in ivory under the Convention on International Trade in Endangered Species of Wild Flora and Fauna.

Mining exploration and development have been forbidden in Antarctica for 50 years under a 1991 accord.

The hallmark of international environment governance to date is the Montreal Protocol on the Depletion of the Ozone Layer. First agreed to in September, 1987, and strengthened significantly twice since then, it stipulates that the production of CFCs in industrial countries must be phased out altogether by 1996. It also restricts the use of several other ozone-depleting chemicals, including haloes, carbon tetrachlorides, methyl chloroform, and hydro-chlorofluorocarbons. Developing countries have a 10-year grace period in which to meet the terms of the original protocol and its amendments.

While this is a momentous international achievement, the world will have paid a heavy price for earlier inaction. Dangerous levels of ultraviolet radiation will be reaching the Earth for decades to come, stunting agricultural productivity and damaging ecological and human health.

The lessons learned in the ozone treaty are being put to a severe test as the international community begins to confront a more daunting atmospheric challenge—the need to head off climate change. Less than two years after it was signed in Rio, the Framework Convention on Climate Change became international law in March 1994, when the 50th country (Portugal) ratified it. The speed with which the treaty was ratified was in part a reflection of the fact that it contains few real commitments.

The pact's deliberately ambiguous language urges, but does not require, industrial nations to stabilize emissions of carbon—the primary contributor to global warming—at 1990 levels by the year 2000. Developing nations face no numerical goals whatsoever, though all signatories must conduct inventories of their emissions, submit detailed reports of actions taken to implement the convention, and take climate change into account in all their social, economic, and environmental policies. No specific policy measures are required, however.

As of late 1994, most industrial countries had established national greenhouse gas targets and climate plans, but they vary widely in effectiveness. Among the most ambitious and comprehensive are those of Denmark, the Netherlands, and Switzerland, none of which have powerful oil or coal industries to contend with. Through the use of efficiency standards, renewable energy programs, and limited carbon taxes, these plans are likely to limit emissions significantly in those nations.

According to independent evaluations by various nongovernmental organizations (NGOs), most of the climate plans issued so far will fall short of stabilizing national emissions and the other goals they have set for themselves. For example, Germany and the U.S., two of the largest emitters, have issued climate plans that fail to tackle politically difficult policies—the reduction of coal subsidies in Germany and the increase of gasoline taxes in the U.S. Neither country is likely to meet its stated goals. Reports from Japan suggest that it, too, is unlikely to achieve its stabilization target. In another failure of will, long-standing efforts by the European Union to impose a hybrid carbon/energy tax have failed so far, despite strong support from the European Community.

Even if the goal of holding emissions to 1990 levels in 2000 is met, this falls far short of stabilizing atmospheric concentrations of greenhouse gases, which will require bringing carbon emissions 60-80% below the current levels. As a result, several European countries and the U.S. have voiced cautious support for strengthening the treaty to promote stronger actions, though they have not said exactly how.

As with protecting the atmosphere, preserving biological diversity is something all nations have a stake in and no one country effectively can do alone. One of the most important achievements of the 1993 Convention on Biological Diversity was its recognition that biological resources are the sovereign property of nation-states. When countries can profit from something, they have an incentive to preserve it.

Genetic diversity is worth a lot. The protection that genetic variability affords crops from pests, diseases, and climatic and soil variations is worth $1,000,000,000 to U.S. agriculture. Over all, the economic benefits from wild species to pharmaceuticals, agriculture, forestry, fisheries, and the chemical industry adds up to more than $87,000,000,000 annually—over four percent of the U.S. gross domestic product. Though international pharmaceutical companies have been extracting genes from countries without paying for years, the convention says that gene-rich nations have a right to charge for access to this valuable resource and encourages them to pass legislation to set the terms.

One widely publicized model of this is a 1991 agreement between Merck, the world's largest pharmaceutical company, and Costa Rica's National Institute of Biodiversity (INBIO). Merck agreed to pay the institute $1,000,000 for conservation programs in exchange for access to the country's plants, microbes, and insects. If a discovery makes its way into a commercial product, Merck has agreed to give INBIO a share of the royalties. Discussing how to replicate such agreements likely will be a high priority for countries that have signed the convention.

Besides providing a forum for future negotiations, the convention calls for a number of actions by governments to preserve biological wealth. Possible steps in the future include discussions of a protocol on biotechnology, as well as deliberations on international standards for biodiversity prospecting agreements.

The oceans are another natural resource whose protection requires international collaboration. Not only did the Law of the Sea receive sufficient ratifications to enter into force in 1994, agreement also was reached on modifications to the original agreement that are expected to mean that the U.S. and other industrial countries will join in. The rebirth of this treaty comes just in time for the world's oceans and estuaries, which are suffering from overfishing, oil spills, land-based sources of pollution, and other ills.

The Law of the Sea contains an extensive array of environmental provisions. For instance, though countries are granted sovereignty over waters within 200 miles of their shores (called Exclusive Economic Zones, or EEZs), they also accept an obligation to protect ecological health there. The treaty contains pathbreaking compulsory dispute resolution provisions, under which nations are bound to accept the verdict of an international tribunal.

Just as the Law of the Sea is coming into force, however, its rules are being overtaken by events in one important area—overfishing. In particular, the original treaty failed to resolve the issue of fish stocks that straddle the boundaries of EEZs and species that migrate long distances. The UN has convened a series of meetings to discuss possible international action to deal with a situation that has seen seafood catch per person fall eight percent since 1989.

## Curbing Land Degradation

The latest addition to the international repertoire of environmental treaties is a convention intended to curb land degradation, adopted in June 1994. According to the UN Environment Program, the livelihoods of at least 900,000,000 people in about 100 countries are threatened by desertification, which affects about one-quarter of the Earth's land area. The degradation—caused by overgrazing, overcropping, poor irrigation practices, and deforestation, and often exacerbated by climatic variations—poses a serious threat to efforts to raise agricultural productivity worldwide.

The desertification treaty supplies a framework for local projects, encourages national action programs, promotes regional and international cooperation on the transfer of needed technologies, and provides for information exchange and research and training.

Protecting the environment and combating poverty are recognized to be interlinked priorities. The Cairo conference looked at the complex interconnections among population growth, deteriorating social conditions, sexual inequity, environmental degradation, and a range of other issues. A sustainable future can not be secured without an aggressive effort to fight poverty and meet basic social needs.

Trends during the last several decades suggest a mixed record on improving human welfare. Even though impressive progress has been made in boosting immunization rates, reducing infant mortality, and increasing life expectancy, one in three children remains malnourished, more than 1,000,000,000 people lack safe water to drink, and about 1,000,000,000 adults cannot read or write. The share of the world's population living in poverty has declined steadily, but the actual numbers continue to rise to more than 1,000,000,000 individuals. Rather than shrinking, the gap between the rich and the poor is growing. In 1960, the richest 20% of the world earned 30 times as much income as the poorest 20%; by 1991, the difference had risen to 61 times as much.

A crucial first step toward turning these statistics around was taken in Cairo, when more than 150 countries approved a World Population Plan of Action aimed at keeping human numbers somewhere below 9,800,000,000 in 2050. It covers a broad range of issues, including the empowerment of women, the role of the family, reproductive rights and health, and migration. The plan calls for expenditures on population programs to more than triple by 2000—from $5,000,000,000 to $17,000,000,000. Of the total, $10,000,000,000 is intended for family planning programs; $5,000,000,000 for reproductive health; $1,300,000,000 for prevention of sexually transmitted diseases; and $500,000,000 for research and data collection. The action plan also calls for accelerating existing UN initiatives aimed at expanding women's literacy and improving their health—though it fails to provide spending targets for doing so.

Vatican opposition to proposed language on abortion rights captured headlines during the conference, but the real news was the consensus forged between the industrial and developing worlds and among representatives of population, women's, and human rights groups during two years of preparation for the meeting. Key elements of this include a recognition that slowing population growth and making progress on a range of social fronts are inextricably linked challenges. It follows from the new consensus that reaching population stabilization goals will require a far different approach than in the past and that family planning programs alone will be insufficient to do so. Equally important are investments in changing the conditions that generate demand for large families—such as illiteracy and a low status of women. In addition, there was widespread agreement that family planning efforts must be noncoercive and integrated broadly with reproductive health programs.

At the Cairo conference, 10 diverse developing nations representing Muslim, Buddhist, and Christian religious traditions joined together to share their experiences with others. Each has achieved considerable success in recent years in bringing fertility rates down. In Indonesia, for instance, the birth rate dropped from 5.6 births per woman in 1971 to three in 1991. In Colombia, it declined from 7.1 to 2.9 over 30 years.

As for poverty, unemployment, and social integration, efforts to combat these problems have decreased in recent years, as recession-ridden nations have found it harder and harder to appropriate funds. Few countries have reached the international target of devoting .07% of their gross national product to development assistance, and the amounts that are spent often are not targeted well. Because donor nations have tended to skew their disbursements toward their own security interests, the 10 countries that are home to two-thirds of the world's poorest people get just 32% of total aid expenditures. The richest 40% of the developing world receives twice as much aid per person as the poorest 40%.

Under the proposed 20:20 Compact on Human Development, developing countries would agree to devote 20% of their domestic resources to human priorities and donors would target 20% of their aid funds for such purposes. If this initiative succeeds, it will be making a major contribution to a more sustainable world.

Additional priorities include progress toward alleviating debt burdens and addressing unfavorable terms of trade for developing countries. Though the financial crisis has been eased for some of the largest debtors, such as Brazil, it remains very much alive in many of the poorest nations. The total external debt of developing countries has grown sevenfold during the past two decades, from $247,000,000,000 in 1970 to more than $1.7 trillion in 1993.

Though the ratio of debt-service payments to foreign-exchange earnings has been declining globally in recent years, it still is on the rise in sub-Saharan Africa, which spends some 25% of export receipts on debt repayments. For many countries, this number is far higher.

To generate the hard currency required to pay back loans, the International Monetary Fund (IMF) and others have urged debtor nations to undertake export-promoting reforms, such as devaluing exchange rates, and fiscal reforms to reduce public-sector deficits. The strategy has been only partially successful. A handful of countries in East Asia and Latin America have boosted exports dramatically, but others with the poorest 20% of humanity have not, accounting for just one percent of world trade.

Trade barriers to developing-country products continue to be a major impediment to boosting exports. Restrictions on textiles and clothing alone are estimated to cost the Third World $50,000,000,000 in lost foreign exchange annually. Though recent negotiations under the General Agreement on Tariffs and Trade (GATT) made modest inroads into the problems, developing countries and the former Eastern bloc are expected to account for a mere 14-32% of the projected global income gains from the revised GATT by 2002. Africa is projected to lose $2,600,000,000 a year as a result of the agreement, as rising world agricultural prices due to the mandated subsidy cuts will boost its food import bill.

Where the push to expand exports has been successful, the benefits often have been unequally distributed. In Latin America, for instance, economic growth has picked up in recent years, but the share of the population living in poverty is projected to hover near 40% through the end of the decade. For some, the strategy is a net loss. Subsistence farmers—frequently women—often are displaced from their land so it can be devoted to growing crops to please the palates of consumers in distant lands. Indigenous peoples are forced from their homelands as forests are felled for foreign exchange revenue.

## Grassroots Opposition to Selling Resources
The uprising in the Mexican state of Chiapas in early 1994 was a wake-up call to some of the failures of this development model. In terms of resources, Chiapas is rich, producing 100,000 barrels of oil and 500,000,000,000 cubic meters of natural gas daily; supplying more than half of the

country's hydropower with its dams; and accounting for one-third of the nation's coffee production and a sizable share of cattle, timber, honey, corn, and other products. However, the benefit from selling these resources is not flowing to many of the people who live there. According to Mexican grassroots activist Gustavo Esteva, "Rather than demanding the expansion of the economy, either state-led or market-led, the [Zapatista rebels] seek to expel it from their domain. They are pleading for protection of the 'commons' they have carved out for themselves.... The [Zapatistas] have dared to announce for the world that development as a social experiment has failed miserably in Chiapas." World leaders would do well to heed his warning that the existing economic orthodoxy needs some fundamental rethinking.

Achieving sustainable development requires protecting the rights of local people to control their own resources—whether it be forests, fish, or minerals. Yet, nations and individuals also are discovering that, if today's transnational challenges are to be mastered, a wider role for international institutions is inevitable.

To respond to this need, considerable reforms are necessary in the United Nations to prepare it for the world of the future. The UN Charter, for example, was written for a different era. Neither "environment" nor "population" even appear in the document. Moreover, though the need for more effective international institutions is clear, people the world over justifiably are worried by the prospect of control of resources being centralized in institutions that are remote from democratic accountability.

As the 50th anniversary of the UN approaches, many ideas are being floated for changes to prepare the world body for the future. Some proposals concern the need to expand membership on the Security Council to make it more broadly representative of today's world. Others focus on the economic and social side of the organization's operations. The UN Development Program (UNDP), for instance, is advocating a Development Security Council—a body of about 22 members to promote the cause of "sustainable human security" at the highest levels.

While these proposals are being debated, another idea merits consideration—the creation of a full-fledged environmental agency. The UN Environment Program (UNEP) has contributed a great deal considering a limited budget which until recently was smaller than that of some private U.S. environmental groups. UNEP does not enjoy the stature within the UN system of a specialized agency, meaning it has few operational programs of its own. Though charged with coordinating the UN response to environmental issues, it has little ability to influence the programs of other agencies with much larger budgets. The time has come either to upgrade UNEP to specialized agency status or create a new environmental agency.

In considering what the functions of such an organization might be, Dan Esty of Yale University suggests that a Global Environmental Organization (GEO) might develop basic environmental principles analogous to widely recognized trade principles advanced by GATT, such as most-favored-nation status and nondiscrimination. High on such a list would be full-cost pricing, the idea that environmental costs should be internalized in the prices of products, rather than passed on to taxpayers. Other proposals include the precautionary principle—that decisions to take preventative action sometimes cannot await conclusive scientific proof—and a right to public participation. Governments already have endorsed these ideas and others in the Rio Declaration, but have not given an organization the task of seeing that they are respected.

In addition, a GEO could play a critical role by serving as an information clearinghouse—as UNEP's Global Environmental Monitoring System already does on a small scale. It also might serve as the implementing agency for some UNDP-financed projects. A GEO could be a partner in recycling or land reclamation. It also might elaborate some common minimum international environmental production standards.

Finally, the time has come for governments to create some form of dedicated funding mechanism to finance investments for the transition to a sustainable society—including environmental expenditures, social initiatives, and peacekeeping costs. Among the possibilities are a levy on carbon emissions, international air travel, or flows of money across national borders. To discourage destabilizing currency speculation, Nobel-laureate economist James Tobin has suggested that a .5% tax be placed on foreign-exchange transactions. This would raise more than $1.5 trillion annually. Even a smaller levy would raise far more funds than are available today. A tax of .003% of daily currency transactions would raise $8,400,000,000.

Even in the best of circumstances, the slow pace of international diplomacy and the rate at which environmental and social problems are growing worse are difficult to reconcile. The best hope for improving the process of global governance lies with people. Just as national policymaking cannot be considered in isolation from public pressure, global policymaking increasingly must consider an organized and influential international citizenry.

The most familiar role for nongovernmental organizations and grassroots groups is within national borders. Around the world, there is an encouraging growth in such activities. In addition to this critical work, citizens' groups are beginning to make their influence felt in international forums. In Rio, the 20,000 concerned citizens and activists who attended from around the globe outnumbered official representatives by at least two to one. More than 4,000 NGOs participated in the Cairo conference, where they widely were credited with helping to shape the terms of the debate. Some of the organizations at these meetings—such as Friends of the Earth, Greenpeace, the International Planned Parenthood Federation, and the World Wide Fund for Nature—represent global constituencies rather than parochial national interests. Taken together, all this activity adds up the creation of a bona fide global environmental movement.

Working through international coalitions such as the Climate Action Network and the Women's Environment and Development Organization, these groups are a powerful force. Daily newsletters produced by citizens' groups, including *Eco* and the *Earth Negotiations Bulletin,* have become mainstays of the international negotiating process. Widely read by official delegates and NGOs during international meetings, they reveal key failures in negotia-

tions and prevent the obscure language of diplomacy from shielding governments from accountability for their actions.

The participation of the international scientific community also is critical. International panels of scientists convened to study both ozone depletion and climate change played instrumental roles in forging the consensus needed to push these political processes forward. The treaties on these two problems created scientific advisory groups that meet regularly and offer advice on whether the agreements need to be updated in light of new scientific information.

The interests of the business community sometimes can be harnessed to positive effect. The Business Council for Sustainable Development, 50 chief executives from the world's largest corporations, were active in the lead-up to the Earth Summit. Though the council opposed language that would have advocated developing standards to regulate multinational corporations, it argued persuasively in its report, *Changing Course,* that sound environmental policies and business practices go hand in hand. The U.S.-based Business Council for Sustainable Energy—a coalition of energy efficiency, renewable energy, and natural gas companies that favor taking action to avert global warming—has begun to participate in international climate negotiations, counterbalancing the lobbying efforts of oil and coal companies.

**Formidable Obstacles**

Despite their impressive contributions, citizens' groups working at the global level face formidable obstacles. International law traditionally has functioned as a compact among nations, with no provisions for public participation comparable to those that are taken for granted at the national level in democracies around the world. There is nothing yet resembling an elected parliament in the United Nations or any of its agencies. Though the UN has begun to experiment with occasional public hearings on topics of special concern, these continue to be rare events. No formal provisions are made for public review and comment on international treaties or is there a mechanism for bringing citizen suits at the World Court. International negotiations often are closed to public participation, and access to documents of critical interest to the public generally is restricted.

The UN Economic and Social Council is reviewing the rules for the participation of citizens' groups in the UN system at large. Some of those involved in the debate advocate making it easier for groups to be involved, taking the Rio experience as their guide. Others resist this view, worrying about the system being overwhelmed by sheer numbers or about whom the citizens' groups are accountable to. The outcome of these deliberations remains to be seen, but it seems likely that the UNCED process has set a new standard for participation that the UN system will have difficulty backing away from.

When it comes to openness and accountability, GATT has been subject to particularly strong criticism for its secretive procedures. When a national law is challenged as a trade barrier under GATT, the case is heard behind closed doors by a panel of professors and bureaucrats steeped in the intricacies of world trade law, but not in the needs of the planet. Legal briefs and other critical information generally are unavailable to the public, and there is no opportunity for citizens' groups to testify or make submissions. Governments are discussing rules on public participation for the Trade and Environment Committee of GATT's successor, the World Trade Organization. Preliminary reports suggest that the fight for public access will be a long and hard-fought battle.

Despite a checkered history regarding openness, the World Bank has instituted two new policies that others would do well to emulate. Under an information policy, more of its documents will be available publicly and an information center has been established to disseminate them. The second change— the creation of an independent inspection panel— will provide an impartial forum where board members or private citizens can raise complaints about projects that violate the financial organization's poli-cies, rules, and procedures. Though both initiatives were watered down in the negotiating process, they nonetheless represent sizable chinks in the World Bank's armor. It will be up to the concerned public to test the limits of these new policies and to press for them to be strengthened—and replicated elsewhere.

Besides access to information, the public must become a fuller partner in the development process itself. All too often, "development" has served the purposes of a country's elite, but not its poorest members. A growing body of evidence suggests that, for a project to succeed, the planning process must include the people it is supposed to benefit. In other words, aid should be demand-driven, rather than imposed from above. Several bilateral aid agencies have developed new ways of fostering widespread participation in the development planning process, and the World Bank has come up with a new strategy along these lines. The challenge, as always, will be moving from words to action.

Despite public support for far-reaching changes, the international response to the interlinked threat of ecological collapse and social disintegration remains seriously inadequate. Fifty years ago, with large parts of Europe and Asia in shambles in the wake of World War II, the world community pulled together with an impressive period of institution-building that set the tone for the next half-century. The time has come for a similar burst on innovation to forge the new global partnership that will enable the world to confront the daunting challenges that await it in the next millennium.

If the changes called for in this article are made and the power of public commitment to sustainable development is unleashed, the planet can head off global ecological collapse and the social disintegration that would be sure to accompany it. However, if complacency reigns and international forums generate lots of talks and paper, but little action, the future does not look bright. The choice is ours to make. ❑

## Questions

1. What does the Montreal Protocol stipulate and restrict?

2. What causes degradation?

3. Under the 20:20 Compact on Human Development, what would developing countries have to agree to do and how would this affect the world?

*Answers are at the back of the book.*

**47** *Ecologists and economists have usually looked at environmental issues from different perspectives. Economists have tended to believe that technological advances can be counted on to solve environmental problems. Ecologists have been less inclined to count on technology to cure or circumvent environmental problems. But recently, there has been increasing cooperation between ecologists and economists. Members of these two professions maintain that although they may have different backgrounds, there is no proof that they hold significantly different values. Both groups have failed to consider sufficiently the input of the other. Better communication is needed between them. There are often conceptual differences between population, resource, and environmental models due to the lack of understanding of the other's fields. Both ecologists and economists can work together productively. Ecologists can guide society in the direction it needs to go in order to avert environmental catastrophe, and economists can devise strategies that would influence that direction.*

# Ecologists and Economists Can Find Common Ground

## Carl Folke

*BioScience*, April 1995

In recent years there has been an encouraging trend of increased interdisciplinary collaboration between ecologists and economists. But, as a general rule, the writings on environmental matters by ecologists and by economists are different in tenor and message. The economists on the whole appear to be more optimistic when regarding the condition of the human environment; in particular, the economists tend to believe that technological innovations can be relied upon to solve environmental problems, while ecologists are less inclined to trust technology to cure or bypass problems.

Do the different attitudes of ecologists and economists reflect different value systems, that is, do members of these professions hold different world views? In short, are ecologists nature lovers, while economists are materialists? And if so, is there self-selection of these types into the two professions? In a discussion in Askö, Sweden, prominent members of the two professions[1] concluded that although members of the two groups may on average come from different backgrounds, there is no evidence that they hold substantially dif-

ferent values. Ecologists have been known to enjoy high consumption levels, while economists have been known to love nature walks. More likely, it was felt, the professional differences were generated elsewhere.

Neither discipline has sufficiently considered the inputs of the other discipline, according to the discussion participants. Models in each field are constructed for specific ends. Not all economic models need include environmental variables, any more than there need be an economic element in all ecological models. However, the economists felt that too many economic models ignore the environmental resource base of material production (e.g., deterioration of mangrove ecosystems into shrimp aquaculture) and the consequences of that production for critical environmental systems employed as sinks (e.g., the atmosphere as a sink for carbon dioxide emitted in the process of burning fossil fuels in rich countries).

Those models continue to postulate unlimited growth in population, unlimited growth of the physical economy by means of capital accumulation and

Reprinted from *BioScience*, Vol. 45, April 1995, pp. 283–284.

substitution, improved organization, and technological progress. The nature of these models, the economists suggested, may well adversely affect their profession's perception of the natural world. They noted too that, as a profession, economists tend to overly stress the ability of markets to allocate resources efficiently. For example, in view of the lack of well-defined property rights in most environmental resources and sinks, failure to consider externalities (which exist when prices do not reflect true social costs) is pervasive. These externalities are not given the prominence they require and in textbooks are still regarded as aberrations.

Another long-standing weakness of the economist's modeling of the environment is that, on the whole, it ignores possible threshold effects, a central concern of ecologists. The economists explained that if threshold effects are significant, the price mechanisms on which economists rely cannot perform well.

The ecologists in turn feel that, when searching for solutions to environmental problems, members of their discipline all too often fail to take advantage of the knowledge of economists and other social scientists, in particular regarding the importance of markets for allocating environmental resources. Frequently ecologists do not bring critical scrutiny to bear on environmentalists who may support central command and control measures when a market mechanism may be more efficient, and vice versa. Ecologists often do not appreciate the underlying economic causes or other driving forces of environmental problems or the indirect effects of remedial measures proposed.

Better communication is needed between ecologists and environmentalists, as well as between ecologists and economists. The ecologists at the Askö meeting also felt that on issues such as the relationship between complexity and stability, they have not sufficiently informed environmentalists of the current state of their science. As a result, environmentalists may use as slogans some notions that are outdated. Ecologists have also tried to move quickly from an understanding of small-scale case studies to predictions about large-scale systems. They may therefore appear more certain than is justified about what they know about the behavior of large systems. In view of the limited ecological understanding, the ecologists at the meeting recommended a precautionary approach to treatment of large systems out of a fear of the consequences of their possible collapse.

The ecologists and economists agreed that there are often substantial conceptual differences between their population, resource, and environmental models due to ignorance of each other's fields. It is bad science when economists build models that are oblivious of ecological knowledge (such as the limited substitution possibilities among resources), and bad science can lead to bad policy and faulty management. By the same token, if ecological models ignore the ways in which economic institutions operate, they too can have unsatisfactory consequences.

The ecologists expressed concern that most economists continue to view as an unalloyed good the growth of the gross national product in rich nations with high levels of wasteful consumption. They emphasized that it was necessary for the material economies of poor nations to grow but that this growth should be balanced by decreasing throughput in rich nations—something they claimed could be achieved with an improvement in the quality of life. They argued that increasing the scale of the global human enterprise (that is, the product of population size and per capita consumption) is a recipe for environmental disaster. Therefore, they are alarmed that economic analyses of the global economy often do not capture the critical relationship of the scale of the human economy to the scale of the ecosystems that support it.

The economists agreed that the gross national product is not an ideal measure of human welfare and that it is all too often misinterpreted in the press and by politicians. They noted, however, that economists have in recent years put considerable effort into devising improved measures. The economists shared the ecologists' concern on the importance of global-scale issues, because they agree that the world's natural capital is increasingly becoming scarce. The two groups also agreed on the need for a careful reconsideration of where and how economic growth and shrinkage should be pursued. An overall conclusion was that the ecologists know more than enough to alert a risk-adverse society to directions in which it should move in order to avoid serious environmental catastrophes and that economists' expertise would be critical in designing mechanisms that would encourage that movement.

## Note

1. The group comprised ecologists R. Costanza, Maryland International Institute for Ecological Economics, P.R. Ehrlich, Stanford University; C. Folke, Beijer International Institute of Ecological Economics and Stockholm University; C. S. Holling, University of Florida; A.-M. Jansson and B.-O. Jansson, Stockholm University; and J. Roughgarden, Stanford University; and economists P. Dasgupta, University of Cambridge, G.M. Heal, Columbia University; K.-G. Mäler, Beijer International Institute of Ecological Economics and Stockholm School of Economics; C. Perrings, University of York, and D.A. Starrett, Stanford University. The meeting, sponsored by Beijer International Institute of Ecological Economics (which is part of the Royal Swedish Academy of Sciences), was held at the Askö Laboratory of the Stockholm Centre for Marine Research, Askö, Sweden, September 5–7, 1993. ❑

## Questions

1. How do ecologists and economists differ in their solutions for solving environmental problems?

2. How do economists feel about many of their economic models?

3. Why are there conceptual differences between the ecological and economic models regarding population, resources, and the environment?

*Answers are at the back of the book.*

**48**

*People are concerned about the environment, but they are also worried about their local economies. However, economic development and environmental protection can be mutually beneficial when advocates on both sides work together for a common goal. One such example is Chattanooga, Tennessee. In the fifties, this industrial city was polluted with toxic wastes from coke foundries and chemical factories. In 1994, the EPA designated 2.5 miles of the Chattanooga Creek as a Superfund site. Environmental and economic problems were identified, and innovative solutions were implemented to bring about a successful cleanup. Change is difficult when it costs millions of dollars, but if communities have an open mind and innovative ideas, results can be accomplished. Chattanooga illustrates sustainable development, the goal of which is to meet the economic and environmental needs of the present without jeopardizing the future.*

# Cinderella Story
## Daniel Glick

*National Wildlife*, **February/March 1996**

*Chattanooga's air was so polluted in the 1950s that when women wearing nylon stockings walked outside, their legwear would sometimes disintegrate.*

By the 1950s, the pollution in Chattanooga matched its gritty industrial image—personified by its famous smoke-belching choo-choo. Its air was so polluted, reported the Environmental Protection Agency (EPA), that when women wearing nylon stockings walked outside, their legwear was apt to disintegrate. The Tennessee River curled through an industrial no-man's land along the downtown riverfront—and its in-town tributary, Chattanooga Creek, was so polluted from toxic dumping by coke foundries and chemical factories that in 1994 the EPA proposed 2.5 miles of the creek as a Superfund site.

Current mayor Gene Roberts recalls returning to Chattanooga in the mid-60s after spending some time in notoriously smoggy Los Angeles—only to find the air was dirtier in Chattanooga. Finally, Chattanoogans got fed up. "It was so bad that people couldn't stand it anymore," says Karen Hundt, an urban designer who has been involved in the city's turnaround since those dark days in the 1960s when headlights were sometimes required at noon. "It was just gross."

It's not gross any more. By almost any account, Chattanooga has transformed itself from a choking, polluted city into a vibrant southern metropolis that *The Washington Post* called in 1993 the "alluring Cinderella of the Tennessee River." But Chattanooga's story is not simply about a successful environment cleanup. While the city still has plenty of problems (polluted Chattanooga Creek, for example, was designated a priority Superfund site in September), it has also become a stand-out example of how environmental protection and economic development can coexist *because of* rather than *despite* each other. Using a range of innovative approaches—from enticing zero-emissions industries to relocate to Chattanooga, to building a freshwater aquarium that became the centerpiece of the city's downtown renewal—the city has become a glowing recommendation for the sustainable-development movement.

Chattanooga is one of 21 case-study communities that have caught the attention of the President's Council on Sustainable Development (PCSD). The council was established in June 1993, with the mandate to "identify and implement policies that will meet the needs of the present without compromising the future." In August, the PCSD praised the "creative work unfolding inside the communities we visited" and promised that its final report would include "practical policy recommendations and concrete measures of progress" to help other communities adopt sustainable-development strategies.

Still, the council has had a hard time agreeing on what "sustainable development" means, much less on how to achieve it. Some conservatives see the concept as a Trojan horse that environmentalists will use to infiltrate big businesses and to slow growth. Some environmentalists, on the other hand, worry that enticements for corporations to act responsibly end up sacrificing conservation principles.

In order to expand the middle ground in this argument, the PCSD shaped its membership from the business, environment, labor, government and civil-rights communities—with participants ranging from Secretary of the Interior Bruce Babbitt, to Chevron Corporation Chairman Kenneth Derr, to Executive Director of the Columbia River Inter-Tribal Fish Commission Theodore Strong. Their mission: to figure out how small towns and large cities can become greener while at the same time boosting the local economy. But sustainable development, like world peace and homemade ice cream, is easier to imagine than it is to crank out. The main idea is simple enough, says Lynn Greenwalt, National Wildlife Federation vice-president for conservation programs. "Don't eat your seed corn." But when that means altering manufacturing practices at a cost of millions or reducing resource extraction to sustainable levels, change can be difficult to achieve. "Getting from here to there is a tedious, uphill, Sisyphean chore," says Greenwalt, who has also served as principal liaison for the President's Council.

But as the President's Council has found, examples from Chattanooga and other communities around the country are proving that sustainable development can work. In projects ranging from home-grown cranberry preserves made from local produce, to furniture constructed in an inner-city factory from landfill-bound wood palettes, enough endeavors have succeeded to encourage others to follow.

In Chattanooga, civic leaders first mobilized widespread community involvement with town meet-ings. The intent was to encourage public-private partnerships (which have accounted for $739 million investments and 1,300 new permanent jobs) and to consider the environmental costs of just about everything. The effort began more than a decade ago with a "Vision 2000" process, which brought together citizens from all walks of civic life to identify the city's many problems. They named 40 goals, ranging from improving the availability of affordable housing to cleaning up the river.

Next, they found solutions. To improve the city's infamous poor air quality, for example, Chattanooga researched and developed a cutting-edge, electric-bus public transportation system. The city is now gradually replacing all its diesel buses with the new, emissions-free models. To encourage the use of public transportation, the city constructed three satellite parking areas on the outskirts of town, and it now uses the parking revenue to finance shuttle buses that riders use for free. These days, the city is selling its homemade buses to other cities around the world. The local economy gets a boost, citizens are discovering public transportation and air quality is vastly improved. Says Molly Harriss Olson, executive director of the PCSD, "There's a small revolution going on out there."

Electric buses are just a start. To help reclaim the Tennessee River front, the city built a freshwater aquarium featuring the river's ecosystem. The aquarium has helped transform downtown from an industrial waste dump to a tourist attraction that generated an estimated $133 million to the city in 1992, its first year, and has drawn an average of 1.3 million visitors annually since opening.

The riverfront face-lift also includes ongoing plans to create a public greenway along the river, with parks and mixed commercial and residential-use buildings. Even the city's recycling center employs individuals with disabilities. "It's not one particular project," says urban designer Hundt. "It's a series of things that are happening simultaneously."

A different kind of test for the notion of sustainable development is taking place in rural areas—especially where dwindling timber, minerals or other now-scarce resources have historically supported the local economy. One example is southern Washington's Willapa Bay, which attracted the attention of the President's Council after local citizens formed the Willapa Alliance in 1992.

Change in the region was inevitable: Oyster harvests from the estuary's productive beds were shrinking, in part because a nonnative grass, spartina, had infiltrated aquatic wildlife habitat. Salmon runs had slowed. Developers stalked the beachfront property, threatening to overburden the county's rural infrastructure with vacation homes. Unemployment rose while per capita income fell. Residents grew concerned, but didn't know what to fix first. "We had never heard the term 'sustainable development.'" says Dan'l Markham, executive director of the Willapa Alliance, a coalition of local interests, "We just knew that our ecosystem was the goose that laid the golden egg. And that was beginning to be threatened."

Enter Ecotrust, a nonprofit organization with roots in international conservation and development. Ecotrust Director and southern Washington native Spencer Beebe wondered if some principles of sustainable development might work in the United States. Ecotrust helped organize the alliance of local fishermen, oystermen, timbermen, cranberry farmers and civic leaders that launched a conservation-based development plan. "We had to move from 'hunt and harvest' to 'managed resource,'" says Markham. The process has meant a lot of "cussin' and discussin,'" with "some oxes getting gored," he says. But the community has realized that if the bay dies from being overextended, so does the community.

For now, all the extractive industries have agreed to more closely monitor their harvests as the development plan unfolds. The alliance has helped fund a $500,000 stream-restoration project and has helped get loans for small industries like a specialty cranberry business that makes jams, condiments and even cranberry fudge. Markham's hope is that the economy eventually will be based on sustainable harvests. "To us," says Markham, "ecology is economy."

Elsewhere in the Northwest, the Sustainable Seattle Project, which began in 1990, highlights the use of environmental and social indicators to track progress. Project leaders count such indicators as the number of salmon running wild in rivers and the number of children living in poverty. In Eugene, Oregon, citizens formed the Eugene Car Co-Op in 1993 to cut down on automobile use and share the expense of operating cars. And in Portland, a group called The Energy FinAnswer has been encouraging the construction of energy-efficient buildings.

Proponents of sustainable-development strategies have discovered that if communities take an open-minded look in a mirror, ideas for projects can follow. Jacksonville, Florida, for example, developed 74 quantifiable gauges, called "Quality Indicators for Progress," to keep the community abreast of how positive and negative trends affect the quality of life. With "gold-star indicators," such as lower infant mortality rates, and "red-flag indicators," such as higher rates of lung-cancer deaths, city planners can focus efforts where they are needed most. In response to a red-flag indicator that water quality in the St. Johns River had been declining, for example, city managers speeded up sewer-line hookups to reduce the need for new septic tanks.

Even on the neighborhood level, reassessments of local resources can pay off. In New York City, a program called Bronx 2000 has a Big City Forest project to recycle wood palettes that manufacturers use to transport goods, saving city businesses $150 million per year in waste disposal costs. At the same time, it also gives workers 15,000 board feet of hardwood to make flooring, furniture and new palettes. "It's a way for conservation and good business to come together," says Director David Muchnick.

Although these and other examples are encouraging, to talk about sustainable development without tackling global issues like overpopulation is like trying to wash a car in a sandstorm. Political realities like entrenched subsidy programs can skew markets—and development strategies—beyond recognition. "There have been a lot of unanticipated and unintended consequences because of how we've conducted our business since World War II," says Olson of the PCSD, citing everything from the hole in the ozone layer to the long-lasting effects of the banned pesticide DDT. But, she adds, "Now there are opportunities to do things differently so they are much more profitable and more environmentally sound."

For longtime Chattanooga resident Gaines Hobbs, who is now an assistant to Mayor Roberts, doing things differently has meant rewriting a few local jokes. Civic promoters have always claimed that the view overlooking the city from Lookout Mountain takes in seven states. "There was always a lot of yuk-yukking about that," says Hobbs, who recalls that coming down from the mountain into the smog in the 1960s, one was lucky to see one state—

Tennessee. On a recent trip to the mountain, however, Hobbs says he experienced the same thrill he felt as a kid up there in the 1950s before things got bad. As for whether one can really see seven states these days, Hobbs demurs. "In any case, there's a lot less yuk-yukking about it," he says. "It's exhilarating again." ❑

## Questions

1. What is the mandate of the President's Council on Sustainable Development?

2. What was the intent of Chattanooga's civic leaders?

3. Due to the successful environmental cleanup, what did the *Washington Post* call Chattanooga?

*Answers are at the back of the book.*

**49**

*Everyone is guilty of pollution in one form or another. We are a throwaway culture. However, the reuse industry is solid. It is evolving into a new and innovative industry from the traditional fix-it businesses. In this time of extreme waste, reuse has become very fashionable for Americans, and the trend is definitely toward the preservation of resources.*

# The Real Conservatives
## Jim Motavalli

*E Magazine*, July/August 1995

*Whatever became of fixing things? A noble tradition is dying, but reuse is still alive and well.*

Everybody on Earth is guilty of fouling the environment to some extent—to be alive, after all, is to be a polluter—but some of us are much worse offenders than others. And what's true for individuals is true for countries. The African nation of Togo, for instance, has 3,500 cars, one for every 200 people. The U.S. has 137 million cars, 35 percent of the world's total, or one for every *two* residents, including people too young to drive.

We here in the U.S. lead the world in fossil fuel pollution, acid rain generation, production of industrial waste and energy consumption. The U.S. creates 19 percent of the world's garbage—compared to 4.4 percent for Japan, 1.1 percent for Australia, and 2.9 percent for West Germany. The U.S. is among the elite 20 percent of the world's population that takes in 82.7 percent of global income. The fortunate few also consume 10 times as much energy and one-and-a-half times more food than people in the developing world.

There were, at last count, over 250 million Americans, and we've created the biggest throwaway culture the world has ever known, with close to 200 million tons of municipal solid waste generated every year—three-and-a-half pounds per person, per day. An incredible 30 percent of the garbage rapidly filling up our 5,800 landfills is packaging. We're chucking out 10 to 20 billion disposable diapers, two billion razors, 1.7 billion pens and 45 billion pounds of plastic every year. Indeed, our plastic waste disposal problem has gotten so serious that we're now exporting 200 million pounds of it every year—mostly to Asia, where it merely gets landfilled there instead of here.

If there's a bright spot in all this gloom, it's that we still retain a solid—though evolving—"reuse" industry. David Goldbeck, in his new book, *Choose to Reuse* (Ceres Press), describes reuse as "making a worn-out product new again, as in retreading a tire." There's also what he calls secondary reuse, in which "the tire is used for something else, like helping to form an artificial reef, or ground up and used in surfacing roads."

Unfortunately, the traditional reuse business is being put on life support just as environmentalists are recognizing its significance. It's unlikely that Greenpeace is going to start a campaign to save the jobs of cobblers and Maytag repairmen, but environmental groups are beginning to encourage the growth of small and innovative reuse industries. One such, The Tutwiler Quilting Project, was launched in the Mississippi Delta in 1988 as a way for women to make money for themselves and their families. Using largely donated textile scraps, about 40 local quilters earn their livelihood sewing blankets, wall hangings, handbags, potholders, table runners and placemats. They're making money and conserving resources at the same time.

And the reuse message is getting through to people. According to Michael Lewis, a senior research engineer at the Institute for Local Self Reliance in Washington, "A new type of reuse organization is emerging to take the place of traditional fix-it shops. We had reuse in the past and now we're getting back to it." Lewis cites extensive returnable bottle programs, as well as nonprofit groups around the country that acquire unwanted office goods or appliances and pass them on to low-income organizations. The Institute is preparing a book on just this kind of reuse.

Reusers don't necessarily identify themselves that way. Joe of Joe's Fix-It Shop often just does what he does, taking quiet pride in returning a worn or broken widget to service. Their crafts very widely, but they share a commitment to reducing the waste stream and smokestack pollution, and saving on landfill space and raw materials. If these people constitute a movement, it's a threatened one. Many of those *E* interviewed say their work is increasingly embattled by cheap imported goods—which make fixing something broken more expensive than buying it new—and disposable designs that don't even allow some new products to be taken apart, let alone repaired.

**Back into Service**

It's becoming a throwaway world," says Dan McMillion, who runs Dan's Volvo Service in Tampa, Florida. "I see big billboards advertising contact lenses that you use for just a day or two and then throw away." McMillion's parents raised him better. He likes to take broken-down Volvos and make them ready for service again. "I've probably done ground-up restorations on 20 or 30 cars," he says. "If we restore them, it keeps them out of the ground for a while." The problem, McMillion says, is that the sturdy 122S and 544 Volvos he favors "aren't worth tremendous amounts restored. You end up with more time into it than the car is worth."

In much the same way, Tom Migliaccio of Beacon Electronics in Westport, Connecticut, admits that the ancient Philco and RCA tube radios he fixes amid the nostalgic clutter of his repair shop are a labor of love. "I don't make any money on fixing

them," he says. "But I like the idea that they'll be around after I am."

Migliaccio has been fixing radios and TVs in Westport since he got out of the Navy in 1946. "TV was a novelty then. They said it would last a few years and then fade. But look what it's become. People come in here, see the old stuff from the 20s, 30s and 40s and it brings back their childhood," he says. Finding parts for old electronic equipment takes some ingenuity. Migliaccio says his replacement tubes come from Russia and China. He also sells such obsolete items as phonograph needles and rooftop TV antennas.

Migliaccio says today's electronics are too complicated for the storefront fix-it man. "I used to have 18 competitors in the phone book, but now there are very few. The new stuff, it's like today's cars—you need computers to fix them. In our day, we'd take a screwdriver and bailing wire and fix our cars ourselves."

Morris Campbell is another take-charge guy who opened his store—Campbell's Clock Shop in Grand Rapids, Michigan—right after World War II. "I've been fixing clocks for 50 years," he says. As he talks, Campbell is surrounded by the gentle revolution of 30 or 40 glass-domed anniversary clocks, most of them German-made. He estimates he is only one of 30 or 40 people in the country who know how to fix this popular postwar accessory.

"It's becoming a lost art, it really is," Campbell says. "Most shops just clean 'em up, put in a little oil and hope for the best. I tried to get my son interested in the business, but he said there wasn't enough money in it and got involved with computers instead." Modern digital clocks, says Campbell, "are really junk," and with their electronic circuitry beyond the country clockmaker's art. Campbell, who's 79, is going to retire and let other people worry about the future of clock repair.

"I hate to see repair places go by the wayside, because they serve a valid purpose," says Allen Blakey, a spokesman for the Environmental Industry Association in Washington who shakes his head at Campbell's story. "But sometimes the economics of the times are stronger than our sense of what we ought to be doing."

Joseph Ancona is another victim of "the economics of the times," but he still needs to feed his family. Ancona runs Economy Shoe Repair in Norwalk, Connecticut, a business his father started in 1929. Americans don't get their shoes fixed anymore, he says, they just replace them. "That's my problem," he said. "They make these injection-molded shoes in China or wherever and because of the molding they can't be repaired. Even if they could be fixed, it would cost more than a new pair. Now we sell workboots, make keys, anything to get a day's pay. The business is just not as good as it used to be—in the last two years we've seen a big drop." Ancona cites a stark example. The new (and fixable) Chinese-made workboots he sells are $35. The cost of resoling those same boots? $35.

Ancona may be gloomy about his prospects, but he's still proud of the work he does. "What we do saves on landfill space," he says. "When you rebuild a shoe, only a very little bit of material is thrown away. And the shoe is often better than it was new."

## Invisible Repairs

Nancy Molleur, who runs AA Reweaving in Albuquerque, New Mexico, is a practitioner of an even more endangered craft. Clothes reweaving, she says, "is a declining skill." Molleur learned her art from 75-year-old Nina Davis, who started the company in 1954.

"It's a very old craft that was used originally during the industrial age to repair fabrics that had flaws in them," Molleur says. "Now we use it mainly to repair garments that have holes in them, or are fraying. Other people reweave Navajo rugs out here. It's a difficult and somewhat secretive skill, and quite wonderful. People are amazed when they see what I can do." Molleur's clients bring in $2,500 suits that ripped the first time out, or priceless heirlooms. But her problem is similar to other fix-its: New products are more difficult to work on. "With polyester, for instance, the threads are not very tangible," Molleur says. "The clothes tend to fray rather than unravel, and it's hard to reweave them back into a garment." Blends of synthetics and natural fibers are better but, with mass-produced imported clothes getting cheaper and cheaper, reweaving appears to have a cloudy future.

If people aren't fixing damaged clothing any-more, the Asian factories are working overtime to keep up with increased demand—and creating a much bigger waste problem. Linda Shotwell, communications director of the Washington-based National Recycling Coalition, says that source reduction and reuse "are very important, because they reduce the need to have recycling and waste management in the first place."

Furniture reupholstering, meanwhile, remains a healthy profession, as many Americans still recover their old couches and sectionals. Ben Saiz of Ben's Upholstery ("One Call and You're Covered"), also in Albuquerque, has been on the recovery scene since 1958. "I think it's a form of recycling," he says. "I love working with solid pieces of furniture, and it's still cheaper to reupholster than to buy new." Again, though, cheap imports are clogging the market. "There's too much junk out there—from halfway around the world. That's what's polluting our planet." Saiz plans to fight back with his own line of sofas and chairs. "You'll get a quality oak or pine upholstered sofa for $800 to $1,000—that's a good deal, isn't it?" he asks.

Donnis Samples, whose voice has the lilting music of the Appalachian Mountains, is getting ready to close the doors at the AAA Appliance Service Company in Chattanooga, Tennessee. for the last time. She and her husband have been fixing washers, dryers and refrigerators for decades, but now they'd rather go fishing. "A lot of people will just go out and buy a new appliance when it breaks down now," Samples says. "We always tell them their unit can be fixed unless there's a bad compressor or something like that. That kind of work can cost $300 or $400 and you might as well buy new."

Jerry Powell, editor of *North America's Recycling Journal* in Portland, Oregon, says shoppers should not be using price as their only motivator. "Consumers don't do enough forward thinking when buying things," he says. "They think about durability and quality only when buying clothes and cars. People care more about what's cheaper or more efficient." Powell says that federal and state governments must lead by example, as in replacing paper milk cartons in schools with reusable lexan plastic designs.

The American Rental Association certainly thinks it's setting a good example. It blankets its member stores with big Earth posters emblazoned with green emblems and the message, "Rental is Good For All of Us."

At the Archdale Rental Center in Charlotte, North Carolina, Manager Kellie Brown says her customers don't have to buy machines or equipment that they'd really only use once a year. "We're talking about things like drain snakes," she said. "Or very specialized equipment like lawn aerators, which you use only in the spring. People will probably only re-tile their bathrooms once, so do they need to buy ceramic tile cutters?" She also cites big construction equipment like jackhammers that the crews don't have the time or expertise to maintain. "I would say that renting helps save our country's resources," says Brown, echoing the association's message.

## Buried Treasure

Two other businesses—pawnbroking and auctioneering—also turn one man's junk into another's treasure. Bob Peltier is the Bob of Bob's Viking Pawnbrokers, in St. Paul, Minnesota. "We recycle everything that comes in," says Peltier. "We refurnish it and it goes back into the system." Hard luck stories often come attached to gold wedding and engagement rings, and these are refined (to remove the brass and copper) and then formed into blocks of "casting grade" gold for reforming into jewelry. "I'd say 80 percent of our customers are working people who get a little short before payday," said Peltier. "We buy their stuff and help get them back on their feet. We try to fix the stuff, but if it's beyond repair, we sell it to auctioneers."

And that's how people like Hank Kessler get their hands on it. Kessler runs the Auction Barn in Cranbury Township, Pennsylvania, near Pittsburgh. "We specialize in estate work," Kessler says. "We take everything, from pots and pans to the washers and dryers. We have many different buyers, from antique dealers to appliance salesmen. Everything's sold at our Friday night auctions. Tonight we're selling the entire contents of a three-bedroom house. People sometimes write into their wills that everything should be auctioned when they die, so the relatives don't fight over who gets what." Kessler said he likes to deal with the older furniture "be-cause it's made better than the newer stuff, which is pressed sawdust. We get young couples come in here, just starting out, with little money, and we can set them up with a solid bedroom set that's going to last at a fraction of the cost of a new one." And, auction fever being what it is, everything is sold down to the last potholder.

## Reuse Reborn

But while older forms of reuse are slowly declining, new and innovative forms are springing up. The Nevada-based Ribbon Factory, for instance, reloads used "disposable" computer printer ribbons and laser cartridges and resells them at half price. Kodak remanufactures about 18,000 copiers for the North American market every year, almost double its production of new copiers. The Xerox Corporation is also going ahead with a new line of "remanufactured" copiers. Asked why American corporations build in so much waste, Xerox communications manager Daniel Minchin says, "The trend is clearly toward the preservation of resources. In the specific case of Xerox Corporation, we do fix things. The machines are returned to us in Rochester, New York, and completely rebuilt from the frame up. They have warranties that are identical to new copiers."

Remanufacturing is also available for automotive parts, office furniture, tools, vacuum cleaners and an assortment of other appliances and equipment. Laser cartridge remanufacture is one of the fastest-growing cottage industries in North America.

## Waste Reduction

The most exciting inroads in refuse reduction have come from industrial "waste exchanges"—regional and national computerized matchmaking services that link businesses discarding potentially usable material with other businesses that can use it. In 1993 an estimated 15 to 25 percent of the 12 million tons of goods listed were exchanged. Even more important is the fact that, in 1993, the number of waste exchanges doubled.

Even modest commercial programs can have significant effects on the generation of garbage. The Neighborhood Cleaners Association in New York City estimates that if customers at each of the 1,100-member drycleaners used reusable garment bags, more than 6.6 million plastic bags would be taken out of the waste stream each year.

In Los Angeles an arrangement between the major movie studies and Re-Sets Entertainment Commodities brings significant cuts in the city's solid waste, particularly wood. The estimated 250,000 sheets of lauan plywood utilized by the region's entertainment industry each year are now finding a second home among nonprofit theaters and cultural groups.

Reuse is hip, and entrepreneurs all over America are coming up with novel ways of making old things dance to new tunes. With a lot of work, we might reach the happy situation of Western Europe, which is on track to recover 90 percent of its packaging waste in 10 years. While it's sad to see the sun set on traditional fix-it industries, reuse is still alive and well.

Contacts: *Choose to Reuse,* $15.95 from Ceres Press, P.O. Box 87, Department CTR, Woodstock, NY 12498; Institute for Local Self-Reliance, 2425 18th Street NW, Washington, DC 20009/(202)232-4108. ❏

---

**Questions**

1. The elite 20 percent of the world's population earns how much of the world's income?

2. What types of businesses are environmental groups encouraging?

3. What are industrial "waste exchanges"?

*Answers are at the back of the book.*

---

## 50

*Environmental regulations are needed if we are to have a healthy environment. The Clean Water Act, the Right to Know Law, the Safe Drinking Water Act, and other regulations serve to protect the public and the environment. Since the 1994 elections, some members of Congress have moved to weaken or cancel many of these protections. This would result in a relaxation of sewage-treatment requirements, would weaken wetlands protections, and would increase the discharge of pollutants into the water. This move partly stems from the influence of politically powerful businesses. However, there are regulations that incorporate economic incentives for responsible companies. These incentives have allowed companies to become more competitive and more profitable while protecting the environment. Studies have shown that environmental regulations are needed to protect citizens and natural resources while stimulating a productive economy.*

# Environmental Regulations
## Who Needs Them?
## Vicki Monks

*National Wildlife*, **February/March 1996**

**We all do, according to people whose health and livelihoods have been protected by these rules and laws.**

During the early 1980s, Diane Wilson, a fourth-generation Texas shrimper, had worried that the prime fishing grounds of Lavaca Bay, on the Gulf Coast, might be seriously contaminated. For years she had watched onshore industries pumping wastes into the waters where she and other shrimpers had struggled to make a living on smaller and smaller catches. She also had noticed disturbing numbers of dead dolphins and birds at sea and washed up on beaches.

Then, in 1986, when the Emergency Planning and Community Right to Know Act became law as part of the Superfund package, requiring industries to disclose their discharges of more than 300 different toxic chemicals, one of the plants on Lavaca Bay proved to be among the worst polluters in the nation—the Aluminum Company of America (Alcoa) plant in Point Comfort. Offshore from Alcoa, the Environmental Protection Agency found toxic levels of methyl mercury and proposed the area as a

Superfund site. The Texas Health Department warned pregnant women that eating one meal of fish caught in the area could cause fetal damage.

Wilson now sees hope for an end to the pollution. In summer 1995, Alcoa signed a "good-neighbor" agreement pledging to work toward zero discharge of wastewater pollutants. In exchange, Wilson agreed not to file a citizen's Clean Water Act lawsuit against the company. Late last year, Formosa Plastics of Point Comfort, a major producer of the polyvinyl chloride, signed a similar agreement.

This corporate change of heart occurred after Wilson had staged three hunger strikes and after other fishermen had joined her in multiple protests and legal challenges. But had it not been for the Clean Water Act and the Right to Know law, Wilson believes, the agreement never would have happened. "When we got Community Right to Know, it was like a light in the darkness," she says. "If it hadn't been for that law, we never would have known how much pollution was out there."

The laws of Texas shrimpers relied on to leverage pollution-control agreements—along with many other environmental laws and regulations—are now targeted for radical change. In response to complaints from some politically powerful businesses, which claim that regulation is a burden, Congress since the 1994 elections has moved to weaken or revoke many environmental protections.

Anecdotes of heavy-handed regulation seemingly have carried great weight with Congress, yet they tell only a small part of the story. "Environmental regulations have empowered citizens to protect their own surroundings and have helped create a cleaner environment for millions of Americans," says Mary Marra, director of NWF's national office. The rules have helped people to breathe easier, live longer and raise healthier children, Marra says, and they have also made good business sense in many parts of the country. "Regulations have changed economic incentives so that responsible companies are rewarded. In many cases, that's meant those businesses also become more competitive and more profitable," she says. The laws have also protected public resources and enhanced our lives through conservation of the natural world. But all of these benefits may be undone or curtailed in the drive to ease regulations.

While many corporations press ahead to weaken environmental protection, individual citizens who have benefited from regulation clearly support existing laws. For instance, Robin Brandt of Rothschild, Wisconsin, recalls how her daughter, Jessica Buckmaster, suffered from severe asthma attacks through most of her childhood in the 1980s. The attacks were brought on primarily by exposure to sulfur dioxide released in concentrated bursts from a Weyerhaeuser paper mill located near her school. The pollutant triggered asthma attacks in many of the children at Rothschild Elementary, but Jessica was so sensitive, teachers sometimes called her "the canary."

According to Jim Harris, the principal during Buckmaster's elementary-school years, a mechanical monitor placed on school grounds by the state Department of Natural Resources often recorded sulfur dioxide levels that exceeded the .4 parts per million known to induce asthma attacks. In fact, readings often surpassed the 5 parts per million the instrument was capable of measuring. On those days kids had to stay indoors, and teachers kept classroom windows shut even in hot weather.

Jessica's health has improved greatly since Weyerhaeuser installed pollution-control equipment in 1991. Today, at 16, she can play volleyball and take walks without getting sick. But she has not forgotten the times when her lips and fingernails turned blue, and she was taken away from school by ambulance. "I was just angry at Weyerhaeuser," she recalls. "I was so mad at them when I was little."

Weyerhaeuser's short-term but intense bursts of sulfur dioxide did not violate regulations because the total pollution emitted over a 24-hour period fell within federally established limits. Even so, after parents protested, the EPA threatened to invoke emergency powers under the Clean Air Act. As a result, the company voluntarily spend $9 million on stack scrubbers to reduce emissions by 90 percent.

Harris, who is now principal at a neighboring elementary school, says the quality of life for the whole village is better. "We saw an improvement at the school, vastly reducing the number of kids having medical emergencies," Harris says.

Because of Jessica's case and others like it, the EPA has proposed new regulations to limit intense, short-term bursts of air pollutants. According to the American Lung Association, more than 13 million Americans—including 4.8 million children—suffer from asthma, and for them, exposure to air pollutants can be dangerous. But the proposed rules may never be implemented. Under some of the risk-assessment and cost-benefit scenarios that Congress is considering, the well-being of the relatively small number of people who are extremely sensitive to pollution may not measure up against the costs to business.

Another example of the power that regulations offer to private citizens can be found among Kentucky residents who live along Yellow Creek, near Middlesboro. In the 1960s, a tannery began piping bubbling, maroon and black wastes laden with toxic chemicals into the Middlesboro sewage-treatment plant, which then discharged partially treated toxic effluent directly into the creek. "Every house here had health problems, leukemia, birth defects, miscarriages," says Sheila Wilson, whose farm animals all died after drinking water from the creek in the 1970s.

Stopping the toxic discharge took more than 10 years and a citizen's lawsuit under the Clean Water Act, but now the creek is once again running clear, and smallmouth bass, beavers and muskrats have returned. Although federal water-protection laws have been in place since the 1970s, they were not vigorously enforced in Kentucky until citizens demanded relief. Says attorney Hank Graddy, who represented Yellow Creek residents, "The Safe Drinking Water Act and Clean Water Act were late in coming to Kentucky, but the citizens of this state are benefiting from those laws now, even if it is belated. To weaken the laws would be an invitation for these tragedies to be repeated."

Yet that weakening is precisely what a powerful cadre of federal legislators seeks at the behest of industry. Last spring, the House approved an overhaul of the Clean Water Act that would loosen sewage-treatment requirements, weaken wetlands protections and allow industries to discharge more pollutants into water. House Majority Whip Tom DeLay (R-Texas) introduced legislation to repeal all of the 1990 Clean Air Act Amendments. Senate Majority Leader Bob Dole (R-Kansas) sponsored a regulatory reform bill requiring proof that benefits outweigh costs before any environmental regulations could be implemented. That bill would also substantially weaken Community Right to Know rules. Both houses of Congress approved appropriations bills that included cuts in funding for drinking-water protection, curbs on EPA enforcement powers and special provisions exempting some industries—such as cement kilns and oil and gas producers—from key regulations.

Linda King of the Environmental Health Network based in Chesapeake, Virginia, which provides advice to local groups on ways to combat pollution, fears the activity in Congress may undo years of work in developing cooperative agreements between industries and nearby communities. "Companies are beginning to back out of agreements that have taken more than 10 years to negotiate," King says. "Looking at what Congress has proposed, they see they may have an out."

That's bad news for the Baltimore neighborhood associations in the heavily industrialized area around Curtis Bay, Maryland. Activists there cite federal regulations as strong allies in winning pledges of reductions in air and water emissions from many local industrial plants. "The regulations are in place, and they don't want to be butting heads with us all the time, so now we sit down and talk," says neighborhood resident Doris McGuigan.

McGuigan got involved in 1971, after her mother died of aplastic anemia—a probable result, said doctors, of years of exposure to contaminated air in her neighborhood. "At the time, I didn't know what to think about the environment," McGuigan recalls. "The only thing I knew was I didn't want anybody to suffer like she did."

The pollution was so bad by the early 1980s that the Maryland Department of Transportation installed warning signs on Key Bridge to alert motorists to the dense chemical fog that sometimes flowed from the complex of industries along the waterfront. A 10-car pileup on the bridge even led to lawsuits that blamed the accident on a cloud of titanium tetrachloride released from the SCM-Glidden paint factory. But reported toxic emissions began dropping dramatically after the Community Right to Know Act made total amounts of toxic releases public. Air and water pollution in the area are now down by 74 percent since 1988.

In August, President Clinton visited the neighborhood to announce an executive order that will require businesses with federal contracts to continue to report toxic emissions publicly even if Congress disables the Community Right to Know Act. Although that law involves little cost or bureaucracy, the President said, it has been one of the most successful tools for environmental progress. Since it has been on the books, reported toxic air emissions have declined 43 percent nationwide. "It's also helped to spur innovation that helps businesses work smarter and cleaner and become more profitable, not less profitable," Clinton said.

Several recent studies suggest that environmental regulations do not harm the economy and may in fact stimulate economic development. In the Los Angeles area, the "most aggressive air-pollution regulations in history" have not interfered with economic performance, according to the Institute for Economic and Environmental Studies at California State University. A detailed analysis shows that during the past 30 years, job, wage and manufacturing growth in the Los Angeles basin have outpaced growth in the rest of the nation. Even the most heavily regulated industries in Los Angeles outperformed their counterparts in regions with looser air-quality rules. The Institute for Southern Studies found similar results in a recent survey: States with the best environmental records had the most productive economies.

Conversely, a degraded environment may do considerable harm to businesses. While pollutants in the heavily industrialized Houston Ship Channel have declined steadily during the past 20 years, spills still occur and contaminants in the water still occasionally catch fire. During crises that shut down the channel, businesses that depend on shipping through the channel lose an estimated $1 million a day.

Similarly, the economy of Belmar, New Jersey, was very nearly ruined when trash and medical waste washed up on East Coast beaches in 1987. "We experienced a huge loss of tourism dollars as a result of the pollution," says Mayor Kenny Pringle.

Through a variety of federal regulations, including the Coastal Zone Management Act and the Shore Protection Act of 1988, controls were tightened on runoff, sewage discharges, burning at sea and garbage and sludge dumping. Today, Pringle says, the quality and clarity of the water rivals any in the country. Tourists are returning, and Belmar's economy is rebounding.

Ollie Klein, Jr., who runs a family restaurant and fish market in Belmar, is worried that Congress will weaken the laws that protect his town. "It won't be a good thing for people in the fishing industry or the tourist business," Klein says. "It won't be good for anyone who depends on the shore. I'd much rather see them make it harder to pollute."

The city of Belmar itself had to invest in sewage and runoff controls because of federal regulations, but Pringle believes the benefits to the economy have far outweighed the investment. The mayor is convinced the beaches here will not stay clean without federal rules. "We can't control New York, where the bulk of floatable pollution came from," he says. "It would be such a crime to turn back. We are just now starting to enjoy the fruits of these regulations."

Some economic benefits can be calculated and weighed against the costs of regulations, but other equally important advantages cannot be so easily measured. For instance, putting a dollar value on the human suffering that results from environmental degradation—such as Jessica Buckmaster's inability to play outside on a beautiful day—is virtually impossible.

Such quality-of-life issues came up recently in New Mexico, where the Laguna Pueblo tribe relied on the National Environmental Policy Act and other federal regulations to negotiate with the Anaconda Mining Company and its parent, Atlantic-Richfield, over restoration of what had been the largest open-pit uranium mine in the world. The impetus for cleanup was not so much a fear of long-term health consequences as an effort to heal psychological wounds. "Culturally, the Earth is our mother, so psychologically we were hurting because the Earth had been torn open," says reclamation project manager Marvin Sarracino, a member of the Laguna Pueblo tribe. "So we've tried to mend it."

With cleanup on the Laguna Pueblo reservation nearly complete, the tribal corporation formed to do the job has signed contracts for restoration projects on other reservations and on federal land and continues to employ tribal members.

Even harder to quantify are the benefits of environmental protection that will not be discovered until sometime in the future. No one can calculate the precise benefits of protecting biological diversity, for example, because no one knows which species will prove to be critical in protecting our health or ensuring our survival in the future. "One-third of all prescription drugs are derived from plants, and yet we've only investigated 5 percent of all plant species for their medicinal value," says Dr. Kevin Browngoehl, a Pennsylvania pediatrician. "We need to ensure that the rest of them will be around when we are ready to look at them. In balancing costs and benefits, Congress should take into account the thousands of people who are diagnosed every year with illnesses that currently are not treatable. We don't know which plants may provide medicines to treat these diseases."

The environmental problems we still face in the United States are a potent sign of the continuing importance of regulations. A Harvard study estimated that as many as 60,000 people die yearly from particulate air pollution. Twenty-eight million Americans with chronic respiratory problems are regularly exposed to harmful levels of smog that worsen their illnesses. Millions more drink water laced with contaminants, including fecal coliform, pesticides, radioactivity, and disease-causing microorganisms. "Far from needing to reduce environmental regulation, we need to sharpen it so that it offers even better protection for our citizens," says Mary Marra of NWF. "Our future and our safety, our health and our children, depend on strong environmental protection." ❑

## Questions

1. What act enabled Diane Wilson to determine that local industries were polluting the water?

2. What are the ramifications of the overhaul of the Clean Water Act?

3. What were the results of the survey conducted by the Institute for Southern Studies?

*Answers are at the back of the book.*

**51**

*We have always had environmental problems. Originally, we were concerned with the scarcity of food, shelter, and other basic essentials. By the eighteenth century, western philosophers were becoming concerned with the possibility that world famine and other scarcities could jeopardize our civilization. Three theories came about in the late eighteenth to early twentieth centuries, each of which has something different to contribute to the solution of environmental problems. The Malthusian doctrine of population growth stipulates that if population remains unchecked, growth will surpass the world's food supply. John Stuart Mill's steady-state economy espouses a voluntary, less consumptive existence. The third theory, the neoclassical economic notion, stresses an efficient marketplace in order to establish production and consumption levels attaining optimal equilibrium. Of the three theories, Mill's steady-state economy may prove to be the most promising solution.*

# Three Theories from Economics about the Environment

## J.E. de Steiguer

*BioScience*, September 1995

For most of its time on this planet, the human race has had to deal with environmental problems in one form or another. The original concern was with the local scarcity of food, shelter, and other essentials provided at least in part by nature (Fisher and Peterson 1976). By the late eighteenth century, western philosophers were beginning to recognize the theoretical possibility of worldwide scarcities and famines that could threaten the existence of civilization (Malthus [1798] 1965).

From the mid-nineteenth century, writers expressed concern that modern industrialization and population growth was degrading the environment (Marsh [1864] 1965, Mill [1848] 1965, Pigou 1932). Environmental degradation did not, however, become a permanent public concern until biologist Rachel Carson in 1962 published *Silent Spring*. Carson's book, which focused on the irresponsible use of pesticides, generated profound public sentiment for improved environmental quality. Thus, by the mid-1960s environmental degradation had joined with the much older concern of resource scarcity to form the two interrelated, central interests of modern environmentalism.

Not surprisingly, numerous theories have evolved in an attempt to explain the causes of and solutions to environmental problems. These theories, while not always being well-developed philosophies (Norton 1991a), nevertheless represent attempts at bringing order to a confusing array of facts and hypotheses about the environment.

Three of the most influential theories contained in today's environmental literature were first formally stated in the work of English economists who lived between the late eighteenth and early twentieth centuries. These theories are: the Malthusian doctrine of population growth and resource scarcity, John Stuart Mill's theory of the steady-state economy, and the neoclassical economic notion of efficient markets as the solution to environmental and resource problems. During the period of intense environmental awareness immediately following the publication of *Silent Spring*, these theories were, in a sense, rediscovered.

In this article, I trace the history of these three schools of economic thought in relation to the environment. I begin with the origins of the theories during the Industrial Revolution (1760–1850), next discuss their reemergence during the years immediately following *Silent Spring*, explore their present status, and finally compare their potential value in the resolution of future environmental matters. Each theory has something different to contribute, and together they present a rather comprehensive scheme for solving environmental problems.

## The Industrial Revolution and the Rise of Economic Thought

Before the Industrial Revolution, Europeans had lived in a society which, for better or for worse, was characterized by stability (Fusfeld 1982). The eighteenth century, however, brought widespread change in the existing order, first in England and later on the European continent. The introduction of coal as a principal energy source followed by the invention of the steam engine and then gas lighting permitted the widespread development of industrial manufacturing (Lombroso 1931). Improved prospects for employment and wages enticed many to migrate from the country to the cities where most manufacturing facilities were located. The rapid increases in urban populations throughout western Europe were well documented (August 1975).

With this change came some improvements for people: death rates fell, and the general human population experienced the beginnings of a major expansion, which has continued to the present (Miller 1994). However, there was also an associated measure of social and economic chaos. Depressions and financial crises reduced the lower classes to a rock-bottom existence with no relief in sight, and laws passed to protect domestic production in England sent consumer prices skyrocketing (Lombroso 1931).

The magnitude of the social change and population growth was sufficient to raise concerns about the fate of civilization. A liberalized atmosphere of inquiry (Lombroso 1931) soon led scholars to wonder about how humanity in the face of change might best ensure its survival and improvement in the quality of life. A distinct academic discipline called political economy arose to address the questions of resource scarcity, allocation, and societal well-being. The objective of these new economic philosophers was as simple as it was grand: to obtain an improved understanding of the human condition (Heilbroner 1986).

## Malthus and the Classical Economists

The first group of economic philosophers to emerge during the Industrial Revolution has been called the classical economists. Their method of study was based on the philosophy of natural law (Heilbroner 1986). They, thus, attempted to discern by reason a naturally endowed set of principles that order human life and community (Finnis 1980). An important member of the classical school was Thomas Robert Malthus. He expressed concern about the potential consequences of population growth. The doctrine of Malthus was set forth in his monumental treatise, *An Essay on the Principle of Population as It Affects the Future Improvement of Society* (Malthus [1798] 1965).

The common interpretation of Malthusian scarcity is: Society has the ability to increase agricultural production only at an arithmetic rate while the number of mouths to be fed increases at a geometric rate. Hence, at some point, population is likely to outstrip food supplies with calamitous results. Discussions of Malthus's ideas often suggest that a complete disappearance of resources eventually causes society to crash. Malthus, however, presented the more sophisticated concept of economic scarcity and its attendant effects on human well-being (Barnett and Morse 1963). Economic scarcity refers to the decreased availability of resources relative to the effort required to obtain them.

The example that Malthus used was agricultural production. To Malthus, land was one ingredient, like labor or tools, used in the process of growing crops. While he argued that the quantity of arable land was fixed and someday might be completely occupied by farms, Malthus also recognized that land could be made more productive through intensive cultivation. With greater effort, farmers could gradually squeeze more produce from that same fixed amount of land but—and herein lies the rub—at decreasing rates per each additional laborer. Thus each new worker sent to the field produces incrementally fewer crops or, as later economists would say, with diminishing marginal returns.

Malthus predicted diminishing marginal returns as farmers sought ways to feed the ever-increasing masses. The economic scarcity would arise because society would have to sacrifice increasingly more to obtain less on the margin. Whether measured by the number of field hands and their hoes, or by the money required to pay for that labor and equipment, the cost of extracting agricultural produce would increase. And, as populations continued to grow and societies were pressed harder to feed their members, there would come a time when these costs would dominate the entire economy. Per capita economic growth would cease and then plummet as people struggled just to scratch a living from the earth. War, plagues, famine, and other catastrophes would periodically thin human populations, and the cycle of diminishing marginal returns to human effort would then recommence.

## Mill and the Stationary State
Following the classicists came the Utopian socialist philosopher John Stuart Mill. During his life, Mill produced an impressive quantity of written work on a variety of topics dealing with ethics, law, morals, and economics (August 1975). His most important contribution with respect to economics and modern environmental thought was contained in *The Principles of Political Economy* (Mill [1848] 1965).

Like Malthus, Mill foresaw that increases in human population and wealth could not continue in perpetuity. At some time, a steady—or, as he said, "stationary"—state would eventually be reached where both population and consumption were stabilized, but perhaps at some low level of human happiness. What was needed in order to improve the human condition, wrote Mill, was a more immediate stabilization of population, reduction in aggregate consumption, and a more equitable worldwide distribution of wealth.

In order to achieve the desired steady-state, Mill advocated a voluntary, less consumptive existence. Thus, Mill did not share Malthus's pessimism regarding the ability of humanity to avoid disaster. Furthermore, the stationary economic state by no means implied to Mill a stationary state of human improvement. There would always be opportunity for elevating mental culture and for moral and social progress. In his philosophy, Mill seemed much a kindred spirit with his US literary contemporary Henry David Thoreau, who had also insisted that our lives needed "simplicity, simplicity, simplicity" (Thoreau 1854). Also, elements of Mill's philosophy anticipated wildlife biologist Aldo Leopold's call a century later for a land ethic where humanity would maintain the integrity of the environment through less resource exploitation (Leopold [1949] 1987).

Mill also introduced a concept that would seem strikingly relevant to twentieth-century economists (Barnett and Morse 1963). It was the notion that personal solitude and natural beauty could be impaired through population growth and industry. So, even though a person may not experience shortages of conventional agricultural produce and minerals, Mill saw that the process of growing crops and mining minerals could result in a paucity of quality human habitat.

## The Neoclassical Economists
The end of the nineteenth century in Victorian England saw the beginnings of the neoclassical school of thought. The unofficial leader of this school was the Cambridge economist Alfred Marshall. Where the classicists had relied upon the philosophy of natural law to derive their theories, the neoclassicists employed the engineer's tools of analytical geometry and differential calculus to develop abstract models of market economies (Christensen 1991). Neoclassical economics—with its supply and demand curves, prices and quantities, and market equilibria—would eventually become the economics of the modern university classroom. All told, it was a sharp methodological departure from the classical school.

Neoclassical theory emphasized the well-functioning, or so-called efficient, market as the means of maximizing satisfaction. According to the theory, as producers and consumers meet in the market place, voluntary exchange prices are established to set production and consumption at optimal equilibrium levels. Furthermore, increasing prices spur discovery of new technologies and raw materials, and they encourage efficiency and substitution both in production and consumption. Any departure from the market system, according to the neoclassicists, results in a less than optimal allocation of resources and, likewise, lower human satisfaction.

A two-part, market-based measure of social well-being emerged from the neoclassical studies of societal welfare. The first part, called producer's surplus, was in essence a measure of profits, that is, the difference between the price received in the market for an item and the cost of producing it. The second measure, called consumer's surplus, was the difference between the value of the satisfaction received from the consumption on an item and the price the consumer must pay for it.

Producer's and consumer's surpluses provided a means for neoclassical economists to begin valuing societal welfare, but the conceptual framework was incomplete. It still lacked some means of accounting for pollution and other side effects that, although they are external to the market transaction, nevertheless still affect human welfare. The missing piece was supplied by A. C. Pigou, a former student of Marshall, in his book *The Economics of Welfare* (Pigou 1932). Pigou realized that these market-external changes in human welfare could have both beneficial and detrimental effects. These effects he called "uncompensated services and disservices" (Pigou 1932).

Pigou (1932) provided an example of an uncompensated service:

> It is true in like manner of land devoted to afforestation, since the beneficial effect on climate extends beyond the borders of the estates owned by the persons responsible for the forest. (p. 160)

And of an uncompensated disservice:

> ...smoke from factory chimneys...in large towns inflicts a heavy uncharged loss on the community, in injury to buildings and vegetables, expenses for washing clothes and cleaning rooms, expenses for the provisions of extra artificial light and in many other ways....(pp. 160-161)

Pigou had hit upon the modern notion of economic externalities—those changes in welfare due to unintended side effects, often of an environmental nature, that are not directly captured in the market transaction. Though simple as a concept, externalities provided a powerful way of incorporating environmental damage into economic assessments. Also, externalities, because of their connection to production prices and quantities, suggested remedies, such as taxes, that could be used to reduce environmental damage. Likewise, subsidies could be paid to resource owners to encourage the production of amenity goods, such as forest aesthetics, for which no cash market exists.

## The Years Following *Silent Spring*

The ten or so years following *Silent Spring* were important both to the modern environmental movement and to the three economic theories. In response to Carson's book, the academic community began producing scholarly works that revived and adapted the older theories of Malthus, Mill, and the neoclassicists to modern situations.

**Malthus.** Certainly the most ubiquitous of the three theories in the post-1962 environmental literature was that of Malthus. However, the basic Malthusian theme of increasing resource scarcity was modified to a modern, neo-Malthusian perspective. According to the new view, in addition to the traditional population concerns, world calamity could result from environmental degradation, which also diminished the natural resource base.

Neo-Malthusian concerns were clearly evident in entomologist Paul Ehrlich's (1968) best-selling book *The Population Bomb*. Its message was apocalyptic: There were too many people on the earth and because of a decrease in the doubling time of population growth, the situation was worsening every day. Within the next nine years the world would see acute food shortages where one in every seven persons would die from nutrition-related causes. The dreadful effects of overpopulation would not be limited to starvation. The environment would deteriorate too, as people used more fertilizers and pesticides, cleared forests, increased the siltation of streams, encountered the greenhouse effect, and engaged in nuclear warfare.

Another appearance of the Malthusian theme was found in *The Limits to Growth* (Meadows et al. 1972). The study used a Massachusetts Institute of Technology–based computer model, which employed several scenarios of future world resource stocks and population. Just beyond the year 2000, according to the model, food production and industrial output suddenly would decline, triggering in approximately the year 2030 the beginnings of a 50% reduction in the world's human population. Increasing population and industrial production in grim Malthusian fashion would severely outstrip limited natural resources, thus crashing civilization.

In their attempt to save the human race, the researchers devised and fed into the model other more optimistic alternative future scenarios. One assumed a doubling, through new discoveries, of natural resource stocks. Other scenarios made energy more freely available, improved resource use, increased food yield, and instituted birth control. But the final outcome was sadly always the same. At some point during the twenty-first century, natural resource stocks would drop followed by a dramatic population decline.

A final example of the Malthusian theme can be found in the writings of economist Kenneth Boulding ([1966] 1973). In "The Economics of the Coming Spaceship Earth," Boulding explored energy entropy as a factor limiting the existence of civilization. The second law of thermodynamics states that due to entropy, the amount of energy available for work will always decrease. Without the introduction of new energy sources to our planet, the second law will see to it that existing energy dissipates into heat and thus eventually becomes useless. In theory then, Boulding thought that the second law of thermodynamics placed an absolute limit on the viability of civilization. The concern he raised regarding entropy was, in effect, the ultimate Malthusian warning. The demise of humanity was now said to be governed by the immutable laws of physics.

**Mill.** Mill's theory about the steady-state economy had been largely discarded by neoclassical economics. In 1973, however, economist Herman Daly pub-lished an article entitled "The Steady-State Economy," acknowledging Mill as his intellectual forerunner.

In his work, Daly lamented the problems of what he termed *growth-mania*. Among the attendant maladies were overpopulation, pollution, and human stress. His solution, like Mill's, was the steady-state economy, where humanity would strive for the maintenance of a constant population level, a constant stock of physical wealth, and a more equitable distribution of economic production among the members of society. In place of economic growth, Daly, like Mill, recommended moral growth in order to replace anxiety about material trappings with a concern for some higher and greater good. Furthermore, Daly said explicitly that the steady-state was compatible with Leopold's ([1949] 1987) land ethic. Daly's writings were responsible for the modern revival of the steady-state theory.

**Neoclassical Economics.** Neoclassical economists made some important contributions to environmental theory during the 1950s. They recognized the common-property nature of environmental resources as the root cause of many economic externalities (Gordon 1954). Because the oceans and the atmosphere belonged to everyone, hence to no one, they were freely exploitable. Common property was then seen as a type of market failure (i.e., no defined property rights) that could reduce social well-being. Thus, economists documented in the literature the importance of common property in environmental matters. (More than a decade later, Garrett Hardin in "The Tragedy of the Commons" [Hardin 1968] presented the common property concept to a large readership of noneconomists. Such interdisciplinary transferring of knowledge appears not to have been a principal interest of the earlier academic economists.)

Despite the advancements of the 1950s, it was not until the mid-1960s that neoclassical economics developed a specialized branch of learning called environmental economics, although economic externalities had remained a part of the standard university economics curriculum. The ideas of Pigou were often cited as the foundation of environmental economics (Fisher 1981). With interest stimulated by

*Silent Spring,* the study of natural resource and environmental economics accelerated rapidly at universities, government agencies, and especially at Resources for the Future, a Ford Foundation think-tank located in Washington, DC. The result was important theoretical and empirical advancements in neoclassical economics as applied to the environment.

### Economics and Environmental Thought Today

It is important to understand that the Malthusian doctrine is a hypothesis (Barnett and Morse 1963). Thus, it is subject to empirical testing. Barnett and Morse (1963) tested the Malthusian hypothesis with data for the United States and found that between 1865 and 1957 most natural resources (the exception being forestry products) had not become scarcer but instead more plentiful from the economics standpoint. The lack of scarcity was evidenced by declines in both extraction costs and resource prices. The reason the Malthusian hypothesis had failed[1] was that rising resource prices had induced new resource discovery, substitution, and more efficient technologies, all of which had lowered extraction costs. Additional tests of the scarcity hypothesis are a continuing part of modern economic inquiry (Cleveland 1991).

Some 20 years ago, Daly restated Mill's thoughts on the steady-state, and the old ideas found new acceptance. The relatively new school of ecological economics, of which Daly is a founder, is undoubtedly the most rapidly growing branch of economic thought with respect to the environment. Like Mill, the ecological economists seem to support, among other things, voluntary constant rates of population and wealth accumulation and a more equitable distribution of the world's wealth. The ecological economists also have promoted the development of national income accounts that reflect resource degradation and depletion. They argue for more incorporation of biology[2] into economic studies (Costanza 1991).

Mill's theory, as rediscovered by Daly, has also greatly influenced sustainable development. This social movement, which attempts to balance economic development and environmental health, currently enjoys worldwide popularity (World Commission on Environment and Development 1987).

The importance of ecological economics notwithstanding, the neoclassical school continues to define the majority of university economics programs. Thus, modern neoclassicism must be regarded as the dominant economic paradigm. Students wishing to study environmental economics draw upon the line of scholarly thought that traces back to the contributions of Pigou and the neoclassicists (Fisher 1981). The body of academic literature generated by environmental economists includes numerous textbooks, hundreds of monographs, and annually more than 250 articles published in approximately two dozen scholarly journals (de Steiguer 1989).

A practical success of environmental economists—that is, of putting theory into action—was the provision for marketable pollution permits in the Clean Air Act of 1990. Long-favored by mainstream economists as the most efficient method of reducing pollution, marketable permits set overall acceptable levels of pollution reduction and then allow polluters to bargain amongst themselves in order to achieve these desired reductions.

Despite the academic and policy successes, however, mainstream economics has sometimes had difficulty establishing itself in major environmental science programs (NAPAP 1991). Norton (1991b) has suggested that environmentalists have not always viewed economists with favor. Society would gain by closer cooperation among economists and scientists on environmental studies.

---

[1]Fisher (1981) reviewed separate studies of resource scarcity conducted by economists V.K. Smith, W.D. Nordhaus, G. Brown, and B. Field in response to *Scarcity and Growth* (Barnett and Morse 1963). These studies indicated that agricultural products, forestry products, and fuels had become economically scarcer, while metals had become economically more plentiful.

[2]The idea of incorporating more biology into economic studies has been a principal theme of ecological economics. It is interesting to note however, that forest economists have routinely used biological models in the form of empirical forest growth and yield functions to determine the economically optimal timing of timber harvests.

## A Comparison of Theories

Which economic theory seems best for today's world? This question may not be appropriate. Malthus had a hypothesis, Mill had a philosophy, and the neoclassicists had a quantitative model for testing hypotheses and making decisions. The more appropriate question is: What can each contribute to the solution of environmental problems?

From Malthus, we derive an unyielding sense of urgency regarding environmental matters. His hypothesis provides a haunting image of what might be should we fail to take natural resource and environmental matters seriously. Since Malthus' own time, his theory has generated reaction, and even outrage, for its implied lack of faith in humanity. Yet, Malthus continues to exert pressure on society to solve its environmental problems. Malthusian-like concerns provide the impetus for much of the modern environmental movement.

The modern neoclassicists in their role as economists have traditionally not been concerned with the philosophical and psychological factors that govern resource consumption activities. Instead, they have dealt primarily with empirical validation of that behavior in response to prices, costs, and other market-related phenomena. The ethical motivations behind an economic response have been of less concern than the response itself. Indeed, the modern mainstream economists generally conclude that the establishment of normative social goals is beyond their role as economists (Ferguson and Maurice 1974), because there is no objective way for them to establish those goals (Just et al. 1982).

Modern neoclassicists have brought practical skills to environmental matters. With rigor and mathematics, they have suggested specific methods of analysis to determine the economic importance of environmental damage, to examine the trade-offs required to control losses, and to suggest specific policy instruments for reducing damages. These mainstream economists provide essential information to elected officials who must draft and vote on environmental legislation.

Finally, the modern steady-state theorists provide important recommendations for closer working relationships between economists and biologists and for establishing better systems for measuring aggregate economic performance. However, Mill's most meaningful legacy is his expression of faith that humanity can control its destiny. Far from being simply an economic man—that pale wraith of a creature who follows his adding-machine brain wherever it leads him (Heilbroner 1986)—Mill's ideal person has a heart and a mind to make intelligent choices that might involve denial of material needs. To many people, Mill's work represents more than an optimistic ideal; it may prove the most promising solution to our environmental problems.

## References Cited

August ER. 1975. John Stuart Mill. New York: Charles Scribner's Sons.

Barnett HJ, Morse C. 1963. Scarcity and growth: the economics of natural resource availability. Baltimore: The Johns Hopkins Press.

Boulding KE. [1966] 1973. The economics of the coming spaceship earth. Pages 121–132 in HE Daly, ed. Toward a steady state economy. San Francisco (CA): W.H. Freeman and Company.

Carson R. 1962. Silent spring. Boston (MA): Houghton Mifflin Co.

Christensen P. 1991. Driving forces increasing returns and ecological sustainability. Pages 75–87 in R Costanza, ed. Ecological economics: the science and management of sustainability. New York: Columbia University Press.

Cleveland CJ. 1991. Natural resource scarcity and economic growth revisited: economic and biophysical perspectives. Pages 289–317 in R Costanza, ed. Ecological economics: the science and management of sustainability. New York: Columbia University Press.

Costanza R, ed. 1991. Ecological economics: the science and management of sustainability. New York: Columbia University Press.

Daly HE. 1973. The steady-state economy: toward a political economy of biophysical equilibrium and moral growth. Pages 149–174 in HE Daly, ed. Toward a steady state economy. San Francisco (CA): W.H. Freeman and Company.

de Steiguer JE. 1989. Forestry sector environmental effects. Pages 251–262 in PV Ellefson, ed. Forest resource economics and policy research. Boulder (CO): Westview Press.

Ehrlich PR. 1968. The population bomb. New York: Sierra Club and Ballantine Books.

Ferguson CE, Maurice SC. 1974. Economic analysis. Homewood (IL): Richard D. Irwin, Inc.

Finnis J.1980. Natural law and natural rights. New York: Oxford University Press.

Fisher AC. 1981. Resource and environmental economics. Cambridge (UK): Cambridge University Press.

Fisher AC, Peterson FM. 1976. The environment in economics: a survey. Journal of Economic Literature 14: 1–33.

Fusfeld DR. 1982. The age of the economist. Glenview (IL): Scott, Foresman and Company.

Gordon HS. 1954. The economic theory of a common property resource: the fishery. Journal of Political Economy 62: 124–142.

Hardin G. 1968. The tragedy of the commons. Science 162: 1243–1248.

Heilbroner RL. 1986. The worldly philosophers. New York: Simon and Schuster.

Just RE, Hueth DL, Schmitz A. 1982. Applied welfare economics and public policy. Englewood Cliffs (NJ): Prentice-Hall, Inc.

Leopold A. [1949] 1987. The land ethic. Pages 201–226 in A sand county almanac and sketches here and there. New York: Oxford University Press.

Lombroso G. 1931. Tragedies of progress. New York: E. P. Dutton and Co.

Malthus TR. [1798] 1965. The first essay on population. New York: Augustus M. Kelley.

Marsh GP. [1864] 1965. Man and nature. Cambridge (MA): The Belknap Press of Harvard University Press.

Meadows DH, Meadows DL, Randers J, Behrens WW III. 1972. The limits to growth: a report for the Club of Rome's project on the predicament of mankind. New York: Universe Books.

Mill JS. [1848] 1965. Principles of political economy. In JM Robson and VW Bladen, eds. The collected works of John Stuart Mill. Vols. II and III. Toronto: University of Toronto Press.

Miller GT Jr. 1994. Living in the environment. 8th ed. Belmont (CA): Wadsworth Publishing Company. ❏

## Questions

1. What does *economic scarcity* refer to?

2. According to Malthus, what would be the cause of economic scarcity?

3. Describe Mill's ideal person.

*Answers are at the back of the book.*

# Answers

## 1. Turning Curricula Green

1. Human behavior is responsible.
2. We must change in the ways we think and act.
3. Students from all 50 states and 22 other countries organized the Campus Earth Summit at Yale University in 1994. They drew up 10 recommendations, beginning with a call to "integrate environmental knowledge into all relevant disciplines." A follow-up conference in February 1995 drew more than one thousand students to the University of Pennsylvania.

## 2. Television Misses the Picture

1. Television celebrity is more important than objectivity.
2. Media operations and entire networks are being taken over by large corporate empires, thereby making it increasingly difficult for independent voices to be heard.
3. Forms of persuasion used on the media include thousands of letters generated and published by members of the Sierra Club, visits to editorial boards, and calls suggesting local environmental angles.

## 3. Slow Knowledge

1. Two factors that drive the twentieth century are rapid technological change and the rise of the global economy.
2. Fast knowledge represents the very essence of human progress.

3. We have been able to count on knowledge that has been gained slowly through cultural maturation.

## 4. We *Can* Build a Sustainable Economy

1. Populations are effectively stable if they narrowly fluctuate around zero growth.
2. The European Union provides a model for the rest of the world.
3. Wind power could replace fossil fuels in the future.

## 5. Mankind Must Conserve Sustainable Materials

1. Paper, steel, aluminum, plastics, and container glass. They contribute to the problems of global warming, acid rain, flooding, and destruction of rivers for hydroelectric dams.
2. Develop comprehensive systems for collecting waste and transforming it into new products, which will be possible only if many consumer goods are redesigned to be reused and recycled easily.
3. An outdated global economic framework depresses virgin materials' prices and fails to account for the environmental costs of their extraction and processing. Prices have continued to fall even as the ecological expenses of the global materials economy have risen sharply.

## 6. Can Technology Spare the Earth?

1. Two basic arguments against technology are that technology's success is self-defeating and

that we lack the wisdom to use technology for worthwhile purposes.
2. The factors of production include energy, materials, land, water, labor, and capital.
3. 1970.

### 7. The Environmental Challenges of Sub-Saharan Africa
1. Deforestation, degradation, and fragmentation.
2. Eleven percent.
3. South Africa, Nigeria, and Zaire.

### 8. Women, Politics, and Global Management
1. *Reproductive rights* refers to the power and resources that enable individuals and couples to make informed and safe decisions about their reproductive health.
2. High-quality reproductive health services.
3. Sexuality and reproduction.

### 9. Ten Myths of Population
1. People were having fewer children around 1965, which decreased the population growth.
2. Most demographers cannot accurately predict future population growth rates because they cannot foresee changes in birthrates or changes caused by large migrations of peoples.
3. Limiting factors are subject to changing cultural values.

### 10. Earth Is Running Out of Room
1. Between 1840 and 1940.
2. Oceanic fisheries and rangelands.
3. Weather and civil disorder.

### 11. Easter's End
1. The palm. It would have been ideal for transporting and erecting statues and constructing large canoes. It was also a valuable food source.
2. Porpoises, seabirds, land birds, rats, and seal colonies.
3. Intensified chicken production and cannibalism.

## SECTION TWO: PROBLEMS OF RESOURCE SCARCITY

### 12. What Is a Wetland?
1. The fundamental problem of wetland protection is that it fails to excite the general public.
2. More than half of the wetlands in the United States have been lost since 1763.
3. Change in a river's flow or direction, subsidence, and erosion can contribute to the destruction of a wetland.

### 13. The Unexpected Rise of Natural Gas
1. No emissions of sulfur and negligible emissions of particulates.
2. Storage of fuel in the vehicle.
3. Russia. It is the largest producer and has the most identified reserves.

### 14. Windpower
1. Wind power does not produce air pollution, acid rain, or carbon dioxide.
2. India
3. Wind power is important to most developing countries because they desperately need electricity.

### 15. Sea Power
1. OTEC has to move a lot of water.
2. Warm ocean water drawn from the surface flashes into 72° Fahrenheit steam in a vacuum chamber. The steam then drives a turbine to generate electricity; the water that doesn't evaporate is discharged. Cold deep-ocean water recondenses this steam into liquid at a heat exchanger.
3. Warm surface water boils pressurized ammonia at an evaporator. A turbine uses this ammonia vapor power to generate electricity. Cold deep-ocean water turns the ammonia vapor back to liquid at a condenser.

### 16. The Truly Wild Life around Chernobyl
1. The study of how radioactive and chemical

pollutants alter the life course of species.

2. This would indicate that mammals in particular are more resilient than once thought.

3. Flaws in the reactor's design and judgment errors by the operators. At least 10 times the amount of radiation released by the atomic bomb.

### 17. Immersed in the Everglades

1. Wetlands are measured in hydroperiods, the length of time each year that a piece of land has standing water.

2. The true Everglades begins at Lake Okeechobee and extends more than a hundred miles to Florida Bay.

3. The ecological ramifications of curtain-wall technology include cutting off groundwater flow east to Biscayne Bay, making the bay hypersaline and prone to destructive algae blooms; stifling underground water flows to Dade County wells; and causing the park to flood.

### 18. Will Expectedly the Top Blow Off?

1. Management plans that are designed as actual experiments, the results of which can be evaluated scientifically.

2. Biological survey, ecosystem management, and adaptive management.

3. Biological diversity.

### 19. The World's Forests

1. Forests protect soils, they play a major role in hydrological cycles, they exert a gyroscopic effect in atmospheric processes and other factors of global climate, they are critical to the energy budget and albedo of Earth, and they harbor a majority of species on land.

2. Lack of scientific understanding of forests' overall values and lack of economic capacity to evaluate many of their outputs.

3. Encouraging sustainable development, enhancing forests' institutional status, removing "perverse" subsidies, calculating the costs of inaction, and promoting forests as global commons resources.

### 20. The Mystery of the Steller Sea Lion

1. Trawlers may catch as much as 350,000 pounds of sea life in a single haul.

2. Ninety percent of harbor seals have disappeared since 1970.

3. In a normal fluctuation, the marine mammal population will decrease slowly from the edges of its range. The disappearance of the sea lion is abnormal due to the heavy population decrease from the middle of its range.

### 21. Nature, Nurture and Property Rights

1. When the right to property is affected.

2. As an unreasonable restriction.

3. Insects, plants, or fungi.

### 22. A Recipe for River Recovery?

1. PHABSIM predicts the depths and speeds of water that correspond to different levels of flow in a river and matches them with the known habitat preferences of fish. Water flows can then be adjusted to maximize those preferred habitats.

2. Adaptive management turns the management of a stream or river into an experiment in itself: Hypotheses are formulated, flows are manipulated to answer them, and the management of the river is adjusted accordingly.

3. High flows are very important for maintaining stream channels.

### 23. Vacuuming the Seas

1. Nine out of 17 major fishing grounds are in serious decline.

2. *Pulse fishing* refers to the practice of fishing area species until they dry up, then moving on to target different species.

3. The "precautionary, risk-averse" approach means that nations must err on the side of the resource if scientists are unsure whether fishing pressure is damaging a particular stock's sustainability.

### 24. Back to Stay

1. Beavers build dams to create a submerged

"lodge" that protects them from predators and serves as a storage for winter food.

2. It was lowest at the end of the nineteenth century. Between 60 and 400 million beavers lived in North America.

3. Beavers use their tails to warn of predators and to prop themselves up while eating or working.

### 25. Common Ground

1. They envision a food system that nourishes the environment and local economies.

2. It concentrates on the garden itself as a source of employment and education. In addition to teaching about sustainable agriculture and environmental issues, it tutors youths in basic science and math and provides a forum to learn about economic development.

3. It builds bridges and sets agendas for environmental and environmental justice groups.

### 26. Labeling Wood

1. We have lost more than 14 million hectares of tropical forest every year over the past decade. This is equivalent to the entire state of Florida.

2. The FAO statistics are based on the presumption that deforestation means the complete removal of tree cover.

3. First, forest products from sustainably managed sources must attract a "green premium." Second, producers must avoid the loss of market access where certification is required or must gain market share where consumer awareness is high.

### 27. Who Owns Rice and Beans?

1. It allows researchers to freely traverse species lines, to insert just one desired quality into a new plant rather than an uncontrolled number of traits, and to create plants that will do just what their designers want them to do—tolerate herbicides, resist insects, or prosper in drought or heat.

2. Industry tends to think of patents as a matter between the company holding the patent and its competition.

3. The advent of biotechnology.

## SECTION THREE: PROBLEMS OF ENVIRONMENTAL DEGRADATION

### 28. The Alarming Language of Pollution

1. By sending false signals to the endocrine system in the body.

2. The temperature of the eggs' environment. Heat produces a female, and cold produces a male.

3. Dioxin.

### 29. Holding the World at Bay

1. Oysters are the natural filter of the Chesapeake Bay.

2. Wetlands clean the bay by purifying water as they soak up both sediment and contaminants.

3. The Chesapeake absorbs pollutants from hundreds of miles of land connecting the bay to its tributaries.

### 30. Sorcerers of the Sea

1. The oceans are the ultimate sink for most pollution, making the need for bioremediation critical in marine environments.

2. Terrestrial microbes are not used in marine environments because they are not adaptable to marine conditions.

3. Nutrient overload, sewage, metals, and synthetic organic compounds are considered the worst threats.

### 31. Drinking Recycled Wastewater

1. Surface infiltration and direct-well injection.

2. They have built new dams, levees, and canals.

3. Wastewater is usually treated with chlorine and less frequently with alternative disinfectants such as ozone, monochloramine, and ultraviolet radiation.

### 32. Particulate Control: The Next Air Pollution Control Growth Segment

1. Volatile organic compounds are removed by thermal oxidation and absorption.

2. Open access transmission and premature closure of nuclear power plants.

3. 50 percent.

## 33. The Sound of Global Warming

1. Scientists believe that the Scripps program can help us learn more about global warming, and animal advocates are concerned that the sound waves will harm marine mammals.

2. The average temperature can be determined by clocking the travel time of low-frequency sound from its source to a receiver.

3. Most of the heat that powers the climate is stored in the seas.

## 34. Verdict (Almost) In

1. Researchers have been looking not just at average global temperature, but also at the geographic pattern.

2. We release six billion tons of carbon and 23 million tons of sulfur, mostly from fossil fuels, into the atmosphere each year.

3. Carbon dioxide spreads around the Earth.

## 35. Complexities of Ozone Loss Continue to Challenge Scientists

1. Chlorofluorocarbons and halons.

2. Milder northern winters.

3. Aircraft, balloons, and ground instruments. The results pointed to widespread chemical destruction of the Arctic ozone.

## 36. Ozone-Destroying Chlorine Tops Out

1. The year 2050.

2. Yes, at least 40 times more destructive. Much of the bromine comes from fire-protection systems.

3. Halogenated CFCs are substitutes for traditional CFCs in wealthy countries. They are weak ozone destroyers.

## 37. Fowling the Waters

1. 90 percent.

2. Areas that have poor environmental laws, an anti-regulatory culture, low wages, and a docile, anti-union labor pool.

3. Decaying animal waste uses up oxygen in fresh water. Because it is rich in nitrates, phosphorous, and other minerals, it encourages algae to grow, which takes up more oxygen.

## 38. Green Revolution in the Making

1. The Blue Angel is "a market-oriented instrument of government" that informs and motivates environmentally conscious thinking and acting among manufacturers and consumers.

2. Waste heat can be used in homes and factories, can operate paper mills and chemical plants, and can generate a few more kilowatts with super-efficient technology. It will boost efficiency to approximately 90 percent, and air pollution will be cut in half.

3. Four to 300 times those of the United States.

## 39. Growing a Healthy Crop for Christmas

1. *Pre-emergence* refers to the use of herbicide to control weeds before they have sprouted.

2. The cover crop provides nutrients for the soil and food for wildlife.

3. The farmers turned to a natural biological-control method.

## SECTION FOUR: SOCIAL SOLUTIONS

## 40. China Strives to Make the Polluter Pay

1. Because most of these industrial enterprises are small, local EPB revenues from fee collection are less than those from larger state-owned enterprises. Since EPBs have limited personnel, they concentrate on the largest polluters first.

2. The objective is to correct deficiencies and propose changes to improve effectiveness and efficiency consistent with a market economy and with ongoing economic and institutional reform.

3. The goal is to develop a pollution levy system that reduces emissions and effluent, achieves environmental goals with the least cost, and imposes minimal administrative burdens on local EPBs and regulated enterprises.

## 41. Microenterprise

1. Instead of collateral, the borrowers form small groups and agree to a pact of mutual liability. If one should default, the others have to pay from their own profits. The participants in a pact often know one another, which creates peer pressure

279

for successful repayment. Microenterprise meets the compelling need for an income source in a place with few other opportunities.

2. These trends include a greater reliance on temporary or contract work; telecommuting and job-sharing; and an understanding that jobs are not as stable as they used to be.

3. Microenterprise's inherent advantages are high flexibility, lack of bureaucracy, and speed of decisionmaking.

### 42. Reassessing the Economic Assumption

1. Pollution, toxic chemical concentrations, forest depletion, desertification, thinning ozone layer, and global warming are six examples showing a strong correlation between economic product and environmental deterioration.

2. In an economy-dominated value system, it is believed that quality of life should be measured in technological terms and that technological advance equals societal progress.

3. Progress is the driving force behind the assumptions of an economy-dominated society.

### 43. What Good Is a Forest?

1. When forests are cut down, water rolls straight into streams, cutting channels, carrying silt, and causing floods.

2. In the last five years, logging declined in the Pacific Northwest. During the same period, the local economy expanded more than in any other part of the nation. The Northwest had the lowest unemployment rate in a generation as new high-tech jobs more than replaced those lost in the timber industry.

3. When the Clearwater National Forest was "salvage-logged," a series of mud avalanches were initiated that caused the devastation of miles of trout streams.

### 44. Selling Blue Skies, Clean Water

1. To stop and think where it wants to be in five years in terms of productivity.

2. Tough regulations and strict enforcement.

3. Producing less waste.

### 45. How to Make Lots of Money, and Save the Planet Too

1. By creating new markets or by protecting the old ones against competitors.

2. Government regulation.

3. Coal producers and oil-producing countries.

### 46. Forging a New Global Partnership to Save the Earth

1. It stipulates that the production of CFCs in industrial countries be phased out by 1996. It restricts the use of several other ozone-depleting chemicals.

2. Overgrazing, overcropping, poor irrigation practices, and deforestation.

3. Developing countries would agree to devote 20 percent of their domestic resources to human priorities, and donors would target 20 percent of their aid funds for such purposes. It would make a major contribution to a more sustainable world.

### 47. Ecologists and Economists Can Find Common Ground

1. Economists tend to believe that technological innovations can be relied on to solve problems, whereas ecologists are less inclined to trust technology to cure or bypass problems.

2. They feel that many economic models ignore the environmental resource base of material production and the consequences of that production for critical environmental systems employed as sinks.

3. This is due to ignorance of the other's field.

### 48. Cinderella Story

1. The council's mandate is to "identify and implement policies that will meet the needs of the present without compromising the future."

2. Chattanooga's civic leaders sought to encourage public-private partnerships and to consider the environmental costs of almost everything.

3. The *Washington Post* called Chattanooga the "alluring Cinderella of the Tennessee River."